SUFI CIVILITIES

Sufi Civilities

*Religious Authority
and Political Change
in Afghanistan*

ANNIKA SCHMEDING

STANFORD UNIVERSITY PRESS
Stanford, California

Stanford University Press
Stanford, California

© 2024 by Annika Schmeding. All rights reserved.

No part of this book may be reproduced or transmitted in any form or by any means, electronic or mechanical, including photocopying and recording, or in any information storage or retrieval system, without the prior written permission of Stanford University Press.

Unless otherwise indicated, all photographs are by the author.

Printed in the United States of America on acid-free, archival-quality paper

Library of Congress Cataloging-in-Publication Data
Names: Schmeding, Annika, author.
Title: Sufi civilities : religious authority and political change in
 Afghanistan / Annika Schmeding.
Description: Stanford, California : Stanford University Press, 2023. |
 Includes bibliographical references and index.
Identifiers: LCCN 2023007579 (print) | LCCN 2023007580 (ebook) | ISBN 9781503633384 (cloth) | ISBN 9781503637535 (paperback) | ISBN 9781503637542 (ebook)
Subjects: LCSH: Sufism—Political aspects—Afghanistan. | Muslim religious leaders—Afghanistan. | Islam and state—Afghanistan. | Afghanistan—Politics and government—1989–2001. | Afghanistan—Politics and government—2001–
Classification: LCC BP188.8.A3 S34 2023 (print) | LCC BP188.8.A3 (ebook) | DDC 297.409581—dc23/eng/20230222
LC record available at https://lccn.loc.gov/2023007579
LC ebook record available at https://lccn.loc.gov/2023007580

Cover design: Susan Zucker
Cover photograph: Annika Schmeding, Ziyarat of Khaja Abdullah Ansari, Gazargah,
 Herat, Afghanistan, 2016

To all Ustads

I am void of *zikr*, thought and affirmations	نه ذکر و فکر، نی اوراد دارم
The sorrow of a city is contained in my screaming heart	غم یک شهر، دل فریاد دارم
Like tulips blossoming in myriad colors	به رنگ لاله هردم میکشد قد
The plains of my breast are scarred with color	به دشت سینه داغ آباد دارم
I am screams, groans, moans and tears	فغانم، ناله ام، آهم، سرشکم
I was born with these potentials	من این سرمایه از ایجاد دارم
By the will of a cruel and unjust world	ز اوضاع جهان بی مروت
My heart is immersed in sorrow and pain	دل آزرده و ناشاد دار
Like a wild desert sprouting flower	من از گلهای داغ نامرادی[1]
It is lit with the bloodied graves of youthful martyrs	چراغان مشهد[2] فرهاد دارم

(From the Diwan of Ustad Haidari Wujudi)

CONTENTS

List of Figures ix

Note on Transliteration xi

Acknowledgments xii

Introduction 1

ONE Navigating the Past: Sufi Strategies of State Alignment, Contestation and Strategic Distance 37

TWO Navigating Insecurity: Mullahs and Sufi Lodges 74

THREE Navigating the Interior: Sufi Poetry as Islamic Education and Heritage 103

FOUR Gendered Navigation: Equality in Difference 144

FIVE	Navigating the Divine through Dreams	168
	Conclusion and Epilogue on Transitions	197
	Glossary	213
	Notes	219
	References	267
	Index	313

FIGURES

2.1	Haji Tamim showing mementos	80
2.2	Haji Saiqal at the *khanaqah* celebration	89
2.3	Haji Saiqal in his mosque in Microrayon	91
2.4	Mohammad Monir Saiqal holding a photo	95
3.1	Haidari Wujudi in his youth	107
3.2	Photo of Sufi Ashqari in Haidari Wujudi's notebook	108
3.3	Sufi intellectuals and literati	110
3.4	Prayer (*du'a*) at Ustad Haidari Wujudi's class	113
3.5	Ustad Haidari Wujudi teaching	116
3.6	Recitation at Ustad Haidari Wujudi's class	118
3.7	Haidari Wujudi receiving honors	131
3.8	Ustad Haidari Wujudi speaking	135
3.9	Ustad Asma Mahjor with images of her father and his oeuvre	139
4.1	Drawing of the human heart by Allama Faizani	157
4.2	Faizani online teaching	159
4.3	Female *murid* speaking at Faizani Conference	165
5.1	Praying at Khwaja Abdullah Ansari Shrine	180
5.2	Salwatiyyah *murids* drinking tea at Pir Osman's shrine	185

NOTE ON TRANSLITERATION

THE TRANSLITERATION HAS FOLLOWED the IJMES transliteration system, with changes. Most diacritical marks have been omitted for clarity of reading. Diacritics in names of books, persons and quotations have been retained. Names of famous poets are spelled in accordance with their common English usage—for example, Saadi or Mawlana Rumi. For *izafa*, *e* is used, not *i* (e.g., *padar-e manavi*, not *padar-i manavi*). Following IJMES guidelines, the common spelling is used for non-English words frequently used in English, such as *agha*, *hajj* and *madrasa*, and they are not italicized.

ACKNOWLEDGMENTS

CONTRARY TO POPULAR BELIEF, writing does not happen in total solitude. I had the good fortune to write in conversation with others and with revisions and guidance gleaned from the engagement with many critical minds. None of this could have been written without people in different parts of the world who were willing to teach, guide and correct me in the process of assembling this book. First and foremost, I thank everyone I met in Afghanistan who taught me through conversation and through allowing me to participate and learn from them. I hope what I documented will do justice to what I have learned from you. Any errors are of course my responsibility.

Over the past few years I have amassed innumerable debts. I received my first books on Sufism in Larkana, rural Sindh, when I lived and studied in Pakistan. Barkat Ali Jhatial, who kindly gifted them to me, predicted that I would one day write a book "about all this." While I did not believe him back then, I concede that he was right and stay indebted to his joking wisdom with which he welcomed me into his home and on this path.

In Afghanistan I benefited from the unwavering support of AIAS, especially from Zaffar Daqiq, Sami Azim and Tarek. I owe Rohullah Amin, then AIAS director, fellow researcher and dear friend, for introducing me to knowledgeable teachers on Sufism, for familiarizing me with terms and understandings of Sufi poetry, for patiently reading and critiquing chapters, for discussing various versions of poetry translations such as the poetry in this volume and for signing many visa support letters. I am furthermore indebted to Michael Barry for the delight of witnessing his teaching about Persian culture and miniature paintings and for having me as his student on Ibn Arabi, Sufism and Herat's Sufi past. In a similar way I am thankful for Safa Kazimian at Ferdowsi University in Mashhad, Iran, for making Mawlana's and Attar's writing come alive in its Persian original, and for Arif Naqvi for laying the foundational love for beauty and multiplicity of meanings through teaching me Urdu poetry. Thanks is due also to my teachers Tamanna Bariawal, Uranus Hamidi, Johnny Cheung and Naser Farahmand for teaching me the beauty of Persian and Pashto.

The book is based on initial dissertation research at Boston University, where I benefited from the solid support, unwavering encouragement, intellectual generosity and guidance of Thomas Barfield, Charles (Chuck) Lindholm, Shahla Haeri, Kimberly Arkin and Robert Weller. I could not have been luckier with such a responsive and caring committee, who have truly engaged me and my work and believed in its viability even when others did not. I thank Thomas Barfield for much sage advice and enduring intellectual guidance, particularly when everything kept changing repeatedly. In the department I gained from exchanges with an exceptional group of colleagues, especially Calynn Dowler, Emily Williamson, Alexander Heywood, Amy Scott, Kevin Boueri, Dat Nguyen, Merav Shohet, Chris Taylor, Omar Sharifi, Carol Ferrara, Mehrdad Babadi, Noha Roushdy, Feyza Burak-Adli, Jeffrey Dyer and Laura Tourtelotte, who read earlier drafts of the chapters and gave valuable feedback. Extra thanks are due to Calynn Dowler and Noha Roushdy, who read the earliest draft forms of thoughts and attempts at formulations in our own reading and writing group. Special thanks go to Dat Nguyen for inviting me to the reading group on *War and Memory* and later on the *Anthropology of Science, Death and War* between the Institute for War, Holocaust and Genocide Studies (NIOD) and the Max Planck Institute, which has been a source of much inspiration and valuable insight while rethinking my initial dissertation material, especially with Peter van der Veer, Tam Ngo, David Henig and Nicole Iturriaga. In particular, for all the exchanges over the years about chapters, conference papers and revisions that found their way into this book, thanks are due to Feyza Burak-Adli for being my conference buddy and support in rethinking anything related to Sufism from Istanbul to Venice to New Orleans.

Chapters of this book have been presented at various conferences and workshops, where I benefited immensely from the feedback, discussions and critique of colleagues, such as Ismail Alatas, David Geary, Irfan Ahmad, Maria E. Louw, Fabio Vicini, Christian Suhr, Lili di Puppo, Robin Sheriff, Matthew Newsom, Jeannette Mageo, Gabrielle van den Berg, Elena Paskaleva, Sara Kuehn, Francesco Piraino, Shobhana Xavier, Ezgi Guner, Hajar Masbah, Marta Dominguez-Diaz, Omar Sadr, Sarajuddin Isar, Harini Kumar, Mudit Trivedi, Joel Lee, Shenila Khoja-Moolji, Amanda M. Lanzillo, Teena Purohit, Ruslan Yusupov, Barry Sadid, Rose Deighton and Razia Sultanova among others. The initial research was made possible by grants from Boston University, the Wenner Gren Foundation, the Global Religion Research Initiative (GRRI) and the Institute for the Study of Muslim Societies and Civilizations. Parts of Chapter 4 have appeared in article form in the *Afghanistan Journal*, and some materials from Chapter 5 appear in an article for *HAU: Journal of Ethnographic Theory*. Thanks to Laura Portwood-Stacer's Manuscript Works Workshop my book proposal got into the right shape and form to communicate what the book is all about. Heartfelt thanks are also due to my editors, Dylan Kyung-lim White and Kate Wahl, who saw the value of this book and patiently shepherded me through the process, as well as the three reviewers, including Sonia Ahsan-Tirmizi and David Edwards, for their valuable input. Thanks is also due to the whole team at Stanford University Press, including Kapani Kirkland, Tim Roberts, David Zielonka, Cynthia H. Lindlof and Sarah Rodriguez.

I reworked book chapters in past years at Harvard's Society of Fellows, where I have found a truly supportive community of fellow researchers who have shared commiseration, encouragement, insights and good spirits, especially among them Tania Bhattacharyya, Rachel Kolb, Sivan Goren-Arzony, Mireille Kamariza, Tara K. Menon, Monica I. Pate, Pedro Regalado, Paris Spies-Gans, Shriya Srinivasan, Manon Garcia, Michael L. Schachter, Suraj Shankar, Camille Owens, Quincy Amoah, Mohamed El-Brolosy, Jason Ferguson, Matthew Moscicki Spellberg, Christopher Spaide, Katie

Ebner-Landy, Gili Kliger, Matylda Figlerowicz, Maria Mendez Gutierrez, Max Brandstadt, Ana Novak and Laura Jakli, to whom I owe the title of this book. Senior Fellows such as Elaine Scarry, Amartya Sen, Peter Galison and Nur Yalman were guiding lights when times seemed darkest.

Fellow researchers and academics have been kind in sharing access, insights and comradery, chief among them Bette Dam, Andrea Chiovenda, Melissa Kerr-Chiovenda, Omar Dewachi, Haider Hameed, Lucile Martin, Mejgan Massoumi, Munazza Ebtikar, Nafay Choudhury, Rod Mena Fluhmann, Scott Flower, Mike Fane, Mohammed Moheq, Khalillulah Afzali, Eva Meharry, Ashley Jackson, Farzana Felisa Hervey, Zach Warren, Zalmai Nishat, Dipali Mukhopadhyay, Romain Malejacq, Omar Sharifi, Wazhmah Osman, Shah Mahmoud Hanifi, Yama Torabi, Kali Rubaii, James Caron, Yousef Baker, Rahmat Amiri, Lenny Linke, Charity Watson, Paniz Mousavi Natanzi, Ping-hsiu Alice Lin, Melissa Cornet, Mohsen Jalali (one day we will get access to that archive . . .), Arian Sharifi, Syeda Masood, Emma Allen, Timor Sharan, Nile Green, Noah Coburn, Jesko Schmoller, Seema Golestaneh, Yakir Englander, Michael Lindsey (thank you for the music!), Ali Abdi and Mirl Redman. I would also like to thank David Edwards for sharing with me transcripts of interviews that he conducted with *murids* of the Faizani community in Peshawar in the 1980s. There are colleagues and friends whom I cannot thank enough for their mental and emotional support as well as their immense intellectual generosity: I believe that the extended voice-message discussions with Marya Hannun would fill its own podcast library if we ever assembled it. Thank you for reading all those draft versions, slashing my German paragraph-long sentences and being the most critical and caring work-wife I could have ever asked for.

The research was helped on every step of the way by the kindness, teasing laughter and helpful insights of a host of research assistants, colleagues and friends in Afghanistan and beyond. Ahmad Rafi Rasuli spent innumerable hours discussing translations, negotiating access and helping in calm decision-making. I shared so much good laughter and commiseration with Tala Kemya, whom I thank for both her tireless work on the research and her insane haggling skills at Herat's lelami market. Tamana Ayazi endured getting up way too early to go to *zikr*, showed incredible persistence and has always offered honest assessments of any situation. Abdul Quddus Mosaddiq provided introductions and support in Herat, as did Grand Hewand in Kandahar. Sami Nabizada set me onto the right path for my research with an incredibly insightful shared tea at Le Bistro and has sharpened my perspective through his analysis since. Farhad Zalmai Sayeed made some of the most impactful connections in Herat and was an amazing sounding board for thoughts and questions. Thanks to Jawad Timoori for helping me with research permissions and to Amin Saraj for enduring not only long conversations but also a drive to Chisht-e Sharif. Among the wonderful research oasis of the Afghanistan Center at Kabul University (ACKU) Jebrael Amin and Fazelrabani Qazizai especially helped me find resources and make them accessible. Shoaib Behrad provided many kind introductions and interesting discussions of material and questions. Thanks to Ghulam Naqshband and family for opening your home and allowing me access to the private photos of Ustad Wujudi's life, whom I also thank for feedback on the chapter. Thanks to Momena and Manija Billah for reading and critiquing the chapter on the Faizani community and for making additional resources on their community available. The one and only Khalid Shahim helped with introductions and not getting killed despite his questionable driving skills. Thanks to Hamed Sarfarazi for taking me into his family, for helping me set up my living in Herat, for being a connector extraordinaire and for being my anchor in Herat with whatever was needed, from flight tickets to dried fruit. Similarly, thanks to Humaira Raziq for the best quruti on earth, uncounted meals and incredible hospitality, practicing Persian with me, raising two of my favorite kids on earth and letting me collapse onto their sofa for naps anytime without questioning. Soraya Afzali helped with discussions, commiserations, visits in Balkh and shared many a tea when times were rough. Thanks to Naweed Hamkar for going with me to events and places even if it was not always directly clear what it all was for, for being the voice of reason when I pushed to go to insecure places, for being puzzled together with me, to some extent, for being my Haji Sahib. Thank you to Fatima Faizi for not only being a dear and beloved friend who gave me a home when I returned to Kabul but also a staunch defender. I am furthermore thankful for friendships that offered reflection time as well as moral sustenance, especially with offering places that let me write and ponder: sincere thanks to Boris Bogdanovic, Nathan W. Stroupe, Richard Dwerryhouse and the

TM crew in Kabul and Amman, to Rada Akbar for the oasis she creates wherever she lives and invites me in, as well as Ann-Katrina Bregovic for the productive writing retreat in Tunis. Thanks to Birte Paulsen for being my home when I needed to rethink and to Julia Schreier for being an incredible technical wizard and fast emergency-thinker friend. Thanks to the Boston CI community for all the dances, particularly Jacob, Frances, James, Derek, Paul, Katerina, Neige, John Adams, Olive, Anvita, Nelson, Funda, Robin, Benoit and Başak. Among the friends who were always there when needed I want to thank Beatrice Barco, Mehrdad Pourzacki, Duygu Demir, Nicole Bogott, Payman Shamsian, Nafise Motlaq, Matt Longmore, Felicity Cain, Abasin Azarm, Sinsia van Kalkeren, Janna Lou, Fathema Mansoorally, Reihane Akhlaqi, Ustad Wafi, Jordan Byron, Kiana Haeri, Maira Küppers, Susanne Eisch, Annika Eklund, James Novakowski, Vic Getz, Patrick Finn, Ruchi Kumar, Hikmat Noori, Berit Muhlhausen, David Mason and Kern Hendricks: thank you for being there when it counted with much-needed distractions, discussions and the occasional motorbike rides.

The last ones to thank were the first ones to always support me. I am deeply thankful to Dietlind and Karl Erich Schmeding, for not only unfailingly supporting me and for letting me go with full trust but also for instilling an unwavering hope that things will come together even when we do not yet know how. Thanks to Alexander Schmeding for being an example of academic excellence and true integrity and for letting me sometimes forget about academia when playing with Jonathan and Jacob. I owe my deepest gratitude to Adnan Rafiq Khan, who was not only the first to support me in this research endeavor but also always the first and last to edit and critique any drafts, discuss ideas until the early morning and be a loving corrective to worries and wayward thoughts. Thank you for enduring Bostonian hardship and celebrating life in Istanbul and Kabul with me. Your critical mind inspires me to be better.

SUFI CIVILITIES

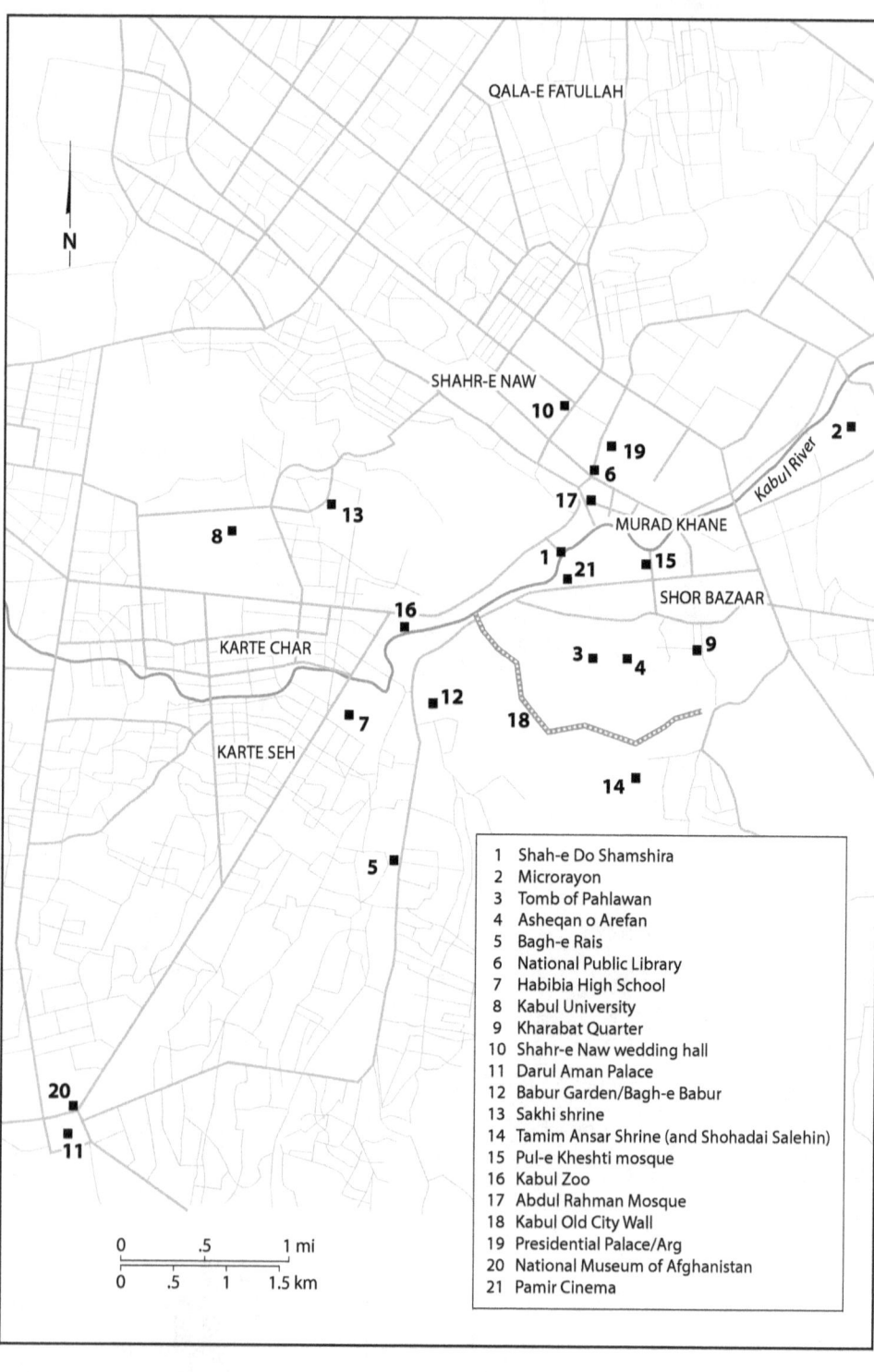

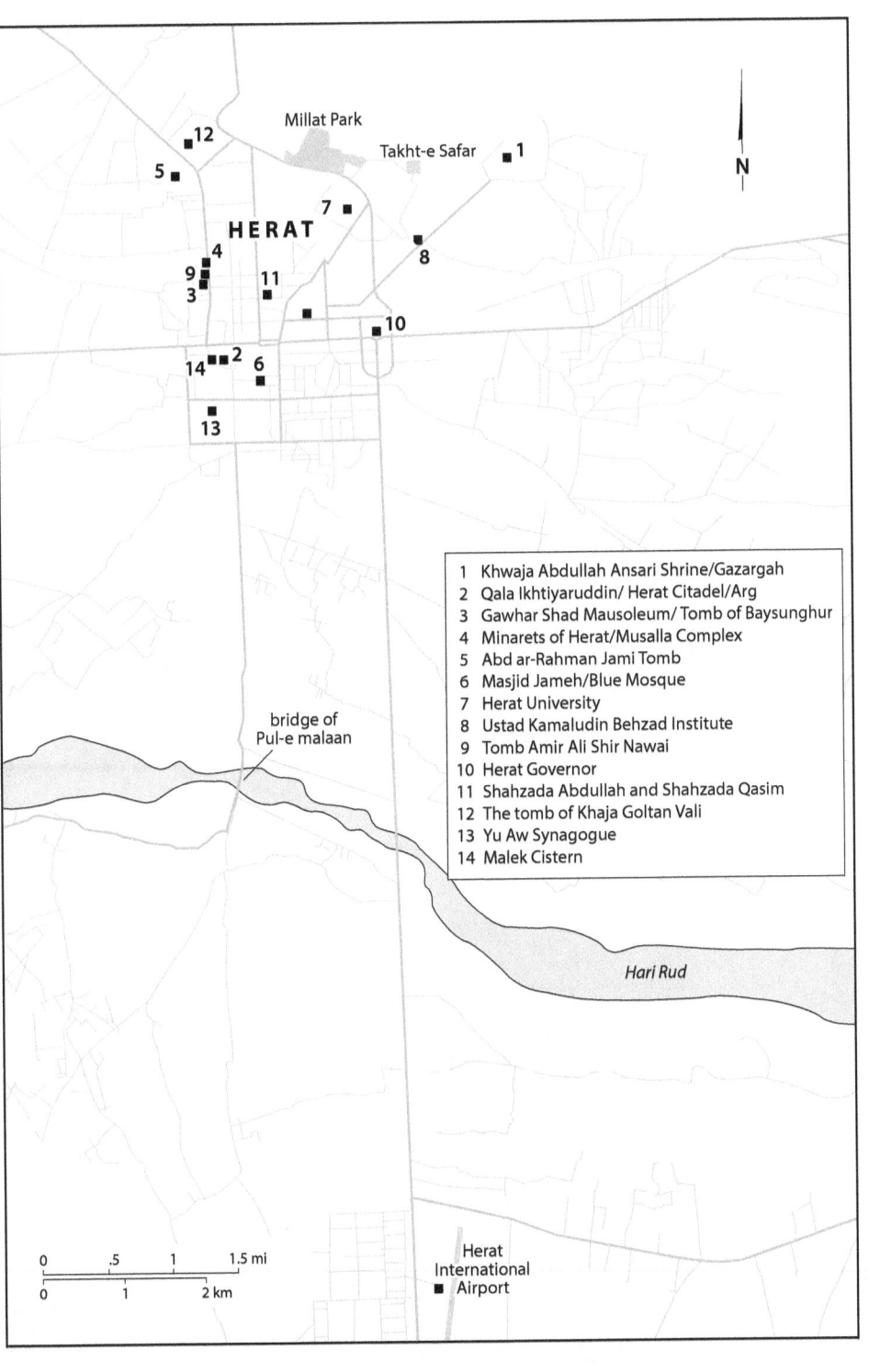

Introduction

BAGH-E RAIS, KABUL, AFGHANISTAN

July 19, 2018

The midday sun had just begun to warm the backs of the guests seated on padded *toshak* mattresses under the half-shade of a willowing canopy when Asma Mahjor, a poet and Sufi teacher in her late thirties, took the podium. Her father, an eminent expert on the poetry of Bedil Dehlavi, who had tutored her in the intricacies of mystic allegories and poetic meter, had passed away a year earlier. This was his annual death celebration (*urs*), an event celebrated for important Sufi teachers or saints. "There are some men who have heroic women and children," Asma's brother said in his introduction for his sister who was about to speak, "and there are some daughters who make their father a hero." Ascending to the podium, Asma greeted the community: "Dear respectful scholars, may peace be with you as I welcome you to the house of Bedil."

As she launched into her speech on love (*ishq*) in the Sufi tradition, a middle-aged woman in the audience next to me whispered: "This is the *real* Afghan civil society," skewering a buzzword of the Western-funded, English-speaking nongovernmental organization (NGO) scene with its lofty goals of rebuilding Afghanistan's society in its own image.[1] The woman herself had a foot in both worlds, interfacing with international donors and their "transformative" agendas as the director of a large NGO as well as hailing from a traditionally influential family. Her grandfather had been a founding member of the Bedil *halqa* (circle) alongside Asma's grandfather. "There's no funding for this, but it exists and continues nonetheless," she explained. "It's the resistance of a nation to organize these social, cultural and religious events, to keep the memory of who we are alive." Her words hinted at the vital role that Sufism had played throughout Afghanistan's history along with other types of voluntary associational groups that have long been a feature of social life in Afghanistan. While individuals might have family connections to a *pir* who led a particular Sufi community, affiliation with a specific order or group was not a foregone conclusion but a voluntary act. It created a group of like-minded people bound together by their common search for knowledge and participation in Sufi ritual practices. As Asma was joined on the podium by a young poet who was a student of the late Mahjor, the woman nudged me out of my private thoughts, declaring: "Look! This is the new generation."

What a casual visitor might not pick up on, but what was perceptible to discerning community members like the woman seated next to me, was that choosing a leader and embodying authority were not a straightforward question of inheritance. Asma was the daughter of the late teacher, but her status as an authority on Bedil and teacher of Sufi insights remained questioned and disputed. She had organized the *urs* celebrations, in which she would speak and disseminate the newest publications of her father's oeuvre, which she had also edited. The event served as an opportunity to demonstrate her ability to mobilize the financial and cultural capital needed to bring these books that honored the memory of her late father into existence. It was a necessary effort concerning the competition for leadership. Her uncle had hosted a competing *urs* event in memory of Asma's father on another day by inviting Bedil aficionados for a *mahfil* (celebration) that many in the community recognized as a competing bid to claim leadership of his brother's followers.

Threats and challenges to authority were rarely expressed openly in these bids for leadership in Afghanistan. Indeed, in this instance, the dueling events could be shrugged off as just alternative dates for people to come and celebrate in another setting. When I asked Asma about it, she simply replied, "We had already printed the invitations when he decided to invite [community members] on another day." But from what I knew of the community and the varying contenders' interactions, it was clear that this discord was not a logistical miscommunication. The choice of guests and speakers, decisions to invite the media or leave it a semi-private affair, the way individual teachers used social media to broadcast or to teach, all lay the groundwork for competing claims for power and leadership. They also embodied very different visions of the community that each contender intended to lead.

The particulars of the Bedil community's struggles over succession were distinct but hardly unique. They arise in many Sufi communities after the death or departure of an established leader. By the time I witnessed the competing *urs* celebrations within a Bedil group, I had become aware of similar struggles, transitions and processes unfolding in other Sufi communities past and present. I had returned to Afghanistan to research how Sufi communities navigated transition phases of different types during the periods of conflict, ideological struggle and migration produced by four decades of war. What I realized after spending months at a time, over successive years, among different Sufi communities was that the choice of leadership was intimately linked with the ways these groups understood their changing environment and their own role in it. Leaders needed to respond to these changes, to give guidance, assurance and support to their communities, sometimes shield them or take the brunt of attacks against them. They needed to show their dexterity in dealing with these situations and skillfully navigating tense and changing social and political environments.

Unlike the power of a state ruler that is often enforced by violence or coercion, authority among Afghanistan's Sufi communities is established through the mutual acknowledgment of teacher and student, leader and follower. If religious authority relies on such interpersonal dynamics, on this continued labor, how could it have not been altered by the intense changes and ruptures that tore through Afghanistan's societal fabric over the past decades? How could it not be challenged by the varying ways in which Islam became a pawn used by all the factions fighting these wars? How did potential leaders in the communities confront these changes and potential contestation to their authority? The communities I researched seemed to have adapted in manifold ways to their changing environments, navigating in turn external changes as well as internal transitions. Yet when I looked for literature to capture or explain these dynamics, I found little about the particulars of these processes. This book explores how leaders like Asma navigated changing social and ideological environments and how the necessity to adapt to these changing conditions affected the way that religious authority itself was legitimized and constructed.

Sufism and the Study of Islam in Afghanistan

This book is a reflection on the navigational dexterity of Sufi leaders and their communities who weather periods of instability and ideological animosity by adapting to an ever-changing world around them. Sufism is as pervasive as it is often contested in Afghanistan. A focus on Sufism, given its deep historical roots and its local, national and transnational salience, allows us to zoom in on particular aspects of change and continuity within Afghanistan's past and present. Centering "Sufis"—a multivalent term on whose definitional disagreement I elaborate later—allows for a more complete picture of the changes within discourses on Islam and brings into focus the lived experience of civilians in conflict and postconflict settings who are often targeted for their particular beliefs or practices.[2] The community-centered perspective from the ground up that this book espouses challenges the flattened, two-dimensional image of Islam so often applied to Afghanistan.

Much of the literature on Islam and Afghanistan tends to focus on the use of Islam in political ideologies and nation building or its gendered dimensions.[3] Islam as a faith is frequently relegated to a position of instrumentalized ideology, especially in regard to the decades-long insurgencies that were often legitimized as a jihad.[4] More recently, religion in Afghanistan has been viewed through reference to the Taliban's version of Islam, particularly after their takeover of the country in 2021.[5] However, Islam is lived in diverse ways among Afghanistan's various Muslim sects—Sunnis, Twelver Shi'a and Isma'ili Shi'is—who have historically lived alongside non-Muslim communities of Jews, Hindus, Sikhs and Christians.[6] Sufism should not be thought of as a separate sect, like Shi'ism or Sunnism, but an orientation within Islam, one that is present within any sect. It is better understood as a lens through which Islam is interpreted, thought of and lived in Afghanistan as well as in many Muslim communities worldwide.[7] Referred to as *tasawwuf* or *irfan* (gnostic mysticism) in Persian, Sufism in its most simplified rendering is the search for the inner meaning of the Qur'an and the Prophet Muhammad's message.[8] It has been part and parcel of a diversified discursive environment, taught in madrasas as religious education, interwoven into seemingly secular socioeconomic networks, viewed as inspiring courtly artistic flowering and inscribed as an essential element of Afghanistan's national cultural heritage.

Forays into the history of interregional Sufi networks that ran from Delhi in present-day India through Afghanistan to Central Asia, Iran and Turkey, as well as Persianate literary studies (which cannot be conceptualized without Sufism at its core), point to the far-reaching significance of Sufism's legacy in today's Afghanistan.[9] However, the lack of contemporary scholarship on Muslim communities and on the nuanced Islamic discourses in Afghanistan has, perhaps inadvertently, played into a "decline hypothesis" that declares Sufism defunct in the contemporary era. In this view Afghanistan had a golden past populated with courtly Sufi statesmen and poets that bears no resemblance to its present state, one characterized by narrow-minded Islamists and suicide bombers.[10] In reality, Sufis never left the stage of Afghan history; they simply reappeared in unexpected roles and places: as resistance fighters and aid workers in refugee camps, as politicians and businessmen, as actors and musicians, as university professors and students, mullahs and mobile phone sellers. We might have to adjust our lens, but Sufis are there, and not as mere bystanders but as active agents in their own history.

Sufi Civilities contributes to and builds on the growing ethnographically informed literature on present-day Afghanistan that was reinvigorated post-2001 after decades of a virtual standstill for on-the-ground research in the country.[11] Anthropologists have since explored changes in local politics and center-periphery interactions, gender relations, memory, trauma and ethnicity, the reconstruction and development nexus as well as international economic and labor networks.[12] With only a few exceptions, significant attention to Islam from an anthropological perspective has been largely absent.[13] Indeed, the post-2001 revival of anthropological research on Islam pales in comparison to the meteoric rise of interest among political scientists and international relations and security studies researchers.[14] Furthermore, the most recent anthropological accounts of Afghanistan's Sufi communities, reflecting a reality that many Afghans have had to face, were conducted among diaspora communities in Pakistan and Germany.[15] *Sufi Civilities* builds on their insights while offering a novel perspective on what happened to Sufis who stayed in Afghanistan or those who returned there.

A "Community of Disagreement"

So far I have used "Sufi" as if it were a self-explanatory and widely agreed-upon term and as if Sufi communities had an uncontested position within Afghanistan's society and the Muslim community of believers (*ummah*) globally. Nothing could be further from the truth. In fact, it has been suggested that "Sufism" is one of the most complex Islamic terms to define.[16] Anyone following the news in recent decades, even cursorily, will have read about a plethora of attacks on Sufis and Sufi infrastructure by fellow Muslims. These attacks are a physical manifestation of fierce debates about what constitutes the core beliefs and boundaries of Islam and, by extension, Sufism. These debates are also finding their expression in the historical and anthropological study of Islam and Muslim communities, transmuted into inquiries into how to study Islam as culturally and locally embedded instantiations derived from universal claims of a singular truth proclaimed by the Prophet Muhammad.[17] Not surprisingly, the question of Sufism figures prominently in most of these accounts. Shahab Ahmed poignantly remarked that "one might say that the community of Islam is a *community of disagreement*" over the question of what Islam is.[18] These disagreements are more than erudite fistfights. As I argue later, they are at the core of understanding shifts and changes within civil society in many Muslim-majority societies.

But what is being fought over? Attempting to delineate the fault lines in the disagreements and divergences in definitions necessitates a look at the various dimensions at play in conceptualizing Sufism. Defined as a system in which Muslims seek a personal encounter and closeness to God, Sufism is often described as an individual path in which a seeker usually becomes a student (*murid*) of a teacher (*pir, murshid*).[19] This educational relationship is sealed by a pledge (*bay'a*) to the *pir* after which the student officially joins the Sufi order (*tariqa*) and participates in its rituals.[20] Sufis practice within and are connected to a Sufi social sphere at meeting circles (*halqas*), shrines (*ziyarat*) and lodges (*khanaqahs*, in other areas called *tekkeh, zawiyahs* or *merkez*).[21] There they meet for classes (*dars*), celebrations (such as the *urs* of saints or the birthday of the Prophet Muhammad) or collective rituals such as *zikr* (lit., "remembrance" of God). Over the course of centuries, various Sufi orders have developed, differentiating along genealogies of learning, pedagogies and devotional practices. Most Sufi orders trace their origin back to the Prophet Muhammad. Affiliation to one of the main Sufi orders, such as the Naqshbandiyyah, Qadiriyyah and Chishtiyyah,[22] which are prevalent in Afghanistan, is not necessarily exclusive; most *murids* with whom I spoke had been initiated into multiple orders or had experiences in practices from more than one order. Some Sufis do not belong to any particular Sufi order at all but coalesce around particular individual teachers who give classes centered around interpreting Sufi poetry in conjunction with the Qur'an and Hadith, such as Ustad Mahjor and his daughter, Asma.[23] Others have built up NGOs as additional outreach. The forms of assembly and the organizational format might change, but common to them is the search for an experiential encounter with the Divine.

Undergirding this understanding of the spiritual path (*suluk*) is a cosmology asserting that the ability to access and know the Divine is not evenly distributed among believers.[24] In Sufi thought, God's ultimate truth (*haqiqa*) is differentiated into many layers, and the Sufi teacher is the guide to a deepened understanding of the Divine with the ultimate goal of closeness to God or ultimate annihilation (*fana*). Some Sufi literature refers to this hierarchy explicitly, such as Khwaja Abdullah Ansari's (d. 1089) *Stations of the Wayfarers* (*Manazil al-sayitin*), which divides the different levels into *amm, khass* and *khass al-khass*—commoners, elect and elect of the elect.[25] A thread that runs through this is an epistemological and hermeneutical authority over deeper, hidden layers of existence that are invisible to the uninitiated. In this hierarchy of knowers who traverse the Sufi path, the claim of a higher level of insight can sometimes set Sufi adherents at odds with other Muslims in regard to practices ranging from the use of music, dance or substances in rituals, to the exalted position of the *pir* as an intermediary with potentially miraculous powers or the visitation of and praying at gravesites.[26]

This brings us to a tension that often surfaces in Muslim communities attempting to mediate between varying truth claims. Sufis' claims to higher understanding of divine knowledge that supersedes that of other Muslims, and sometimes nullifies Islamic law itself, sets up a potential competition between *shariʿat* and *tariqat*.[27] Some legal scholars have criticized behavior and actions arising from Sufi Islamic interpretations, and some Sufi writers have derided the limited philosophical insight of legalists. This conflict has often been described in simplistic terms and tropes that locate these various positions in mutually exclusive and often antagonistic roles, such as the jurist and the Sufi. Within Orientalist and colonial writing, which also influenced later postcolonial and Muslim reformist writing, Sufism and Islam were separated and located within different personas: the *alim* who studies the Islamic sciences was set in contrast to the Sufi who sees beyond them.[28] In reality the two were not so distinct: most traditional scholars of Islam (*ulama*) were simultaneously legal scholars (part of what one might consider the orthodoxy) and Sufi thinkers, leaders and guides. Far from being mutually exclusive roles, they were often combined in one person. Indeed, some of my interlocutors, such as Haji Saiqal in Chapter 2 and most members of the Sufi Council in Chapter 5, were both part of the traditional ulama *and* Sufi teachers and leaders. They did not fit neatly into either of these categories, inhabiting both without any sense of contradiction. Thus, my work contributes and builds on a growing body of literature that challenges compartmentalized depictions through an ethnographically informed look at the heterogenous Sufi sociosphere in which the idea of orthodoxy is not external to Sufism.[29]

But if not in easily identifiable roles and job descriptions, where are the tension and conflict to be located? Critique can come from many places, both from outside a Sufi community and from within. A particularly productive area of scholarship in Islamic studies has outlined the internal criticism of reformers within the Islamic tradition, even positing that at the very base, religion itself is a way to critique how to live one's life.[30] These scholars are mainly focused on understanding Islam through its long tradition of textual discourses and disputation.[31] Others, meanwhile, have pointed toward extradiscursive ways that individuals and communities manifest consensus or dissent on matters of community vision and truth claims, for example, by voicing skepticism and aspirations.[32] Indeed, most Sufis I researched with did not explicitly criticize one another. This would have been considered bad form in terms of their own character and spiritual development. I often heard Sufi leaders say that "there are many different paths up the mountain" or "they are different paths, leading to the same goal" when trying to diffuse views that could be seen as critical of another order or *pir*. They relied on alternative ways of making their stances heard: a choice of one leader over another, for instance; a donation in favor of a particular publishing venture; a disavowal of a particular book that describes a community vision or a shrine built over the grave of one *pir* next to the abandoned grave of another. All these are also ways to make positions clear and to claim ground, to exalt one teacher and diminish or criticize another. Fault lines within the community of disagreement also run within Sufi communities themselves and between various Sufi groups who do not necessarily agree on rightful conduct, praxis and leadership.

Sufism has also been discursively attacked by Muslims and non-Muslims, reformers and traditionalists, scholars and laymen alike as to whether or not it belongs (wholesale or in part) to Islam.[33] Not only fundamentalists have criticized Sufis, as Deepra Dandekar and Torsten Tchacher have suggested; a surprising rapprochement can be found between non-Muslim rationalists and Muslims who criticize shrine visitation as superstition.[34] Sufism has been part of Islam's past for almost as long as the religion has existed, and for just as long questions of whether Sufism should be part of Islam's present and future have provoked debate that has led to certain Sufi practices being condemned as *bid'a* (wrongful innovation) or *shirk* (polytheism).[35] This reference to heresy has come recently into prominence for its association with Salafism. According to some scholars, rejecting something as *bid'a* is a core characteristic of Salafists.[36]

The turn to increased and strict moral codes in conduct have been researched by anthropologists focusing on the formation of new ethical subjectivities.[37] These examples of piety movements focus on what Shahab Ahmed calls "prescriptive authority" based on following the behavior of the Prophet Muhammad and the *salaf* (the first three generations of Muslims). He notes that, historically speaking, this type of self-cultivation based on the *salaf* has not been the norm and obscures other modes of religiosity, many of which are part of a Sufi-infused practice and environment that would better be captured by what he labels "explorative authority," alluding to the historical freedom of Muslims to explore meaning, value and truth through a multiplicity of ways that include philosophy, Sufism or artistic expressions steeped in Islam.[38] Drawing on starkly differing understandings of what constitutes a legitimate base for authority fuels debates on heresy and, because the definition of what constitutes heresy has always been highly contentious and Sunni Islam lacks an ultimate religious authority figure who has the power to make such a determination, such debates inevitably remained unresolved. But while critiques of Sufism are opinions and not dogma, this does not stop some of them from inciting violence.

While most media and academic literature cover the conflict between Sufis and Salafis, the more subtle impact of the debate among Sufi communities themselves remains largely unexamined.[39] The existence of the critiques that can end in physical violence and destruction is a specter that Sufi communities confront through their own mediation, including the potential restriction and policing of each other's practices and behavior. This book variously describes adaptations that Sufi communities make to navigate ambiguous and complex environments in which animosity and insecurity can mix in volatile ways. Chapter 5 describes in more detail one response in which a number of Sufi communities in Herat came together under the umbrella of an ecumenical Sufi Council founded in 2004 to respond to the heightened discursive environment in which they have experienced an increase in attacks. The council published information about Sufism to legitimize its practices. However, as I show in the case study, it also criticized other Sufi communities and started to police them for their conduct, especially in their choice of leadership. The community of disagreement is found not only "outside" a Sufi community but also among various teachers and Sufi communities in relation to each other.

Sufism as a Lens on Afghanistan's Civil Society

One of the arguments this book makes is that a focus on Sufism reveals an unacknowledged sector of Afghanistan's society. It provides a lens for viewing civility and the seemingly uncivil arguments Sufism often provokes about the boundaries of the acceptable and the desirable, of aspirations and sociability. My own perspective on Sufi communities shifted after hearing the comment of the woman seated next to me at the *urs* commemoration, deriding the lack of understanding among foreigners about the *real* Afghan civil society.

Why did I see these two—Sufism and civil society—as separate, especially considering that in so many places, the United States and Europe included, large parts of the civil sphere are in fact run by religious groups?[40] How did a particular definition of the term "civil society," influenced by Western Enlightenment definitions and neoliberal development policy, prevent me from noticing the horizontal ties that held these groups together, forming a crucial part of the civil sphere in Afghanistan's society? To conceive of Sufi groups in their various capacities necessitates a paradigm shift that enables a critical distance toward how civil society has been conceived of mainly in the Enlightenment tradition that influenced the rhetoric of the post-2001 neoliberal peace-building efforts of the international community in Afghanistan.

Civil society has been of special interest in the neoliberal development policy driving the post-2001 state-building process in Afghanistan, financed and directed by leading NATO members. It has been framed as a way to "effectively assist implementation of government liberalization reform and efficiently fill service-delivery functions not sufficiently taken care of by the state or the market."[41] For this reason, as the woman's joke at the beginning of the chapter suggests, civil society in Afghanistan has been mainly understood as a project championed by the English-speaking, NGO-connected strata of society that was engaged to serve as local implementers in the development and reconstruction sector.[42] While this, in itself, is not uncommon in the global development sector, it should be acknowledged that many of these civil society actors and organizations were framed as central to the post-2001 peace- and state-building process. This means that projects and programs were designed to create and support a particular framing of the civil society sphere, and donors supported formally established organizations that could provide services catering to this end. Overlooking a complex, preexisting associational landscape and working with technically oriented NGOs for aid delivery is, of course, not unique to Afghanistan.[43] Indeed, a substantial body of critical analysis of such an approach already exists, illustrating how its dependency on international aid can lead to a "rentier civil society."[44] This is not to say that these organizations did not contribute in often meaningful ways to Afghanistan's society but that our understanding of the full scope of the civil sphere remains limited if it is conceived of only through the persons and organizations connected with the international community.

The guiding concept of civil society is based on a Western Enlightenment framework, which originated with the idea that voluntary institutions play important mediating roles between individual, family and state.[45] As an intermediary realm, these associations were seen as connected to particular standards of voluntarism, independence from kin ties and normative criteria of civility, seeing it as something inherently "good" and "civil." The term "civil" has roots and resonances in ideas of "civilization" and colonial civilizing missions, which also reverberated in the rhetoric of post-9/11 neocolonial development contexts.[46] Terms such as "good" and "civil" are, of course, just as much constructions as "bad" and "uncivil" and subject to the set of values used to construct what are seen as inherently positive/productive or negative/destructive characteristics.[47] Normative approaches can artificially narrow the focus and exclude other actors in the civil sphere that do not fit into these conceptions, such as the National Rifle Association or the Muslim Brotherhood.[48] With the transformation of post–Soviet Eastern Europe, as well as popular struggles against autocratic and pseudo-democratic regimes, especially in the Middle East, the concept has gained renewed traction in recent decades.[49] However, the revived enthusiasm it has engendered has also spurred criticism about the applicability of the term in non-Western contexts.[50]

Formal organizations in the civil sphere have been useful in the NATO-led war of the last two decades. In the attempt to further humanize the war, NGOs were considered by political and military elites in the United States as "a force multiplier" and "an important part of our combat team," as General Colin Powell stated in 2001.[51] In 2011, the US Senate Committee on Foreign Relations reiterated the decisive role of humanitarian and development actors, acknowledging that development complements the work of "defence and diplomacy" and, as such, supports military gains.[52] Building an effective civil society was also part of counterinsurgency strategies intended to show that services were delivered to constituents and cast the international community in a positive light. In regard to foreign policy in Afghanistan, both the George W. Bush and Barack Obama administrations built on this approach to the Afghanistan War in their respective national security strategies.

This book argues that Afghanistan was not, and has never been, without its own civil society groups anchored in indigenous movements. Looking to the civil and political movements that emerged in the wake of 2001 shows they have been varied in their political ideologies and religious anchoring and included grassroots civil disobedience movements. Movements, such as the Junbesh-e Roshnayi (Enlightenment Movement), advocated for political and economic rights of Hazaras from 2016 onward.[53] The Helmand Peace Convoy, or People's Peace Movement, marched across Afghanistan to Kabul in 2018 to push for a cease-fire and mediation to end the fighting. The elite youth political movement of mid-career professionals of the Harakat-e Afghanistan 1400 (Afghanistan 1400 Movement) sought to honor victims of war and strengthen democratic values,[54] and the Muslim Brotherhood–inspired Jamiat-e eslah wa inkishaf-e ijtem'ai Afghanistan (Association for Reform and Social Development of Afghanistan, henceforth Jamiat-e Eslah) advocated for bottom-up Islamization.[55] All of these movements could be rendered as part of Afghanistan's civil society sphere that do not neatly fit into the NGO formats. What sets them apart from most Sufi groups is that even in their stark differences in terms of ideology or social positioning, all interfaced with the political sphere: over half of the founding members of Harakat-e Afghanistan 1400 were part of the Afghan government, and Junbesh-e Roshnayi as well as Jamiat-e Eslah had clearly defined political demands. Some of these groups also had formal institutional setups, such as Jamiat-e Eslah, which was registered from 2003 at the Ministry of Justice.[56] Others, such as many of the Junbesh-e Roshnayi, were active within the NGO scene.[57] So while these groups clearly worked within the purview of political organizing, which can—but does not have to—be an aspect of civil society, they also represented a sphere of organizing in which groups or movements came together because of shared values or causes.

Afghanistan also has a long tradition of informal, resourceful civic engagement that long predates formalized NGOs, in which people come together in their communities on a volunteer basis to improve local infrastructure (*ashar*), support people in need (*khairat*) or mediate disputes through councils (*shuras* and *jirgas*). Neamatollah Nojumi terms these intermediaries as part of "grassroots democratization" that enables participation and democratic representation.[58] These forms of collective organization, however, come into view only when the definition of "civility" is expanded to include both informally organized and religion-based civil groups.[59]

My approach to Sufism—as a lens through which we can better understand Afghanistan's society—builds on work by anthropologists who have questioned the narrow usage of the term "civil society" and opted instead for an expanded definition of "civility."[60] The term itself might be misleading when viewed only as morality, manners or an attitude of holding civic virtues, although anthropologists have pointed out alternative genealogies of the civil originating in *adab*—represented in the ethically correct-acting Sufi adherents who live faithfully.[61] However, in analyzing Sufi communities as actors in the civil sphere, I do not aim to measure their level of virtue or morality but to aspire to locate an alternative notion of civility that "is based on bottom-up embodiments and social understandings of the respectable, the debatable and the disreputable."[62]

Expanding the view on civil society and civility to include informal interpersonal groups that work neither as neoliberal development providers nor necessarily as proponents of democratization, we can perceive these groups as creating social networks of trust that in turn define identities and belonging. They fulfill important functions for socialization and social cohesion, public communication of ideas, social security and resource distribution, as well as mediation and conflict resolution.[63] Recently, Armando Salvatore has argued that Sufi orders, with their horizontal networks, vertical hierarchies and translocal connectedness, were a "versatile source of civility" in the history of Islam.[64] Spiritual experiences anchored within ritualized collective practices also facilitated wider social bonds, such as between master and disciple (what he calls vertical and dyadic) and between *murids* (horizontal and transversal).[65] Sufi lodges historically served as nodes for long-distance travelers and were often considered sanctuaries. *Pirs* were regularly recruited to mediate problems in local communities and to intercede in conflicts, either to resolve them or to at least prevent their spread. Ultimately, Sufi orders proved able to connect a wide variety of individuals belonging to a diverse set of social classes, regions and economic backgrounds. That remains so today, as the case studies in this book show.[66]

An examination of this historical background offers an understanding of the types of communities that Sufis have built over centuries and how they became a locus of civil interactions. This understanding can then in turn inform an ethnographically embedded analysis on how Sufi communities engage in societal self-organization that is vital for horizontal structures of participation, accountability and exchange. Furthermore, it provides a vantage point from which to observe how change is introduced in ways that are seen as socially acceptable.

The example of Sufi teachers such as Asma Mahjor, whose speech began this Introduction, points to the civic sphere in which Sufi leaders and their communities are active and sets the parameters that differentiate them from their NGO counterparts. As a teacher and leader, Asma engaged in the "typical" activities of a Sufi leader—organizing yearly Sufi celebrations, offering Bedil lessons and publishing books for the spiritual nourishment of her followers. But she was also active in service-delivery functions, which are often seen as the purview of formalized organizations or institutions. In 2022, she collected donations online to drill a well and make safe drinking water available to the mountainside community residing close to her father's grave. Unlike that for formal organizations, however, the construction was not financed through approved international grants but crowd-sourced from the wider Sufi community inside Afghanistan as well as its diaspora. Once the drilling and construction of the well had started, the estimated costs doubled and superseded the amounts that Asma had at her disposal. She thus reached out again to her wider community:

> Because I didn't have that money to pay, I asked the circle of friends of the Bedil school, with whom we are working. I published it on the Facebook page, and I told them that it is the right time to help people. We always say this, that we are patriots, that we love our country, and we love humanity, and now is the time that you show humanity and help those people. I told them, I will post your name, I will share the contact details for the company that is digging this well and everything will be transparent. And so, happily, they helped.[67]

The accumulated donations were, in the end, more than what was needed for the well. A Malaysian company donated a substantial sum, which Asma decided to gift to the imam of a nearby mosque to install solar panels, demonstrating that the financial circuits accumulated by the Sufi leader extended beyond her own community and reached into the wider religious community. When asked by a neighbor, an army general who had previously unsuccessfully attempted to establish a well on the mountainside, how she had managed it, Asma recounted that "it was a good deed, and maybe it was that our intention as a good deed for the people is why we got the water."

Asma's horizontal approach to funding and implementation set her apart from the broader NGO-ized civil society milieu. The publication of donor names online was not meant to advertise the goodwill of those who had contributed, as is often the case with donor-funded projects in the development sector. "It's not about getting acclaim," Asma told one of her donors. "It is about transparency. I have rivals, and because I am posting it on Facebook, these rivals will say that I am taking money out of it for myself. But that is why I posted everything there." As a teacher and leader in her community, she was aware that civil action did not always produce civil responses, particularly in the embattled sphere of Sufi authority, where such actions could also be interpreted as bolstering one's own position as a leader.

Navigating those complexities is no easy task. On the one hand, *Sufi Civilities* sees individual groups as potential sites for understanding civility and civil action, but I also argue that a look into present-day Sufi communities offers a wider scope for understanding the discourses and disagreements in which these communities are enmeshed and how they pertain to many other aspects of Afghanistan's society. These include changes and continuities in areas of religious education, questions of how national heritage is negotiated, ideas of how authority is constructed, the waxing and waning of the ability to voice divergent opinions and tolerate coexistence, as well as strategies for keeping communities safe when the state turns predatory. Crucial in this perspective of how communities are positioned are their teachers and leaders.

Navigational Dexterity

The anthropologically grounded literature on authority in Afghanistan has focused mainly on secular political leadership, as it arises, is maintained and contested.[68] The position of religious leaders, by contrast, is often taken for granted, and their roles are determined by the titles and the reverence (or lack thereof) ascribed to them.⁶⁹ But apprehending how religious leaders are positioned in relation to the community can be difficult to determine. David Edwards argues that, unlike secular leaders who received titles based on an individual's tribal, kin, occupational or regional affiliation, religious leaders in Afghanistan historically had "the power to name themselves rather than having a name imposed upon them."⁷⁰ Religious titles such as "Ustad," "Pir," "Sahib," "Mawlawi" or "Akhund" that are accorded to learned teachers with a following tell us little about how the authority of specific individuals was established, projected, submitted to or challenged, let alone what changes might have occurred within religious communities in the past decades.⁷¹

Ignoring such complexities belies the fact that there is a significant difference between how authority might be imagined and how it works in practice. Authority, as Hannah Arendt remarked, "is commonly mistaken for one form of power or violence" because it always demands obedience.⁷² However, in Arendt's rendering, where force is needed to materialize it, authority has failed. She therefore defines "authority" as a hierarchical relationship that is seen as rightful and legitimate by both those exerting it and those submitting to it. In short, authority hinges on recognition and acquiescence—it is relational and contingent.⁷³ If prospective Sufi students do not recognize a teacher as their rightful *pir*, they will not follow the person as a leader and teacher.

Theorists have disagreed about the qualities and characteristics of such authoritative relationships and whether authority is lacking if it can be questioned or if it is dependent on persuasion.⁷⁴ Within Sufism, an ideal type of mentoring relationship is that of total dependence of the student on the teacher. The jurist and Sufi Al-Ghazali described this unquestioned reliance as the disciple accepting that "the advantage he gains from the error of his sheikh, if he should err, is greater than the advantage he gains from his own rightness, if he should be right."⁷⁵ In reality, however, a teacher's authority rarely goes unquestioned. As Muhammad Qasim Zaman notes in his study of modern Islamic thought, authority is not only often questioned, but "it is often *recognized* as being questioned."⁷⁶ He points to the historical dimension of the crystallization of authoritative structures such as the legal schools in Islam that took time and effort to coalesce. Equally, individuals can seek different legal scholars' input and fatwas to decide on questions they seek to resolve.[77] Authority is therefore "not a stable endowment but one that is always exposed to implicit or explicit challenge," as Zaman puts it, and "waxes and wanes in response to the pressures bearing upon it."[78]

This description of authority is helpful in pointing to its malleability, but it runs the risk of reducing authority to a spontaneous by-product of challenge and response. In his work on authority of Islamic religious leaders in Indonesia, Ismail Alatas stresses that the production and maintenance of relationships of authority and discipleship involve a process of continuous labor.[79] For him, the role of authoritative leaders is to connect with the Prophetic past and adapt it to manifold locally situated communities in the present.[80] Through a focus on the process of establishing religious authority, transmitting teachings and cultivating a community, he steers the analysis away from a Weberian understanding of religious leadership imbued through charisma and cemented through routinization. He intimates that charisma as a dialectic emotional relationship between leader and follower might be more useful in understanding the founding of a community rather than the labor required of a postfoundational religious authority.[81] Indeed, there is considerable labor involved in establishing religious authority, especially in a Muslim *ummah* where the correct way to interpret and live according to the Sunna is subject to multiple, competing visions. It is not a particular leader's charismatic aura or competence alone that produces the individual's authority. Authority is also derived from the interplay of taking on responsibility for the care of others and, in the process, coming to represent the social world and its structures.[82]

The cases in this book build on these approaches to offer an on-the-ground perspective of how religious authority is established and challenged in Afghanistan. Focusing on how individuals and communities have navigated transitional moments, both historically and contemporaneously, brings processes of authority into sharper relief. What capacities, within and beyond Sufi communities, are needed to negotiate these tumultuous times? I contend that the question of authority becomes particularly salient in moments of transition. Much like a rite of passage, with phases of separation, transition/liminality and incorporation, the process of succession can leave a community changed.[83] Similar to other liminal times, the open-ended question of who takes on the leadership role next lays bare both the rules of the game and the ways in which these rules can be subverted. This is the reason why attending to succession within Sufi communities helps us understand how communities and likely contenders navigate transitions and attempt to establish legitimate authority. In Sufi communities, neither the existence of a male biological heir nor a highly learned student marks either out as an automatic successor. In spite of this reality, most of the literature presents the process retrospectively, as if the outcome were never in doubt, without inquiring into the process of deciding on that leader. In a rare discussion of the different ingredients that need to come together to mark out a successful successor, Mark Sedgwick notes that lineage alone cannot make a leader (even if it can work as an "endorsement") nor can the possession of charisma, divine *baraka* (blessing, grace, "beneficent force") or scholarly erudition.[84] Instead, "a shaykh's authority often derives more from the preconceptions of his followers than from any quality of his own."[85] This is produced by the contextual interplay between "followers' expectations—of what constitutes sanctity, of what constitutes piety, of what the Sufi path is—[which] prove more influential [than the written literature of the order]."[86] This shows, again, the importance of understanding the situationally produced, relationally negotiated and context-bound nature of the recognition of authority. But the reverse is also true: we can learn from their preconceptions how ideas about authority have been influenced and transformed by the shifting discourses of the changing times that produced them.

To explore these questions, my work begins with the premise that authority is not static but under constant negotiation in the interactions with each other, be they potential followers, their community, other contenders or outsiders, and it applies the lens of social navigation. The term "social navigation" has been used variously in social scientific writing, often as an undefined shorthand for acting in a particular, rapidly shifting environment or as a description of how actors seek to escape confining situations. Inspired by Ralf Dahrendorf's concept of "life chances,"[87] as well as Pierre Bourdieu's "theory of practice," Henrik Vigh has explored the term as an analytic lens to grasp the life choices of people caught in situations of uncertainty and change.[88] In contrast to terrestrial images of a physical landscape in which navigation functions akin to map using, Vigh argues that fluid environments emphasize "the construction of tentative mappings and a constant dialogue between changing plots, possibilities and practice"—a process of mapmaking in which both movement and the map "are constantly shaped and attuned to each other."[89] Such social navigation is not a matter of whether or not one lives in a war zone—everyone navigates social situations—but the heightened intensity, fluidity and speed of social change produced by an unstable environment requires more vigorous, creative and sometimes desperate maneuvers to manage.[90] Social navigation thus shows the interaction of two kinds of change: the change of social formations as well as the movement of social agents.[91]

Not all is fluid in social interactions, and some ideas and social formations display a remarkable longevity. In his study of Muslims in Central Asia, David Montgomery investigates how his interlocutors are also constrained by organizational forms, pressure from peers or political and moral restrictions.[92] Following a Barthian approach to knowledge, Montgomery applies the idea of social navigation to how Muslims in Central Asia (Kyrgyzstan and Uzbekistan) manage their everyday by drawing on social organization (the economic and political structures), different forms of knowledge transfer (oral, textual and experiential) and a corpus of knowledge (schooling, profession, frames of reference).[93] Montgomery's addition to Vigh's approach shows how Muslims draw on a socially embedded tradition of knowledge and a rich past to weather the present and create a future. It is useful for my discussion of how different social and cultural "tools" are used by my Sufi interlocutors. Publishing, poetry recitation, the format of the *shura*, dream divination and technologies as divine vehicles are all used to position contenders for leadership within moments of transition.

In Montgomery's analysis, authority can stem from different sources (orality, literacy, community history as well as prestige from external sources). But the actors he describes are positioned as rather stable and established.[94] By contrast, none of the contested positions in the communities I researched were automatically passed on through titles, and all required community engagement and approval before they became stable. These situations required an *adaptational dexterity* not only to navigate particular situations but also to craft new possibilities.

It might be tempting to describe Sufi communities and their leaders as resilient. After all, in the face of various governments, power brokers and insurgents, internal challenges and challengers and external shocks, didn't they "survive"? But the framing of "resilience" as the capacity to rebound, returning to its past form, unchanged by the shocks just weathered, is problematic. Emerging in the 1980s as a keyword in ecology, economy, psychology and characteristic of political systems, "resilience" is thought of as a complex adaptation or as "the capacity of a system to undergo disturbance and retain its basic structure and function."[95] Discourses on resilience have been particularly criticized for obscuring the role resilience plays in neoliberal economies, in which individuals are expected to withstand ever-greater challenges to their physical and mental well-being in order to "make it through." If they fail to do so, they are blamed for not being resilient enough—a move that focuses on the individual capacities of victims while distracting from the structures of violence that act on their everyday life.[96] In the humanitarian sector, resilience fetishism can lead to a kind of justification that individuals and communities can adapt, or can be made to adapt better, and therefore do not need an amelioration of circumstances or wholesale political change.[97] In the securitized post-9/11 world, some authors have argued that resilience talk has led to a conservative stance of keeping the status quo at all cost, stifling political imagination of how things could otherwise be.[98]

While some suggest retaining a revised version of resilience that does justice to these various layers of the term and its discontents,[99] I argue that using a lens of resilience runs the risk of obscuring two salient dimensions. First, the adaptations of Sufi communities are more than mere scraping by and surviving; they show the agentive existence of these communities that do more than resist erasure; they mark a presence and keep cultural identities alive.[100] More than survival, through their adaptational dexterity, Sufi communities I research demonstrate a plurality of ways to navigate, the potential for an otherwise and the ability to not only keep but also create community in a civil sphere of their own making. Second, a look at their navigational dexterity shows that there is an interdependence that comes from the mutual influence on both the ones who are navigating and the very thing that is being negotiated (ideas about authority, community, belonging). Both agents and ideas emerge potentially changed from the encounter.

While this argument might seem abstract, it comes alive when delving into the various worlds the communities inhabit, navigate and craft. Consider the example of Sufi poetry: Muslims in the Persianate world learned about Islam not only through authoritative texts such as the Qur'an and the Hadith but also through the poetry of Rumi, Saadi and Hafiz. It was a regular component in madrasa education, entering the oral realm through memorization and informing the everyday socioreligious experiences of Muslims.[101] While a Sufi poetry teacher's authority was based on the elucidation and interpretation of the text, which was traditionally acknowledged as part of Islamic education in Afghanistan, Sufi communities were also actively involved in crafting Sufi poetry as a national intangible heritage through cooperation with musicians and politicians. They could then claim this cultural heritage as a basis for their authority (see Chapter 3). The link between a particular understanding of Islam through Sufi poetry was not only retained but also transformed into various, more widely circulated mediums. These in turn influenced conceptions of authority within the wider religious civil sphere.

Another example of these varying sources of authority is the opportunity for Muslims to personally participate in divine revelation provided through revelatory dreams.[102] Dreams have an important, albeit contested, place in Islamic cosmology: they are mentioned in original sources (Qur'an,[103] Hadith), and Islamic dream theory has been developed by writers over centuries.[104] In one of the Sufi communities portrayed in Chapter 5 the collective negotiation of dreams influences a wide range of decision-making, from establishing a new Sufi order and changing *zikr* practices to ordaining a new Sufi leader. Dreams, dream induction (*istikhara*) and inspirational visions were the ways in which the community navigated the subtle shifts and granular decision-making both for their individual lives and their community. While dreams are often thought of as solitary experiences of a mind immersed in the imaginal sphere, an ethnographically grounded perspective on the negotiations within this Sufi community shows the relational aspect of establishing authority through dreams. A potential next leader needed to show that he had developed the inner capacity and the spiritual levels of perception and readiness to receive the dream. Community members needed to acknowledge his capacity in various realms of Sufi authority, recognizing it to be on the right level to both lead the community and receive such a guiding dream. While dreams have been part of orthodox Islam throughout its history, they have become contested in reformist readings and are today challenged from several vantage points—so much so that the dreams of leadership have become a new realm of contestation among various Sufi communities in the civil sphere.

Following the processes in these communities, I show not only how potential leaders adapted to constant political change but also how, in their ways of navigating their surroundings, a multiplicity of authoritative discourses emerged in the daily lives of Sufis in Afghanistan. These include how poetry is perceived and lived as an expression of Islam and how dreams guide the actions of believers, sometimes even through the anticipation of dreams that have yet to reveal themselves (dreams-in-waiting). The individual chapters of this book focus on various mediums, such as poetry, *zikr* or dreams, in which Muslims explore realms of the Divine, stake authority in guiding others through their expertise of these spheres or contest other leaders' claims.

Communities and Methods

The problematics of what Sufism is, who is a Sufi and who is excluded from this category does not end with book-length explorations. Nearly every interview that I conducted over the course of several years touched on this question, with each interviewee giving me a different definition of "Sufism." In writing an account of various Sufi communities, I am not claiming to give a complete overview of all forms of Sufism in Afghanistan or of all the different Sufi groups.[105] There are limitations and a selective bias of which communities I portray in my cases: all of them are set in urban Afghanistan, mainly in Kabul and Herat. The observable spatial, gendered and security patterns might therefore be different from those of rural areas. There are also other urban areas that are well-known historically for Sufi activities, such as Mazar-e Sharif, Kandahar and Ghazni, which offer future anthropologists the opportunity to extend this research. I initially started my research focused solely on Herat because it was known as the *khak-e awliya* (earth of the saints) due to the many mystic luminaries whose graves and shrines dot its urban landscape.[106] I reasoned that its history of a strong Sufi presence in the past would make a good comparison to contemporary changes and continuities within Sufi communities there. However, after considering security concerns, I decided to adapt the research to be multisited, as this allowed me to lighten my physical footprint by traveling between both cities on a more itinerant basis. What had initially been a decision based on security concerns turned out to be beneficial for my research, as I was able to explore the interconnections between Sufi communities in each city.

I have often been asked how numerous the Sufi communities are as well as how many Sufis exist in Afghanistan overall. Both are questions that I cannot conclusively answer for the following reasons. Afghanistan has never conducted a comprehensive national census, and even if it did, I doubt the state would consider the category of Sufi one to measure. More significantly, the very question of what makes someone a "Sufi" is (as I have argued earlier) a matter of contestation and negotiation, not a public badge of identity. For example, when I saw only thirty followers attend the weekly *zikrs*, leaders estimated that there were hundreds of thousands nationally, assuring me that individual local groups had a few hundred to a few thousand members. While one could discount those numbers as exaggeration, they could also very well represent individuals who are connected to followers of the path and are influenced by a particular leader, even if they do not actively participate in every week's activities. Most groups usually had a dedicated core of followers and a more fluid outer circle of students. I myself was surprised, for example, when I attended a conference of the Faizani community at Kabul's Polytechnic University. I had usually seen about thirty to fifty women in the weekly *zikr* meetings. However, at the conference the whole auditorium was filled with men and women connected to the Faizanis.

The Sufi communities that we meet in the following chapters belong to a wide range of socioeconomic, class and ethnic groups.[107] While most of the interviewees were native Dari (Persian) speakers, some of the interviewees spoke Pashto at home and conversed with other community members in Dari. Most interviews and conversations were held in Dari, though some interviews were conducted in English. The interviews in Kandahar as well as with former Taliban officials were conducted in Pashto (for my use of research assistants and translation, see discussion later). Socioeconomic standing and class varied among community members and teachers of the communities, from working class (shopkeepers, cobblers, clerks, soldiers) to middle class (imams, schoolteachers, university professors, students, government workers).¹⁰⁸ They appeared at the elite level as members of the politically prominent Mujaddidi and Gailani families who had provided the leaders of politically powerful Sufi orders at the national level for well over a century and held elevated governmental positions in the post-2001 government. Education or affiliation with the internationally financed state, as well as migration and life abroad, sometimes translated into class mobility. However, connections to the international community through work in international organizations seemed rarer in these communities than in other circles of Afghans who focused on upward mobility through learning English, studying abroad or working for international NGOs, NATO countries or the UN.

All the communities I researched were well educated. Sufi affiliates (both students and teachers) had usually attended primary and high school; many of them had received higher education or held university degrees. This high level of education was remarkable in a country with an education system in shambles after decades of war and with an urban illiteracy rate of 43 percent.¹⁰⁹ Most of the men and women studied, worked or did both. They attended Sufi gatherings in their free time with primary gatherings on weekends (Thursday and Friday). My main interlocutors were Sunni Sufis, although one of the groups that I researched had both Sunni and Shi'a followers in the past and claimed to still have followers of each affiliation. My research, however, focuses on Sunni Sufis in Afghanistan. A proper study of Sufi beliefs and practices among Shi'a communities in Afghanistan is therefore still lacking.¹¹⁰

This book is largely based on ethnographic observations, interactions and conversations (also called participant observations) as well as formal interviews. First contacts with the communities happened through myriad and often serendipitous connections and channels. Having worked and researched in Afghanistan since 2011, first as an intern to the Afghan government, then in the NGO sector and in research, I asked everyone in my extended network of friends, former coworkers and acquaintances whether they knew people who considered themselves Sufis or who might be knowledgeable on Sufism. They usually first said they did not but then remembered an uncle, a cousin, a driver, a work acquaintance who might know. I asked fellow Afghan academic friends as well as journalists to introduce me to anyone who had knowledge of Islam and Sufism in Afghanistan. Many introductions led to lengthy back-and-forths but were ultimately unproductive. Others led to kind referrals and introductions to Sufi teachers and their followers.

Once in touch with them (often initially through formal interviews that lasted between one and two hours, followed by invitations to their events and meetings, as well as informal gatherings), I asked them whether they knew other communities, gatherings or teachers. Such an approach is of course fraught with bias, as I met, spoke with or interviewed only the people who were reachable through this personalized snowball approach. However, dealing with groups that can be relatively secretive about their actions within their own society made working through trusted introductions a necessity. While I interviewed and interacted mainly with people who were explicitly affiliated with Sufi teachers and Sufi communities, I also spoke to imams without Sufi affiliation; with teachers within the religious field, such as members of the Jamiat-e Eslah; as well as with politicians from former Afghan governments, such as the Communist People's Democratic Party of Afghanistan (PDPA) of the 1980s, Mujahidin fighters from the 1980s and 1990s and the Taliban's Islamic Emirate of the late 1990s. For these interviews I relied on professional contacts from befriended foreign and Afghan journalists. These were, however, one-time-only interviews in contrast with those of the Sufi communities, whom I not only interviewed but also spent time with at their *urs* celebrations, at their *zikr* meetings and in the homes of Sufi students and teachers. Several Sufi students and teachers became friends during this time, and we met each other for tea, lunches and dinners. However, some chose to retain distance and maintain more formalized relationships throughout my research.

Most of the ethnographic research in Afghanistan was conducted between 2016 and 2021, with two full consecutive years (2017–2019) spent in the communities in Herat and Kabul with follow-up visits in 2021 and 2022. I frequented different Sufi poetry circles (*halqas*), such as the one of Ustad Haidari Wujudi in Kabul's public library and the circles associated with the late Ustad Mahjor and his family. I also researched different Sufi orders (Qadiriyyah, Naqshbandiyyah, Chishtiyyah—now Salwatiyyah) through visiting their weekly gatherings and teachings, attending their annual *urs* celebrations and partaking in some of their nightly or early-morning *zikr* sessions. Visits to *khanaqahs* and *zikr halqas* that were ultimately not included in the book nonetheless offered rich implicit comparative material for the cases that I present. Many of these occasions gave rise to discussions and informal conversations. Some of them led to close relationships with Sufi teachers and students that offered me the opportunity to spend time in their homes and with their families, sharing meals, doing sports together, visiting graves, drinking tea and discussing books. I videotaped and photographed speeches, recorded and traded MP3 recordings of *zikr* sessions and lectures with other students and delivered newly published books to followers abroad when I was traveling, which offered opportunities to talk with the members of the diaspora of these Sufi circles. While the latter are not the main focus of my research, they inform my understanding of the communities and my analysis. In addition to these informal occasions, I also conducted (often repeated) semistructured interviews with Sufi teachers and students as well as religious preachers that lasted from one to three hours. I supplemented these oral sources by collecting and selectively translating books that the Sufi teachers had published, videotapes of celebrations and copies of newspaper articles that covered events at the *khanaqahs* or religious foundations. I also analyzed the online presence of the teachers through social media.

In between visits and stays, I remained in touch with community members and leaders online, who shared with me photos and videos of celebrations and news from the community. I also shared chapters of the book as it was developing with individual teachers and community members and discussed the material with them, taking into account their feedback and concerns, which gave rise to additional discussions that inform my understanding of situations and dynamics. This dialogical approach to research and writing has become increasingly utilized as a way toward participatory research and accountability.[111] The comments from individual teachers on my writing, for example, the feedback of Ustad Momena and Ustad Manija on the chapter about their community (Chapter 4), made me aware of implications and alternative readings of particular phrases that I had not considered previously. We engaged in dialogues about sections that could be misunderstood by various audiences, particularly in the fast-changing political environment that they navigated, and I made changes accordingly to the text. I also discussed with individuals in the groups themes and topics that could be considered compromising for their security setup, and we decided together which parts to exclude.

As will have become clear in this overview, my main research was conducted in Afghanistan's NATO-supported Islamic Republic (2001–2021) before the renewed governmental takeover by the Taliban. The main descriptions in this book reflect the situation of Sufi communities in the time before these political changes. However, I have updated viewpoints, sensibilities and realities of the communities, where possible, guided through online conversations and in-person visits in late 2022. While I reference these changes selectively in the chapters, in the concluding chapter I reflect most on the current realities that these communities and their leaders face. It is clear that the ongoing challenges of economic decline/depression, closures of *khanaqahs* through the de facto governmental authorities and attacks on congregational places and spiritual leaders make up another chapter in an ongoing struggle to preserve communities, their culture and learning.

Security, Belief and Layers of Positioning

Security, or the lack of it, was a constant concern for me, the people who helped me in my research and my interlocutors. Anthropologists have long worked in highly unstable environments, from Guatemala to Iraq, Sri Lanka to Cambodia.[112] This has prompted Leah Zani in her work on military waste and contamination to suggest that "war zones demand their own cultural and area studies."[113] Far from fetishizing research in potentially dangerous environments, this call actually points to the long-term social and cultural impact of war, dismantling the binaries of war and peace to discover how conflict is intertwined in the ongoing processes of social change even in moments of relative peacefulness or in "postconflict" settings.[114] This call for seeing commonalities between war zones also points to the global military industrial complex that produces interlocking structures of militarized oppression.[115] On the methodological level it attests to the fact that research in such settings is deeply influenced by the many constraints that such an inquiry needs to adapt to in order to keep everyone involved safe.

The parameters of what was safe for either me as a researcher or the people I talked to and spent time with constantly changed as violence escalated in its various guises. Direct risks such as bomb and suicide attacks, targeted killing of religious personnel as well as a generalized danger of kidnappings mixed with the threat of being associated with a foreigner or being seen as foreign funded. While bombs can hit anyone indiscriminately, kidnapping was a particular threat to wealthy Afghans as well as foreign nationals. Herat was dubbed the "kidnapping capital in Afghanistan," with the children of Afghan businessmen or politicians being especially under threat for extortion through kidnapping.[116] A responsible research setup also needed to take into account that short-term research stints for interviews are qualitatively different endeavors than setting up long-term research within communities. This meant that I kept an open dialogue with interlocutors, whether long-term contacts or one-time interviewees, about what they considered safe ways of interacting with each other, as they often had a much better sense of the constantly changing security scenarios. The associated difficulties and ethical quandaries help explain why longer-term ethnographic research conducted in Afghanistan over the past twenty years was still a rarity in comparison to that in other disciplines.

As a response to this environment, I changed my research to multiple sites and varied my daily routine and travel routes. Becoming a "moving ethnographer" meant a loss of detailed engagement with only one group (a pursuit on which most traditional anthropology prides itself).[117] But it turned out to be a fitting strategy to follow topics, themes and opportunities as they arose. Frequenting multiple Sufi communities in differing time intervals also had its own risks, opening up questions about whether I was a spy—a suspicion that was usually shared with my research assistants more than with me.[118] Given anthropology's complex disciplinary history with European colonialism and foreign governments, but also the wider structures of violence in the "War on Terror," this accusation was not too far-fetched.[119] While anthropologists have worked with the military and government agencies, this practice has also been sharply criticized within the discipline.[120] Regardless of the researcher's position, scholarship on Islam of the past twenty years is embedded in the geopolitical realities of the post-2001 "War on Terror," which continues to shape lives with its ongoing structural, physical and epistemological violence. This also impacts the research and those whose work does not directly confront it. Muslim communities have been surveilled and targeted, both within the wars spurred by the "War on Terror" as well as the increased surveillance apparatus in Western countries.[121] One Sufi community decided to discontinue our conversations because they feared the combination of my being a woman and a foreigner could compromise them ethically in local eyes and lay them open to the charge of being foreign funded, an accusation that could potentially not only discredit but also endanger them.

I tried to respond to this complex environment by being as transparent as possible about the scope and rationale of the research, as well as the dangers that I saw in it, so that individuals could make an informed decision about whether and how to participate in the research. Often this seemingly straightforward dictum was difficult to achieve. As an international researcher with a Western passport I was aware that I could leave at any time, but my interlocutors were mainly not part of a passport elite who could extract themselves if the situation turned on them for my association with them.[122] Furthermore, the security environment kept changing, and increasing numbers of teachers with whom I interfaced experienced threats or were targeted for their teaching and preaching overall. While I recorded the interviews, there was usually an unrecorded time after the interviews, if sensitive data were shared with me, in which I discussed whether interviewees wanted their name or other identifiers mentioned or which information they wanted associated with themselves and what should be used anonymously. For the book I am using the real names only of leaders and public personas who gave me permission to do so, many of whom are also publishing under their own names in Afghanistan. The names of any of the *murids* or other community members have been categorically anonymized in my account.

In Herat, where gendered segregation in the public sphere was stricter and more socially enforced in a city with a much tighter social network than Kabul, I partnered with a local media and civil society organization to set up a living-working arrangement. During my three years of repeated stays I financially supported the office of their organization and in turn used it as a meeting place so that it oscillated between being a public place (through its function as an organization's office) where I could meet men on my own, because I was not inviting them to my own private place, and simultaneously a more private venue than a café or restaurant, because the office was used only for workshops and meetings that were prearranged and thus offered a calm meeting place. As it was situated in a nondescript apartment complex, interviewees could attend meetings without any further association with an organization that could otherwise put them at risk.

Researching within predominantly male groups, my experience oscillated between experiencing my gendered emplacement as an asset or liability.[123] Many of the male groups accommodated my requests to attend all-male *zikr* sessions, talk with them individually and in groups or to visit their homes. Especially in communities where I researched long term, I often experienced a successive integration in which both I and the communities I researched came to accommodate each other. I was invited in, one door at a time, seated where it seemed appropriate and incorporated in manifold, often kind ways.

Working with research assistants was an asset in navigating different places and groups. While I worked with a female research assistant in the all-women's groups, my male research assistants formed a socially acceptable contact point in most formal interview settings in which the more conservative male interlocutors seemed to feel more comfortable not only by having present a fellow Afghan man but also in addressing him when speaking. I used the group of research assistants as a sounding board for questions about security and safety as well as feedback on how they experienced aspects of the communities we visited. Research assistants helped with translations, particularly in the beginning when I was still learning more of the specialized vocabulary and including those from Pashto. Our conversations teased out the nuances and multilayered references, particularly when discussing recordings of interview sessions. My research assistants were not part of the Sufi communities I researched, but they were interested in Sufism, and I learned from their views as non-Sufi Afghan Muslims about the communities we researched.[124]

One of the questions that both I and my research assistants had to answer repeatedly was the status of my personal beliefs and whether I was a Muslim or aspiring to become one. The inquiry into my status ranged from well-meaning, supportive questions directed at a foreigner who showed interest in another religion, to more outright dismissal evidenced in several refusals to meet and talk, as when a Chishtiyyah *murid* replied that since I was not even a Muslim, how could I then claim to understand or write about Sufism? These attitudes—apart from the general proselytizing thrust—underlie another specific idea about understanding. It might be particularly pronounced for Sufi adepts because "the experiential character of the Sufi path means that its knowledge becomes embodied in those who have traversed it."[125] But knowledge is always situated, and, as will become clear in later chapters, there are many different types of knowledge.[126] William James makes this point in quoting al-Ghazzali's instruction on the different types of comprehension: "Knowledge about a thing is not the thing itself. You remember what al-Ghazzali told us in the Lecture on Mysticism—that to understand the causes of drunkenness, as a physician understands them, is not to be drunk."[127] Taking al-Ghazzali's words to heart, I am therefore not speaking from the point of a believing practitioner, but I take practice as well as doctrine and belief seriously.

More often than not, an inquiry by my interlocutors into my own motives for this research and my own background in terms of belief led to intriguing comparisons as research interlocutors tried to place me vis-à-vis themselves, often gauging whether my research was driven by a personal quest to convert. While I might have disappointed quite a few interview partners with my lack of interest in conversion, our different experiential backgrounds made for stimulating discussions. As a daughter of a Catholic mother and Protestant father, we often discussed how splits in Christianity varied from the ones in Islam. I had married into a Muslim family, and many knew my husband, who visited me at my field sites, which made for quizzical joking whether he would not be cross with me for not converting yet. Some discussions also led us to discuss influences of Buddhism in Afghanistan because of my own extended familial ties to Thai Buddhism through intermarriage. While for some it was unusual that a Western non-Muslim was interested in Islam to such an extent, at the same time it also seemed self-explanatory to many of my Sufi interlocutors. In their view it was the right path and made sense that I would be interested in exploring it. These conversations resulted in acknowledgments of how personal affiliations are multifold and how spiritual pathways can be complex. Often, the openness to discuss our personal backgrounds informed our way of approaching a topic.

Chapter Overview

The following ethnographic accounts examine the different navigational strategies employed by a variety of Sufi leaders over the past four decades. While aspiring leaders drew on customary socioreligious tools embedded within a range of Islamic traditions, the social legitimation strategies they employed left room for maneuver and contestation. The question of who was supposed to lead a community was far from a foregone conclusion, despite retrospective justifications that attempted to portray it otherwise. The individual chapters offer a view into how Sufi leaders react to moments of transition and outside change within a highly insecure environment in which the very foundation of Islamic authority is contested.

Chapter 1 lays the groundwork for understanding how Sufi leaders and their communities were positioned in the recent social, cultural and political history of Afghanistan in relation to the state. In the past four decades, Afghanistan has undergone drastic political changes. While there is no univocal approach of Sufis to politics per se, Afghanistan's historiography shows Sufi communities have remarkable dexterity in their ability to adapt. The chapter is not an exhaustive overview but instead focuses on strategies that Sufis adopted toward the state. Focusing on *state alignment, resistance* and what I term *strategic distance*, the chapter shows how the three approaches have been adopted circumstantially as environments shifted and changed over the course of the twentieth and into the twenty-first century.

The next chapters zoom in on how individuals and groups in the post-invasion reconstruction era after 2001 employ a variety of religio-cultural tools to legitimize their claims of authority, including Sufi poetry as Islamic education and heritage, publishing as spiritual service, investigation of the Self as an exploration of God and dream divination. Each chapter highlights a different community and its particular struggles while also focusing on a specific realm of navigation.

Chapter 2 focuses on the case study of an imam from Kabul's Soviet-built Microrayon neighborhood, who was tasked with taking over leadership of one of Kabul's oldest Sufi lodges (located in the old city, part of Asheqan-o-Arefan) when its *pir* fled the country during the 1990s Civil War. The case shows how the situation of war, insecurity and consecutive migration brought about new patterns of authority and enabled new alliances between Sufis and a lower class of ulama (religious scholars), who stepped in to protect Sufi orders and shrines. The chapter questions the prevailing narrative in Central Asian and Middle Eastern studies of the antagonism between ulama and Sufis by contextualizing its formation in colonial narratives and its impact on multiple discourses among Muslim reformers, as well as how local communities utilized these perceptions to shield themselves during times of discursive change and violent attacks. Narratively following the imam and his friend, the caretaker, in how they used these conceptions to shield their newly acquired congregation from harm, while having to sometimes look on as the lodge was looted and bombed, I tease out the navigational tactics of such an alliance and their impact on the rendering of Sufi authority in an environment of insecurity.

Chapter 3 examines the purported conceptual splits between orthodoxy and Sufism, lived Sufism and Sufism as literary heritage and the different types of authority they engender. Historically, Sufi poetry used to be one of the most significant forms of transmission of Islamic knowledge in Afghanistan. Paired with authoritative texts such as the Qur'an and the Hadith, the poetry of Rumi, Saadi and Hafiz was a regular component in madrasa education, entering the oral realm through memorization and informing the everyday socioreligious experiences of Muslims. While Sufi poetry as Islamic education has become contested, groups of literary students keep this tradition alive. The chapter follows Sufi poetry circles whose teachers not only taught individual students but also worked on crafting Sufi poetry as intangible national heritage through collaborations with musicians throughout the twentieth century.

Chapter 4 integrates themes of the previous chapters of state-Sufi relationships, as well as the use of poetry and literature, to show how the navigation of authority in all of these realms is also gendered. While drawing on similar aspects of Sufi knowledge as their male counterparts, female teachers and *zikr* leaders navigated restrictive norms that limit women within Islamic leadership positions. Through the case study of a Qadiriyyah Sufi order in which women not only practiced *zikr* but also taught it to other women and became speakers and teachers in the civil society arm of the order, I investigate community processes to legitimize their role. Taking a community-centered view illustrates that female leaders' agency was embedded in the community's strong ethos of male allyship and its oral history of the inclusion of women by their deceased *pir*, who still served as a moral exemplar directing contemporary behavioral patterns. The community overall adapted gender-segregated meetings for spiritual practices in Afghanistan (although not in its diaspora chapters). Yet discursively they engaged in an overt argument of spiritual equality that stood in contrast to the exclusion of women in the institutionalized religious sphere in Afghanistan. The community legitimized women's participation through recourse to the spiritual psychophysiological organ of the heart, rendering divine connection a nongendered endeavor that transcends social categories.

While the previous chapters deal with attempts at continuity, struggle for leadership and development of new Sufi teachers, Chapter 5 takes the reader into the heart of an extended moment where a community either reinvents itself or dissolves. The case study concerns a succession debate within a Sufi community of former Chishtiyyah Sufis in the western city of Herat. The community attempted not only to transition to a new leader divined through dreams (*ruya*) but also to establish a new Sufi order altogether (the Salwatiyyah). We encounter the devotees and potential future leaders while waiting for a dream—which needed to be received by the chosen leader and confirmed by dream insights through other members of the community—to ascertain the authority of the future leader. Developing the thread of navigating Islamic learning and mystic insight, the chapter investigates the power of divine dreams to establish authority. These decisions become a public negotiation in the wider Sufi sociosphere when Sufi adepts publish a community history that is evaluated by the local Sufi Council.

The cases highlight various scenarios of transitions within Sufi communities and how they draw on different socioculturally embedded religious resources to negotiate their place in a drastically changing environment. The Conclusion and Epilogue offer an overview of how various groups and individuals of the Sufi civil sphere have coped with the political changes post-2021 and life under the Taliban de facto government. These ongoing challenges are part of the struggles that communities in Afghanistan face and navigate. While ongoing and ever changing, many have their origins in earlier tensions and developments. The next chapter analyzes the navigational strategies of Sufis toward the state and power brokers in the last decades.

ONE

Navigating the Past

*Sufi Strategies of State Alignment,
Contestation and Strategic Distance*

FROM THE TWENTIETH TO the twenty-first century, Afghanistan has undergone drastic political changes, transitioning from relatively stable, albeit dynamic, polity until the early 1970s to various stages of reinvention over the past half century. It has existed as a constitutional monarchy from independence in 1919 until 1973, and in the years since the state has styled itself as a Republic (until 1978), then a Democratic Republic (until 1987), renamed a Republic (1987–1992), an Islamic Emirate under the Taliban (until 2001), an Islamic Republic (2001–2021) and again an Islamic Emirate in its current manifestation (2021–). Over the past four decades, people in Afghanistan have also experienced a revolution and a coup, social and political upheaval linked to rapidly changing socioeconomic conditions, the Soviet invasion, resistance, civil war, international intervention/occupation, counterinsurgency operations and terror attacks. How were Sufi communities positioned in relation to these drastic changes?

Historians dealing with the relationship of Sufis and political centers have cautioned that there is no univocal Sufi approach to politics per se. Surveilling the historiographic record and my oral history interviews shows that Sufi communities have shown remarkable dexterity in their ability to adapt.[1] Contrary to the image of quietist mystics concerned only with their relationship to God, Sufis in Afghanistan have both supported and opposed governments, sometimes joining a political regime, at other times disengaging from it, sometimes fleeing its repressive policies and sometimes actively fighting back. This lack of a predictable or generalizable rule governing Sufis' relationships to power centers does not, however, leave us with an absence of an analytical framework with which to describe those relationships. Indeed, the dexterity itself *is* the framework. How Sufis establish and maintain authority in Afghanistan is directly influenced by the stability and religio-ideological position of the state or empire within which a Sufi group must operate. Some adaptational strategies, I argue, show surprising continuity over time, while others shift in response to the massive ideological changes of successive regimes while still drawing on the Sufi community's previous positioning within the political arena.

One important shift that this chapter makes in viewing the adaptive success of Afghanistan's Sufi groups is to approach Afghanistan's historiography from a different vantage point that includes Sufis in various positions, not only within the state apparatus. This makes two salient points: First, there is a broader tendency in Western historiographic accounts of Afghanistan to view the country through the prism of its recent wars, framed as a purely political narrative from the vantage point of various governments, with a focus on state formation, or as particular ethnic histories.[2] This plays into the prevailing narratives of perpetual state failure over these last decades that plague not only Afghanistan but also so-called developing nations more broadly. Afghanistan has often been described as "failed," "fragmented" or "collapsed,"[3] a framework that erases international liability (for instance, the destructive impacts of colonialism, proxy wars and interventions/occupations), local agency and global interconnectedness through the application of a reductive, prejudiced and dehumanizing lens.[4] Even humanistic and historical inquiry seems to cleave to this trajectory of decline. Surveilling the studies of Islam on Afghanistan, Nile Green comments that uneven research foci skew realities to suggest a transition from "a past of poets and Sufis [that] seems to bear no relation with a present of Islamists and suicide bombers."[5] But the reality is that Sufis never left the scene. Sufi communities have existed during past ages, when historians tended to describe them as either mendicants or courtly advisers, to the present, where they have taken up arms supplied by international backers, supported fellow Afghan refugees in soup kitchens or kept the literary heritage of their nation safe. They have never been mere passive bystanders at the periphery but active agents in their own country's history.

This also makes the second point that Sufis have been variously positioned vis-à-vis the state, both within its structures and outside it. As part of the state-centered approach to historiography, the narrative is often told through the focus on two elite Sufi families, the Mujaddidi and the Gailani, who are connected to the state through positions and intermarriage in the past. Not diminishing the tremendous work that has been done on tracing their changing position, their history is but one facet in the history of Afghanistan's Sufi communities.[6] As I am basing my portrayal on available historiographies, their narratives are particularly pronounced in the following sections when analyzing Sufi-state relations, especially for state-aligned Sufis. However, narratives coming out of oral histories of how the status and relationships to power of non-state-connected communities shifted and changed decenters a univocal approach to history writing and offers new avenues beyond the existing narratives.

Continuously Adapting Patterns

This chapter provides an overview of the recent history of Sufi groups and their relationships to changing state and social structures, using both existing literature and oral history narratives collected through interviews with various Sufi communities that are portrayed in more depth in the following chapters. It is not intended as a comprehensive history of Afghanistan's recent decades but as a compass for gaining a rough understanding of how Sufi groups were positioned within the changing political and social order. In tracing this history, I have retained the periodization of different state forms and propose three "relational types" to describe the strategies adopted by Sufis in relation to the state: *state alignment, resistance* and *strategic distance*. These three approaches do not always map neatly onto particular actors or groups but are adopted circumstantially as the environments shift and change.

State Alignment

The two most prominent Sufi-state alliances in Afghanistan are the Gailani family and the Mujaddidis. While both families' origins lie outside the current nation-state of Afghanistan, they have become a fixture in its politics, attesting to long genealogies of interregional connections.[7] Sufi-state relations have long-established patterns, even as they have shifted in response to changing times. Over the centuries, many rulers in various parts of the world have attached themselves to Sufi *pirs* or followed their guidance, including the Seljuqs of Rum (1037–1308) and the Mevlevi-guided Ottoman rulers. Connections between the Chishti order and the Mughal Empire (1526–1857) were particularly close, and the Iranian Safavid dynasty (1501–1736) drew legitimacy through its allegiance with the Safaviyya order.[8] The Timurid Empire (1370–1507), which shaped much of what is today's Afghanistan, was no exception. Leading Sufi figures such the Naqshbandiyyah shaykh Abdur Rahman Jami (1414–1492) and vizier/poet Ali Shir Nawa'i (1441–1501) secured, through their influence in royal courts, royal approval and financial support for Islamic figurative artists who painted manuscript illuminations that employed Sufi literary motifs in their visual art, producing masterpieces that brought a Sufi perspective on Islam into the cultural mainstream.[9] Other forms of royal patronage of the arts, from Sufi-inspired poetry to tile work, as well as support for building projects, included pious endowments (*waqf*), which were bestowed on well-established shrines such as the complex of Abdullah Ansari at Gazargah in Herat and the shrine of Ali ibn Abi Talib at Balkh, present-day Mazar-e Sharif.[10]

Another prominent shrine is the one of Sayyid Hasan Gailani (1862–1941) in Charharbagh outside Jalalabad, who was buried there after his death from a brain hemorrhage. Sayyid Hasan, who was also known as the Naqib of Charharbagh as well as the Naqib of Baghdad, was the leader who brought the Gailani family to Afghanistan. The family's origins lie in present-day Iraq, where the eponymous founder of the Qadiriyyah Sufi order, Abd-al Qadir Gailani (1078–1166), a Hanbali Sunni preacher and theologian, is buried.[11] He was famed for his preaching abilities during his lifetime and in subsequent centuries was a widely popular saint whose shrine in Baghdad became a major pilgrimage site.[12] The Qadiriyyah order began as a localized Sufi order centered in Baghdad with family branches in Damascus and Hama (present-day Syria).¹³ Sayyid Hasan Gailani, the father of the late *pir* Sayyid Ahmed Gailani, traveled from Baghdad to Afghanistan in 1905, where he was welcomed warmly by its then ruler, Amir Habibullah. Afghans had long looked toward Baghdad as a center of learning and were well acquainted with the saintly lineage. The amir paid him a monthly allowance of thirty-five hundred rupees and built him a winter residence near Jalalabad.¹⁴

The Gailanis, of course, were not Afghanistan's first prominent Sufis on the political scene. Indeed, the alliance between Sufi leaders and Afghan rulers had long-standing antecedents with another Sufi family, the Mujaddidi, who had settled several centuries earlier in Afghanistan. The Mujaddidi family's arrival in Afghanistan was more winding and complex than the Gailanis', characterized by the meanderings and exchanges of teachers and disciples who flowed among the many networks of *khanaqahs* and madrasas in the region. The Naqshbandiyyah order, to which the Mujaddidi branch belongs, was founded around Bukhara (in present-day Uzbekistan) in the thirteenth century and spread widely throughout Central Asia and Khurasan.¹⁵ By the fifteenth century, the Naqshbandis operated several *khanaqahs*, shrines and soup kitchens in Kabul.¹⁶ However, the Naqshbandi-Mujaddidi branch that settled in Afghanistan as the Mujaddidi family was a later arrival and originated not in Central Asia but in Mughal India under Shaykh Ahmad Sirhindi (1564–1624).¹⁷ This Naqshbandiyyah shaykh was called the Mujaddidi Alf-i Sani (reviver of the second millennium) for his attempts to confront the "crisis in Islam" by searching for answers to questions of spirituality within authoritative sources.¹⁸ It was an approach to law (shari'a) with an emphasis on religious duties that deemphasized the role of the *pir* as spiritual mediator.¹⁹

Sirhindi and his descendants initially built Sufi madrasas, mosques, *khanaqahs* and shrines in Sirhind, north of Delhi in the Punjab. The main *khanaqah* was passed down through the generations of Sirhindi's sons, and spiritual deputies (*khilafas*) were appointed to serve a far-flung network of dependencies as far away as Bukhara, Hyderabad and Istanbul.²⁰ As the Sufi order extended its reach, the disintegrating Mughal Empire and the wars its collapse precipitated accelerated the process of forcing *pirs* and their disciples to migrate to new regions, including present-day Afghanistan. Two of its most notable *pirs* traveled westward during this time and became the founding figures of the Naqshbandi-Mujaddidi suborder in Afghanistan during the time of the second ruler of the newly founded Durrani Empire, Timur Shah (1772–1793). The first was Fazl Ahmad Ma'sumi (also called Jiu Sahib Peshawari), who settled in the Durrani winter capital of Peshawar, today a part of Pakistan.[21] The second was Khwaja Safiullah Mujaddidi (d. 1798) who established the famous *khanaqah* in Shor Bazaar in Kabul.[22] The Naqshbandi-Mujaddidi became one of the most influential religious families in Afghanistan, as symbolically expressed in Khwaja Safiullah performing the coronation ceremony (*dastarbandi*) for the Durrani ruler Zaman Shah (r. 1793–1800). In her study on religious response to political change Senzil Nawid points out that new sovereigns sought out the most prominent religious leader to conduct the ceremony to indicate their own level of influence and political power.[23]

Patronage could stem from a ruler's own individual affinity to Sufi interpretations of Islam, but these alliances also had tangible benefits. As Waleed Ziad shows in his study of the Naqshbandi-Mujaddidi alliances with rulers in the region including Afghanistan, for instance, newly established states often lacked historical legitimacy and required the backing of a spiritual institutional base that could provide blessings and social capital.[24] Sufi scholars offered historically grounded symbolic capital that worked to integrate various rural, tribal and urban environments through political, commercial and spiritual mediation.[25] While rulers drew their legitimacy from these alliances, Sufi scholars similarly used the economic and political advantages afforded to them to bolster their claims of authority. Prudently, and tellingly, many were also cautious to maintain a private economic base of support from disciples and land endowments so that when rulers became intolerable, these scholars possessed the capital to organize along their networks of followers against the ruling class.[26]

The longevity and depth of the state-Sufi relationship that anchored the Mujaddidi, and later the Gailani Sufi family, in the political landscape of Afghanistan should not obscure the fact that the relationship was not always amicable.[27] The Mujaddidi family, for instance, actively opposed King Amanullah's modernizing policies and instigated large demonstrations against the king in 1928.[28] However, not all Mujaddidis who settled in Afghanistan became so politically active; for example, its Herat branch was less politically influential than the Kabul branch.[29] But the general pattern of integration with power centers persisted into the twentieth-century, post-independence nation-state: King Nadir Shah (r. 1929–1933) made the Hazrat of Shor Bazaar, Fazl Omar Mujaddidi, the minister of justice; his son-in-law, Fazl Ahmad Mujaddidi, the deputy minister; and his brother, Mohammad Sadeq (Gul Agha), the ambassador to Egypt.[30] Many other Mujaddidis later became senators and ministers.[31] Later, some members of the Mujaddidi family who were at odds with Afghan president Daoud Khan moved to Egypt when he became prime minister in 1953 and established close ties with the Muslim Brotherhood.[32] However, the opposition remained within the framework of political contestation in an institutional setting, and the overall affiliation remained intact until 1979.

Resistance

Sufi communities have not only served as allies of the state but also as key figures of resistance. Indeed, in many parts of the Islamic world, Sufis were, and in some cases still are, known to be fierce critics of the powers that be and an opposition force to be reckoned with. Especially during the time of colonial expansion, as colonial administrations dethroned former leaders and elites, Sufi *pirs* and brotherhoods were often one of the few authoritative structures left intact to oppose the political takeover.[33] They were often at the forefront of Muslim resistance, engaging in the religiously approved strategy of jihad against the colonial enemy.[34] Resistance to colonial power by Sufi orders spans many countries and continents, exemplified in the attacks by Amir 'Abd al-Qadir against the French in Algeria, Naqshbandi shaykh Shamil's independent state that attacked the Russians in the Caucasus until 1859 and the Sanusi resistance against Italian occupation with the head of the Sanusiyya *tariqa* becoming king of the independent Libyan kingdom.[35] Closer to Afghanistan, in British India and at the Afghan-Indian frontier, several Sufi groups fought colonial powers as well: Sayyid Ahmad Barelwi's Muhammadiyya *tariqa* attacked the British, along with the Hadda Mullah and Saidullah Khan, who was dubbed the "Mad Mullah" by his British enemies.[36]

Not surprisingly, "Mad Fakir" or "Mad Mullah" was used loosely and profusely by the colonial power to delegitimize opposition to its rule. It became a common derogatory term for any religious scholar or spiritually enthralled *pir* who fought against the British colonial administration,[37] who portrayed them as frightful demagogues with fanatic followers who would lay down their lives for their masters.[38] While followers attributed their devotion to divine inspiration bolstered by miracles and righteous fervor, and saw it as a strength, their opponents ascribed it to madness.[39] The dehumanizing terminology was not merely a failed attempt to fathom the charismatic strength needed to rise defiantly against a superpower, knowing that one would most likely perish if unsuccessful, but also a strategic move to delegitimize opposition. As a populist tactic to discredit native critique and opposition, using the motif of madness expanded on familiar tropes of past decades of the exotic, crazy and out-of-bounds mystics.[40]

Sufi resistance to what was seen as illegitimate authority did not come to an end when the British left the subcontinent in 1947. Indeed, the continuation of Sufi critiques of Afghan national governments shows how a critical stance, particularly in terms of rule and its legitimacy, had become deeply intertwined within the practice of Sufism in Afghanistan. One such example is Allama Faizani, who was active in Afghanistan's political scene in the 1950s–1970s but whose trajectory was outside the statist Mujaddidi-Gailani trajectory. Born in 1924 in Herat into a family of *miagan* (descendants of a venerated saint) and religious scholars, the teacher and Islamic scholar Allama Faizani initially established a *khanaqah* near Pul-i Khumri in northern Baghlan but later moved to Kabul, where he set up a library near the Pul-i Khishti mosque in 1970.[41] The Qadiriyyah *pir* hosted classes and *zikr* circles that attracted a growing following among the educated, such as teachers and students, as well as military officers and governmental officials.[42] He had a captivating way of combining descriptions from the natural sciences with Sufi insights that appealed to a young, urban-educated core who proved increasingly disenchanted with traditional religious authority structures, a feature of the Afghan intelligentsia more broadly at the time, which included the blossoming left-wing ideologies and Islamist circles at Kabul University.[43] The seminary for teaching the Qur'an, which Faizani started, was first known as the Madrasa-e Qur'an (School of the

Qur'an).[44] After establishing alliances with other Islamic associations, the movement came to be known as Maktab-e Tauhid (Monotheism School) and Hezb-e Tauhid (Unity Party).[45] Allama Faizani not only organized a spiritual movement, but he also spoke out in sermons and public speeches against the government. In one instance in Mazar-e Sharif, he condemned "the corrupt practices of clerics, government officials, and feudal landlords,"[46] a scathing critique of virtually the entire ruling class for which he was imprisoned. During the 1970s, Allama Faizani was in and out of prison for his political stances.[47] His last prison sentence ended in his disappearance around the time when the Communist regime took over and many other prisoners were "disappeared," meaning that they were likely killed.

Allama Faizani shared some key features with his Sufi predecessors who resisted colonial rule: for instance, the use of his platform as a spiritual leader and the group networks his position afforded him to criticize and, therefore, in a sense, resist government encroachment and incorporation. But he was different in that his goal was not revolution but reformation through political dissent, demonstrations and critique.[48] Earlier movements of resistance took on the form of open militancy, usually against non-Muslim entities such as colonial powers. The Afghan government was not declared illegitimate wholesale, but it was seen as highly flawed and in need of reform. Generally, however, what both Faizani and the Sufi oppositionist leaders who came before him shared, and what gave an air of legitimacy and authority to their criticism, was their distance from the center of power. Unlike the Gailanis and Mujaddidis, they were seen as untainted by the machinations of power.

Strategic Distance

Historical records focusing on the literary and artistic production of Sufi scholars at imperial courts—an obliquely political act given the intertwining of politics and religion at the time—as well as records of colonial administrators describing Sufi groups as potential threats skew the history toward Sufis as political actors. These records, however, represent only a part of Sufism's textual past, though it is often disproportionately used to describe that history. In contrast, Sufi communities have primarily existed as localized social groups affiliated to particular *pirs* or high-ranking students (*khalifas*) with teaching authority invested in them by their affiliation to a *pir* without any overt political affiliation to central government structures. Their stories are told more succinctly through the training manuals they used for adepts, through the ways their knowledge intertwined with oral poetry that carried Islam into wider regions of the world or through the material history of local mosques and lodges, retreats (*chilla khanas*) and shrines that physically manifested their enduring community-level engagement.[49]

This kind of distance to centers of power likely emerged as a feature of daily life rather than a sought-out strategy that Sufi communities honed for survival. However, in times of political turmoil and drastic change this remoteness from contested power centers could well have, by default, become a shielding mechanism, a feature that is explored in more detail in the sections that follow. Nonalignment does not mean that the communities would have remained unaffected by the political turmoil wrecking the areas where the communities lived. Communities would have had to make decisions concerning whether they thought they could remain in an area or whether they would have to move. Indeed, one of the most famous Sufis of all ages, Mawlana Rumi, was himself a refugee of the tumultuous Mongol onslaught that ravaged Central Eurasia in the thirteenth century and propelled his family to move from Balkh in present-day Afghanistan to Konya in present-day Turkey.[50]

In the context of political upheaval, this way of life could also become what I call "strategic distance." The difficulty in terming it "strategic" is obviously imputing intent. For example, distance might sometimes just be an unintended consequence of a community's particular position in regard to centers of power at a given point in time when turmoil is on the horizon. Particular behavior might not be a conscious choice but just a general habitus of a leader or community. However, a pattern that I have seen emerging in interviews with various communities is that an apolitical, power-avoidant stance became a conscious choice at particular times.

What I call strategic distance can mean literally seeking out physical distance from the source of power and the potential for violence. This can come in the guise of avoiding interaction with governmental representatives or insurgents, regional reallocation to a different, less-affected place or wholesale migration to a different region or country. While this can be an individual or household decision, in the case of Sufi communities, it has also sometimes meant the (re)establishment of *zikr* circles and libraries in neighboring countries as their main place of communal gathering and ritual performance. It can also mean discursive distancing within the community or stances held individually or communally. For example, an acclaimed poet who is being wooed by a government to join might choose nonalignment with the reigning regime. He might not take up a governmental office, decline an invitation to speak at a government's event or decide not to write poetry that can be used in national hymns or speeches. Strategic distance could mean a quietist stance toward politics at times when politics are at the center of social debate, of not getting involved and withholding political opinions to keep the community out of the limelight. It could entail the changing or curtailing of rituals to draw less attention to the community through their performance. Writers and communities could engage in self-censorship or offer depoliticized interpretations when speaking or publishing under their own name and restricting modes of expression. It could also mean selective engagement with the government as needed but otherwise trying to fly under the radar.

While it is just an unquestioned characteristic of some groups in peaceful times, this distance becomes strategic at times of upheaval when people and groups are expected to take a political stance. At those moments Sufi groups can continue to exercise distance, which becomes a strategic act. In some settings, such as purges after coups, this strategy might not work, given that the mere existence as a consolidated group or community with a meeting place might paint a target on their backs. But at times of ideological or authoritarian pressure that rewards submission to a central power and that shrinks the place for civil society, strategic distance and quietist, apolitical stances might become a valuable tool to shield a community and keep it intact.

We see all three of these rough typologies surfacing across space and time in the Sufi communities whom we meet in the following pages. The rest of the chapter traces how they appear in Afghanistan's more recent history. While readers might be familiar with the general contours of these time periods, the particular experiences of Sufi teachers and students offer nuances and new perspectives on these otherwise well-known developments.

PDPA Coup, Purge and Rule

From the tumultuous period starting with the Soviet invasion of Afghanistan in 1979 until the present day, each Sufi community in Afghanistan, whether cohesive or loosely defined, had unique experiences. In these four decades, Afghanistan's political leadership has changed hands repeatedly and the country has undergone varying phases of war. Nonetheless, common denominators emerged in the way these times were remembered by my Sufi interlocutors. In the following sections I trace some of these common experiences and how Sufi communities navigated the impact of the political changes that reconfigured Afghanistan as a nation-state.

In the 1970s, Afghanistan reaped the outcome of the economic and educational reforms initiated under the leadership of Prime Minister Daoud Khan (1909–1978) in the late 1950s and 1960s, which led to the expansion of education and higher levels of enrollment of both men and women.[51] These young educated Afghans, who often came from the provinces to study in the capital, remained in the city, despite high unemployment rates, and became politicized, particularly in the contentious sociopolitical milieu of Kabul University. As in many other parts of the world at this time, radical ideologies from opposite ends of the spectrum—Islamist and Communist—flourished. However, much of this organizing was forced underground because political parties were illegal in Afghanistan.[52] The bottling up of these ideologies led to radicalization and an exclusionary mentality, which produced clashes between Islamists and Communists on the streets and at the university.[53]

In April 1978 the contestations between various factions and the ruling elites under Daoud Khan escalated to a coup d'etat, later called the Saur Revolution (Inqelab-e Saur),[54] enacted by a Marxist-Leninist political party, the People's Democratic Party of Afghanistan (PDPA). The two Communist parties (Khalq and Parcham), who had jointly carried out the coup, split up and fought each other in the subsequent struggle for power, with Khalq taking control of the government.[55] This was followed by extensive purges of all perceived opposition, what Thomas Barfield describes as a "frenzy of bloodshed at a level not seen in Afghan politics since the nineteenth century."⁵⁶ In addition to Prime Minister Daoud and his family, other key political figures and members of minority groups (Hazara, Nuristanis) as well as Islamists and established ulama were killed.

Sufis, too, were caught up in these purges. Due to their political alliance with the previous government, the Naqshbandi-Mujaddidi family was a particular target of the Communists and suffered especially heavy losses: Hazrat Muhammad Ibrahim Mujaddidi of Shor Bazaar was arrested with 138 members of his family in January 1979 when the PDPA government started to focus on the religious establishment. According to contemporary witness and anthropologist Louis Dupree, more than two hundred other relatives and followers of the Mujaddidis were also arrested in Herat, Kandahar, Paghman and Logar. At least ninety-six male members of the family were killed on the night of their arrest in Kabul.⁵⁷

While the magnitude of reprisals against government-aligned Sufi families was exceptional, other Sufi orders who were perceived to belong to the religious establishment were targeted as well. Olivier Roy reports of the arrest and disappearance of three hundred Chishtiyyah *murids*, rumored to have been buried alive.⁵⁸ Religious scholars, such as Allama Faizani, who had been prisoners of the previous government, were presumably executed in prison, although documentation of their deaths is patchy at best. Many of my interviewees recounted stories of family members who disappeared after being arrested. Some were never seen again, such as Haji Ahmad Jan, who taught at one of the oldest Sufi lodges, *khanaqah* Pahlawan, in Kabul before he was taken away to Puhl-e Charkhi prison. The current caretaker of the *khanaqah*, Haji Tamim, recalled the incident: "It was during the time of Hafizullah Amin [organizer of the Saur Revolution who ruled Afghanistan as general secretary during 1978–1979]. Haji Ahmad Jan was the one leading the *khanaqah*. They came into the *khanaqah* and dragged him out with them to arrest him. . . . He never came back."⁵⁹ Many families would not hear for decades about their loved ones, who in all likelihood had been executed after being detained. It was not until 2013 that the Dutch Prosecutors' Office published a list of 4,785 people who were detained and killed in 1978 and 1979 in the first twenty months after the Saur Revolution. It was the first publicly available list of its kind in Afghanistan, giving names, professions, places of birth and the "crimes" they had been accused of.[60] However, during the Taraki and Amin governments (1978–1979), between fifty thousand and one hundred thousand people disappeared, with mass arrests targeting the ulama, intellectuals critical of the government, liberals, Maoists, ordinary people arrested under pretexts and disciples and teachers of Sufi orders.[61]

After the initial years of ideological class struggle, closures of *khanaqahs* and arrests and executions of religious personnel, including Sufis,[62] the PDPA government soon realized that it had a shallow popular base and was struggling for legitimacy in the eyes of the majority of the population.[63] Its strategy then developed from positioning the government as nonoffensive to Islam to attempting to gain religious legitimacy through appeals to religious leaders, new rhetoric positioning and the formation of religious institutions.[64] The PDPA set up a General Department of Islamic Affairs within the Prime Minister's Office as a central node for religious organization.[65] The department included a High Council of ulama (Shura-ye 'ali-ye 'ulama wa ruhaniyun) as a consultative body appointed by the prime minister. This department became its own, separate ministry in 1985 (Wizarat-e Shun-e Islami wa Auqaf), tasked not only with facilitating basic religious functions—hajj (pilgrimage), maintaining mosques, assisting religious research and so on—but also ensuring control over the kind of religious learning that was disseminated.[66]

Chantal Lobato, writing in 1985 about the changes of government from Taraki/Amin in 1978–1979 to Babrak Kamal (1979–1986), describes the latter's government as "far from underestimating the religious factor. It wants to control and monopolise Islam for want of the power to destroy it. Religious affairs have, therefore, been institutionalised."[67] This meant that the newly created departments took charge of the *waqf* endowments and the construction and renovation of mosques, transitioning all religious personnel who continued to work with Karmal's government to officials of the Afghan state.[68] While Lobato acknowledges the notable changes brought about by these tactics, she also notes that they were limited in reach. The policies from the Ministry for Islamic Affairs and the KHAD (Afghan secret services) were applicable only in Kabul, with religious functionaries outside the city largely remaining independent or linked to the resistance.⁶⁹ The regime's preferences concerning religious personalities once again shifted, attempting both to engineer a diverse religious elite and avoid those with questionable loyalties. Avoiding a direct confrontation with Hafizullah Amin's previous choices, religious leaders were gradually replaced; for instance, Abdul Aziz of Kandahar, who "had been chosen by Amin for his anti-Sufism and Wahhabi inclination[s]," was replaced by the Al-Azhar-educated Sayyed Afghani in the Department for Islamic Affairs.⁷⁰ Religious leaders for the government were mainly chosen for their perceived loyalty and support for the regime.

By 1986, the PDPA claimed to have twelve thousand mullahs on its payroll.⁷¹ They were continually reaching out to ulama as well as Sufi intellectuals such as Ustad Haidari Wujudi, one of the foremost teachers on Mawlana's *Masnawi* and one of my interlocutors, whom I repeatedly interviewed. Wujudi remembered the attempts during the PDPA government, as well as successive politicians, to integrate him into the state apparatus:

> This happened later with Marshall Fahim,⁷² but also earlier under Dr. Najib [Dr. Najibullah, president of Afghanistan, 1987–1992]. Sayed Ali, the minister of Hajj, he sent a friend to me and said that "Mr. Haidari is getting old, he needs a car and an office, please invite him." I knew they had a *jirga* [political assembly] coming up and they wanted support.⁷³

Wujudi had remained in his office in the public library for most of the decades in which changes swept through Afghanistan's political arena. Officially, he was a library clerk. Unofficially, his acclaim grew over the decades as a poet as well as public intellectual. I wondered how the PDPA government had heard about him at a time when he was still relatively young, and Wujudi recounted how his involvement in Bedil poetry circles got him noticed:

> I was invited to a Bedil meeting in Kolala Poshta [central part of Kabul city]. I was respectfully taken in. Then I saw the cabinet ministers of Najib there and the head of the *shuras* and councils. A lot of officials were there. And there was a flagpole where everyone ties colorful clothes. The minister of hajj went to tie a flag to that stick and make a speech. But when he went

to that stick, people shouted that he is not to touch that: "You are not supposed to tie anything there." Because he was the minister of that Communist regime, people could forbid him from going close to something that they would consider as belonging to religious symbols and rituals. He tied that cotton anyway, but they did not allow him to speak. They were shouting that I should speak. "Haidari, Haidari, Haidari." And when I spoke a little bit, that was taken to Dr. Najib.[74]

Haidari Wujudi's memories of advances by the Communist regime, as well as the people's reactions toward the minister of hajj's attempts to insert himself into religious symbolism and practices, attests both to the PDPA's efforts to recast its anti-Islamic image at a Sufi poetry gathering and its failure to do so in the people's eyes. Considering that the refusal of government advances could have had serious consequences for him, given the government's previous proclivity for making Sufis and intellectuals disappear in the early days of its rule, Wujudi seemed unperturbed: "I asked to be kept away from Dr. Najib and any other regime afterwards." His distance to power was also facilitated through the establishment of Sufi poetry as a religio-cultural heritage of the kind political powers could use, but still a separate realm to be mastered. He was sought after as a prominent figurehead that could be beneficial for establishing religious and cultural credibility of a regime, but he was not a threat to it either.

Not only did the PDPA government try to build up its own religious institutions, but it also initiated a process of "symbolic desecularization." This included such efforts as reintroducing "Bismillah-e Rahman-e Rahim" (lit., "In the name of God, the most gracious, the most merciful," used as a benediction at the beginning of an action) at the start of speeches and public announcements, changing the national flag and the official name of the country again, reinserting religious symbolism in speeches and mandating that high officials participate in all public religious functions.[75] Both Babrak Karmal and Najibullah wove Islamic legitimizations into their speeches, with mixed success.[76] However, as evidenced in Wujudi's recollections, the PDPA's attempts were not taken seriously by many, who saw in them mainly cosmetic attempts to appease the public.[77]

Exile, Mujahidin Resistance and Civil War

While some Sufi poets and scholars who had survived the initial purges during the PDPA takeover remained in Afghanistan and worked to strike a balance between strategic distance and proximity to the state, many others left the country altogether, seeking exile in neighboring countries such as Iran or Pakistan or farther abroad in Europe or the United States.[78] Indeed, the majority of communities I researched had some of their members living abroad in the years that followed the Soviet invasion. They were part of the overall out-migration of Afghans fleeing the country, which was at that time described as historically unparalleled:[79] "The Afghan crisis," as it was called back then, referring to the fight between the Soviet-backed Communist government and the Mujahidin resistance, caused the deaths of more than one million people and prompted the exodus of roughly one-third of the population.[80]

Once they arrived in neighboring countries, Sufi affiliates became part of the refugee population. Most scholarly accounts depict Sufism as having gone underground. For example, Asta Olesen writes that Sufism was "only practiced in a very withdrawn and almost clandestine way among the Afghan *muhajir* [refugees]."[81] However, in my more recent interviews, members of communities recall a different experience. Some communities established *khanaqahs* in exile and organized weekly *zikr* meetings. Others convened poetry recitations and celebrated the *urs* (death anniversary) of poets such as Bedil. Some even became active in organizing supportive livelihood strategies for fellow Afghans. The Faizani community, for example, established a library and *zikr* meetings in Peshawar, in addition to support programs for Afghan refugees such as infrastructure programs, food kitchens, carpet weaving, agricultural education and vocational training.[82] These activities were advertised in brochures as well as on the historic background section of their community on their contemporaneous website, suggesting that the community views the engagement with and service for their society—no matter whether in their country of origin or in exile—as an integral part of their spiritual calling.[83]

While individual Sufi leaders and their communities attempted to envision a more peaceful future for their country, other actors ignited ever-new cycles of violence. In the wake of the PDPA's seizure of power and the arrival of Soviet troops to prop it up (December 27, 1979), resistance parties (*tanzimat*) had started organizing in Peshawar and sought support from the Pakistani government, led by General Muhammad Zia ul-Haq (1977–1988). The Soviets had assumed they would restore order and remove their troops after a few months, but Afghans mobilized a massive uprising that led to a decade-long protracted fight against the occupation that lasted from 1979 to 1989.[84] The resistance became broader and more international in scope under the leadership of Afghan Islamists, who had been exiled in Pakistan after their failed uprising against Daoud's government in the mid-1970s. Events played out in a Cold War theater in which these opposition groups fought a proxy war funded and armed by foreign powers such as the United States and Saudi Arabia. The Soviets took control of the major cities and transport routes; however, despite brutal countertactics such as air bombardments, torture and disappearance of suspected collaborators and the laying of land mines, the Soviets were unable to extinguish the resistance.[85]

Some of the Sufi families who had been state aligned with the previous regime opted to join the resistance and form parties of their own.[86] Pir Sayyid Ahmad Gailani founded the National Islamic Front (Mahaz-e-Milli-e Islami), and Hazrat Sibghatullah Mojaddedi established the National Liberation Front (Jabha-yi nejate-i milli).[87] They were both considered "traditionalist parties" in comparison to the more radical Islamist parties, Jamiat and Hizb-e Islami.[88] They also received less international funding, including aid and weapons transport payments, because they were considered too nationalist (*watani*) in outlook and were often regarded with suspicion by Arab Islamists.[89] Though damaging to the parties' abilities to wage war, such disfavor provided them a greater degree of independence than that of other parties; for instance, leaders such as Sibghatullah Mojaddedi used to publicly denounce the Pakistani secret service's (ISI) interference and favoritism among the Afghan resistance leaders.[90]

However, not all Sufis joined these two organizations; others formed their own resistance groups or were subsumed within other, bigger parties.[91] Olivier Roy, who researched the resistance and its various factions, chronicles his observations of the Sufi-led resistance fighters in Dehsabz (Kabul vicinity) and in Herat as tightly interwoven, possessing high morale, resistant to penetration by informers—since they all knew each other—these groups are efficient from the military point of view.... In most cases the local *pirs* delegate their military authority to a *murid* who is often older (the cadres originating from brotherhoods are older than those provided by the so-called fundamentalist parties). The two *pir*[s] of Cheshtiya are the only ones who personally direct military operations. In the west a large number of *pir*[s] took refuge in Iran, leaving command in the hands of their favorite disciples. This departure of the *pir*[s] is explained by the fact that most of them are very old, many of their children are not up to this task.[92]

The *ziyarats* (the tombs or mausoleums of a *pir*) became "assembly points, places of political indoctrination and also refuges," as it was believed these holy places were protected by God and could not be destroyed by bombs.[93] While Roy observed that many smaller Sufi groups such as the Naqshbandiyyah in Herat were assimilated by the much larger Jamiat-e Islami,[94] some of my interviewees recalled Sufi orders in Herat as having felt a stronger affinity for Hezb-i Islami during the later stages of the resistance.[95] Regardless of their specific affiliation, the fighting groups led by Sufi orders were minority parties compared to the larger Islamist parties that fought the jihad and received the lion's share of funding, weapons and international support.[96]

Nonetheless, the few of my Sufi interviewees who counted themselves as Mujahidin during the jihad remembered their fighting time with pride. One professor at Herat University, who was also a *murid*, rebuked me when I wondered how Sufism and fighting could go hand in hand: "Of course it can! They [the Soviets] were invaders, and it was our duty to defend Afghanistan! We were doing *zikr* with rifles in our hands at times when we had to wait or keep watch. And then we fought and won."

As the war waged on, it became increasingly costly for the Soviet Union, who looked for a way out. They accepted peace negotiations in 1986 under a UN-sponsored withdrawal agreement, and the troops left the country between May 1988 and February 1989.[97] Before the Soviets left, they made the former head of the secret police, commonly known as Dr. Najib, the leader of the PDPA. In the following years (1989–1992), the Mujahidin struggled to get rid of the surviving Soviet-backed Communist government under Dr. Najibullah, who had modified his name to give it a more Islamic flavor.[98] But when the Soviet Union collapsed in December 1991, Najibullah's government lost its patron and was deposed in April 1992. The victorious Mujahidin then turned on each other in their quest for power, which resulted in a brutal war that destroyed much of Kabul city during what became known as the Civil War period (1992–1995). In 1993 alone around ten thousand Afghans were killed across the country as the Mujahidin fought each other.[99]

Many Sufi affiliates reflected on how their perception of the Mujahidin shifted during this time. The sons of a former *pir* in the vicinity of Herat, who had been affiliated with the Mujahidin parties during the jihad, felt bitter about this checkered past:

> [Our] house was used for fighting and it got destroyed.... Our relationship with Jamiat was also finished after the jihad finished. They were using us, unfortunately. I don't have any card [membership] of the Jamiat, because I don't believe in their goals. They are using the Jamiat for their own benefit. For example, the Mujahidin were fighting in Afghanistan, but their children went to school in other countries, they are buying a lot of houses for themselves, they take the passports of other countries but the people here don't have bread! We see the leaders of the Mujahidin; they have a lot of money, a lot of castles. This discrimination is not accepted by us, by the new generation. My brother [current caretaker of their *khanaqah*] also doesn't believe in them, because they use the people for their benefit, but not for Islam.[100]

The shifting of public opinion away from the Mujahidin as Islamic freedom fighters to thugs who destroyed the country in the ruthless Civil War of the early 1990s has become a common perception, especially among the urban Afghan population, who had to endure the trench warfare of the different factions.[101] Fatima Gailani (b. 1954), the daughter of Pir Ahmad Gailani and spokesperson for the Mujahidin during the Soviet War when she was based in London, pointed out to me in an interview in Kabul that her family chose to stop fighting once the Soviets left and once the justification for jihad had disappeared as Muslims turned on Muslims during the Civil War:

My father said that "fighting has been imposed upon us. A superpower has invaded this country, and I have the power of calling upon the people to come together... and because of the same reason as soon as the last Soviet troop, the last soldier crossed the border, the fight is finished, and anyone in my name [has to] stop the fight." Yes of course there are people like Gul Agha and others who joined for someone else to carry on the Civil War, but the people who were truly in love with the name of the Qadiriyyah, the name of my father, they quit. So, he didn't participate in the Civil War; he didn't fight; he left when everybody was taking sides and destroying Kabul.[102]

It is beyond the scope of this work to parse out the web of alliances between Sufi groups and Mujahidin parties. Oral history accounts of the 1980s and early 1990s were sometimes difficult to disentangle, in terms of whether interviewees had always been critical of the Mujahidin or became so in the course of the decade (which also showed ample infighting between the groups) or in the subsequent Civil War.[103] One factor complicating people's memories was the broad application of the term "Mujahidin" during various stages of Afghanistan's recent history. The term was applied irrespective of whether the period referred to was the actual time of the jihad, the Civil War or the post-2001 period when Mujahidin leaders transitioned to political players.

The Civil War period in which the Mujahidin continued fighting each other was remembered by many Sufis in urban *khanaqahs* as a time of relentless attacks and hardship. Haji Tamim, the caretaker of *khanaqah* Pahlawan in Kabul, recalls this time vividly in contrast to other periods of the past:

> Even though the Communists disappeared people and took their nails off their hands, we were more afraid of the Mujahidin, because they have done so much to us. They were not Mujahidin [fighters for God]; they were *monafaqin* [hypocrites].[104] Mujahidin came, they burned this *khanaqah*; they looted and burned all the stuff that was in here. They took out all the dishes and all the stuff from the mosque [*masjid*] and from the *khanaqah*.[105] They took even the carpet from the *masjid*! First the *khanaqah* was burned,

and then it was destroyed by rockets that were flying around and then they also hit here. That's why the roof and upper floor had to be rebuilt two times. And then after that when the Civil War stopped, we rebuilt the whole *khanaqah* as you see it now.¹⁰⁶

Because the war against the PDPA and the Soviets had been framed as a jihad, it had united many Mujahidin factions who were now not divided over ideology but who would hold power in a fight where the victims were again the Afghan population.¹⁰⁷

Taliban in the 1990s

At the end of 1994, a movement that came to be known as the Taliban arose in response to the factional fighting between the Mujahidin and the brutality they were inflicting on Afghans. In 1995, the group rapidly took control of many of Afghanistan's districts, particularly in the south and the east. By September 1996, the Taliban had captured Kabul. In the coming years, there would be attempts to take over the rest of the country, leading to several massacres in the north and a stalemate with the last remnants of the Mujahidin factions.¹⁰⁸ The Taliban drew on Afghan discontent about the ongoing war and their disillusionment with the power-hungry Mujahidin. In Pakistani refugee camps, they recruited young men who had not fought as Mujahidin and gave them a chance to fight instead for what they pitched as an idealistic cause, a new jihad sanctioned by their own clerics. Inside Afghanistan they promised stability and security to a population that was still reeling from the chaos of the Soviet collapse and the factional fighting that followed.¹⁰⁹ The strict regime the Taliban instituted did, like other brutal authoritarian movements before it, provide security and swift justice (or at least, a kind of justice of the Taliban's own rendering). In doing so, it also made the Taliban synonymous with the brutality and restrictive policies implemented toward women.¹¹⁰ The Vice and Virtue Police enforced strict dress codes, banned women from attending schools or working outside the home and instituted draconian punishment for those violating their laws.¹¹¹

The brutality of the Taliban writ large was, and remains, undeniable. At the same time, the movement was not without internal contradictions and ideological competition. Because the Taliban was a decentralized agglomeration of local groups, there was always a range of beliefs among its military commanders and ideologues that vied for supremacy. Sufism is one arena where those contestations played out. The Taliban's relationship to Sufi scholars and Sufi communities more broadly was complex. Taliban officials of the first generation, who were in power in the 1990s, regarded some forms of Sufi practice as rightfully Islamic while attempting to regulate or delegitimize others. Thus, Sufi affiliates faced a spectrum of realities because the Taliban themselves did not have a unified national policy in regard to Sufi communities. Several cross-cutting issues, from musical expression to gender, as well as Taliban commanders' personal stances, guided engagement and circumscribed the navigational space that Sufis had for negotiating varying practices.

Notwithstanding the fact that they bear the same name, it should be clear that the current post-2021 Taliban are not the same as the ones my interviewees remembered nor the ones that I myself interviewed from the 1990s government. The movement has changed considerably, and at the time of writing the full scope of the change remains unclear. In this section, when I talk about the Sufi communities' experiences with the Taliban, I am strictly describing events that occurred during their first government between 1995 and 2001.

The politically aligned Sufi families—the Mujaddidi Naqshbandiyyah and the Gailani Qadiriyyah—who had created oppositional fighting groups during the anti-Soviet jihad but had declined to participate in the Civil War remained in exile during the 1990s and chose to return only post-2001, after the fall of the Taliban regime. However, as Fatima Gailani, who was working in London at the time, illustrates, Afghans engaged the Taliban from a distance. In one exchange, on a BBC Pashto talk show, she recounts her own efforts to directly challenge Taliban policies:

> There was one session... with the Taliban [member] on one side and I was on the other side. He said, "Bibi, with all your titles, do you think that education is much more important than honor of a woman?" I said, "Well, you have a government in the name of God, and I have come here to talk about this. If God says, 'Iqra' [read] first,[112] then Fatimah says, 'Iqra' first. Had

God said 'Iffah' [modesty] first, Fatimah would have said 'Iffah' first. But now God said, 'Iqra'; the first thing God said was 'Iqra' and 'ilm-e qalam.' So I don't have the audacity to say, well, I know better than God. Do you?"[113]

Fatima Gailani chose to challenge the Taliban on their own terms—within the framework of Islam. Of course, she had the advantage of physical distance that allowed her to be blunt without risking arrest, or worse. Even so, this strategic approach, and more broadly the engagement of ordinary Afghans and Sufis with the Taliban, or indeed with any of the varying ruling classes at the time, is often underappreciated in most histories that focus on the top-down metrics of who ruled and how.[114]

Meanwhile, Sufis in Afghanistan had to continually negotiate space for their existence and often did so with surprising success. My own conversations with Afghans who were in the diaspora at the time reflected surprise at the ability of Sufis to carve out a place for themselves in Taliban-ruled Afghanistan. Fatima Gailani was perplexed by the apparent contradictions:

> There were *khanaqahs* in cities, especially in Kabul and Herat, that continued. We were out [of Afghanistan], but it continued, and we heard that even in the ranks of the Taliban they would do the *zikr*.... For me that was a puzzle. How can these two things that are totally in conflict continue? But this is Afghanistan; there are a lot of things that are in conflict that continue.... The head of the armed forces in Jalalabad during the Taliban was Mullah [Abdul Salam] Rocketi, and he always had *zikr* gatherings in the shrine of my grandfather.[115]

Though based on hearsay, Fatimah Gailani's information about Taliban participation in Sufi rituals is supported by other accounts from inside Afghanistan, which begs the question of what the core beliefs of the Taliban were concerning Sufi practices. It is one thing for an intolerant group to tolerate certain practices; it is quite another to participate in those practices. But in many of my interviews, in disparate parts of Afghanistan, it does seem like some members of the Taliban did. For instance, a Herati interviewee in the northwest recalled: "My father was Qadiriyyah. He died two years ago. From him I know that even during Taliban time, in our mosque, after the Friday prayer there was *halqa-e zikr* happening, and there were several Taliban who were taking part. There were Taliban who were followers in the Qadiriyyah and others who followed the Naqshbandiyyah." Another interviewee from Kandahar remembered that the Hazrat Sahib of Sevon/Seven was respected even during the Taliban time and that the four sons of his own *murshid* were all in the Taliban as low-ranking soldiers while also participating in the social sphere of the Naqshbandiyyah and Qadiriyyah orders.

Leaders of the Taliban are often characterized as being raised in refugee camps and educated in radical madrasas in Pakistan, but Alex Strick van Linschoten and Anand Gopal have argued persuasively in their analysis of the genealogy of the Taliban's ideology that the Afghan Taliban have been influenced by Sufism both through their Deobandi education and through "village-based traditions." Of the original Taliban leadership, 48 percent received their education in a *hujra* in Afghanistan, with the number swelling to 59 percent when including other forms of Afghan education such as madrasas and *maktabs*.[116] The Afghan *hujra* is an informal system of learning, culminating after about ten years in a turban-tying graduation ceremony to a mullah.[117] The curricula varied but usually ranged from anatomy lessons to poetry and herbal medicine to sexual taboos. Linschoten and Gopal also describe how *hujras* used excerpts of Deobandi curricula "because certain features of the school resonated with the pre-existing logic of cultural practice within Afghanistan . . . [such as] Deobandism's intimate link with Sufism."[118]

These leaders also ascribed to other sociocultural practices such as taking advice and directives from dreams.[119] While psychologically oriented interpretation of dreams is mainly focused on dream interpretation as the excavation of the workings of the unconscious, in the Islamic tradition, dreams are situated in spaces where humans and the Divine can potentially interact. Taliban officials practiced *istikhara* (dream incubation) as a device to make professional decisions, and Mullah Omar is reported to have shared dreams for interpretation regularly with a close circle of confidants.[120] Dreams were more than individual experiences; they could be crucial in political discussions, as the former Taliban finance minister Mutasim Agha Jan details in an example from a strategic political meeting on the eve of the American bombing campaign post-9/11:[121]

Most of our ministerial meetings were held in the presidential palace. When the bombardment started, we were supposed to hold the meetings in our houses instead of in Arg.... The deputy minister was Mullah Muhammad Hasan, [who] came with some other ministers, such as the minister of defense, Mullah Obaidullah, to my house to hold the meeting.... The meeting started by asking the question, who has had a dream? I responded that I had a dream last evening. The dream had two parts. I dreamed of black rain and standing in a place that had a pool, where I collected some stones for ablution and praying. When I took some water from a pipe, suddenly the water turned brown. I looked for the reason [of this change in the water] and found that one part of the pool's wall had fallen down and the clean, white water changed to be dusty and full of clay. When I shared the dream, Mullah Mohammad Hassan and all our friends said that we wouldn't be able to stay in Afghanistan. Afghanistan was our home, but a black rain had come and we needed to withdraw from it. We had clean water, but we weren't able to use it.[122]

Dreams formed a shared religious-cultural idiom among various Afghans, and dream sharing and collective interpretation of dreams were practices in Sufi communities and among the Taliban leadership. This did not make the Taliban Sufis, but it shows how a similar educational background and enculturation led the two groups to share the same widely held—and fundamentally Islamic—beliefs in divinely inspired dreams.

Apart from the shared educational background, in which Sufism played a role, and shared socioreligious practices, some leading Taliban officials had connections to Sufi *pirs* and orders through family ties. One of the early members of the Taliban who spoke to me about his connections to Sufism was Mawlawi Pir Mohammad Rohani. He served as the chancellor of Kabul University under the Taliban but laid down weapons post-2001 and was integrated into Afghan politics in 2005 as head of the Supreme Court's administrative affairs department and, in 2010, as a High Peace Council member.[123] In an interview at his residence in the Darul Aman area of Kabul, he told me:

I am myself part of the Qadiriyyah through my family. It's not possible to go into Sufism without having the knowledge of the physical or outer knowledge [*zahir*]. In our university with the permission of Amir ul mumin [Mullah Omar], there were four ulama in every faculty assigned to teach all these outer subjects. Without this, nobody can enter Sufism.... I was visiting my *pir* every six months or every year, and he taught me how to do *zikr*. My *pir* is in Musair district of Kabul; his name is Nur Mohammad Jan Shaver. His son is now in charge, Abdul Waseezada. I went to the *khanaqah*, and my family members are still going there.[124]

Surprised by his admission (I had no idea he was a *murid*), I asked how he would define Sufism. He framed it as a thread that extends through every school of jurisprudence, as a deepened and immersed piety.[125] However, he also clearly saw the limitations of Sufi practice, criticizing certain *zikr* practices for veering into innovation. While it might be unusual to have a former Taliban official admitting to his Sufi connections, it points to two important nuances: First, Sufism is a spectrum that includes a host of beliefs and practices. With a restrained and reformed understanding even a Taliban official can claim to be a Sufi. Second, and more important, it shows that Sufism was deeply embedded into the Pashtun culture from which the vast majority of the first generation of Taliban emerged in the 1990s.[126]

While individual members of the Taliban had family connections and affinities to particular forms of Sufism, it has remained a much-discussed question in Afghanistan whether the reclusive leader of the Taliban, Mullah Omar, had Sufi connections himself. Mullah Omar was educated in the Afghan *hujra* system and as a child received education from Sufi teachers such as Haji Baba. He has been described as visiting shrines in Kandahar on a regular basis.[127] I asked one of Mullah Omar's closest confidants, the former Taliban finance minister Mutasim Agha Jan, about Mullah Omar's visits to *pirs*. He framed the relationship as one of respect toward an Islamic scholar who was simultaneously also a Sufi *pir*:

Some *pirs* would come to meet Mullah Omar. But there was also a man named Salahwat Haji Baba, who was in Panjwai district in Kandahar. I visited Haji Baba together [with Mullah Omar] twice, but the third time when we arrived, we came to the tomb where he had died. We decided to go to his grave and pray. It was not about Haji Baba being a Sufi, but he was also a good religious scholar and very popular in Kandahar, and people highly respected and believed in him. So it is not for me to say that Mullah Sahib Omar had gone to see *pirs*, but they came to him themselves. We went to some shrines together,[128] such as Mohammad Jan Agha, in the village of Mirbazar, Ahmad Shah Baba shrine, the shrine of Mirwais Khan's grandfather, and occasionally Mullah Omar went to his father's shrine, also in Nada district.[129]

Mutasim Agha Jan's deflection, classifying Mullah Omar's relationship with Haji Baba as more scholarly than spiritual, is a common strategy to reframe the discussion along ideologically fitting terms. The *pir* to whom Mullah Omar paid visits is dead now, making it impossible to ascertain the nature of the visits or the exchanges between the two. Certainly, visits to a *pir* do not in and of themselves make anyone directly a *murid*, and it is not known whether Mullah Omar ever took a *bay'a* (oath of allegiance) to any Sufi *pir*. Its impact on Sufi-state relations seems negligible. Omar never instituted a policy or approach to Sufis under the Taliban rule. Rather, the salient point these visits make is that he remained open to consulting with an individual widely known to engage in Sufi practices. This suggests Mullah Omar was at the very least not opposed to these practices and their intertwining with how Islam is lived and interpreted in Afghanistan.

This apparent tolerance for Sufism clashed with beliefs of other high-ranking members of the Taliban movement, a fact that was not lost on most Sufi affiliates. "During the Taliban regime there were some *talibs* who were Wahhabi, and they had problems with Sufis," one Naqshbandiyyah *pir* in Herat told me. "Some of them [Taliban] were Sufi as well, so they had discussions and conflict among the Taliban themselves."

Today, the term "Wahhabi" has evolved to become broadly derogatory in Afghanistan, denoting a religious extremist who attacks local and regional configurations of religious experience. Usually, "Wahhabi" is shorthand for a Salafi-leaning religious interpretation. In the Afghan political consciousness, it referred to multiple periods of history and groups, such as the influence of Arabs and Arab fighters during the anti-Soviet jihad of the 1980s; Arab support in the establishment of the Taliban in the 1990s;[130] and most recently, post-2001, to the emergence of mosques, associations and preachers that are seen as supportive of, connected to or assumed to be directly financed by Saudi Arabia or Gulf Arab countries.

Tensions over the contours of belief persisted both within the Taliban and between the Taliban and Arab fighters who came to Afghanistan during the anti-Soviet jihad.[131] The latter, who called themselves the fedayeen (self-sacrificers),[132] are commonly known as the "Arab Afghans"[133]—a misleading term as the group was neither Afghan nor entirely Arab, with some hailing from Turkic, Malay and other ethnicities.[134] While their numbers were comparatively small, their impact on shifting the discursive environment and transforming the Afghan national jihad into a global enterprise was significant.[135] Influential ideologues such as Abdullah Azzam (1941–1989) and Osama Bin Laden (1957–2011), who initially gave organizational, financial and logistical support but later became more prominent as an ideologue, especially after Azzam's death, formed the institutional and ideological backbone of the Arab involvement during the jihad as well as in later political alliances.[136] These Arab volunteers were known to clash with their hosts over the widespread Sufi practices and shrine visitations common in Afghanistan. As one of my interviewees recounted of their initial arrival: "Arabs came into the jihad. They destroyed shrines, cut flags on the shrines and graves. But sometimes they were faced with strong reactions against them from the people. That's why they did it at nighttime."[137]

While my interlocutor saw these as clandestine acts of destruction, other historical narrations document earlier pervasive and open tension between Afghans and these foreign fighters. At least on one occasion, the leader of one of the Afghan Islamist parties, Maulvi Khalis, had to travel to Kandahar to mediate a dispute after Afghan Arabs removed flags from a grave.[138] Afghan Arabs viewed this practice as unlawful *shirk* (polytheism), whereas, as David Edwards has phrased it, "given the moral calculus of sacrifice, in which the living owed a continuing debt to those who had died in battle, the Wahhabi interdiction against prayers and flags at the graves of martyrs can be seen from the Afghan perspective as both sacrilege and immorality."[139] Warnings to respect Afghan beliefs and customs were issued by several Mujahidin leaders, such as Sayyid Ahmad Gailani and Abdulrab Sayyaf.

The presence of these advisers as well as differing stances of Taliban officials toward Sufis and their practices created a complicated environment for Sufi communities to navigate. What would strategic distance look like in an environment where commanders could be favorable—and sometimes even join *zikr*—or turn out to be anti-Sufi, imprisoning *pirs* and burning literature?

One solution was a kind of negotiation over how rituals were performed that allowed certain Sufi practices to continue in a form that would not necessarily raise the wrath of the Taliban's more Wahhabi-leaning members. Most Sufi communities recounted that meditative *zikr* rituals still occurred during the Taliban era but that the Taliban government was concerned with the specifics of their practice, especially whether they were accompanied by music. The Taliban were renowned for forbidding video, imagery and music during their rule.[140] Many musicians were unable to make a living after the Taliban prohibited singing and dancing at weddings. The Taliban also destroyed recorded music such as cassettes and banned music from the airwaves, transforming Radio Kabul into the Voice of Radio Shariat.[141] For some of Afghanistan's most prominent Sufi *tariqats* such as the Chishtiyyah, whose long history in the country included the combination of *zikr* with music, this was a problem. However, when I pointed this out to Mawlawi Pir Mohammad Rohani in an interview in 2018, he dismissively rejected my line of inquiry, arguing that there were no Sufi groups who used music with *zikr* under the Taliban and that these were aberrations found in other countries. This denial of a well-known fact simultaneously legitimized the practice of *zikr*—for it was not the practice he was denying—while it delegitimized the practice of *zikr* if accompanied by music. However, *zikr* with music had long existed in Afghanistan, and many musicians who had played for *zikr* gatherings came back from self-imposed exile after the fall of the Taliban.[142]

Musical accompaniment with instruments was, however, not the only type of *zikr* that was under scrutiny during Taliban rule. Several Sufi affiliates reported Taliban who restricted the practice of vocalized *zikr* (*zikr jahr*), in which the voices of participants alone form the rhythm of the ritual.¹⁴³ Again, the core issue was music: the rhythmization of this *zikr* was perceived as too close to music, with a potential of inducing trances that could lead to dancing. Mutasim Agha Jan, the former Taliban finance minister and close confidant of Taliban founder Mullah Omar, argued in an interview that *"zikr* should be in the heart, secretly."¹⁴⁴

While limiting, this view on *zikr* did create space for negotiation and offered Sufis varying ways to deal with Taliban restrictions. Some Sufi communities hid certain forms of *zikr* and foregrounded approved practices as a shielding mechanism. Haji Saiqal, who led one of the oldest *khanaqahs* in Kabul, described how the community sometimes played a cat-and-mouse game with the authorities: "We have never stopped the *zikr jahr*. When we knew that on that day a Taliban [official] would come, we would stop for that time with *zikr jahr*, because of the problems it might create, but after that we continued." The caretaker of the same *khanaqah*, Haji Tamim, added: "They believed that we are the people of the Qur'an and Hadith and that we pray. That's why they didn't have any problems with us."

Haji Tamim's comment seems innocuous, and perhaps even superfluous considering the *khanaqah* was led by a mullah, but he intimates another strategy Sufi communities used to protect themselves from Taliban reprisals: a kind of religious misdirect. Establishing religious bona fides with the Taliban invited less scrutiny. Another former Sufi affiliate from another order told me that "during the Taliban time, the cover for the *khanaqahs* was *khatm*, reading thirty chapters of the Qur'an. People would come together under this cover, but then they would also read poems and get high through literature."¹⁴⁵

Engaging in self-censorship, offering depoliticized interpretations and restricting modes of expression were common responses to keeping communities and practices intact during this time, as part of strategic distance to the government. This was especially true when newcomers who might be sympathetic to the government or who came directly as government intelligence joined Sufi gatherings. Also, importantly, none of the Sufi groups that I researched organized female gatherings during this time. The female teachers and students of the communities who had been active in earlier years mainly practiced outside Afghanistan in the diaspora or in hiding.

Karzai, Ghani, Indifference and Insurgency

After the toppling of the Taliban regime in 2001, the focus of the internationally financed Afghan government shifted to the reconstruction of the country, gender mainstreaming and building up state institutions.[146] The first two decades of the twenty-first century are often described as the "reconstruction" era.[147] Islam was acknowledged in the constitution and inscribed in national laws.[148] But most perceived the state as rather technocratic compared to that in previous decades, in which fervor against religion, motivation to fight for Islamic principles (however earnest or shallow), destruction in the name of Islam or punishment along strict ideas of the setup of Muslim society had been at the forefront of national players' rhetoric.

Some Sufi communities returned from years in exile to build up new lives in Afghanistan, while others remained abroad, supporting the communities in their country of origin with remittances and occasional visits. Among the returnees were the former state-connected political Sufi families, the Gailani and Mujaddidi, who took little time in reinserting themselves into elite Afghan politics. Sibghatullah Mojaddedi served as chairman of the 2003 Loya Jirga that approved Afghanistan's new constitution. He was then appointed chairman of the upper house of the National Assembly of Afghanistan (Meshrano Jirga, reappointed in 2011), chaired the *jirga* on the Bilateral Security Agreement (BSA) in 2013 and served on the Afghan High Peace Council.[149] The Mujaddidis, primarily through Sibghatullah, remained a highly visible political presence. The Gailani family straddled the line between symbolic roles and civil society engagement. Syed Hamed Gailani became the first deputy speaker of Afghanistan's Senate,[150] and Fatima Gailani, who had served as a spokesperson for the National Islamic Front (NIFA) in the West during the 1980s, served as the president of the Afghan Red Crescent (2005–2016). During the "peace process" with the Taliban, starting in 2018, she served as a member of the Afghan government's negotiation team.[151] Both families retained their symbolic roles in government as advisers.

Apart from these two political families, most Sufi communities remained largely undisturbed by but also unconnected to the government.

Their practice and community services were now positioned within the private realm of individual decision-making and semipublic congregations. Some Sufi shrines, such as Gazargah in Herat and the Hazrat Ali mosque and shrine in Mazar-e Sharif, became symbolically charged for political purposes.[152] However, generally the governments of Hamid Karzai and Ashraf Ghani initially showed no interest in connecting with, supporting or targeting Sufi communities. Selectively, individual politicians saw it as beneficial to renovate and care for infrastructure that was used by Sufi groups, but this was not general policy.[153]

As the Taliban-led insurgency against the Afghan government and the international troop presence grew in the 2000s, the question of Muslim identity and Islam became increasingly politicized.[154] As Abdulkader Sinno argues, the strategic use of religion, religious language and symbols plays an additive role in a religious Muslim country, and the post-2001, largely technocratic Afghan government was pushed into a defensive stance on religious issues.[155] While other actors (Taliban, ulama councils, political actors using Salafi and Islamist language) were able to make active demands, the Afghan government was obliged to engage with these claims in a reactive capacity.[156]

The Taliban increasingly relied on religious leaders to legitimize their rule. As Ashley Jackson observes in her study of how individuals negotiated with the Taliban over the course of the US intervention, "village religious figures are often co-opted into Taliban structures and play an influential role in collecting information and acting on the Taliban's behalf."[157] However, religious leaders who opposed the Taliban were harassed, threatened or killed. In 2017, the *New York Times* reported on the targeted killing of religious scholars in Afghanistan's provinces, noting that those scholars who spoke out against the Taliban and for a more open, pluralistic or moderate view of Islam were killed by bomb blasts or shot.[158] The BBC estimated that more than eight hundred religious scholars who confronted the Taliban by calling their insurgency un-Islamic and unlawful in their sermons and teaching had been killed by 2013.[159] The attacks were not limited to outlying areas in the provinces: high-ranking ulama, such as the deputy of the national Kabul Ulama Council, were shot and killed in Kabul as well.[160] Some of those killings appeared to be linked to the ideological stance of the scholars.¹⁶¹ Others were part of a wider pattern to discredit ulama who were supportive of the government or the peace process, such as the macabre irony of a suicide bomber targeting the ulama *shura* in 2018, which was convened to support the government in peace negotiations and sought to condemn suicide bombings.¹⁶²

These killings culminated during my research in the tragic bombing of the Uranus wedding hall during the celebration of the Prophet Muhammad's birthday (*Mawlid*) in November 2018.¹⁶³ Some Sufi students from the communities I researched decided to join the celebration at the wedding hall, where two different Sufi groups had organized celebrations simultaneously with a mixture of Sufi affiliates and ulama. My research assistant and I decided to join them and were getting ready to go when we heard about the blast. Our interlocutors survived, but the bomb took part of two floors of the building down, ultimately killing more than fifty religious scholars and Sufis.¹⁶⁴

Attacks in Afghanistan are usually claimed by one terrorist group or another. Some attacks, however, remain unclaimed, possibly due to the negative public reaction to them. Many of the attempted or successful assassinations and attacks in Kabul and elsewhere in Afghanistan did not make it into international or even national news. Some were shared on social media, while others were kept under wraps, such as the burning of the shrine at Chardah Massoum in the musicians' district of Khoje Kharabat, which was officially designated as an electrical fault.¹⁶⁵ However, the community unofficially discussed with me threats they had received that culminated in, they claimed, an act of arson. Not all killings and attacks are so easily identifiable as having ideological motives, especially when no one takes responsibility for them.¹⁶⁶ There were murders of caretakers of Sufi places, such as the one targeting a mountainside *chilla khana* in Herat, but it is unclear whether that was a personal dispute or a hate crime directed against a Sufi.¹⁶⁷ A few years earlier, a shooting in a mosque that doubled as a *khanaqah* in Kabul was reported, but no one took responsibility, and it is unclear whether this was an insurgent attack or a private feud.¹⁶⁸ The people I interviewed had varying opinions about it; some security sources even thought the place was attacked because it was connected to Tajik insurgents. The one common thread in these accounts was that they were all a mixture of half-knowledge and guesses. Many Sufi affiliates felt that the environment of unaccountability hit them particularly hard because no investigations were instigated or legal actions taken in most cases.

In the last years of the National Unity government under Ashraf Ghani and Abdullah Abdullah, a silent consensus developed within parts of the government that it would be beneficial to take a more active stance toward the type of Islam that should be promoted in Afghanistan. Apart from the killings and attacks, there were reports of increasing radicalization at madrasas and institutions of higher education, which were seen as potential recruiting grounds for the insurgency.[169] In 2017 an interministerial coordination unit on deradicalization cochaired by the chief executive of Afghanistan, Abdullah Abdullah, and the Ministry of Hajj and Religious Affairs was instituted to advise the government in policy planning and strategy. Getting a handle on how the government was positioned in regard to Islam was portrayed as a major pillar for how to win the war against the Taliban as well as legitimize the government. An internal memo stated that "the moderate understanding of religion is under siege by extremist ideologies" and a "lack of a policy of promotion of a moderate understanding of religion (de-radicalization) has been one of the biggest deficiencies of the government of Afghanistan in the past 16 years."[170] Tasks for the unit included formally registering mosques, assessing school and university curricula "with an objective of improving and reforming them for promotion of an indigenous and mild understanding of Islam" and working with the Ulama Council to "disseminate the indigenous understanding of Islam."[171] The document never defines what is meant by a "moderate" or "indigenous" understanding of Islam, apart from clarifying that Afghanistan's legal bases had been Hanafi jurisprudence, described as "quite distinct from the Wahabi [sic] interpretation promoted by extremist groups."

In January 2019, President Ghani invited a group of religious leaders and Sufis to Kabul. He announced that he intended to create a new position within the Ministry of Hajj and Religious Affairs that would honor Afghanistan's Sufi legacy and take Sufism more into account in charting the course of Afghanistan's future. As I watched the TV coverage, I saw several of my interviewees in attendance; some even gave speeches. I wrote to one of these scholars, who had been invited to Kabul and taught *Masnawi* classes in Herat, asking him what he thought of this initiative. His response was cautiously hopeful. He said he hoped that Sufi scholars, both their insights and concerns, might be heard more widely in the future. After a few months passed and I stopped hearing about the initiative, I wrote to him again, wondering how it was developing. The *ustad* wrote back, but the sliver of hope had vanished, replaced by a sobering realization. "They gave all these promises and nothing happened. The only thing that happened is that the media attention brought new threats against me." In a volatile environment like that in Afghanistan, where the internationally connected state was a main target of the insurgency, affiliation with the government was seen as taking sides. The *ustad* received death threats, escaped an attempt on his life and withdrew from public teaching at the university.

Further outreach and promotion of Sufi Islam were contemplated at the time in circles around President Ashraf Ghani, but political events such as the peace negotiations and the intensifying war after the withdrawal agreement signed between the Taliban and the United States took the focus off these plans.[172]

Afghanistan was not the first Islamic country to flirt with making Sufism a centerpiece for religious reform, nor was it the first to suffer from political and societal costs because of it. Alix Philippon's research in neighboring Pakistan shows that since the beginning of the "War on Terror," Sufi saints have been promoted as "true" Islam and an ideal for the Pakistani nation.[173] While the aim might have been to give legitimacy to Sufi interpretations of Islam, it effectively led to the radicalization of Barelwis and the taking up of arms by the very actors described as peaceful, who had become targets for their association with the state.[174] State acknowledgment and affiliation can have many unintended effects, and in a volatile environment such as Afghanistan's in the first two decades of the twenty-first century, it could have made Sufis more of a target through association with a government that was seen by nonstate actors as illegitimate and affiliated with the West and NATO forces.

What this short overview of the different phases of recent historic changes in Afghanistan shows is that there are multiple configurations of Sufi-state relations. Especially in times of stability it has been beneficial for Sufi leaders to ally themselves with the government for resources and prestige. However, particularly in times of transition and change in which ideologically legitimated regimes targeted religious leadership and in times of generalized insecurity, many Sufis found themselves targets, and strategic distance or even resistance to the different regimes was the preferred option. As we have already seen, the state was rarely the only player within the political sphere in Afghanistan. Nonstate actors and other governments, regional and international entanglements played as large a role as the actual governments that ruled the country.

This chapter has given a general overview of the historical developments in Afghanistan and some of the Sufi communities' responses to the changing environment. The next chapter delves into a particular case, that of Haji Saiqal and the *khanaqah* Pahlawan, in order to show how the community navigated to ensure its survival and a sense of community coherence during tumultuous times. The case further illustrates how the ideological changes that undergird the changing state formations impacted the choice of leadership and relational establishment of authority within the particular community.

TWO

Navigating Insecurity

Mullahs and Sufi Lodges

ONE DOOR CLOSING, ANOTHER opening, and between them the winding alleyways of old Kabul, their intricately carved wooden entryways and fluttering curtains offering fleeting glimpses into courtyards with kids immersed in play, teenage boys running errands, women preparing meals. Surrounding those domestic tableaus, Friday's late-morning calm, the only time everyone, no matter whether government employee, businessman, NGO worker or shopkeeper, had off, at least until after noontime prayers. In the mornings, the streets were unusually quiet, unburdened of the multitude of honking horns, growling motors and cursing drivers who formed the sludge of choking traffic that defined this overpopulated city on any other day. Except Friday.

On Friday, before the faithful rushed out of their homes to their local mosques, you might have found Haji Saiqal dashing along the empty streets between one of Kabul's oldest Sufi lodges (*khanaqah*) and a modern mosque in Microrayon, one of Kabul's Soviet-built quarters, the keys for both dangling in his hand. As he switched roles, his uniform remained the same: white *pirhan tumban*, a modest turban, a well-groomed white beard. Haji Saiqal was what some of my Afghan friends, as well as Western policy makers, would call an oxymoron, a man who somehow occupied two supposedly incompatible worlds.

Uniting the *pir* and mullah in one person might seem to be a contradiction. The term "mullah" is dripping with cultural connotations, not all of them favorable.¹ In the most benign sense, a mullah is an educated Muslim trained in Islamic theology and sacred law, holding an official post in a mosque as an imam. But the term can mean so much more, ranging from respected leader to ridiculed dogmatist. Mullahs are often portrayed as illiterate foot soldiers of a tradition they know little about.² They are feared for their putative power to whip up crowds or mobs, particularly when fulminating on political issues at Friday prayers and, in the case of Iran, for the geopolitical influence they can wield.³ But they can also be the target of lighthearted ridicule, as in the well-known Mullah Nasruddin trope of the wise fool—the satirical character in the folklore from the Balkans to China, who at times witty, at other times wise, dispenses pedagogical humor to criticize the powerful and humble the listener.

Whether respected or ridiculed, mullahs are often seen as the antithesis of Sufis.⁴ And there is a long-standing tradition in the popular imagination as well as academic writing of portraying Sufis and the religious class of ulama, exemplified here through the position of a mullah, as mutually exclusive categories.⁵ The binary opposition between religious scholar and Sufi is also reflected in more recent literature that often singles them out as individual groups, with the authority of Sufi *pirs* resting on experience and example, in contrast to the ulama, whose authority rests on religious knowledge through Islamic education.⁶ So how does it come about that a mullah like Haji Saiqal, who is supposed to be antagonistic to Sufi thought and practice, can become a Sufi leader, taking on both the mantle of esoteric knowledge and protector of a Sufi community?

For a historian of Islam, this dual role would hardly seem surprising. Historically, many ulama were simultaneously Sufi leaders and guides. However, in the contemporary world, as well as during Afghanistan's Civil War when Haji Saiqal was chosen as leader of Kabul's Pahlawan Sufi community, a conceptual rift has opened between what is perceived by many as a Sufi Islam that stands in stark contrast to a legalistic "mullah Islam."⁷

This chapter follows the trajectory of colonial, Muslim reformist and Western epistemological categorization and critique that has created these two not merely distinct, but competing, groups and discusses how this dichotomy has had profound effects on Muslim communities' own perceptions and categorizations. The ability of religious communities and their leaders to survive shifting social terrains in times of war and insecurity is bound up with the socio-ideological shifts in their environment that enable and disable particular practices and styles of leadership. The case of Haji Saiqal is instructive in this regard as it oscillates between the varying understandings of his position as a traditional Muslim leader. Why was he chosen to be the leader, and how did he fare during those decades of unrest? What happened to the previous leaders of the Sufi lodge, and where are they now? What does it take to shield a Sufi community during wartime? What tactics did the leadership revert to, where did they fail and how did they succeed? And what is the impact of wartime cooperation on the long-term constituency of the community?

While there are no general rules determining how this would work itself out for varying communities, the case of a mullah shielding a Sufi *khanaqah* is instructive for several reasons. In following the case of leadership transition within the *khanaqah* Pahlawan, we see not only how a Sufi lodge survived but also how this survival had far-reaching implications for continuity, practice and the development of the community—and in turn, how Sufi authority was defined and positioned. Violence in this case shows its dual faces of destruction and creation. Whether targeted, as in the killing of religious teachers and leaders, or generalized, as in bombings and destruction that spurred migration, violence precipitated change and also opened up room for potential leaders to take charge. It pushed the need for cooperation between groups of Islamic leaders who had previously not worked together but who found it advantageous to do so now.[8] While other studies on the generalized impact of cooperative behavior induced through war view cooperation as an indicator and end in and of itself, I argue that the types of cooperation people choose shape their communities for years or decades to come.

Khanaqahs as a Family Business

The Sufi lodge that Haji Saiqal would take over was situated in the western part of the old city of Kabul, an area filled with numerous graves of saints that is fittingly called Asheqan-o-Arefan, "Lovers and Mystics." The Sufi order (*tariqa*) connected to it was established in the eighteenth century when ruler Timor Shah moved the Afghan capital from Kandahar to Kabul. Among the people who moved north along with their king was Sufi Sher Mohammad, who bought land in Asheqan-o-Arefan, and his son Mir Mohammad, popularly called Pahlawan (wrestler), who formally established a Sufi lodge there.⁹ Seeing the *khanaqah* for the first time, I was less struck by its long history as I was by how the algae-green walls stood out against the otherwise earth-tone, dried-mud walls of the surrounding cityscape of old Kabul. The paint bore witness to the multiple renovations that the community had financed and managed in the absence of state or outside funding.¹⁰

After stepping through the gate of the cube-shaped building, one might notice a stone plaque with a lengthy inscription installed in the enclosed courtyard. Framed with ornamental leaves it described the *khanaqah* as the place "where shari'a is shining, where the doctrine of Mohammad lives, as well as the speech of the friends of faith" and "where the sickness of body, soul and heart is healed." Below this introductory praise commenced the community history in the form of the *silsila*, the chain of leadership and learning, that ran from the founder of the Sufi lodge and his Naqshbandiyya *pir* to its current leader.¹¹ What is remarkable is that since its establishment in the eighteenth century, the *khanaqah* remained in the hands of a single family until, in 1993 (1371), a mullah took over leadership.

Even though a Sufi's knowledge and abilities might be measured by the individual's learning, insight and immersion in the Sufi path, Sufi leadership has often been passed down through biological or spiritual patrilineality. This means that the leadership of a Sufi community and the inheritance of its property, rights and titles is passed down to related male kin. While many of my interviewees criticized this practice as "new" and part of the "decay of true Sufism," it has been a practice in many Sufi communities for centuries.¹² In his study of the Naqshbandiyyah Sufi tradition, Itzchak Weismann argues that while hereditary succession was denounced by the founders of the order, it became accepted as a rule around the fifteenth and sixteenth centuries.[13] Historically, the leadership of the Naqshbandiyyah *khanaqah* at Sirhind in India was passed on to members of Sirhindi's biological lineage, and the network was then expanded through the various *khulafas/khilafas* (deputies/highest-ranking students), who appointed their own representatives.[14] The *khilafa* system is thus a "surrogate progeny" linking disciples through a line of spiritual transmission, "which functions as a kind of genealogy in giving status and position to those included in them."[15] Spiritual transmission through a *khilafa* system also exists in Afghanistan. However, many of the *khanaqahs* I visited were run by families employing a biological hereditary model. The same used to be true for *khanaqah* Pahlawan: over its more than 250-year history, it was led by generations of the same family, passed on from one man to another in a line of hereditary transmission and spiritual service to the Sufi community. So how did a mullah who had no family affiliation with the Pahlawan line fit into this pattern of succession?

As I stood in front of the *silsila* stone inscription, a man in his mid-fifties, clothed in a walnut-brown *shalwar kamize* and black vest, a white skullcap on his head and turquoise ring on his left hand,[16] appeared, his bespectacled eyes wandering over the stone inscriptions he knew so well. Haji Tamim was the caretaker of the *khanaqah* and mosque complex. Making tea for guests and *zikr* participants, cleaning and caring for each nook and cranny, he seemed to have become quintessential to the place. He lived close by with his family, his granddaughters often strolling along and playing in the *khanaqah*'s courtyard.

I asked him if he had been with the *khanaqah* when Haji Saiqal took over leadership. "Yes," he said, his face beaming with pride about the fact that he had been coming to the *khanaqah* since he was around six or seven years old. "My maternal uncle and my father both came here in the time of Zahir Khan. In the time when Daoud took control, they still came. When they tried to close the *khanaqah*, I came and opened it again. I was a very naughty kid," he laughed. But then more solemnly, as if talking about a living, breathing entity that needs a protector to stay alive, he added: "I didn't let anyone touch the *khanaqah*. That's why they gave me the guardianship from that time until now." The warm and jovial Haji Tamim was *khanaqah* Pahlawan's soul and internal guardian, while the wiry and clever

Haji Saiqal was its official outward face and representative.

As we walked through the various rooms of the *khanaqah*, it became apparent through Haji Tamim's memory-laden explanations that even though he tried, he was not able to fully shield the *khanaqah* from the destruction that ravaged many parts of the city. "We had to rebuild the roof and upper floor two times," he told me, explaining that they were hit by rockets. "Then the Mujahidin came; they burned this *khanaqah*; they looted and burned all the stuff that was in here. They took out all the dishes and all the stuff from the mosque [*masjid*] and from the *khanaqah*. They took even the carpet from the *masjid*!" The *khanaqah* also housed a small mosque on the first floor. During the Mujahidin time the *khanaqah* sometimes lay within the fault lines of fighting, and the community decided to gather instead in a mosque in Shahr-e now for *zikr* and classes.

While material destruction scarred the building, it was the persecution of religious personnel that set in motion the changes that were now visible on the *silsila* stone panel. Entering the main congregational room on the second floor—a rectangular room with red carpets, lit by several chandeliers, equipped with an audio system and decorated with colorful posters reminding the attendants to care for the development of their hearts[17]—Haji Tamim walked me to the dark blue metal cabinet in the corner of the room.

Climbing onto a tall chair to access the cabinet, he removed the padlock and, one by one, began taking out relics, holding them as the material manifestation of the *khanaqah*'s history. He first held the walking stick that was used by its founder, Pahlawan Sahib, over 210 years ago. Haji Tamim leaned onto the half-moon saddle at the end of the stick while explaining the history of the other items that he extracted from the cabinet. One of them was the cap that belonged to Pahlawan Sahib himself. A second cap belonged to Haji Ahmad Jan, a teacher at the *khanaqah* who was taken away to Pul-e Charkhi prison by the Communist regime. "It was during the time of Hafizullah Amin," Haji Tamim recounted, unfolding the cap, taking his mind back to the first few months after the Communist coup in 1978 when religious scholars fell victim to a campaign to control religious education. "Haji Ahmad Jan was the one leading the *khanaqah*. They came and dragged him outside and arrested him. When they manhandled him, he lost his cap. It fell to the floor. He never came back." Haji Tamim looked pensively at the

Figure 2.1. Haji Tamim showing mementos from the *khanaqah*'s history, 2018.

cap, holding it as if to weigh the cataclysmic changes that came after that fateful day. The three main relics kept by the caretaker in the little cabinet in the corner of the main room where the *zikr* usually took place marked both the beginning of the *khanaqah* and the turning point under the Communists when repression forced the family who had run it into migration.

Later, on a subsequent visit to the *khanaqah* during its 252nd anniversary in mid-August 2018, Husnia Samadi, the daughter of the Pahlawan family, now in her late fifties, told me about her family's exodus from Afghanistan. Sitting with me in a side room adjacent to the main celebrations, she recounted that it was not only Haji Ahmad Jan who had been arrested but also other members of her family. "It was in the Communist time," she recalled. "My brother-in-law was arrested for doing *zikr*. He was arrested and then detained for four years. His arrest was what made us scared and what prompted us to go abroad. He was arrested two more times after that."[8]

Some of these arrests ended with the disappearance and likely death of these teachers; others were released after a certain time in prison. But one never knew when a loved one was taken whether the person would be seen again. Uncertainty connected to the ever-present threat against religious personnel forced the family into exile. "By now, I have been in the United States for thirty-three years," Husnia said thoughtfully. "When we left, we first went to Pakistan, and then one and a half years to India before settling in the US, where we had a sponsor. This is my first time in thirty-seven years that I have come to Afghanistan."

After arriving in California, Husnia Samadi built a new life but remained in touch with Sufi practices through weekly *zikr* in her mosque community. Her main language remained Dari while her children excelled in English. Our conversation, a mixture of English and Dari, was interspersed with moments when we both fell silent and listened to the celebratory speeches that would float in from the main room attended by male Sufi followers. Husnia participated in the prayers from the side room in which we sat, and looking through the dark-rimmed glasses that framed her thoughtful eyes, she told me how their exodus proceeded in stages: "We used to live here in a house next to the *khanaqah*. I was born here. But now it is destroyed and we couldn't rebuild it. It was my father who was in charge of the *khanaqah* before we left. Afterward it became my cousin, Daud Dastageer, who started to coordinate events here. You know, Sufism goes from generation to generation."

While affirming the chain of hereditary transmission that was inscribed in stone at the entrance to the *khanaqah*, Husnia also admitted that she herself was not fully aware of how the transfer of power had taken place. "Women did not come to the *khanaqah*, even before the Communists. Women were wearing the *chadori* and were not allowed. I was a small child then. I have only come one other time before to the *khanaqah* in my life before today, which was when I was twelve years old."

Sitting in the *khanaqah* only for the second time in her life, Husnia shrugged off my question about how it was in the past: "I don't know much about how it came about with Haji Saiqal taking over," she said. "Maybe my husband knows more about that."

Despite belonging to the family who had initially established the *khanaqah* and led it for centuries, as a woman she was still excluded from certain decisions that are traditionally made by men. But as we turn toward Haji Saiqal's story and its intertwining with the political developments of his time, it will soon become clear why he was the prime choice for leadership of the *khanaqah*.

The Making of Enemies

The answers to these questions, as with so many other conundrums, lie in colonial history and its enduring impact on many societies officially occupied or indirectly influenced by it. Writing about the politics of representing Sufism, anthropologist Katherine Ewing attests to a double conceptual split that began in Orientalist literature during the colonial period and carried on through the Cold War politics of Islamic studies funding in North America.[19] The split also informs today's perception of Islam in Muslim societies and globally, particularly in the context of the "War on Terror."[20]

The first split is the conceptual divide between a perceived legalistic Islam as separate from mystic Sufism as an individual, liberal pursuit.[21] Early colonial envoy Mountstuart Elphinstone (1779–1859), for example, describes three categories of religious functionaries: the "moollahs," the "holy men" (sayyids, dervishes, *faqirs* and *qalandars*) and the "Soofees," whom he considers a minority sect of philosophers.[22] Setting aside the misrepresentation of Sufism as a sect, Elphinstone saw mullahs and Sufis as diametrically opposed enemies in the religious field, as Sufis were "held in great aversion by the Moollahs, who accused its followers of atheism, and often endeavor[ed] to entrap them into some doctrines which are liable to punishment by the Mahommedan law."[23] Far from embodying a dual orientation as a scholar and mystic, Sufism and Islam were separated and located within different—and antagonistic—personas.

The second conceptual split, which is also represented in Elphinstone's categorization of "Soofees" as separate from "holy men," is the delineation of Sufism as the philosophy, high art and literature of mystic poetry in contrast to living, contemporary Sufi *pirs* who were often seen as flawed. These views are an extension of descriptions by Western travel writers who focused in their accounts of contemporary Sufis on the outward behavior of "faqirs" and "dervishes." Not surprisingly, such writers were obsessed with behavior that they considered strange and alienating, interpreting Sufi rituals and practices as exotic and peculiar without understanding the context in which they were produced. In many of these encounters Sufis became a "staple of the wonders of the Orient" who frequently appeared in illustrations and travelogues as solitary ascetics either inflamed by a fervent passion for God, when portrayed positively, or as frauds misguiding the people.[24] While the living "holy men" were studied and carefully managed by colonial administrators, Sufi mystic poetry and literature were to be deciphered by Orientalist scholars—the conceptual split thereby also engendering different areas of expertise.[25]

Ewing asserts that regardless of the evaluation of the practices—"whether Sufism was 'good' in its sophisticated mystical inspiration and Islam was 'bad' because of its legalism, or the inverse, in which Sufism was 'bad' because of its ties to superstitious rituals and Islam was 'good' because of its rationality and strict monotheism"—it is indeed the very split itself, "its political and rhetorical force in the colonial environment that was to be crucially significant for the subsequent evolution of Sufism/taṣawwuf."[26] We can see this split at work not only in political polemics during the colonial period but also within the writing of Muslim reformers of various persuasions, and as impacting politicking in Afghanistan since the 1980s. While many examples could be given to substantiate the far-reaching impact of these conceptualizations worldwide, I will take up three movements—Muslim modernists, Deobandi ulama and Islamists—that interpreted these conceptual splits in varying ways and have influenced public opinion, scholarly debate and everyday life in Afghanistan. I am interested here in the impact of these conceptual differentiations on the perceptions of Muslims and in the politics enacted toward them in the wider intellectual, educational and political spheres, because those are the ones that Sufi communities, such as the one connected to *khanaqah* Pahlawan, had to navigate over the past decades.

Western ideas and sustained colonial critique were not confined to the echo chamber of political agents sipping whiskey in drawing rooms but also found their way into Muslim intellectual thought patterns and views on Sufism. In her overview of anti-Sufi sentiments, Elizabeth Sirriyeh aptly describes this process as the absorption of Christian and post-Christian Western ideas into existing arguments of indigenous critique of Sufism by Muslim modernists.[27] Early Islamic modernists such as Sayyid Ahmad

Khan (1817–1898), who was born into a mystically inclined family in India,[28] sought to bring Islam into accordance with the laws of nature, in turn criticizing Sufism for its propagation of belief in miracles.[29] For him, Sufism came to be equated with obscurantism and an obstacle to development and modernity.[30] This move can be seen as an essential development in the response to the "empiricization of reality" in which only what is measurable or written in accepted canonical texts such as the Qur'an can be an object of knowledge or truth. In Shahab Ahmed's view, this "re-calibration of the human relationship with reality has led modern Muslims to the intellectual, practical and social depreciation and invalidation of the authority and Truth-value of the practices and discourses" of philosophy and Sufi approaches within Islam,[31] while appreciating and validating the authority of more narrowly defined text-based practices and discourses.[32]

Sayyid Ahmad Khan was a Muslim reformer in British India, but his approach to Sufism and its role in knowledge production reverberated among intellectual reformers in Afghanistan. Recent scholarship has emphasized the long-standing and historically interregional ties between India and Afghanistan, which influenced many areas of society, including the education sector.[33] The first institution of higher education, Habibia College, for instance, was modeled on Sayyid Ahmad Khan's Anglo-Indian College of Aligarh.[34] Staffed with Indian Muslim teachers and Afghans who had studied in India, it followed the British Indian curriculum in its educational model.[35] The former principal of Islamia College of Lahore, Abdul Ghani Khan, led Habibia College as its director and was later appointed as Afghanistan's director of public instruction, spearheading one of the most important educational initiatives at the time.[36] These political and educational ties demonstrate the influence that intellectual developments in India exerted on Afghanistan.[37] Such state-connected reforms were aligned with ideas forged in interaction with Western notions of education and societal restructuring, with reformers who saw reason and an emphasis on textual discourses as an important corrective to perceived decline.

These so-called "modernist" reformers were not alone in exerting influence on Afghanistan's state, religious and intellectual developments.[38] While Habibia College educated Afghanistan's aristocracy, future members of its bureaucracy and burgeoning middle class, many gifted members of the ulama continued to be educated at the Deoband Dar ul-'Ulum madrasa in India, a school that offered a more nuanced approach to engaging Sufism than Aligarh's rationalization.[39] Throughout the late nineteenth and twentieth centuries, Afghan ulama learned and taught at Deoband, often making up the majority of foreign students there.[40] Once trained, they would return to Afghanistan and what is now Pakistan, "contributing to the world of print, education, and jurisprudence in ways that continued to shape Islamic practice there."[41]

The schools at Deoband and Aligarh were both established after the failed rebellion of 1857 against British rule in India. However, in contrast to Sayyid Ahmad Khan's loyalty to the British in his approach to educational reform, the Dar ul-'Ulum madrasa's primary goal was not to directly influence the people through education but to return to religious observance and spiritual life through shaping a new generation of ulama.[42] This undertaking had far-reaching and varied outcomes. Contemporary Afghanophiles will likely conflate Deobandi schools with the satellite madrasas in Pakistan, which were the socialization and recruitment grounds of the Taliban in the 1990s.[43] But the relationship between these madrasas and the Deoband school in India is much more complex.[44] The Deobandi madrasas at the Pakistani-Afghan frontier became known in the media as a place of "rote memorization of the Qur'an."[45] The development of the Pakistani Deoband movement and the origin of the Taliban within the Deoband education system is, however, far from straightforward: Brannon Ingram argues that the writing of the Dar al-'Ulum Haqqaniyya, which is often credited as being the Deoband branch that educated the Taliban, still shows support for Sufism and condemns the destruction of shrines. He calls on scholars to take a closer look at the politics driving attacks rather than search solely in religious stances as motivators behind violence.[46] Indeed, the origin of these madrasas (and the thousands of madrasas that spread in South Asia) lies in a reformist Sufi project.[47]

The school of Deoband in India could be termed a Sufi project in a double sense as many of the school's personnel had a common allegiance to Sufi orders, predominantly to the Chishti order, and furthermore for its actual teaching of Sufi insights and the teacher/student relationships it fostered. Many of the teachers doubled as guides into Sufism for their students. They were, however, not bound to a specific *tariqa*. A single teacher might train a student in a combination of approaches from different orders or might train one student in the silent *zikr* of the Naqshbandiyyah and another in the loud Qadiri *zikr*.[48] However, while Deoband students were often students of Sufism themselves, they were particularly concerned with the reconciliation of the mystical path (*tariqa*) with Islamic law (shari'a), leading to a preoccupation with defining what constituted "orthodox" and therefore an acceptable version of Sufism.[49] Deobandi scholars criticized customary celebrations and practices, including excessive saint veneration at tombs (*ziyarats*). Deoband scholars exemplified an orthodoxy embedded in particular understandings of Sufism.[50]

The impacts of colonialism initiated some soul searching among both the modernists and Deoband reformers, though how each group reacted differed, with modernists seeking out answers in Western concepts and institutions and Deobandi reformers turning inward, to their own past and traditions. Both streams of reform also influenced intellectual developments and politics in Afghanistan. While the Islamic modernists valued technological development, Western educational models and religious rationalism, Deobandi scholars mediated between a prescriptive Islamic observance with circumscribed, but nonetheless some measure of, space for the experiential side of Sufism. Sufism was part of orthodox thoughts and practice, even if certain expressions of Sufism were seen as aberrations. While all these streams still mediated the varying spaces for Sufism within society, sometimes with disdain, sometimes as integral, the 1980s and 1990s would rewrite many of these competing notions because of the influx of Islamist and Salafist concepts of authority and leadership.[51]

The jihad against the Soviets had far-reaching effects on the restructuring of political and religious authority in Afghanistan. Before the onset of the conflict, traditional claims to religious authority were based on religious knowledge, clerical training or Sufi lineages, credentials that Islamist party leaders lacked.[52] Islamism developed in Afghanistan's urban university milieu in the 1950s and 1960s, and most leaders of Afghanistan's emerging Islamist parties, all based across the border in Peshawar, were university-educated men with no traditional religious training. Instead, they legitimized their claims to leadership with the fact that they were the first to initiate jihad against the Communist government in Kabul and had access to weapons and money through the assistance of Pakistan and other foreign powers. David Edwards argues that by defining the ideological territory of the jihad through the production of propaganda material (photographs, magazines, pamphlets, etc.), the Mujahidin created and controlled the cult of martyrs, which established their religious authority.[53]

The shift in Islamic discourse that emerged out of the war against the Soviets was connected to the legitimization of the war effort but also to the recruitment of foreign fighters. The national jihad that the Afghan resistance parties started developed into a global enterprise through the ideological, institutional and financial support brought by a rather small group that was to be later called the "Afghan Arabs."[54] Their involvement introduced, on the one hand, tensions between fighters from differing backgrounds, such as between Afghan Mujahidin and Arab fighters who criticized local customs such as flags on shrines and graves. On the other hand, it also sparked a broader process, which one of my Afghan friends, a businessman in his thirties, described as "social erosion":

> The circles of elders who had been using Sufism were delegitimized by the new rulers. It was a shift in different respects: education, at school, the government, in society overall. I would call it social erosion, a change that affected all parts of society. It changed society overall, how people interacted with each other. It changed the interaction of men and women—where there had been a lot of respect before and certain codes of behavior that were accepted, they changed, and it was very painful for the women. Suddenly the men would not shake their hands anymore. They wouldn't eat at the same table with them anymore. Things changed.[55]

What he describes was the reorganization of everyday life, of the ethics of how to be together, how to greet each other, with whom to eat, how to worship and whom to listen to for advice. The change was more than a shift in emphasis; it was a restructuring of the way of being and thinking, of how to be good and lead an ethical life, which was intimately bound up not only with everyday Islamic norms but also with the question of who holds power to enforce rules and set norms. Contrary to the way the Mujahidin were publicized and celebrated in the West during the anti-Soviet jihad, their

Islamically justified restrictions and rules were similar to those of the Taliban who followed. Veiling increased, music was outlawed in parts of the country and the living situation for women worsened.[56] While the Mujahidin justified their monopoly on the use of violence and religious authority through the legitimizing cover of jihad, in many places they still relied on the support of local power structures. Romain Malejacq describes how Mujahidin leaders such as Massoud "published newspapers to be used by mullahs in their Friday prayers" and how warlords were "a new form of khans" in the sense that they relied on relationships with local powerbrokers who needed to be satisfied for the warlords to retain their power and influence.[57]

This utilitarian relationship of formal respect and reciprocal recognition between Mujahidin and ulama positioned Haji Saiqal to take over the leadership of a Sufi *khanaqah* during the time of the anti-Soviet jihad and the Civil War. Religious authority based on Sufism had still been an integral part of society and the rendering of religious authority in Afghanistan before the war, exemplified even in Islamic reformist movements such as Deoband, which vied for influence against other modernist strains of reform. However, the war effort privileged brokers of Islamically justified violence such as the Mujahidin, or local religious functionaries such as mullahs, who were legitimated through their title and position within communities. At the time when the Taliban—who were, in fact, mullahs or mullahs-in-training themselves—took over, being a mullah had developed into a real asset for shielding a Sufi community.

Hiding in Plain Sight

When I asked the caretaker Haji Tamim how the community kept itself safe during these past few decades, he told me that it was about their outer appearance, their image as upright and pious believers that shielded the Sufi community: "They believed that we are the people of the Qur'an and Hadith and that we pray. That's why they didn't have any problems with us."

In an environment of both raw destruction and more fine-grained societal change, in which the external performance of piety was either linked to a position within the war as Mujahidin or as a recognizable authority through title and position, Haji Saiqal proved to be the right man for the hour for two

Figure 2.2. Haji Saiqal at the *khanaqah* celebration. Reproduced with permission.

key reasons: his position and training as a mullah and his personal pragmatism in dealing with expectations of powerbrokers.

His position as a low-level cleric made him recognizable to Mujahidin commanders and Taliban officials as a respectable, though nonthreatening, conservative religious scholar, someone whose official position in his mosque they recognized and whose rank would mark him out in a way as "one of them"—a rightful cadre of religiously legitimated authorities. Among other aspects, Afghan Islamists also saw the hereditary nature of Sufi families as delegitimizing Sufism as a representation of Islam.[58] An unconnected mullah, however, was marked out through his learning and not through his genealogical, hereditary status. He could project the respectable status that the caretaker Haji Tamim alone, by virtue of lacking a formal position and Islamic credentials, could not. He could face officials when they came for visits to check on what was going on at the *khanaqah*, and he could present an image of respectability through asserting that ritual practices were situated within the strictures of Islamic law.

The neighborhood mosque that Haji Saiqal led in the Soviet-built neighborhood of Microrayon seemed to be a physical manifestation of his adeptness at social camouflage.[59] When I first arrived at the mosque, I found most remarkable its utter unremarkableness. The simple concrete building, rectangular walls, empty halls and plain red carpets were a far cry from the intricate Islamic architecture of Central Asia and the Persianate world, adorned with dazzling tiles, arches and impressively constructed domes. I had somehow expected a more outwardly beautified place as the seat of a Sufi leader. As it turned out, the mosque was a repurposed depot and distribution center where Afghans used to come to redeem their food stamps during the PDPA government time. Later, it became one of the 155,000 estimated unregistered mosques in Afghanistan.[60] The environment that Haji Saiqal had chosen as his base for teaching and preaching was inconspicuous—one mosque among many, one imam among hundreds.

The only place in the mosque that stood out was the *mihrab*, the niche indicating the *qibla*, the direction of the Kaaba in Mecca, which Muslims face when praying. Dazzlingly decorated with a modernist rendering of stylized flower motifs, calligraphy and the Kaaba, the artistic piece reminded me of a Pakistani truck-art version of inlaid *pietra dura* or *parching kari*, the image-creating precious stones replaced by colored, light-reflecting mirrors. But the *mihrab* was set back from the main rooms in a backroom, hidden like a treasure to be known only by those who ventured deeper. It reminded me of the interplay between visible and hidden, outward title and inward secrecy.

While the powerbrokers who took control of Kabul—whether Mujahidin or later Taliban—were focused on outward compliance of conduct and representative titles that met their expectations for religious credentials, the Sufi family of the Pahlawan line who chose Haji Saiqal knew him by his character and deeds. They had seen him growing up, from the time when he was a young boy who sometimes joined his father on his visits to the *khanaqah* Pahlawan for *zikr*. This long-standing acquaintance was what made his character and personality known to the Pahlawan family when their last family member was faced with deciding to whom to entrust the future of the *khanaqah*. Haji Saiqal was judged to be a good choice, as Daud, a member of the Pahlawan family, summarized to me another time when I met him alone to talk about Haji Saiqal's status in the community: "Now most of the people know him as the *pir*, because since the beginning, he has had a calm, honest character." Daud compared his experience of how Haji

Figure 2.3: Haji Saiqal in his mosque in Microrayon, 2017.

Saiqal led the *khanaqah* to other Sufi orders that he had seen in the region: "In Pakistan and also sometimes in Afghanistan, there are some people who join politics through using Sufism. But Haji Saiqal stays out of politics."

"Staying out of politics" is a multivalent description for a behavior that we also find in later chapters. Its connotations range from the inner-community judgment of honesty and trustworthiness through nonalignment with corrupted and corrupting forces (not being a "sellout" so to speak), to being inconspicuous in the eyes of changing governments, who might pick out and throw in jail a religious leader for failing to meet their varying definitions of a "good" or "legitimate" leader. Staying out of politics meant keeping a strategic distance. It was thus simultaneously a character judgment as well as an appraisal of Haji Saiqal's navigational strategies, an acknowledgment of his ability to manage political powerbrokers and potential state repression. By staying out of politics himself, he kept the community out of politics, out of the attention of governments that had imprisoned and tortured previous teachers, had bombed and looted the lodge and made being a Sufi unsafe.

While Haji Saiqal's official title and position contributed to his success in taking over the Sufi lodge at this critical juncture, it was not his title alone that marked him out as a successful leader of the Sufi community. It was also his canny ability to analyze the volatile environment and to position himself within changing discourses. Part of that positioning was knowing which aspects of the community's practices to keep secret so that the community would not be targeted.

Writing about violence and socialities of secrecy among Guatemalan ex-guerrillas, anthropologist Silvia Posocco observed that secrecy "seems to amount to a survival strategy," noting that it was "about concealment and misdirection, but as a predicament, activity, or endeavor, it inherently implied partial relationalities and a sociality of possible selective disclosure."[61] Secrecy was never complete but situational, positioned with selective amounts of trust. The relations that were forged among guerrillas as well as between guerrillas and the outside world were marked by partiality: Whom to trust with which aspects of the truth? How to conceal or disclose certain aspects of information? How to establish trust and partially let someone in on a forbidden activity in an environment of repression and violence? While Sufis in Afghanistan are a world away from guerrilla fighters in Guatemala, Posocco's insights about relations engendered in the negative through secrecy, dissimulation and only partial disclosure are fitting for understanding Sufi leaders' actions in the violence-saturated environment in which they attempted to keep their community safe.

"He is the one who resisted them and continued the *khanaqah*," Daud told me about Haji Saiqal. Daud was the last member of the Pahlawan family to leave the *khanaqah* during the Civil War. He was the person who handed over the keys to his friend when he himself left for Pakistan. After staying in Pakistan for years, Daud returned to post-2001 Afghanistan and opened up several clothing stores in Microrayon not far from the mosque that Haji Saiqal led. The two men saw each other regularly, and Daud also traveled with Saiqal and his wife for *umrah* (Islamic pilgrimage). The two remained friends, but Daud left the running of the Sufi lodge to Haji Saiqal. On a summer afternoon when they had just returned from their recent travel to Mecca, we sat in a side room of the main prayer hall on a dark-red *toshak* (cushion), eating potato *bolani* (flat bread with filling). Haji Saiqal was incessantly pouring green chai for my research assistant and me as we discussed the history of the *khanaqah*.

"Until 1371 [1993] the *khanaqah* was in the hands of my family," Daud recounted. "After that Haji Saiqal has been responsible, and since then he has been leading the *khanaqah*. Even during the Taliban regime, he worked a lot when the Taliban were making trouble."

Haji Saiqal chimed into our conversation: "At the time of the Taliban regime we had the problem that we couldn't do *zikr jahr* [loud *zikr*]." *Zikr*, which literally means "recollection," is a meditative technique that comes in different shapes and forms. It can be silent, called *khufya*, or involve speech, recitation and chant, voiced *zikr*, or *zikr jahr*, as it is called in Afghanistan. I had heard about allowing certain types and forbidding others during the Taliban time. While the Taliban had no overarching policy toward Sufi communities and their practices, they regarded some forms of Sufi practice as rightfully Islamic while attempting to regulate others. The connection of some forms of *zikr* to music was one of the most troublesome aspects under the Taliban government. The Taliban were renowned for forbidding video, imagery and music during their reign. Other types of *zikr* without musical accompaniment but involving vocalized chants in groups and physical movement could fall under a category that the former finance minister of the Taliban and close confidant of Mullah Omar, Mutasim Agha Jan, told me should be outlawed.[62] The disunity among the Taliban also threatened the Sufi community. While some commanders could decide that their conduct and practice were lawful, another might decide that it was not and take action against them.

I wondered how that worked, especially as I was curious about the implications of defying the Taliban. I remembered the one time when I had arrived late for the morning session of *zikr* at *khanaqah* Pahlawan. The men's aspirated voices were audible outside the building in the street, filling it with its rhythmic chant. In that sense, *zikr jahr* was not very discreet and hard to hide once a group of Sufi *murids* came together. People living in adjacent buildings and in the surrounding neighborhood must have heard them. Was this a public secret, generally known but not articulated?[63] Were neighbors, while secretly knowledgeable about it, feigning unawareness when asked, knowing exactly what not to know? Many forbidden cultural practices continued like this under the Taliban in the 1990s in the cities—

forbidden CD and movie sales, outlawed girls' schools—all run by communities who disagreed with the Taliban's dictums and who kept them safe by collectively harboring their secret. So why not also hidden Sufi *zikr* chants?

Memories of interactions with the Taliban differed: I had asked Haji Tamim about the *zikr* gatherings, and he told me that the Taliban had come and hit participants, enraged about the gathering. However, later on the Taliban agreed to let the *zikr* happen, and even sometimes participated themselves, arguing that they had been initially against it because they had thought that the *zikr* would be performed with music, which turned out to be a wrong assumption. However, not all Taliban were of the same opinion, even when it came to vocalized *zikr* without music. Haji Saiqal and Daud remembered a more continuous bargaining process with Taliban officials over time.

"There were some problems with the Taliban regime, but they never arrested anyone," Daud observed,[64] raising a finger in a gesture indicating he wanted to draw a line between the Taliban, the Mujahidin and the Communist regime. "We never stopped the *zikr jahr*, even during that time," he added. "We have been doing the *zikr jahr* for three hundred years. Usually at night, but now because of security we do it by day."

Haji Saiqal weighed in, divulging some of the tactics surrounding the practices: "Occasionally we would come; it was not during every Thursday/Friday. Sometimes we made the *halqa* [meeting circle]." What sounded so casual was actually a practical piece of navigating repressive rule. Irregularity is a widely practiced strategy to avoid surveillance, state repression, bandits or insurgencies. I myself kept an intentionally irregular schedule when commuting, setting up interviews or staying at field sites to avoid overt patterns that could facilitate tracking and kidnapping. It made sense to me that inconsistent meeting times would conceal their practices to some degree. But in the end, they would still meet in the *khanaqah* and practice *zikr* together. The voices of *murids* would still resound in the old city streets surrounding the *khanaqah*, and Taliban patrols would hear them.

I could not make sense of it until I talked with Haji Saiqal's son. The middle-aged Mohammad Monir Saiqal, a then government employee who worked for the Independent Election Commission, had the calm demeanor of someone who observed more than he let on.

"There is no doubt that my father was very smart," he told me over tea

Figure 2.4. Mohammad Monir Saiqal holding a photo of his late father, Haji Saiqal, 2021.

and cake in their upper-floor apartment in Microrayon. He had been close with his father, especially as a young boy, following his father around to the *khanaqah* and into the mosque. He said that he had been worried, especially during wartime, about what could happen to his father, so Haji Saiqal had taken him wherever he went for his meetings and official trips. "He understood how to talk to different people, be they officials, local shopkeepers, people with different vocations. He talked with everyone on the level of their own understanding. The Taliban tried a lot to close our *khanaqah*, but my father somehow dealt with them and could keep it open." When asked how he achieved that, Mohammad Monir pointed out his father's ability to communicate with various types of people in conjunction with his role as an imam in the mosque:

> The Taliban were not unified, were not one group. They came from different parts or institutional groups. For example, some would come from Amr-bi al maruf;[65] they had their own system, their own leaders and com-

manders, and another group was from the Ministry of Justice. Whenever they sent someone from the Ministry of Justice, my father would find someone among his students or his contacts who could solve it through that ministry. And when the Taliban came from the Amr-bi al maruf, then my father searched and found someone who had connections there. This is the way that he solved it, and this is how he kept the *khanaqah* open.[66]

Negotiations are ongoing social processes. As Ashley Jackson argues in her work on civilian negotiations with the Taliban at the time when they were still an insurgency, negotiations are "not a one-off deal but a socially embedded dynamic of interaction."[67] Haji Saiqal leveraged personal social connections and networks to influence official stances and positions of the Taliban. His interest was to keep the *khanaqah* and its community safe and running. While Taliban stances could vary on these issues and the particular reasons for their acquiescence to these requests remains shrouded in history, it becomes clear that the Sufi lodge was not the only place Haji Saiqal had to fight for. The imam had to navigate to keep the critical eye of the Taliban off the *khanaqah*, but his own position in the mosque also hung by a thread for years. His disagreement with Taliban edicts became visible every week when he disregarded one of their decrees, as Mohammad Monir recounted:

> The Taliban didn't like the people who were educated but who decided to stay outside the Taliban. My father was an educated person; he understood everything in terms of Islam, but he was not a member of the Taliban. On Friday prayers we have the *khutbah* [sermon]. The Taliban asked all imams to use the name of Mullah Omar, the leader of the Taliban, for the *khutbah*, but my father did not, because Mullah Omar is not on the level of the Prophet Muhammad.[68]

This decision proved consequential, because during the Taliban time of the 1990s *khutbas* were surveilled, and not reading the Friday prayer in the name of the supreme leader brought Haji Saiqal into open conflict with the regime. But while they tried to remove the obstinate mullah from his position, he also mobilized his own defenders. His social circle stepped up for him not only for his decision in the mosque but also on the issue of keeping the *khanaqah* open and practicing vocalized *zikr*: "A lot of talibs were privately students of my father," his son remembered. "Whenever the Taliban wanted to make a decision about my father, his students stood against the other Taliban's decision. That went on for four years like this. After that time, the issue that he did not read the *khutbah* in Mullah Omar's name as well as the other issues such as the *khanaqah* became exceedingly sensitive. When it was taken then to the Ministry of Justice, they ordered a change of leadership in the mosque." Just a few months before the fall of the Taliban in 2001 his negotiation with the Taliban soured and Haji Saiqal was deposed of his position at the mosque in Microrayon. The *khanaqah* kept a low profile during this time, and he stayed at home while another imam ran the mosque in the neighborhood. However, not even half a year later, the Taliban government fell. Mohammad Monir's eyes shined while he remembered that time: "After the collapse of the Taliban regime, the people gathered and they brought my father back into the mosque. They carried him from his house back into the mosque."

Post-2001 Coda

Compared to the tumultuous times that came before, the first two decades of the twenty-first century seemed to be a period of stabilization for the Sufi lodge and its community. Haji Saiqal remained its leader, overseeing the reconstruction and renovations of the *khanaqah* building during the Karzai era. In addition to carpeting for the main rooms, fresh paint jobs for the walls and new posters for educating visitors, the rooms were equipped with modern stereo systems that could transmit the *na'at* singers' voices who accompanied the *zikr*. The community library was extended with books ranging from local history and hagiographies of saints to the writing of Haji Saiqal and other Afghan Sufi writers such as Sufi Ashqari and Haidari Wujudi. Community members could sign out books in a ledger kept by Haji Tamim, and he kept a supply of printouts of *zikr* formulas and instructions for teaching *murids*. The library also housed CDs and videos from the annual celebrations that were recorded for posterity. Apart from the weekly *zikr* sessions on Friday mornings, the community coalesced around annual celebrations such as the anniversary of the *khanaqah*, the celebration of the Prophet Muhammad's birthday and the birthdays of important Afghan Sufis such as the poet Sufi Ashqari. Those celebrations were also a tangible manifestation of the connection that the community retained with the Pahlawan family, who now resided in Germany and the United States. The "nephews of Pahlawan Sahib," as they were called, sent money for the celebrations annually, especially for the *khanaqah*'s anniversary and the anniversary of Fazl Ahmad, one of the last *pirs* of the family who had led the *khanaqah* before Haji Saiqal took over. Abdul Tarin, the nephew residing in Germany, was mainly concerned about the maintenance and updating of the *khanaqah*'s infrastructure, hoping to renovate the kitchen on the upper floor, which was regularly used for cooking food for hundreds of *murids* and visitors on celebratory occasions.[69] Haji Tamim was the main cook for the community, helped by four kitchen aides. "When we have the big celebrations," he told me, "we maybe have four hundred or five hundred people. Then you need twenty-two *seer* [a seer is approximately seven kilograms], and it's a lot on my shoulders to cook for so many." But Haji Tamim had learned cooking when he was seven years old in the *khanaqah* under the previous cook. He took the job seriously. "I learned under Daud, who was a good cook, and I learned it well; therefore I am taking care of it. If we bring someone from the outside, we cannot trust them." Serving and building up the community through nourishing it was as important a job in peacetime as defending it in wartime. But it turned out that this would not be Haji Tamim's only position in the *khanaqah* community.

In October 2019, Haji Saiqal died from cancer. He would not see the return of the Taliban roughly two years later, nor would he be privy to the heated conversations within the *khanaqah* over how to replace a man who had so valiantly defended and supported the community. Though the wider community mourned, not everyone had been a fan of Haji Saiqal in his lifetime. The criticism had been mainly muted, expressed indirectly. Some of the criticism came, like many challenges to authority in Afghanistan, through remarks about the decline of the *khanaqah* and its current state. One of the community members, a man in his fifties who had visited the lodge his whole life, remarked to me:

> This *khanaqah* didn't used to be like this. Before—thirty, forty years ago—

there were other rules within these *khanaqahs* in Kabul. For a *murid* to even come from the doorsteps to where the *pir* sits, he needed to have ten to fifteen years of a moral, ethical education process to get there. But now the situation is different and the people are not so much into this anymore; that's why this situation exists that the people come and only do *zikr*. That is sufficient right now, and we are satisfied with it. We don't have *khalifas* and certification of *khalifas* here anymore like in the past. They didn't used to have papers to give as a certificate, but they would do a prayer as a ceremony for his capability. Haji Saiqal got the *khalifa* certificate from the Alauddin *khanaqah* and then came to us.⁷⁰

He saw a general decline of *khanaqahs* that was also visible in the *khanaqah* Pahlawan itself, becoming an empty husk of a Sufi lodge rather than an active center of learning. When I inquired into these dynamics, he concurred evasively: "Of course, if anyone comes, their questions are answered. If not, it is the usual gathering on Friday after Saiqal Sahib comes and we do the gathering."

The underlying tensions came to the fore after Haji Saiqal's passing, and as is the case with many struggles, the varying parties had different opinions about what happened and why it had come to pass that way. Haji Saiqal's son, Mohammad Monir, remembered that his father had settled his affairs when it became clear that the cancer was incurable and in its late stages, selecting a community member to succeed him:

> The reason that my father selected this person, besides that he was an athlete and had many good traits, was that he was eligible and qualified. He knew how to manage the *khanaqah*, he was a very good *na'at* reciter and he understood everything about the *khanaqah*, knew what was needed for its running. But then there were some people who were against my father, even when he was alive. They used to interfere in his work in the *khanaqah*. When my father passed away, they said, we need to select another person. But when they selected the other person, presumably because he had a white beard and he was older than the other, they said that he could manage the *khanaqah* well. But after they chose him, there was again a discussion among themselves about this decision.⁷¹

"Whitebeard" is a colloquial way to refer to older men in Afghanistan who are given respect due to their seniority. While senior members of society usually sit on community assemblies such as *shuras* and *jirgas* and are often selected to give advice and make decisions, the choice of this older leader turned out to be a troublesome one for the community. "He was a bit tough with the people, and his behavior wasn't good," a member remarked when asked about the choice. This opaque comment referenced cutting off *murids* when they were reciting the Qur'an, taking the microphone from *na'at* reciters in a rough fashion and giving it to others—expressions of disrespect and slights that left a bitter taste with the community and might have offended many Afghans, for whom politeness in social conduct is of utmost importance. There were even reports of him slapping a follower, breaking out into a brawl. The community conferred with one another and with the Pahlawan family abroad and decided to name him a leader only for a transition period, to be superseded by another. One of the men who had served the *khanaqah* community his whole life and had worked closely with Haji Saiqal in keeping the lodge safe was selected to lead it now: Haji Tamim.

Haji Tamim was known to everyone who had ever set foot into the lodge. The shopkeeper who sold mobile phone cables in a corner store to make a living and who had defended the *khanaqah* his whole life during the various phases of war, defying orders to close it and supporting the previous *pir* in all his dealings, became the leader of the community. A communal ceremony officially conferred title and position on him. Showing me videos of the ceremony on his mobile phone, he also connected his choice to the former leader: "Saiqal was very interested in me. During his illness, I was the one who was always with him. Every Friday I went to get him from the fifth floor of his apartment in Microrayon and brought him here for the *zikr*. A few times, he said to me, 'This position is yours. Don't let others take this position.'"[72] Haji Tamim had taken over the *khanaqah* at the precipice of another political change in Afghanistan's history. When we sat together in the main congregation room of the Sufi lodge in August 2021, a mere week before the Taliban takeover of the government, I asked him how he saw the changes that everyone knew to be afoot in one way or another. He was unfazed by the prospect of the Taliban's return to power. Taking a page out of Haji Saiqal's pragmatic rulebook, he merely said in a matter-of-fact way: "We will talk with them."

An Oxymoron, a Reality or a Strategy?

The case of Haji Saiqal shows multiple navigational strategies at work during various phases of conflict and ideological struggles. Violence, whether targeted, as in the killing of religious teachers and leaders, or generalized, as in bombings and destruction that spur migration, precipitated change and opened up room for other leaders to take charge. It also pushed the need for cooperation between groups of Islamic leaders who had previously not worked together but who found it advantageous to do so now.

Sufi Islam used to be the normative Islam in what is present-day Afghanistan. This means that most traditional scholars of Islam were simultaneously legal scholars and part of what one might consider the orthodoxy *and* Sufi thinkers, leaders and guides. Those positions were not mutually exclusive but could often fall to one and the same person. With such a historic intertwining, one might wonder where all the tropes of the limited understanding of mullahs and *mawlawis* in Persian poetry as well as in popular humorous themes come from. But being part of a religious class did by no means shield them from humor or critique. Intra-Islamic critique has variously singled out and warned against undesirable characteristics and tendencies of religious personnel, criticizing the ones who did not live up to their holier-than-thou facade. Prose, poetry and popular tropes have unceasingly offered pointed criticism against an overreliance or sole focus on the outward, external (*zahir*) aspects of religion. Such critique was often voiced through a pointed commentary on particular types of religious personnel, such as the mullah. Nonetheless, mullahs, *mawlawis*, and *akhunds* were historically not cut off from Sufi thought but often furthered and taught Sufi perspectives as part and parcel of Islamic education.

However, within Orientalist and colonial writing, Sufism and Islam were separated and located within different personas—the *alim* was set in contrast to the Sufi poet. Not unified in one person anymore, but positioned as antagonists in the religious marketplace, they were described as mutually exclusive categories. This discourse disassociated the literature-based individual mysticism of Sufi poetry and writing, anchored in a supposedly peaceful past from the colonial powers' present experience of Sufi-led resistance movements against colonial occupying forces. The "mad mullahs" (who were actually also Sufi *pirs* in the Afghan-Pakistani frontier region of then-British India) seemed to have little in common with the love-and-divinity-infused sweet poetry that the English had read in translation. This line of thinking also influenced Muslim reformers and had profound effects on Muslims' own perceptions and categorization of Sufis.

A particular shift in discourse on religious authority emanated from the legitimation of jihad against the Soviets. The ideological environment that formed during the time of the Mujahidin and the Taliban emphasized outwardly conforming Islamic conduct as a prime characteristic of legitimate Islamic leadership. While Haji Saiqal claimed the traditional position of both imam and *pir*, his outward appearance as a conservative and conventional mullah played to these requirements for religious leaders. The community, deprived of its own leadership through migration and death, adapted to the shifting environment, which predominantly privileged prescriptive authority over exploratory authority, through appointing an outwardly fitting leader. More than that, however, the imam used his own contacts and connections through his students in the mosque to negotiate support for the Sufi lodge and his own position, even though he defied certain rulings at the time.

While this chapter focuses on Haji Saiqal's journey with the *khanaqah* Pahlawan, he was also embedded within the wider Sufi sociosphere. Sufi teachers such as Asma Mahjor and Haidari Wujudi, whom we meet in the next chapter, knew him personally. Ustad Wujudi sometimes visited the Saiqal's lodge to teach Sufi poetry, and Haji Saiqal frequented Wujudi's teaching circle in the public library. The various teachers were appreciative of each other, knowing that they shared a common goal of furthering Sufi interpretations of Islam while their centers of gravity for followers, their teaching foci and some of the strategies with which they positioned themselves differed.

THREE

Navigating the Interior

Sufi Poetry as Islamic Education and Heritage

"Sufi teachers tell the truth in beautiful words," my friend Sami told me as if he were letting me in on a secret. "Even if they say something outrageous, they talk sweetly. But in their eyes, there are storms raging, there are debates happening and those are not easy or tame."

He had come to the house in Qala-e Fathullah, where I was renting a room, for a cup of tea and another round of our frequent debates about the nature of the spiritual path in Islam and the state of Sufism in Afghanistan.[1] Sitting in the living room with a view of the budding trees of late spring in the courtyard, so typical of old Kabuli houses, I had returned with new ideas for research, but Sami was doubtful about its prospects: "The problem is that there are very few real Sufis left in Kabul, or in Afghanistan in general," he said.

A filmmaker and writer in his thirties who made a little extra money on the side offering media training for NGO projects, Sami had been an avid seeker on the Sufi path when he was younger. Growing up, he had supported his family through carpet weaving whenever he was not attending school. During this taxing period, the poems and stories about ingenious Sufis that his uncle told had inspired dreams of developing extraordinary powers to escape the exhaustion of his dreaded daily routine. "I thought that when one becomes a Sufi, one also gets spiritual powers and I would be able to rid myself of this life. So, I grew up; I learned about *tasawwuf*, but I never got the spiritual powers I desired," he told me, with a wry smile.

Still, he persevered, engaging in individual study and visiting *khanaqahs* but ultimately lost his faith in ever finding the leading authority he was searching for. "Most teachers and knowledgeable *pirs* have died in the last years," he lamented. "These days Sufism is like uncooked bread. People have the ingredients and the knowledge about technical aspects, but they eat it raw, trying to sell you as if it were the real, tasty thing."

In the literal sense, I caught his meaning: Afghans are proud of the steaming flat bread, often eaten fresh out of the tandoor (oven), with cream or jam. But I could not quite follow the parallel with baked goods and mystical knowledge. "What do you mean by that?" I asked, wondering if he was maybe referring to the experience of the Divine that Sufi writers have termed *dhawq*, which literally means "taste."[2]

> If you have ever tasted freshly baked bread, then you know that it is something that you experience not only by tasting but with all senses: the smell in your nose and the sensation of warmth emanating from the piece in your hands. These people's knowledge of Sufism is like *khami*, unbaked bread. They recite the poetry of Mawlana and Bedil, but it is one thing to say those things and another to live by them.

Sami paused for dramatic effect before picking up the thread: "In that regard there are not many people left like that. Haidari Wujudi might be the last *arif* [gnostic/mystic] left in Kabul or in all of Afghanistan. Wujudi walked the walk; he has seen true ups and downs. He not only knows the literature, but he also lives it. He is a true Sufi."

It was not the first time I had heard this. The octogenarian teacher Haidari Wujudi had functioned like a lighthouse in my research.[3] Whenever I asked friends, acquaintances or Sufi affiliates whom they knew as currently teaching Sufism, I was referred to the famous Ustad Wujudi. His name was synonymous with erudition; his speech, despite his stammer, clear and concise in thought. People's endorsements were not mere accolades for an accomplished master but a warning: "You should go and see Haidari Wujudi; without that, your research will be incomplete."[4]

Figures like Wujudi are positioned prominently in the ethos of Afghanistan's Sufi heritage. In Afghanistan, the teaching of Sufi poetry can confer a knowledge-dependent form of religious charisma,[5] exemplified by Wujudi because the very poetry these teachers draw on was also, at one time, a crucial locus of Islamic education. While these individual teachers are seen as offering a particular connection to the Divine that is akin to Shahab Ahmed's concept of "exploratory authority,"[6] the embedding of Sufi poetry as Islamic teaching in religious schooling indicates that Sufi poetry is not a fringe phenomenon among a small group of literati but a widely accepted way of teaching Islamic ethics and principles that was, and to a lesser degree remains, embedded within Afghan society.

More than that, however, this chapter argues that Sufi leaders and communities both benefited from and fostered a vision of Sufi poetry as national, intangible heritage—an idea with impact not only in the way that communities were positioned during past decades but also in the way they installed themselves as teachers and leaders of communities. The larger Sufi social sphere of poetry *halqas* and their outreach and collaborations with nationally revered musicians, discussed later in the chapter, illuminates how groups consciously crafted the dissemination of Sufi poetry through popular media.

This chapter builds on two bodies of literature to showcase how they surface and interweave in navigations of authority: ethnographic approaches to poetry as religious practice and poetry as intangible heritage. Ethnographic approaches to literature use in various societies has pointed to the ways that poetry and literature are an essential aspect of Muslims' lives and sometimes part of their religious practices.[7] Sufi poetry is a multilayered sociocultural signifier, not only offering Islamic education but also operating as part of an intangible cultural heritage of Afghanistan's nation.[8] Contenders for leadership within Sufi communities are vying for followers in these multiple realms. In making this case, I am drawing on a recent turn in heritage studies that extends the term "heritage" from architectural and archeological preservation to the social and political construction of cultural expressions that are connected to a people's past.[9] The cultural forms of heritage are in this approach not seen as merely given but acknowledged as necessitating work in the ways they are imagined, created, affirmed and performed (what Ananda Breed and

Ali Iğmen call "culture work").[10] A regional example of the affective dimension of this culture work and its relation to the nation is the performance tradition of *aitys* (oral improvisational poetry). Eva-Marie Dubuisson describes how poetic performances in Kazakhstan have come to stand for a cultural ideal and also become deeply national in the ways that they express pride and grief. While pride might be an emotion to be expected from cultural production connected to the nation, Dubuisson argues that shared grief, as a "recognition that these traditions may have been partially lost or suppressed in the past" during Russian and Soviet colonization, also functions as a marker for shared nationness.[11] Similarly, Sufi poetry in Afghanistan can bring out feelings of pride as well as fears of endangerment through other nation-states' encroachment on poetic heritage, political usurpation of poetry by various governments or the fear of losing the capacity to decode and teach Sufi poetry through a loss of these master teachers.

As Laurajane Smith remarked, heritage is also about the negotiation of how individuals and groups can use the past to express individual and collective identities.[12] A look into the Sufi poetry sphere reveals the multiple layers with which intangible heritage was crafted and how it offers another aspect of cultural authority and status to these teachers. The last part of the chapter shows how this has created new manifestations of claims to Sufi authority based on book publishing, building of cultural organizations and online outreach, which can spark strife between different contenders for Sufi teaching authority.

Between What Is Said and What Is Lived

The first time I came to meet Haidari Wujudi in the upper rooms of Kabul's public library, the guards at the entrance, with whom I needed to leave my bag as a security precaution, only asked whether I was there to see the *ustad*, the teacher. Despite a library full of researchers and dedicated library administrators, there was only one person to whom the designation of master and teacher was given. Carrying pen, paper and recording device in hand, I wandered through relatively empty rooms that were just being renovated with shiny new plaster and white paint, passing a group of young volunteers who were busy indexing books and newspapers in a room downstairs.

Figure 3.1. Haidari Wujudi in his youth, 1959. Reproduced with permission of Ghulam Naqshband, son of Haidari Wujudi.

Ascending a plain staircase and crossing rooms full of yellowing newspaper volumes bound and numbered by year, I found Wujudi at his desk beside a window overlooking the Malik Azghar intersection. The muted cacophony of car horns from the chaos of vehicles wedged into a perpetual traffic jam drifted through the musty air. For a moment, I could imagine the *ustad* a half century earlier, working as a library clerk, not yet the respected teacher he would become, in this very room, only slightly changed, filled with books and a simple table to sort periodicals.

Born in 1939 in a small village in Panjshir Province as one of five children of a cleric, Wujudi had completed only his sixth grade of formal education when he moved to Kabul at the age of fifteen. For a fifteen-year-old boy from the countryside, Kabul must have seemed like a place teeming with opportunities. There he met a person whose acquaintance would shape his approach to literature, life and belief on a fundamental level: Ghulam Nabi,

Figure 3.2. Image of Sufi Ashqari in Haidari Wujudi's notebook. Reproduced with permission of Ghulam Naqshband, son of Haidari Wujudi.

otherwise known as Sufi Ashqari (1271–1358/1892–1979), one of the foremost mystical poets of his time.

He owned a bookbinding business and a small shop for chewing tobacco in the city's Kharabat music district. Growing up in poverty after his parents died, Ashqari led a simple life, although he was known as a great cook who hosted many fellow poets.[13] "There were many knowledgeable persons, but the only one who was living *tasawwuf-e naab* [pure Sufism] was Sufi Ashqari," Wujudi told me. Ashqari included Haidari Wujudi in the group of poets who met regularly, and an unlikely friendship between the teenager and the Sufi poet in his sixties developed so that years later, Wujudi became the custodian of Ashqari's unfinished work, which he prepared for publication. "He called me *Baba* Haidari, even though I was much younger than him," Wujudi remembered with a glimmer in his eye. *Baba*, literally "father," symbolized the respect and deep friendship that both shared. Ashqari and the group became such an integral part of Wujudi's thinking and working that he came to integrate them as touch points for measuring the depths of his despair and loneliness in his poetry:

> The book/record of my patience was in pieces last night
> my heart pounded uncontrollably in my chest
> eager to see you, oh Mecca of desires
> I was all in *zikr*, affirmations and *istkhara*...
>
> my tears of desire flew until dawn...
>
> neither Shayiq Jamal, nor Ashqari were there
> neither Aref, nor moon piece
> no songs of Majeed, nor his comforting voice...
>
> shoulders of Haidari, will I ever forget
> were rented by the world for its sorrows until the light of day[14]

As Wujudi transforms suffering into poetry, describing his body as a vessel and instrument for the expression of the sorrows of the world, he laments that he was so alone that not even his poetry companions were with him. All the names in these couplets are actual people who surrounded Wujudi at the time, such as his mentor and friend Sufi Ashqari and Majeed, who was a singer from Haidari's native Panjshir. Decades later, with Wujudi himself retired with a modest pension, he was still tending to publishing Ashqari's and his own poetry, as well as teaching a class twice a week titled "The Society of Lovers of Mawlana."

After finding him on that day in the backrooms of the library, I joined their community for many weeks either on Monday or Wednesday when they were meeting. Seeing Wujudi laboring away in his office, over half a century after his arrival at the library, I wondered whether the silent persistence of his chosen vocation was the recipe to his success during four decades of upheaval in Afghanistan. On one occasion when I sat down with Wujudi for a more focused interview, I asked how he managed to survive the various regimes and periods of war and semi-peace he witnessed during

Figure 3.3. Intellectuals and literati (right to left): Sufi Ashqari, Sher Muhammad, Shayiq Jamaal, Haidari Wujudi (in back), Shayiq Marhum Nawabi and two older gentlemen. Reproduced with permission of Ghulam Naqshband, son of Haidari Wujudi.

his time at the public library. "My policy has been to stay away from the government and powerful people," he explained. "I got invited several times [to join governments], but I knew that it was best for me to stay away."

I wondered though, did he simply hide away behind yellowing periodicals and decomposing books? Was this all it took for Sufi teachers to survive the slaughter of intellectual religious leaders and the carnage of indiscriminate civil war shelling, to keep their heads down, focused on the slow death of cellulose and lignin in the pages of books, to hope for better days, to wait out the coming and going of governments and rulers? On the surface, this is what Wujudi seemed to be saying. However, when I stepped back from that topical narrative of war and political instability, another, more complex picture came into view. In that four-dimensional rendering, it was clear that Wujudi, and others before him, had been actively building the foundation for Sufism's continued survival in Afghanistan. Because of their diligent work in obscure library offices and publishing houses, Sufi poetry had become an essential part of both Afghanistan's Islamic education and its national heritage.[15]

Sufi Poetry as Islamic Education

Writing about the ways in which mystical poetry is a crucial companion to individual prayer as well as communal religious experience for Persian speakers in Iran, Niloofar Haeri suggests that poetry is both a religious ethical scaffolding for people's lives and an Islamic educational tool.[16] Through poetry, Persian speakers not only learn to evaluate ethical questions, how to conduct themselves and express their feelings but also to think about religion in imaginative and often even paradoxical ways. Classical poetry, which in Iran, much as in Afghanistan, is overwhelmingly steeped in Islamic mysticism, provides a "complex and multidimensional kind of education" that "offers a vocabulary, social types, paradoxical scenarios, and images—in sum, social analysis—through which one becomes tutored in the ways of religion and the world."[17]

The co-imbrication of poetry and Islamic learning is a long-standing tradition in Afghanistan similar to the situation described by Haeri in Iran. It might not become directly apparent for a Western audience when reading Persian Sufi poetry in its English translations, but many phrases within the poetry come directly from the Qur'an or echo its spirit.[18] A telling example of the different reception and understanding of what Sufi poetry is might be the writing of one of its most prominent exemplars: early thirteenth-century Jalal ad-Din al-Rumi.[19] Rumi has become a best-selling poet in the United States over the past decades. He is revered by Deepak Chopra, Madonna and Coldplay, quoted on shower curtains, on iPhone cases and in Facebook inspirational phrases.[20] However, Rumi's main opus, the *Masnawi*, consisting of fifty thousand lines (twenty-seven thousand couplets), one of the longest mystical poems ever produced by a Muslim scholar,[21] is called in Afghanistan the Qur'an in Persian. My research assistant Khalid, a businessman by day and lover of Sufi poetry and thought, used to quote this popular saying when we talked about Mawlana: "The opus of our master is a Qur'an in the Persian language. What shall I say about his excellency? He is not the Prophet, but he has a book."[22]

Several Afghan interlocutors, unaware of the different interpretations of Rumi's poetry abroad, wondered whether so many Westerners had suddenly opened up to Islam, as for them, one could not read Rumi without understanding its Islamic roots and resonance. However, they had not taken into consideration what gets lost in translation. While Mawlana Rumi was translated into English by many able and prominent translators such as R. A. Nicholson, A. J. Arberry, Jawid Mojaddedi and Annemarie Schimmel, most people today know his writing through Coleman Barks, who has been accused of being "not a translator so much as an interpreter... [who] transforms nineteenth-century translations into American verse" cleansed of references to Islam.[23] Working from Victorian-era translations of Persian poetry to rework them for a Western audience,[24] Barks defends his practice of erasing Islamic references while retaining allusions to Christian figures such as Jesus and Joseph, as he found the Qur'an "hard to read" and he "used to memorize Bible verses, and know[s] the New Testament more than ... [he] know[s] the Koran" through his Presbyterian upbringing.[25]

While it might not be important to Afghan interlocutors how Rumi is understood in the West, the actual salient point is one of immersion into a sociocultural realm in which a particular interpretation of a text becomes self-evident to a reader because of the multiple resonances it has within its religious intertextuality. It is telling that the same process of being steeped in a certain religious-cultural setting produces captivating poetry that speaks to a varying readership. While Coleman Barks memorized Bible verses and crafted poetry that speaks to a spiritually inclined Western audience, writers such as Mawlana Rumi were deeply embedded within the Islamic tradition. Mawlana was an Islamic theologian, but more than that, he lived in a spiritual environment in which expressions were made through reference to, and intertextuality with, the Qur'an. Many people had memorized the Qur'an and had become a *hafiz*, so they were able to understand Qur'anic references with ease. Mawlana drew on something that Paul

Figure 3.4. Prayer (*du'a*) at Ustad Haidari Wujudi's class in Kabul.

Nwyia has called the "koranization of the memory": Qur'anic vocabulary not only colored poetic expression and influenced the poetry in its imagery and symbolism, but Sufis were able "to understand everything in the light of one or another Koranic sentence."[26]

This is also how my interlocutors understood the poetry that they read, memorized and interpreted side by side with the Qur'an and Hadith corpus. And to miss this crucial element, as Omid Safi so prudently put it, is an act of "bypassing, erasing, and occupying a spiritual landscape that has been lived and breathed and internalized by Muslims."[27]

This cross-fertilization of Islamic learning and Sufi poetry is exemplified by the history of religious education in Afghanistan, which intertwined reading and memorizing the Qur'an and seminal works of Sufi poetry.[28] The prewar educational environment of poetry teachers such as Haidari Wujudi before the Soviet invasion is a telling example. Growing up, Haidari Wujudi learned to write the alphabet, read the Holy Qur'an and interpret both literature and religion through reading *Panj Ganj* (Five treasures), a collection of rhythmic Persian prose and poetry that contains normative principles of Islamic beliefs and practices. These ranged from the necessary and private—such as the fundamental tenets of the faith, ritual purity, procedures for ritual cleansing, performance of *namaz* (prayer) and religious duties—to the social and political, like relations within families, public duty performance, conditions for prosperity or downfall of rulers, condemnation of ignorance and discussions of the existence of the unitary God.[29]

In the past, learning about Islam through poetry was not a fringe phenomenon but a mainstream educational approach in Afghanistan's madrasas.[30] Until the beginning of the war period, Islam was taught in Afghanistan's madrasas through reading the Qur'an and gaining an understanding of the Hadith as well as through reading the poetry of Rumi, Saadi and Hafiz, both in urban and rural contexts.[31] Nazif Shahrani reports in the 1990s that copies of texts such as *Panj Ganj* and *Kulliyat-e Chahar Kitab* (The complete four books) first existed in handwritten form and, since the nineteenth and early twentieth centuries, in lithographs and printed editions. They were produced in Lahore, Peshawar, Bukhara and other Central Asian cities and made available by itinerant traders and professional book peddlers. Shahrani argues that the use of these Persian poetry texts within religious settings was as widespread in Turkic- and Pashto-speaking communities as it was among native Persian speakers, attesting to Persian as a lingua franca in Afghanistan.[32]

The insights and ethical-religious guidance of these collections is presented with literary devices such as repetition, recapitulation and analogies that encourage the memorization of the material, which is already in narrative form. In comparison to the Qur'an, which is taught and memorized in Arabic, a language that most Afghans neither speak nor understand in depth, Persianate Sufi poetry is far from a passively memorized canon. While written centuries ago, Persian has not changed as much as English in the same time frame,[33] so the poetry is directly accessible as a body of resources that practitioners can draw on in their production and reproduction of action and judgment, in meaning making, ethical decisions and evaluation of Islamic claims. Louis Dupree observed in the 1970s that many literate and nonliterate people in Afghan society can recite Persian poetry by heart, giving both groups the same general opportunities for expression. Dupree concluded that "Afghanistan, therefore, is fundamentally a nation of poets."[34]

While most Afghans had access to Sufi poetry through its widespread use in Islamic education, this nation of poets also had master teachers, revered for their particular insights that they offered to individual seekers on the Sufi path. When talking to Wujudi's students—some who had come for decades to his lessons, others who were more recent additions to the approximately thirty people congregating each Monday and Wednesday—they ascribed to him the position of a guide to divine insights. Wujudi might have seen himself more as a seeker among like-minded individuals, as he describes in his poetry, but students saw him as way beyond their own level.[35] One young law student in his early twenties, with whom I chatted after one of the lessons, compared him to a "spiritual father" (*padar-e manavi*) who takes care of one's inner, spiritual needs. "Scholars of *irfan* [mysticism] mostly have influence on the heart." He explained:

> For example, Mawlana or Bedil or Hafiz, they might be not in this world physically, but they are in this world spiritually. And the world of poems influences the heart. Just as Ustad Haidari Wujudi is here both physically and spiritually, so his words and everything he does affect the other person a lot. Especially when people come into difficult situations, when they cannot organize their thoughts, Haidari Wujudi is like a straight path; he helps you deal with these lessons.[36]

Intrigued by that description, I asked him to elaborate further on what he meant by helping, as it sounded like more than mere literary explanations. "He does not only explain the poem, what you read, the theory, the *qal*, but he gives more explanations of other concepts, like *hal* [lit., "state"], which takes you in, attracts you and influences you. Ustad is very good at *hal*, and he gives *duas* [supplications], which work really well. That is a special thing about him."

In making the distinction between teaching the words (*qal*) to be analyzed through literary exegesis and the mystical state (*hal*) that can be experienced as ecstasy and indicates epiphany-like insight through closeness to the Divine, the student's descriptions reflect an implicit commonplace in Sufi cosmology, that there is a hierarchy of knowers who traverse the Sufi path.[37] Some Sufi literature refers to this hierarchy explicitly, such as Khwaja Abdullah Ansari (d. 1089) in his manual *Stations of the Wayfarers* (*Manazil*

Figure 3.5. Ustad Haidari Wujudi teaching.

al-sayitin), which divides the different levels into *amm*, *khass* and *khass al-khass*—commoners, elect and elect of the elect.[38] The unevenly distributed ability to access and know the Divine has been described variously in Sufi literature, but it was succinctly defined for me by a Sufi *murid* (student) in his sixties when he told me that he thinks of it like an innate ability of each person: "Think of electricity. Some people are like copper; others, like wood. Some are good, and others are poor conductors." Haidari Wujudi was therefore seen not only as insightful but also as able to transfer divine insight through his teaching—a powerful conductor.

For becoming such a teacher or spiritual conductor, a Sufi must have experienced firsthand these levels of closeness to the Divine. Wujudi alludes to these experiences in his poetry:

> You wouldn't know how much I have burned
> until I crafted every word in the temple of fire and art[39]

The process of becoming closer to God, and being able to communicate it afterward in an intelligible way to a student, is described through the imagery of burning. Fire becomes the purifier of sins, inclinations and the ego. The end product is a matured, purified version of the self, cleansed through the process of struggling. In another couplet, Wujudi plays with multiple allegories, combining them with his typical mental agility:

> In the memory of the moon, lost in the world of dreams/
> the imaginal
> Who else has the sky voyager desire that I have?[40]

Lost is the beloved, the moon, which is a common poetic scenario with verses produced in the absence of the beloved. In Sufi poetry, the oscillation between references to earthly lovers and God is retained through keeping the imagery unexplained. The *allam-e ruya*, which could be translated literally as "dream world" or "world of the imaginal," is a crucial locus, conceptualized as an in-between space where spirits communicate. Wujudi jests with the exploration of these realms through assigning himself a "sky voyager desire," or the dream of traveling to the heavens, challenging the reader in a playful tone to match his unmatchable desire for exploration. While Wujudi might be remembered as the grave master of poetry, having met him changes the reading of these texts. Even in his old age, he had a joking, boyish humor about him, a twinkle in his eye as he taught his students. This lightness of being was remarked on by another student, who had known him for years and who saw it as an elevation above the world, as "it seems as if he knows so much more than he might ever tell; he only needs to allude to it with a smile." It was this particular closeness to the Divine, of the immersion in Sufi poetry opening up one's inner being to insights otherwise foreclosed, that singled out a Sufi poetry teacher as more than a literary scholar. Teachers like Wujudi and others leading poetry *halqas* created their leadership position through exhibiting a particular kind of authority—knowledge dependent but beyond the content of the poetry itself. It was the experience of these mystical states (*hal*), and the ability to help students navigate personal struggles and inner states through this experiential knowledge, that established these teachers as knowledgeable guides.

While many students described to me their attachment to their chosen

Figure 3.6. Recitation at Ustad Haidari Wujudi's class at the public library.

poetry teacher as a "matter of the heart" (*dafa-e qalb*), grounded in a spiritual search for understanding the Divine through poetic insight, the general Islamic educational environment had pivoted away from poetry as central to Islamic teaching in the decades just prior to the time I researched. What was once a mainstream approach to learn about the core ethical insights of Islam had been pushed to the margins. Islam as an unacknowledged backdrop, an "all-encompassing way of life," which was naturally embedded in people's lives,[41] was put to the test during the decades of war that were in one way or another infused and legitimized with the veneer of Islamic and Islamicized language. Islam itself became a locus of contest.[42] I conducted my ethnographic field research during the second decade of the twenty-first century in a relatively open democratic system that enabled public debate. However, the bases of religious education emerged as a decisive point in discussions that also measured shifts in the type of religiosity that people sought out.

Mirroring this shift, an Afghan-American interviewee recounts a childhood memory on the decision about religious education in the late 1990s:

Sufism was never much formally talked about, but it was a normal part of life that was always there, at the same time individual and very communal. I remember when my parents talked about which mosque to bring us to, to learn to read the Qur'an. We looked at several places. One was too Arab; the other one had a strong Pakistani leaning. My mother found that okay, but my father said, "No, they are against Sufis and I don't want my children to grow up learning that." I remember sitting in the back of the car and them talking about it. It was very much a part of everything, not separate.[43]

While this memory fragment resonates with observations on the embedding of Sufism into everyday life, it also shows that religious education had become a conscious choice and Sufism a matter of debate. According to many of my interlocutors, Sufi poetry, which was once taught along with the Qur'an and the Hadiths in Afghanistan's madrasas, was being increasingly erased. One interviewee explained that "in the past, there was oral knowledge on how to understand, recite and sing poetry. Until the Soviet time, the mosques were teaching next to the Qur'an also poetry, such as *Panj Ganj*, which was a collection that was used. . . . Now there is only learning by heart, no analysis."[44] The extent to which this erasure was taking place is difficult to measure as no comprehensive data exist on the curricula taught in Afghan madrasas.[45]

While much has changed since my research with the withdrawal of the international troops and the Taliban's takeover of the government, the findings presented here offer a window into discussions among Afghans in the last decade pertaining to the negotiation of authority to interpret and teach Islam in various ways—negotiations that are ongoing to the present day, albeit with different powerbrokers in charge. At the time of research, academic and public discourse on madrasas in Afghanistan mainly restricted itself to the question of "radicalization," which typically referred to an indoctrination of particular politically charged religious views.[46] Before the renewed takeover of the government, the Taliban themselves were a point of comparison for particular interpretations. For example, public discussions after the release of an Al Jazeera film on a madrasa in Kunduz, which was said to impose "an even stricter interpretation of Islam" than the Taliban,[47] led to a petition to the president to review religious educational curricula.[48]

Some have pointed out that social media was used to radicalize students, even at universities.[49] In a similar vein, another publicly contentious discussion centered on rewriting the curriculum of compulsory Islamic lessons (*saqafat-e islami*) at the university level because it allegedly contained anti-democratic biases.[50] Curriculum reform was a contentious issue, although even if a national curriculum could have been established, it would have been another question altogether whether and how it would have been taught, as the reach of Kabul's national institutions was still limited. In all of these discussions, the Afghan government was seen as not fully in charge of curricula, pedagogical approaches and educational content and appeared bound by inertia unless prodded by civil society to act. Even though the form of government has changed since, with the Taliban currently in charge, much remains unclear about religious education as of the time of writing.[51] Most public debates center around access to education, particularly for girls and women. The Taliban have instituted mandatory Islamic lessons for all university departments and also seem to be working on an overhaul of how Islam should be taught.[52] Even if the government decided that Sufi poetry should be purged of educational curricula, would they be more successful than the previous Afghan government in implementing and enforcing a nationwide curriculum reform? The forms and content of Islamic education are not yet decided. However, if the last decades are any indication, the place of Sufi poetry as a vehicle for religious understanding might remain a shifting indicator in the struggle to define the type of Islam to be taught and transmitted.

The erasure that was felt by my interlocutors in the past twenty years influenced the public perception of Sufi poetry as not belonging to Islamic teaching per se and positioned it instead in the field of culture and cultural national heritage. However, this process did not occur in a vacuum; it was not a passively endured process but intertwined with a development that was actively supported by Sufi poetry teachers themselves. Sufi poetry has always had a particular oscillating, or "opalizing" quality,[53] in which one is never quite certain whether the object of a poem's longing is the Divine or an earthly beloved, whether it is an expression of supreme religiosity or the earthbound, cultural expression of a humanistic love of life in all its forms. This ability to morph and be interpreted either as the key to the doors of divine perception or age-old expressions of cultural and national heritage has created new ground for claims of Sufi authority. Teachers themselves have, while navigating the complexities of sociopolitical upheavals, both embraced aspects of the poetry they teach and crafted it as national heritage.

The Production of National (Intangible) Heritage

"Maulana (Rumi) belongs to present day Afghanistan and yesterday's Khorasan. It is the responsibility of the Afghan government to take swift action about it to protect our heritage," Ustad Haidari Wujudi told TOLO news in June 2016.[54] A social media storm had been brewing on Twitter after it came to light through the Afghan embassy in Tehran that Iran and Turkey planned to list Rumi's *Masnawi Ma'navi* with UNESCO as the common heritage of those two countries, excluding Afghanistan. An online petition decried that Afghan culture had been "manipulated by so many outside sources" that it could not "afford any more loss." Particularly, most outsiders had failed to "define the authentic Afghans, Afghanistan and Afghan culture," at the inalienable core of which the writers saw Mawlana Rumi's poetry.[55] The event culminated in what Radio Free Europe called a "diplomatic frenzy" with the Ministry of Foreign Affairs seeking talks with UNESCO and the governor of Balkh, Atta Mohammad Noor, penning a letter to the UN condemning Iran and Turkey's "imperialistic" attempts at appropriating Rumi and disregarding Balkh as the esteemed poet's "motherland."[56]

This incident, in which regional and national heritage is openly negotiated on the stage of international cultural diplomacy, reveals that Sufi poetry has become a site of mediating identity, belonging and, potentially, exclusion. The narrative of the protection from appropriation and disregard reverberates with previous fraught experiences of Afghans in Iran.[57] Many Afghans who lived as refugees and temporary workers inside their Western neighbor experienced discrimination or abuse. The exclusion from what they saw as a shared cultural heritage was seen as another slight in a condescending attitude toward Afghanistan as a country. It showed how heritage discourses are about negotiating the past to deliberate present-day identity.[58]

Considering both tangible and intangible cultural heritage, Laurajane

Smith argues that places, artifacts or practices are not inherently valuable and meaningful—"what makes the collection of rocks in a field 'Stonehenge'—are the present-day cultural processes and activities that are undertaken at and around them, and of which they become a part."[59] What gives heritage its strong emotional valence is how people imbue it with value connected to their own notions of peoplehood. This section addresses how Sufi poetry *halqas* have been involved in promoting Sufi poetry as valuable national heritage, which opens up the discussion to an assessment of how these understandings have changed claims to Sufi authority within the poetry sphere.

The alleged attempt at appropriating Mawlana Rumi's work through the UNESCO designation may have been the trigger for the outcry over cultural heritage in Afghanistan—Rumi is, after all, the world's most famous Sufi poet—but one cannot fully appreciate the depth to which Sufi poetry is intertwined with Afghan culture without including another of Afghanistan's giants, Bedil Dehlavi (1642/1644–1720).[60] Four centuries Rumi's junior, Bedil is less known in the West but is an integral part of the experience of poetry in Afghanistan. *Halqas* coalesce around teachers such as Wujudi who explicated both poets' works. Tracing Wujudi's own educational genealogy reveals not only his individual trajectory of learning but also how it is embedded within larger Sufi sociality and attempts to popularize the classical poets. The literary role models of Ustad Wujudi, as well as of his friend and teacher the bookbinder and poet Sufi Ashqari, were also Rumi and Bedil, and like them, he used classical forms such as the *ghazal* to express himself, albeit in a simpler language. Although Sufi Ashqari and Haidari Wujudi might be remembered in Afghanistan as individual Sufi poets, they were connected to a wider group of Bedil lovers.

As there are many streams that feed into a river, there is certainly not one group or single person who crafted a vision of Persian poetry as cultural heritage. And certainly, there were many more than those I name in this chapter. But some of these groups were part of seemingly diffuse but consolidated efforts to craft literary, artistic and cultural perceptions of Persianate poetry that anchored their understanding in state and popular notions of national cultural heritage. I trace how a particular *halqa* formed around the Naqshbandiyyah Sufi Qandi Agha (1290–1373/1911–1994) anchored itself in literati circles,[61] exemplifying an upper- and middle-class infatuation with Bedil and Mawlana's poetry, and how it then expanded its reach through collaboration with prominent musicians. Bedil, just as Mawlana, became both the cherished national pastime of upper-class literati and a shared cultural heritage sung and hummed by everyone.

I first saw a depiction of Qandi Agha in a wall-sized pastel painting that dominated a home library in an old Kabuli house close to the polluted banks of the river in Bagh-e Rais, halfway between the two royal gardens of Bagh-e Babur and Chilsetoon. Engulfed by more recent urban decay, the area felt less than royal these days. Crossing the bridge from the main street, I watched the remnants of the once-flowing, now-trickling Kabul River, which carried more plastic trash than water. Entering the enclosed courtyard from the maze of winding streets bracketed by high mud walls, I felt like I was setting foot into a parallel universe of a verdant flowering garden full of Russian willow trees, grapevines and birds chirping from hanging cages. In awe, and still slightly dazed by the contrast between the outer decay and inner paradise, I was led into the house and placed before the larger-than-life-size painting of a man with a neatly cropped white beard, peacefully looking into the distance.

"That is Qandi Agha," a voice from the side of the room commented as I stared at the hypnotic and perhaps slightly pensive expression on the man's face in the painting. The voice belonged to an older gentleman in his early seventies with long white hair and a kind, open face. It was Ustad Mahjor, as I would come to know him. He motioned me to sit down across from him, asking whether it would be all right for him to smoke. I nodded as we sat down, and he reached for a pack of cigarettes that lay next to two inhalers and an oxygen mask.[62]

"Who was Qandi Agha?" I asked him.

"My father," he answered, giving the painting a look that I could not quite decipher. "I am his older son."

"How was he?" I naïvely asked to get a sense of the man. Ustad Mahjor inhaled a drag on the cigarette, giving the question some thought. "My relationship with my father was very friendly, but we had a formal connection with each other. I never smoked in front of him," he said, while toasting me with his cigarette. "I have never called my father '*tu*,'" indicating that he always addressed him formally in Persian. "But the last time I met my father when he was dying, he said: 'Come son, and hug me.' And that was the only time that I hugged him."

Surprised by the sudden frankness about this intimate final moment between a father and son, I remained silent. Ustad Mahjor took that as a sign to explain further: "Every father gives something to his son, a heritage [*miras*]. The only heritage that I have from my father is the book that he has left for me." He took out a notebook from his bookcase. It was filled with selected poems of Bedil, written down and commented on by Qandi Agha. I came to understand that it was a family legacy that Ustad Mahjor was describing, the heritage of keeping the memory and furthering the learning about a particular Sufi poet, mainly through teaching his poetry in a poetry circle (*halqa*) and commemorating his legacy through death commemorations (*urs*), akin to festivities for Sufi saints.

I had come to discuss with Ustad Mahjor how an Indian poet of the seventeenth century had risen to become one of the most beloved poets in Afghanistan, while he remained largely ignored in the Iranian Persian poetry canon. Mawlana Abul-Ma'ani Mirza Abdul-Qadir Bedil, also known as Bedil Dehlavi or simply "Bedil sahib" as some in the *halqa* called him, was a poet of the Safavid-Mughal period who was born in Azimabad, present-day Patna in northern India, in 1644.[63] "But his family was from Afghanistan," Mahjor pointed out in our discussion, referring to Bedil's family pedigree of Turkic Central Asian descent, belonging to the Arlas tribe of the Chaghatay.[64] He is therefore often considered an Uzbek and claimed in Afghanistan as an Afghan.[65]

The foremost representative of the "Indian style" of Persian poetry, he is also widely recognized as "the most difficult and challenging poet of that school."[66] This difficulty is often traced to his complex metaphors and sentence structure,[67] as well as his interweaving of exotic wordplay and unusual literary devices such as colloquial Indian words and expressions. The challenge might be further compounded by "Bedil's predilection for ambiguity bordering on obfuscation that made him a great mystic as well as a great poet."[68] One might even wonder if he knew how he would be read by later audiences when reading his statement: "Unhesitatingly, I conceal unconcealed meanings / not blinking made a riddle of the world."[69]

While his impact on Indo-Persian and Central Asian literature has been debated widely, Bedil's influence in northern India itself and the Persianate world remained circumscribed, and until recently,[70] his oeuvre has been ignored in Iran, even in literary circles.[71] Bedil might have remained a normal poet among many in the long literary history of Persian poetry if it were not for the development of a distinct school of Bedil (Maktab-e Bedil) dedicated to *Bedil Shenasi* (Bedil studies) in Afghanistan. But how did it come about that while most of the world forgot about this Indo-Persian poet, a group of Bedil aficionados, often glossed over in current overviews as "a cultic group,"[72] started to champion the serious study and appreciation of him?

It is difficult to pinpoint the exact beginning of Bedil studies, as poetic circles have a long tradition in Afghanistan. Historically, Kabul and Herat were important places for Persian literary circles, while Ghazni together with Peshawar in Pakistan were a center of gravity for Pashto literature.[73] Some of my informants traced the beginning of Bedil studies in Afghanistan to Timur Shah Durrani's time (r. 1772–1793), who is said to have brought back books from India and started poetry circles.[74] This view fits neatly into lines of argumentation developed in the twentieth century attempting to build a coherent national literary heritage to support the nation-building process. Historian Nile Green argues that literature was a key nation-building tool exemplified by the state-led creation of literary societies in the 1930s and 1940s, publications of distinct histories of "Dari" and Pashto literature,[75] as well as the furthering of a school of Bedil studies.[76] He points out that Afghanistan faced a dilemma in establishing its own national heritage: while many classical Persian and Pashto poets spent parts of their lives in the territory that later became Afghanistan, other countries such as Pakistan and Iran laid nationalistic claim on these poets through casting their works as national epics, naming universities after them and physically laying claim on them through monument building.[77]

The development and promotion of a national Afghan school of literary criticism and appreciation championed premodern writers such as Bedil Dehlavi and Mawlana Rumi, who had genealogical ties to Afghanistan as a geographic unit. The study of Bedil gathered momentum "in partial reaction to the modern Iranian denigration of the metaphysical Persian poetry of the 'Indian School'" as well as against the backdrop of both the new nation-states of India and Pakistan, which in 1947 officially "disowned" Persian as a language, because neither country listed it as a national language in its constitution.[78]

Afghan literary scholars increasingly claimed and celebrated Bedil studies as part of their own heritage. Over time, many influential intellectuals and political figures became enamored with Bedil. The father of the great intellectual Mahmud Tarzi, Sardar Ghulam Muhammad Tarzi,[79] is said to have organized *majalis* (meetings) on Bedil consisting of several hour-long recitations followed by discussions.[80] High-ranking political figures such as Prince Nasrullah, the brother of King Habibullah, are reported to have been lovers of Bedil.[81]

By the early to mid-twentieth century, several of these circles had emerged, such as the one that met in the house of Ustad Hasham Sheiq Efendi (1887–1924), a former diplomat from Bukhara who became an Afghan national after the Bolshevik takeover in 1920.[82] Efendi was a writer, editor and educator, teaching at Kabul University. His home Bedil circle was held in the old city of Kabul in Bagh-e Ali Mardan, close to Murad Khane.[83] His family members remembered that the circle was frequented by famous Afghan poets and literati such as the poet and parliamentarian Ustad Khalili,[84] the poet and Hadith commentator Ustad Bitab,[85] as well as the poet and calligrapher Mawlana Khasta.[86] In addition to the discussion rounds about Bedil's poetry, the circle began celebrating the *urs* of Bedil around 1913 or 1914.[87] While the meetings seem to have initially involved a literary circle with distinguished poets and writers in attendance,[88] it became a family legacy after Efendi died and one participant of the group, Ustad Muhammad 'Abd al-Hamid "Asir" (Qandi Aga, 1911–1994),[89] took over organizing the weekly sessions and the yearly *urs* celebration.

The list of participants for the original Bedil circle reads like a who's who of the political and cultural elite of early twentieth-century Afghanistan, showing how Sufi poetry as national heritage grew symbiotically in cooperation between the literati and those members of political and cultural society who reciprocated reverence for this religiously imbued poetry. While not everyone would see Bedil's oeuvre as situated within the Sufi canon—some spiritually inclined Afghans I talked to saw him more as a secular commentator on humanistic existential questions—his poetry was used as Islamic education in Bedil *halqas* and simultaneously celebrated as Afghan cultural heritage. However, Qandi Agha started to chart his own course in respect to furthering Bedil's reception within Afghan society, which included reaching out to and collaborating with prominent artists.

Popularizing Sufi Poetry through Music

When I sat down with Ustad Mahjor to talk about Sufi poetry, we were joined by his daughter and son, who served tea and cookies but also offered further insights into how Qandi Agha involved other artists in crafting Sufi poetry as intangible cultural heritage. "Our family has actively worked on changing the reach and reception of Bedil." Arezo, the son of Ustad Mahjor, chimed into the conversation. Himself a father in his mid-forties (b. 1976), Arezo was a man with flair: sporting a dark mustache and a well-cropped chin beard, he had acted in multiple films, including one in which he had played Mawlana Rumi. Working in the Ministry of Culture by day, Arezo and his sister, Asma, herself a published poet, were both enamored with Bedil studies. One of the ways that the family had managed to spread Bedil's work was through collaboration with one of Afghanistan's most renowned musicians, Mohammad Hussain Sarahang (1924–1983).

Famously referred to as the "Great Mountain (of Music)" (*koh-e boland*) or "Father of Music" (*Baba-e Musiqee*), Ustad Sarahang was educated in classical music in India at the Patiyala School of Music before returning to his country of origin.[90] One of my interviewees recounted how Ustad Sarahang met Qandi Agha:

> Ustad Sarahang finished his studies in India and came to Afghanistan. He came to Baba Wali [restaurant] and was singing there. There was a man, you know, sometimes you realize that someone is a Sufi because of the look that person has. So there was this man, who was Qandi Agha. Ustad Sarahang did not know him, but he had an inkling. So he played his best songs. Still, the man just left after a few songs. Ustad Sarahang ran after him to ask, "Did I not play well enough?" Qandi Agha told him that he thought he had a beautiful voice but that he did not have good taste in poetry yet. So Qandi Agha introduced Ustad Sarahang to Bedil.[91]

The son of Qandi Agha, Ustad Mahjor, who was at the time of this research in his seventies, became an assistant to Ustad Sarahang as a young boy, helping him with adapting Bedil verses into song. They met regularly in the Bedil *halqa*, as Mahjor remembers: "Ustad Sarahang was one of his [Qandi Agha's] students, and I was one of the counselors of Ustad Sarahang. He was illiterate, and so I was the one who was writing his songs down." Ustad Sarahang performed the *ghazal* verses on the radio program *De Ahangoono Mahfil* (The music gathering), which he cohosted in the 1960s and 1970s.[92] He and Ustad Rahim Bakhsh were among the only artists permitted to perform live on air on the new Radio Afghanistan.[93]

Music is often the first contact outsiders have with Sufism. Sufi musical gatherings, Qawwali music and *sema* dance performances are some of the most prominent marketing tools of Sufism, but music is also one of its most divisive elements for its connection to bodily movements and altered states of mind.[94] While music has the alluring power to induce these altered states for practitioners and connect them with the Divine—an aspect explored, for example, in the Chishti order in India and Pakistan[95]—the collaboration between Qandi Agha and Ustad Sarahang played out in a different context. The ethnomusicologist Lorraine Sakata argues in her ethnography of musicians in Afghanistan that "music is often described as *ghezaye ruh* in Afghanistan, meaning 'spiritual food' or 'nourishment,' an idea derived from Sufism."[96] And indeed, in the earlier Sufi tradition, *sama* (lit., "listening") referred to "listening to chanted or recited poetry that might or might not be accompanied by musical instruments."[97] A powerful voice could convey the poetry's beauty and intensity, and, in this sense, music was less a rhythmic instigator for meditative or ecstatic states than a conduit for delivering poetic texts.[98]

Partnering with one of the most renowned singers and musicians in Afghanistan was a clever strategy to reach a wider audience beyond the demographically and geographically limited world of home-based poetry *halqas*. Arezo explained: "In the past it was only scholarly circles who had access to and knowledge about Bedil. But through our *halqas* and introducing the literature through music, for example, with Ustad Sarahang, the circle of people who know about him grew wider. Our family has worked on this for seventy years."

Indeed, Ustad Sarahang became famous for using Bedil poetry, and Bedil poetry became more widely known through him. When the production of commercial audiocassettes of Afghan music began in Kabul in the early 1970s, Ustad Sarahang was featured as the first release from the first recording studio established by Ahmad Hamidi in 1972.[99] He is said to have recorded roughly five hundred *raga* performances and *ghazals* in India and at Radio Kabul.[100] Hailing from a traditional *kharabati* music family and simultaneously connected to Zahir Shah's court and to the public promotion of classical music, he straddled the popular and high-art genres.[101] Ethnomusicologist John Baily argues that to this day, Ustad Sarahang is one of *the* classic musicians whose music is shared and revered by Afghans as well as the Afghan diaspora. While the reception and depth of understanding of the audience of these programs cannot be ascertained from today's point of view, it shows that poetry existed in its dual capacity, from popular uses to religious ethical guidance, as a shared discursive realm, pervading music, private discussions and religious education and became part of a more widely shared cultural heritage that retained its Sufi content.

Politics and the Use of Poetry as Heritage

But where there is heritage, there is also the question of power and politics. In commenting on the narratives that heritage privileges, anthropologist Kristin Kuutma fittingly observes that heritage "emerges from the nexus of politics and power."[102] It is a value-laden concept that creates identities but also contested narratives.[103] This dimension became woefully apparent in the weeks and months after my visit to the Mahjor family. Mere weeks after my interview with Ustad Mahjor, he passed away from a pulmonary edema in the spring of 2017. Arezo called us and invited my research assistant and me to the commemorative ceremony to be held downtown in the ostentatious Shahr-e Naw wedding hall. One of the biggest auditoriums, which usually houses lavish weddings, had been prepared for guests and speakers ranging from laureate poets such as Haidari Wujudi to speakers from the Academy of Science (Academi Oolomi) and representatives of regional governments who had come to pay their respects. When I sat down next to Asma Mahjor in a separate area for women, Ustad Naseer Ahmad Fahramand from the Social Organization of the Green Path (Sazmane ijtemai-rawand-e sabz) was delivering condolences in the form of a speech from Amrullah Saleh, at the time the organization's head (later vice president of Afghanistan, 2020–2021). As fellow poets, local politicians and representatives of regional governments such as Mazar-e Sharif took their turns delivering praise and prayers, I contemplated the complex relationship of politics and poetry as heritage in Afghanistan.

Successive governments have been aware of the fact that poetry has a strong salience among Afghans' sense of belonging, and they have attempted to utilize this cultural value accordingly. During the Communist PDPA government (1979–1989), the Parcham faction established a poets' and writers' association within the Ministry of Culture and Information, as well as a committee within the PDPA Central Committee in an attempt to bring existing literature and traditions in line with state ideology.[104] Ethnomusicologist John Baily reports that "radio and television artists who complied with the new regime were treated well; they had good salaries, received medical care, and in some cases were allocated apartments and even motorcars."[105]

As described in previous chapters, the government also reached out to Sufi intellectuals and poets such as Ustad Haidari Wujudi. When Wujudi remembered the advances by the Communist regime, he told me that he asked to stay uninvolved with the government. He also linked this stance to his own upbringing in a poor family with no political ties (unlike the Mujaddidi family, who experienced massive losses during the early purges). This would have given him the means of contentment with the little he had and, potentially, the moral superiority of not having to work for consecutive regimes, as well as being able to keep a strategic distance. Perusing his poetry, however, shows that he responded to the Communist regime and the atrocities they committed. In a poetry collection just published in the year after the Communist takeover and just before the invasion of the Soviet Union, he criticizes the regime and praises the resistance in his native Panjshir. This year is usually called the year of choking (*khafaqan* or *ikhtenaq*) for the political oppression that Afghans experienced. Wujudi writes about the darkness of the time and the sun rising in the valleys, offering poetic support for horizons better than what he was experiencing and potentially

Figure 3.7. Haidari Wujudi receiving honors from the queen on Mother's Day, 1971. Reproduced with permission of Ghulam Naqshband, son of Haidari Wujudi.

also for the Mujahidin resistance, if the poems were interpreted in that way.

While the regime wooed Wujudi, other artists ran into trouble for their usage of Sufi poetry.[106] An interviewee in Kabul remembered an incident with the famous singer Farhad Darya. Now one of the foremost musical stars of Afghanistan, Darya had first been a member of the famous band Gorohe Baran (Rain Band) that he cofounded.[107] Another interviewee remembered that the government at the time sponsored and supported bands like this: "The government at the time supported groups like the Gorohe Baran. They wanted to distract people from politics and jihad, so they created these groups of musicians and groups of poets, artists and painters. The music group Gorohe Baran was the most successful one."[108] But their success did not prevent strife about the messages delivered through traditional poetry: "He [Farhad Darya] used a Mawlana poem, singing, 'I come back to break the shackles of the prison, I come back to break the shackles of oppression, . . . I have come to smash that demon into pieces.' Poetry has that language, but KHAD discovered the metaphoric messages of the poem. As soon as he sang that song, Dr. Najib chased Farhad Darya."[109]

The PDPA, however, was not the only regime that tried to leverage poetry to establish its legitimacy and that suppressed certain forms when it saw them in opposition. While the Communist government supported poetry on the nation-state level, its opponents, the Mujahidin, burned thousands of the books published by the Communists as fuel in their heaters and instead established their own cultural committees (*komita-e farhangi*) in which poetry also played a part as expression and propaganda.[110] Poetry became a "vehicle for political struggle," from resistance poetry to poetic expressions of the suffering in refugee camps in Pakistan, where many Afghans were stranded during the war years.[111] In a radical move against poetry, the Taliban officially closed all literary associations and cultural organizations in the 1990s, while poets and professors of literature kept them unofficially running as hidden "sewing circles."[112] Reports emerged of unofficial yet systematic burning of Persian books and manuscripts at this time.[113] However, the Taliban have become known since through their own poetry genre in Pashto, bridging "their political and ideological version of Islam and nationalism [to use it for] . . . a wider audience and as a tool for recruitment."[114]

Notwithstanding that some of these developments are in the realms of creative writing and publishing of new poetry, they also show how the place of different genres of poetry has continuously shifted within Afghan society overall, while remaining a crucial aspect of national identity and nation building. Politicians in post-2001 Afghanistan were also well aware of poetry's salience: Haidari Wujudi's rooms within the public library would host political visitors, such as Amrullah Saleh, whose colleague gave the speech at Mahjor's commemoration. Men of state such as Abdullah Abdullah, former chief executive officer of Afghanistan, a post that had been invented after the contested election between him and President Ghani, were known for giving poetry collections as gifts to their dinner guests. Sufi poetry had inscribed itself as a crucial locus of Afghanistan's heritage.

Neither literature nor education is immune to the political environment in which it is received. Quite the contrary, both are enmeshed in the very developments of a society. Weathering the different phases in which regimes tried to appropriate poetry for their own nation-state construction, the Mahjor family was portrayed by condolence speakers not only as the relatives and descendants of an influential poetry teacher but also as guardians of Bedil studies in Afghanistan.

"I am conveying condolences to all of Afghanistan's national family and to the ones who have the knowledge of mysticism [*farekhtegane farhang-o irfan*], and to the companions and friends of Ustad Mahjoor [*yaran-o dostaran-e Ustad Mahjoor*], from the Bedil gathering in Iran," Abed Sayidi Kiafzali, director of the International Bedil Foundation in Tehran, told the gathering at Ustad Mahjor's funeral through a written message. "Mahjor was the one who kept the heritage [*miras*] of Bedil in the correct way to pass it onto us. When I give my condolences to Ustad Arezu, Ustad Hasib Mowahed and to their families, who are the son and grandson of Qandi Agha, who preserved Bedil's way, we say that we want you to preserve it in the way that your father and grandfather did." [115]

But what does preserving mean when that which is to be preserved is inherited and disseminated as a way of teaching and learning? And how is it decided who inherits the authority to teach in the future? Sitting next to Asma Mahjor, who was busily coordinating the event on her phone from behind the screen where the women sat, and watching both her brother and uncle officially chair the event, I had only a faint inkling of the strife brewing in the Sufi poetry sphere. But while I was unsuspecting, others were well aware that when there is something to inherit, there is usually conflict on the horizon. We now turn to the ways in which the intersecting realms of Sufi poetry as Islamic education and cultural heritage also create competing positions to claim authority within Sufi communities. By tracing competing claims to Sufi authority through divergent actions of descendants attempting to establish leadership, it becomes clear that these varying bases of authority have created space for both a greater variety of contestants and more room for strife.

Heritage Inherited

Over the next two years, a pattern of invitations and counter-invitations emerged. For every death anniversary and commemoration of either Bedil, Qandi Agha or Ustad Mahjor, I received two calls: one from Ustad Mahjor's younger brother, Abdullah Mowafaq, and one from Mahjor's daughter and son, Asma Mahjor and Abdul Qadir Arezo.

Mowafaq had been Qandi Agha's cook and servant, an important position in the Sufi social hierarchy because students' acts of servitude show their humility and unconditional love. In traditional Sufi orders, acts of service "broke down the novice's sense of identity and 'polished' away impurities of personality."[116] He took over the *halqa* meetings when Ustad Mahjor moved to Pakistan during the first Taliban time (ca. 1998/1999). Mowafaq was an established Sufi poetry teacher who had authored a book about Bedil's poetry and philosophy, and it seemed that he had been biding his time to fully take over the mantle of teaching and guidance from his brother after his passing. But he had not calculated his niece's interest in Bedil's heritage.

Asma Mahjor was an unexpected contender for Sufi authority. With her kind demeanor and casual outfits of pants and shirts, her main focus seemed to be the editing of her father's oeuvre and the publishing of books. An aspiring poet herself, who initially wrote in free style (*nima*), she told me that her father had educated her about rhyme structures and metric impact, about poetic traditions and how a spiritual message can be cultivated through its poetic enunciation to grow inside a reader's mind. While Mowafaq continued to lead the traditional Bedil *halqa* that he had inherited from Ustad Mahjor and Qandi Agha, Asma started to teach interested students online through Skype, give television interviews and invite people to celebrations and commemorations in parallel to her uncle.

It had already been a year of competing social events, and I was wondering whether their competition was going unnoticed by participants or would just become the new norm. But then Haidari Wujudi took the stage at the first death anniversary celebration of Ustad Mahjor. It was a sunny mid-July morning that was quickly turning into a scorching hot afternoon. A group of about eighty men had gathered in the enclosed courtyard of the late teacher's house, sitting on red carpets and *toshaks* that had been laid out under a billowing textile canopy erected for the occasion. Most women were seated inside the house and watched the event from behind a curtain through a window. Asma had asked me to join the male-dominated space to videotape and photograph her speech from there. After an initial Qur'an recitation, the stage was opened for different speakers to talk about and honor the work and legacy of Ustad Mahjor.

Figure 3.8. Ustad Haidari Wujudi speaks at *urs*.

A sudden calm descended on the crowd when Ustad Haidari Wujudi took the stage. The white-haired, bespectacled teacher, who has been recognized as a national treasure, the "Star of the Wise Sufis" (Najm ul Orafa / نجم العرفا), had known the deceased Mahjor, whose life and legacy this *urs* was honoring, as well as Mahjor's father and teacher, Qandi Agha. Wujudi launched into a historical discussion about the deceased Ustad Mahjor and his father and teacher Qandi Agha, emphasizing the space the latter created for differing opinions:

> Qandi Agha worked hard to let the students fly in the mystic environment. Ustad Mahjor sometimes contradicted Qandi Agha's interpretation, and he used to say that he was not convinced by the interpretation that Qandi Agha had offered. So when Mahjor criticized the poems and interpretations, Qandi Agha never stopped him from criticizing. As a father and teacher, he never wanted him to be annoyed; that's why he let him be free to criticize. It is also because he wanted to create an environment in which everyone can express their ideas and opinions freely.[117]

Initially I thought that Wujudi's speech would culminate in a regular praise of the teaching environment of Qandi Agha and Mahjor's school of Bedil. Then, unexpectedly, he turned to the current generation of Bedil experts, pointing out their indebtedness to their father and teacher:

> Arezo, Mowafaq and his other brother Aziz were actually introduced by Mahjor to this Bedil school and that they are still continuing in this path is because of the introduction made by Mahjor for them.

He then delivered his final punch in the form of a prayer (*du'a*) before leaving the stage:

> Supplications for the people who died before me, for Qandi Agha and Mahjor, and the ones who are in the circle, for his family, his children, so that they can continue steadfast on this way, and don't make any disagreement, to be away from pride, selfishness and disagreement and be well in their life.

The prayer might have seemed benign and even benevolent if seen in isolation. After all, who would not appreciate well wishes for unity and a prosperous future? However, for the ones who were in the know in the audience, it was a sniping remark through its wording, its silences and its allusions. Afghanistan is known for its extreme hospitality, kindness and formal politeness, expressed in lengthy greeting formulas, elaborate rituals for hosting and protecting guests and secretly racing to pay the bill for each other in a restaurant. However, even extreme politeness can sometimes not conceal criticism when it needs to be voiced—indirectly, through stories or even packaged in supplications.[118] After all, how better to chide someone than through prayer that they might behave better in the future?

Haidari Wujudi would later tell me when I asked him about this moment that he thought that Bedil circles were "a good tradition that needs to be kept, but they seem to be in competition among themselves, and I always advised them not to make these materials and circles a matter of rivalry or competition." Ultimately, he judged that "scholars like Bedil deserve better than that."

Whether the chiding remark was met with general approval or support for one side or the other was difficult to tell, as the audience retained its equanimity. On the face of it, Mahjor's younger brother Mowafaq might have been the more obvious choice for leadership of the school of Bedil studies in the Afghan context: he was the younger son of Qandi Agha and therefore within the genealogical line. He was the elder of the contenders, with age playing a reinforcing factor in authoritative judgments in Afghanistan. He was male, which played an important role in this hereditary system, and he had been teaching the Bedil circle for many years since the Taliban government at the end of the 1990s, a feat that would have been difficult to achieve for a female authority like Asma. This seemed all rather clear-cut in terms of inheriting the authority to teach Bedil in the future.

But then I saw the books, stacked in the corner of the *urs* celebration, ready to be distributed to the attendees. Asma had made an astute move in the game of chess that succession can sometimes be. In the year following her father's death, she started to edit, clarify and self-publish his writings while also raising funds from his former students in Afghanistan and abroad to bring out these volumes. Self-publishing still has a connotation in Western societies and in academic circles that the author has not been able to persuade an agent or a publisher to take on the book. However, the implications in Afghanistan were completely different: lacking a strong publishing scene, most books were imported from Europe or the United States and sold to the few international foreigners and wealthy Afghans who could afford the hefty price tag. Most literate Afghans would not buy these books, although they might buy pirated reprints sold for a fraction of the price. The market in which Afghans bought books was saturated with those printed in Iran and Pakistan. The few local Afghan publishers formed the Association of Publishers, established in 2010 (with a total of 250 printing presses in Afghanistan in 2014).[119] But Afghan authors remained, if they did not seek publishers abroad, mainly self-published, not because their books had been rejected by an agent or publishing house but because the infrastructure of large-scale publishing and recognized publishing houses did not exist.

Self-publishing, therefore, carried other connotations. To be able to publish a book meant that authors needed to raise the money themselves. Most authors were not independently wealthy and did not have the funding necessary to publish their writing. This meant that they needed to find other Afghans in their wider community, or Afghans abroad in Europe,

Australia or the United States, who were wealthy enough to sponsor printing these books. Those patrons needed to have the necessary finances to donate to the book publishing venture and to buy into the vision of the particular book they were backing or, at the very least, the author who had produced it. When authors succeeded in raising the money, their audience knew that they had not only succeeded in getting the book printed but that others believed that the content of the book was worthy of publication. This seal of approval, or legitimacy, was manifested in the form of the book itself.

At the *urs* of Mahjor, when the books appeared—stacked in piles at the corner of the carpets that were laid out for the audience—they were the visible manifestation of Asma's ability to mobilize the financial and cultural capital necessary to bring them into existence. Even before anyone had read their contents, they could be used as proof that someone had believed in her vision and in the distribution of this project.

However, there was more to the books than their material manifestation, which demonstrated Asma's clever use of books as a medium for subtly affirming her spiritual authority. While she edited, set and prefaced the volumes of writing, she published the books in her father's name. She was also always clear to ascertain that she saw it as a collaborative effort, as she explained to me one afternoon when we had tea together: "Four people are working on collecting notes and publishing of my father's book: Arezo, Tayeb Shikeb, Mir Mahmood Baktash and myself. We do not add anything; it's pure. We collect whatever my father wrote in his notebook, in its original. The only thing we add from our side is Ustad's detailed introduction. We do not have the right to add anything else to his book, and we do not repeat things from one book to the next one." She presented her own position as service to her father's work, insight and legacy, in which her brother helped in the promotion and the others helped with typesetting and layout.

While Ustad Mahjor's popularity and support gave his daughter the "name, fame, and visibility ... to enter the games of succession,"[120] publishing his writing demonstrated her understanding of her father's thought and insight. Even if his name was on the book, it was clear to everyone in the broader Sufi community that she was the editor. By publishing her father's work instead of her own, she positioned herself positively in several ways: First, she showed her own knowledge (*ilm*) through her ability to edit her

Figure 3.9. Ustad Asma Mahjor with images of her father and his oeuvre.

father's writing, therefore also setting herself up for future teaching opportunities about his insights and knowledge of Bedil. Second, through service to her father and his legacy of teaching, she inserted herself into the genealogy of teaching and learning, despite her being a woman, through an act of service, which holds significant currency within Sufi communities. Charles Lindholm argues that "the emphasis of unconditional love distinguishes the murid from the scholarly talib, who was obliged to obey, but not to adore, his teacher."[21] Acts of service are a spiritual exercise for a Sufi student as much as for a true Sufi teacher, because servitude in its basic sense is usually understood as being a servant of God. However, in an extended sense, we can also see the same attitude in the teachings of Sufi associations in which the students serve their teacher and start with menial tasks such as making tea, or cleaning, and rise in rank during their training under a certain Sufi *murshid*. Publishing her father's work positioned Asma in this generally understood sense of service for a greater cause that was also religiously inspired.

While poetry has the chameleonesque ability to morph into being "mainly literary," a "social commentary," a "theological argument" (or all in one), depending on interpretation, situation and level of insight in decoding it, it also offers the opportunity as a literary publishing venture to be a setting well-suited for a female teacher to claim exploratory authority in the realm of decoding the Divine from between lines of poetry without having to "say" outright that she claims religious authority. The one initiated into the different registers of Sufi insight will understand her allusions and level of insight. Asma furthermore showed resourcefulness in thinking through possible solutions to her teaching problem. While from a conservative rationale in which men teach men and women teach women, it seemed unthinkable that she would teach an all-male group, she started teaching students inside and outside Afghanistan through online Skype sessions. While certainly an important aspect within the navigation of authority, the gendered aspect of claiming authority is further explored in the next chapter.

The online sphere had become an extra layer of interaction with other students and experts on Bedil. Mowafaq and Asma were both curating Facebook pages about Bedil and Mahjor's teaching legacy, on which they posted Bedil poetry and photos of Mahjor as well as meetings with other Afghan intellectuals. However, both used the online sphere differently. Mowafaq focused on posting poetry of Bedil and photos of his meetings with other literati and students, showing them in circles in which they debated, which transposed the *halqas* that he was leading onto the virtual sphere. Asma did not post photos of herself, an online adaptation of maintaining respectability, mirroring the fact that many Afghan women decide not to post photos of themselves online. The focus of her social media posts was instead on the books she was editing or on contemplative images such as candles and texts paired with poetry and explanations along with photos of her father. Her virtual presentation showed herself in line with the way she presented herself in the offline sphere at events, projecting social respectability.

While Sufi poetry was seen as vanishing from the formal madrasa educational curriculum, Asma's plan was to extend the reach of Bedil teaching through publishing, online discussions and the development of a cultural organization that she intended to establish in which she would market not only her own writing but also that of other Bedil experts who could publish through the institutional base of the foundation. Unlike authority that is mainly based on teaching a group of (in Afghanistan, often all-male) Sufi followers in the experiential realms of the content connected to one's spiritual path, which often excludes female authorities as possible teachers, Asma had shifted the focus to an institutional setting in which she could find a place as a woman in a group of leaders and where the main focus would be on publishing as well as celebrations like the *urs*. This change in focus was enabled through the position of Sufi poetry as intangible cultural heritage, which her family nurtured over the course of the last century.

Recognizing Poetic Sufi Authority

I wondered how other members of the Bedil expert community felt about this contestation of authority and leadership, from the dual celebration of the death anniversaries to competing online presence. As to be expected, attendants at Mowafaq's teaching circle considered him to be the rightful teacher, granting him the erstwhile authority over Bedil poetry and spiritual insight, which he could lead as a result of his own immersion and learning in these subtle internal states.

Other participants at the *urs* celebrations found the contestation to be a disgrace that should end, although they did not position themselves in favor of one or the other as a leader. The comparatively small size of this literary elite that focuses on teaching Sufism through Bedil poetry also meant that disagreements and friction were hard to conceal. However, most followers did not want to talk directly about the conflict. I wondered whether the fact that Asma was a woman would rule her out generically as a potential teacher-leader in most people's view. However, when I asked this question to Rahimi Ghafari, a Qawwali musician, who also attended the *urs* celebration and had known the family for decades, he just laughed and responded with an analogy: "If a lion is coming, you don't ask whether it's female or male; you are afraid,"[122] insinuating that Asma's gender made no difference and that her level of learnedness, insight and knowledge marked her out as the rightful leader of the school of Bedil studies. These discourses on the nongendered dimension of spiritual authority are also reflected in other accounts such as Faizani's approach explored in the following chapter. However, while these ideals of spiritual equality persist in the discursive realm, the actual experience is often one of unequal access to teaching opportunities and leadership of groups. Societal prejudices necessitated other navigational prowess from contenders for leadership, such as Asma showcased in her publishing and online ventures, in which she positioned herself.

However, while both claimed leadership of Bedil studies, their ultimate focus differed somewhat. With his focus on teaching the *halqa* and offering one-on-one instruction in Bedil's insight, Ustad Mowafaq was establishing himself in the same way as Wujudi had done—through invocation of Sufi poetry as part of Islamic education and through Sufi poetic authority as resting on the exploratory nature of guiding students to insights about the Divine encoded within the verses. While Asma's goal might have been the same, her main entry point for claiming authority was the understanding of Sufi poetry as a cultural intangible heritage, which needed guidance, care taking, publishing and dissemination, a position that she intended to take on through developing organizational structures. The diversification of the bases of Sufi authority offered varying entry points for the contenders to assert themselves at this crucial moment of transition.

One of the unsettling aspects in recounting these experiences is that they fail to lead to a neat and tidy conclusion that would delineate an outcome to this contestation. When I left the field—and to this day of analyzing, writing and contemplating their lives and my interactions with them—both potential leaders were still putting on rival celebrations, visiting each other as family, with the overlying tension of what would become of Bedil studies after Mahjor's death, the liminal space of a succession in suspension still unresolved. All of the possibilities were still on the table: that Asma asserts herself as a foremost authority, supported by her brother; that her uncle Mowafaq keeps the tradition himself and that Asma is sidelined; or that both find a place with differing spheres of influence. There is also the possibility that someone else from the general community will appear who is not part of the hereditary line but who proves knowledgeable. Some aspects that already played a part in this chapter, such as the varying bases for spiritual authority and the differential impact of gender in regard to claiming positions of leadership and authority, are explored further in the next chapters, which deal with dreams as a basis for Sufi authority and with the ways in which women have become Sufi teachers in an official Sufi order. While they have already claimed their position, the case represented in this chapter remains unresolved.

FOUR

Gendered Navigation

Equality in Difference

"Both men and women have spiritual needs," Ustad Shukria instructed me, sorting through her book of notes and *zikr* formulas. "Women have to work just like men do; there's no difference." A middle-aged mother of three, Ustad Shukria was holding her weekly *zikr* sessions in the living room of her house in Herat. *Zikr* is one of the practices through which Sufis seek closeness to God or even spiritual unity with the Divine through a process described as the cleansing of the heart (*qalb*). It is a meditative technique in which verses from the Qur'an, the names of God or the *shahada* (Muslim profession of faith) are recited or chanted repeatedly. When Ustad Shukria suggested there is gender equality on the spiritual path, she was referring to the women seated at the other end of the room, around the edges of a large, rectangular white bedsheet that demarcated the space for the collective *zikr* sessions on the carpeted floor. But she was also referring to herself and her role in leading the roughly thirty women who assembled every Friday morning in her circle. Along with her daughters, Ustad Shukria led the practice, based on the writings of her order's founder, Ustad Allama Faizani (1924–ca. 1978).

As I recorded their sessions, I began to wonder how other Sufis and Afghan society at large viewed female leadership as a *sar-e halqa* (lit., "head of the [*zikr*] circle") and how such leaders legitimized and navigated participation in Islamic Sufi practices against a backdrop of an otherwise predominantly male Sufi sociosphere. Women like Ustad Shukria have received little, if any, attention in scholarship on contemporary Afghanistan, in large part due to the perceived and actual limitations placed on their public and institutional engagement. The Faizani community was, at the time of my research, one of the only Sufi orders in Afghanistan that I encountered in which women were not only allowed to participate in the *zikr* and tread the Sufi path but also encouraged to lead *zikr*, recite the Qur'an and teach Sufi insights to other women. The founder, Allama Faizani, actively supported this involvement, as did the teaching and work of the current *pir*, Ustad Mazhabi Billah (b. 1964). His wife and daughters also encouraged other women to take on teaching and leading *zikr* circles, teaching them both in person and through weekly online lessons by the wife of the *pir* from the United States. The Sufi order (*tariqa*), which was active in Europe, the United States and Afghanistan, had regional chapters in Mazar-e Sharif, Herat and Jalalabad led by both male and female teachers. Classes on spiritual learning and *zikr* were gender segregated in Afghanistan but gender mixed in the diaspora.

In this chapter I follow my interlocutors on the path to a more nuanced understanding of female Islamic leadership, revealing how individual women, in conjunction with their communities, navigated restrictive norms to create space for women as religious actors and leaders. Contemporary community practices, structural male allyship and the community's use of a nongendered discourse affected the inclusion of women in an area that was usually exclusively male in Afghanistan. I begin by addressing the uneasy location of women as religious actors within broader debates about gender in academic and popular studies of Afghanistan. I then investigate the teaching and lives of the Faizani Sufi community and their inclusion of women within formal, institutional Islamic settings. The example of the Faizani Sufi community shows how the establishment of religious authority is linked to demonstrating mastery over certain techniques that direct the internal activation and development of the nongendered psychophysiological body. More than mere kinship connection to the *pir*'s family, it is the legitimacy and authority that these women contextually and relationally develop that translates into an overall position of respect within the wider community and their cultural organization.

Women as Religious Actors and Leaders in Afghanistan

The paucity of writing on women as actors and leaders in the religious field is closely connected to debates on the general representation of Afghan women. The intense politicization of the "women's question" in Afghanistan draws on a long genealogy of state interventions (both Afghan and foreign) throughout the twentieth century.[1] In 2001, the rhetoric of the "liberation" of "oppressed Afghan women" was used in what anthropologist Julie Billaud calls the "moral grammar mobilized to rally popular support for the military invasion of the country."[2] Liberation rhetoric undergirded the military intervention itself and found myriad new expressions in a rights discourse that fused universal human rights, Western-style modernity and a "women's empowerment" rhetoric of the reconstruction agenda and development interventions throughout the first two decades of the twenty-first century.[3] Underpinning development rhetoric and its translation into practice presumes "Islamic" and "traditional" practices limit women's subjective agency.[4] Women are represented as a rather homogeneous group with similar aspirations facing comparable challenges, a calculation in which Islam is treated as a simple tool that is mobilized to either constrain or legitimize their actions.[5] Women are rarely considered Muslim actors who contribute to shaping or formulating Islamic practices and discourses.[6]

Intended as a challenge to the rhetoric of "oppressed Afghan women," what I call "the trap of singular success" has been haunting media representations of Afghanistan.[7] Addressing the complex realities in which women struggle and succeed, as well as fail, in the structures in which they find themselves, the English-speaking print media reports periodically on Afghan women "firsts": the first female mayor, one of the first female pilots, first female orchestra, first female mountain climbers, first female ministers or first recycling plant owners.[8] While these stories try to "write against" the trope of the powerless Afghan woman, they also affirm the status quo as the norm against the backdrop of the exception.[9] These scholarly and popular approaches first and foremost complicate how to address and represent cases of female leadership in an environment in which Afghan women are either categorized as the oppressed Other, lacking any agency, or the singular success story, possessing a heroic form of agency.[10]

The discussion of agency has a long genealogy in scholarship on Muslim women, starting in the late 1960s with feminist anthropological scholarship.[11] Scholars have remarked how European colonizers, local elites and policy makers have used the status of women as a measuring device for the level of progressiveness and modernity of a society.[12] In a prescient critique of reigning theoretical conceptions of agency, Saba Mahmood posited that devout Muslim women's worldviews were left unaccounted for by feminist conceptions of agency that recognized it only as resistance. Mahmood argues that for the women in the mosque movement in Egypt, which she researched, the ultimate goal of agency was not "freedom" but "piety."[13] An act that seems to be submission can be part of the person's agency to master a talent, for example, piano playing, which initially requires subordination under a teacher.[14] The goal or telos might be different from what certain Western feminists would strive toward, but it is nevertheless a choice and an end toward which these women aspire. As Mahmood argues, a subject constitutes itself within the historical, cultural and societal boundaries, and a researcher needs to consider their desires, goals and self-understanding with their motivation to act. Mahmood's perspective is helpful in shifting the focus away from the binary of freedom and oppression, bringing into view other modes of sociality and goals toward which people strive.[15] Since her intervention, researchers have widened the body of work onto the manifold areas of Muslim women's lives, investigating Muslim women's involvement in youth culture, arts, sports and many domains of ordinary life.[16]

In research on women in Afghanistan several studies attempt to capture the manifold facets of Afghan women's lives by locating them within their social networks and gender-bending practices and in conjunction with oral histories that have offered counternarratives.[17] However, I contend that while these narrative framings attempt to craft a vision of women as individuals with complex agency, scholars have still not examined women as religious actors and leaders in Afghanistan. In most writing on women in Afghanistan, Islam and Islamic cultural traditions are perceived as a backdrop to the lives of the actors—sometimes unobtrusive, at other times patriarchally oppressive—rather than an active dimension of social life that women could also creatively engage with or lead.[18] I argue that the portrayal of Islamic injunctions and a religiously sanctioned patriarchal system that women either need to endure or fight against encapsulates two aspects of erasure: it narrows Islam to a definition of orthodoxy or tradition that excludes different variants, and it silences women as religious actors in their own right.[19]

To be sure, scholars have examined particular aspects of female religious practice in Afghanistan. Mid-twentieth-century anthropological literature explored women as visitors to shrines and as targets of possession by jinns but also as female shamans performing cures, divination, exorcisms and obstetrics.[20] Accounts by Ingeborg Baldauf as well as an article by Micheline Centlivres, Pierre Centlivres and Mark Slobin described women as leaders of all-female ceremonies that combine shamanic seances and Islamic elements of *zikr* in Turkmen, Arab and Uzbek communities in Afghanistan's north.[21] And as Razia Sultanova has suggested, such ceremonies continued in the mid-2000s, albeit with a stronger emphasis on Islamic precepts.[22] The women who were involved in these accounts saw their own healing practices as embedded within an Islamic framework. Yet none claimed to belong to an organized religious institution such as a Sufi order or mosque group. This apparent lack of affiliation raises questions about whether the religious involvement of women in Afghanistan is entirely informal or situated within the domestic sphere, particularly because some accounts have pointed to the practice of secrecy and to public and male disapproval of women's religious gatherings.[23]

By contrast, the women in the Qadiriyyah Sufi order of the Faizani belong to an official institutional order and are supported by their male counterparts as students and teachers of Sufi knowledge. One might be tempted to single out the women of this community as a post-2001 success story highlighting women breaking into a formalized religious sphere. But this runs counter to the group's own narrative of its origin and development.

The few anthropological accounts of twenty-first-century Afghanistan that do address female religious authority take place at the margins.[24] For example, in tracing the development of a pilgrimage place (*ziyarat*) of a young woman killed in the 1990s, Baldauf sketches the relational establishment and contestation of authority of a deceased female saint, Bibi Nushin, whose authority and saintly power are ascribed to her by the pilgrims to her shrine.[25] Another recent, ethnographically rich account by Sonia Ahsan-Tirmizi portrays the countermorality of a group of women who lived in a safe house (*khana-yi aman*) in Kabul. While Ahsan-Tirmizi argues that these women formed their position of oppositional piety at the margins of society, they could not, by virtue of their position as being seen as promiscuous, serve as role models for the outside.[26]

Building on this newly strengthening line of inquiry into the social navigation of the religious sphere by female actors, I focus on women in institutional arrangements such as mosques and Sufi orders, where women are not situated at the margins but are claiming participation in mainstream Islamic groups.[27]

From Absence to Presence: Women within Institutional Sufism

Notwithstanding the sizable number of historic female Sufis, female Sufi leadership is still a rarity.[28] In the past, women have been acknowledged as *sheikhas* or *pirs* even if they had not been formally appointed. Jürgen Frembgen reports that *khanaqahs* were initially places exclusively for men but that by the twelfth and thirteenth centuries Sufi lodges headed by a female *sheikha* existed in Cairo, Aleppo, Baghdad and Mecca, and up to the beginning of the twentieth century in Kashgar and Yangi Hissar in eastern Turkestan. The North African 'Aisawa and Haddawa as well as the Iranian Ni'matullahiyya initiated women, according to Frembgen's account.[29] Though it is unusual for women to lead men, it has occasionally happened: al-Sanusi's aunt was a teacher, and the Rahmaniyya in Algeria were led in the late nineteenth century by a woman, Zaynab al-Rashidiyya (1880–1904).[30] Kelly Pemberton argues that female Sufi leadership is more likely to occur in "associational" configurations outside institutionalized settings where "women who are considered saintly or spiritually powerful operate as de facto pirs."[31]

While the regional literature showcases some contemporary examples of female *pirs* and *sheikhas*, initially I did not encounter female participants in institutional, formal Sufi settings in my field research in Afghanistan.[32]

Based on her interviews among the Afghan diaspora in the 1990s, Almut Wieland-Karimi argued that women cannot be formally initiated into a Sufi order in Afghanistan. Their only way into a Sufi order would be informal connections through fathers and brothers, but they would not be able to participate as *murids* of a *pir*.[33] Indeed, the prevalence of women in informal settings such as shrines seemed to confirm the impression that female religious practice in Afghanistan was characteristically embedded in shrine visitation and in the sphere of the household. Interviews with women visiting *ziyarats* in Kabul, Herat and Kandahar and discussions with female members of the Mujaddidi and Gailani political Sufi families seemed to indicate that their religious practices were also largely carried out among family and in the home sphere, not extending beyond the immediate family members in attendance. While I did not meet women at other *khanaqahs*, I attended other *zikr* gatherings at shrines that also had women in attendance (for example, at the early-morning *zikr* at the Pul-e Khishti shrine or the Tamim Ansar shrine, both in Kabul). However, in those settings women were seated in a different room from where they listened, sometimes mediated through a recording system, to the men's *zikr*. The women had no guidance on *zikr* and no classes in either setting, and they were largely observing and listening rather than actively participating.

I had often asked the men in charge at other *khanaqahs* whether there could be women in their circles.[34] They would often emphatically say that women were welcome and that women sometimes joined. They explained that women, when they attended, would stay in a separate room adjacent to the location where the *zikr* or teaching took place so they could listen and partake from there. However, when I asked to talk with these women or to meet them once they joined, I encountered a complete void. No women came to the sessions I attended, and in my visits, I remained alone among men.

This changed when I met the Faizani community, which is a Qadiriyyah Sufi order named after its founder, Allama Faizani. Faizani lived from 1924 until 1978, when he vanished and was most likely killed in the infamous Pul-e Charkhi prison in Kabul when the Communist regime took control in Afghanistan.[35] In her comprehensive overview on Islam and politics in Afghanistan, Asta Olesen describes the founding *pir* Allama Faizani as "an unorthodox *a'lim* and *pir* in the sense that he started a Sufi order without connection to any established *tariqat* and without himself having been under any guidance of a *pir*."[36] However, the current *pir* of the community, Ustad Mazhabi, the son of Allama Faizani, disputes this characterization, asserting that Allama Faizani took the *bay'a* (pledge) from Naqib Sahib of the Qadiriyyah order. According to Ustad Mazhabi, apart from this primary affiliation, Faizani was also initiated into the ways of other major *tariqas* (Naqshbandiyyah, Chishtiyyah and Suhrawardiyyah) with knowledge of their teaching and rituals.

The Herat-born teacher Allama Faizani initially established a *khanaqah* near Pul-i Khumri in northern Baghlan and later moved to Kabul, where in 1970 he opened a library near the Pul-i Khishti mosque in the old part of the city. The teaching and *zikr* circles that he hosted attracted a large following, "particularly among teachers, students, and mid-level military officers and government officials."[37] He taught individual lessons on *tafsir* (religious exegesis) and Sufism as well as a regular Thursday-evening class on the *Masnawi*. Allama Faizani's political activities led to the establishment of a political movement called Hizb-e Tawheed (the Party of [Divine] Unity), with which he built alliances with other Islamic associations.

Historical writings tend to lump Faizani together with other religiously minded reform critics who denounced the Communist PDPA and the government for promoting public unveiling, social reforms and women's education.[38] Perhaps because it is found in the community-internal oral history, a lesser known aspect of Allama Faizani's life is the space that he created in his teaching and in his practical demeanor to include women on the Sufi path. According to Momena Billah (b. 1990), granddaughter of the *pir*, "Allama Faizani supported and encouraged women to be in *zikr* circles and to be very active. But not only that. One example that I might give to you is his wife, who is my grandma ... she used to lead the women."[39]

Momena Billah explained that Allama Faizani taught his wife to read and write, after which she began to give literacy classes to other women, whom she also led in *zikr* circles. Two *murids* who attended the *ustad*'s teaching circle in the 1970s recounted that Allama Faizani back then "taught women, children, everybody." While one *murid* remembered that "there was a curtain between men and women or sometimes there would be a special place or room for women," the other one recalled that "there was a microphone for the women. If they had a question they would ask through loudspeaker and also heard their answers. He taught families this way."[40]

The current *pir* of the Faizani community, Mutasim Billah Mazhabi (b. 1964), the eldest son of Allama Faizani who was approved for leadership by the community in 1986, also confirmed that the community's inclusion of women was rooted in his father's vision.[41] However, when he took over after his father vanished in prison, Ustad Mazhabi realized that his father's inclusive conduct was exceptional and could lead to discrediting his community:

> This open mind about women I learned at home with my father. . . . I even prayed behind my mother and mother-in-law and other women [as a child], and that of course had an effect on me. For us this was not something strange. With that mind-set, when I came to Peshawar, I did the same thing [include women as active members of the community]. . . . Ah! A lot of fatwas came up against me! *Kafir!* And this and that! First I thought, oh, did I make a mistake? This is normal in our house! People pray like this, and they are doing *zikr*. . . . For me, this was not a particular service—I grew up like that! My father said: "Why are we putting so many *burqas* on women? It is because our heart is diseased! We are pushing the women to put on the *burqa*, but God also told the men to put their eyes down."[42]

The experiences that Ustad Mazhabi recounts from growing up within the Faizani community are significant as they exemplify the equality of women within Islamic practice in this Sufi community. They served as a guide for their children while also revealing conflict with an increasingly conservative environment in the Pakistani refugee camps under the Mujahidin. While the Taliban are often singled out for strengthening prescriptive rules and Islamically justified restrictions, the Mujahidin also outlawed music in parts of Afghanistan, and veiling intensified within the camps, which tallies with the Faizani community's experiences of tensions over their practices.[43]

In this context, Allama Faizani's approach to Islam must have seemed more exceptional than before. Within the Faizani community Allama Faizani was a "moral exemplar." Feyza Burak-Adli makes the fitting connection between the ways in which exemplars not only represent virtues or norms but also engage their followers in particular ways to work on their own ethical dispositions. She argues that in the Rifai Sufi tradition in Turkey *pirs* become moral exemplars for their ethical responses to daily life decisions.[44] Similarly, James Laidlaw argues that "an important dimension of how people grasp and understand moral values is through their engagement with exemplars."[45] Allama Faizani manifested and exemplified through his conduct and teaching particular values that are still held within the current community as aspirational objectives for their own ethical and spiritual development. Stories and memories of Allama Faizani were shared concerning his conduct with other scholars, encounters with prison inmates with whom he shared a cell and his conduct with male and female *murids*. Community members referred to their founding *pir* as the point of origin, as well as the guiding principle for their own current practices. While Faizani might have been an exceptional individual during his time, the salient point is that his attitude and conduct inspired an ethos among a whole community of devotees, initiating long-term and more broad-based change.

While prominent Sufi luminaries of the past have often become exemplary models to emulate because of their kind disposition, spiritual insight, closeness to God or selfless outlook, Allama Faizani became a moral exemplar in his community for the way he approached technological and political modernity as well as diversity, which includes women. He operated in the polarized political environment of the 1970s, when Afghanistan began to see the effects of the economic and educational reforms initiated under Prime Minister Daoud in the late 1950s and 1960s, which led to the expansion of education and higher levels of university enrollment of both men and women.[46] These young, educated Afghans became politicized in the urban environment at institutions of higher education.[47] Faizani reacted against the strengthening Marxist and Communist forces at the time and the Islamist rhetoric that opposed the Left by outlining a third approach. His middle way incorporated both an openness to technology and science, which responded to the development-focused Communist rhetoric of his time, and an Islamic path, albeit with a Sufi interpretation, thus challenging the Islamist rhetoric. This third way also included women within his inclusive vision of a Sufi community.

That spirit, current Faizani disciples told me, continued in the present in the organizational structures the order has developed. They continued with the traditional *zikr* meetings while operating a separate Cultural Center in which introductory courses on Faizani's Sufi thought were offered alongside classes in computer literacy and English. The disciples told me that the establishment of the Cultural Center, which matched formats for associations and organizations prevalent in the post-invasion NGO-saturated environment, was rooted in their founding *pir*'s approach pioneered in the 1970s and followed the same adaptive strategies. It was not, they emphasized, a contemporary innovation, rejecting the idea that their broad-based societal engagement and involvement of women was part of the post-2001 NGO-driven discourses on women in Afghanistan. Instead, in their view, women's leadership and gender equity were inherent within the Sufi interpretation of Islamic precepts and duties, as advanced by Allama Faizani.

The community described Allama Faizani as ahead of his time, a visionary, even a modernizer, a core characteristic that influenced its own contemporary Sufi practice and outlook. His openness to science and technology—seeing it often as a metaphor for the intricate workings of the Divine—translates into their contemporary classes that involved biology and technology.[48] This integrative outlook on Sufism attracted a wide variety of followers, both Sunni and Shi'a, Pashto and Dari native speakers, men and women, and at the time of his teaching both pro-government as well as opposition.

From Inside Out: The Anatomy of Sufi (Non)gendering

According to his followers, Faizani's outlook on women was based on his view of the insignificance of gender as a factor within the spiritual journey. A young male Faizani *murid* in his twenties, whom I met in the Kabul office of the *tariqa*, explained to me:

> Mawlana Faizani's way of thinking about women is totally different from other ways all over the world. As I told you from the start, it's about the human, not about Muslim or non-Muslim; it's about the human soul, me, myself as a human, just as we are. He said that finding God is part of being human, not man, because you [addressing me as a woman] have the thing

that can get you to God, I also have the thing that can get me to God. He said that three things are necessary to take you to God. One is the *ruh*, the soul. I have it; you also have it. Next is *aql*, wisdom; I have it and you also have it. And the other thing is *qalb*, the heart; I have it and you also have it. So if we both have it, you can do that, we can do that and the person who is a street sweeper can also do that. Or the person who is addicted to smoking, he can do it; he also has it. Everyone in the world can do it. This is the way of thinking. There is no woman, there is no man in his way. It's only human.[49]

Students and teachers in the Faizani community argued that divine connection transcends gender, as well as other social categories, and should be understood as a nongendered human endeavor. This approach was grounded within Qur'anic example, which depicts women as spiritually equal to men. However, medieval Islamic as well as philosophical and Sufi writing often equate women with the lower soul (*nafs*) and describe them as lacking in reason (*aql*), interpretations that have served to cement the common notions of women as spiritually inferior.[50] Despite this departure, neither the women who taught and studied in the community nor the male *murids* spoke in terms of a radical break from norms; they simply stated that striving for a relationship with the Divine, being a Muslim and student of Sufism was the right of every person.

Declaring the exception as the norm is a strategy also observed by Joseph Hill in his work on female Senegalese Sufi leaders. When asked whether anyone had ever opposed the female *sheikha* in performing an otherwise typically masculine role of the spiritual guide, the female Senegalese leader responded, "Like childbirth, the perilous process of Sufi initiation requires a guide who is naturally inclined to nurture and care for new initiates, as they are most often young people in particular need of guidance."[51] However, in contrast to Hill's example, where women declare their womanhood and motherhood to be a distinguishing feature as female *sheikhas*, students and teachers in the Faizani community argued that spirituality transcended gender and should be understood as a nongendered human endeavor. Their own discourse of gender equality in the spiritual realm, indeed, of the unimportance of gender as a category on the spiritual path, justifies women participating in and leading *zikr*, Qur'anic recitation and Islamic learning. Mirroring insights that originated in Ibn Arabi's thought,[52] the *pir*'s daughter Momena Billah described a quintessential Sufi worldview of embodiment: "There is the big universe, and we as human beings are like the small universe. This relationship with God, it's never ending because we are in it in ourselves and [through] our heart. We have so many facets of us to explore."[53]

The qualifications that the Sufi affiliates spoke about reference inner dispositions and capacities that a potential teacher needs to develop. The Sufi understanding of the body extends beyond the mere physical corporeality and anchors the seeker's self in what many Sufi writers have developed as a sophisticated spiritual psychophysiology.[54] Built on the foundational distinction between the overt exterior (*zahir*) and the hidden interior (*batin*), the visible physical body is always described as connected to a nonmaterial, imaginal body, such as the spirit (*ruh*), the (lower) self (*nafs*) and the heart (*qalb*).[55] The heart is thus more than a physical muscle or a metaphor for the seat of emotions; it is a primary sense organ. As a perceptive organ, the heart is indispensable for receiving and transmitting information beyond the scope of other sensory organs.[56] As Al-Ghazali explains: "[The] heart has a window which opens on the unseen world of spirits. In the state of sleep, when the avenues of the senses are closed, this window is opened and man receives impressions from the unseen world and sometimes foreshadowings of the future. His heart is then like a mirror which reflects what is pictured in the Tablet of Fate."[57] This perspective sees the body as a "conjoiner of physical and metaphysical aspects of existence,"[58] in which the heart acts as a conduit between divine insights and human perception. In this sense, the heart itself is an intermediary place in which divine infiniteness and the limited human individual meet.[59] However, more than a passive receptor, the heart is thought of as a training ground. As Scott Kugle explains, referring to how these subtle organs are described in a historic Sufi training manual, "the human body and especially the heart [can] be trained to adopt postures and motions that have transcendent ethical effects, so that the body itself can become a mirror for a just cosmic order."[60]

Faizani wrote prolifically about the internal dispositions that a student of Sufism needs to develop. He saw part of the goal of walking the Sufi path

Figure 4.1. Drawing of the human heart by Allama Faizani. Reprinted with permission of Faizani International.

as nurturing an inner mentality of sincerity, love and compassion that is expressed in an imagery of spiritual light and inner wisdom, which resides in the spiritual heart. This centrality of the heart is nothing new in Sufi writing and cosmology, but Allama Faizani took it to a new level, subdividing the spiritual heart into cells that he described as the seat of intelligence, understanding and emotions, and delineated a list of attributes—moral, carnal, loving, patient and merciful—attached to them.[61] Faizani provided anatomical drawings of a heart that included a place for Satan (*makaan sheitan*) as well as a monotheistic core (*hastah tawhid*), including a dark spot called the "self-pride core" (*hastah ananiyat*). He used anatomical drawings to package classic Sufi ideals in ways that were amenable to reaching the young and educated urban class of his time.

In this sense, his Sufi affiliates described to me practices such as *zikr* as "cleaning or purifying the heart," "polishing the heart" or "calming the heart"—a physical feeling and a desired outcome of the practice. This imagery is also reflected in Sufi manuals and Sufi writing on *zikr*, which frequently evokes the imagery of the purification of the heart, the heart as the mirror that has to be polished to reflect God's light and the cleansing of the soul.[62] For the Faizani community, whether the heart and soul resided within a female or male body was inconsequential.[63]

From Daughters to Teachers: Extending Kin Ties to Spiritual Bonds

While the narratives of inclusion of women seem to indicate an unbroken practice throughout the decades since Allama Faizani established the *tariqa*, the sociopolitical realities to which the community needed to adapt tell a more complex story. At the time of the Taliban government, some in the community left Peshawar for Kabul, where they kept reading Faizani's books and practiced *zikr*. Meanwhile, the family of the *pir* established a new life in the United States, where they started to expand the community internationally. Activities in Afghanistan were somewhat subdued during that time: teaching and publishing continued but on more modest terms in an environment where it was unclear which activities might draw the Taliban's ire. Interviewees generally said the community was able to operate, although individual members were occasionally imprisoned for possessing Allama Faizani's writings, and women were not included in the teaching circles.[64]

After the US invasion in 2001 and the subsequent fall of the Taliban government, the community adapted once again, setting up a public cultural association, which later supported the political campaigns of Ustad Mazhabi, and organizing internal gatherings in nondescript, secondary locations.[65] In a sign of the changing times, the Cultural Center began holding computer and English classes like those of other institutes that have sprung up all over the capital to prepare students for university entrance exams (*konkur*) or for English exams such as the Test for English as a Foreign Language (TOEFL). Spiritual classes called *khudshenasi/khudashenasi* (knowing yourself/knowing God), named after one of Faizani's books, were also offered and focused on the path of seeking God through profound inner reflection. In setting up a cultural organization, the Faizanis were responding

Figure 4.2. Faizani online teaching.

to an urban public sphere saturated with NGOs that catered to the interface between state and citizenry through capacity building.⁶⁶

Computer knowledge and the mastery of English were often prerequisites for employment by foreign NGOs and international institutions. By offering this training to young Afghans, the Faizanis implicitly hoped to kindle interest in more spiritually aligned topics that could be taken up alongside the technical classes. Participants who showed an interest and aptitude in religious topics got invited to the weekly *zikr* meetings that took place in rented rooms in Kabul, while in provinces such as Herat the women met in the private house of the *sar-e halqa*.

The teaching of women and their full inclusion within practice and learning were reinvigorated when the granddaughters of Allama Faizani, Momena and Manija Billah, moved back from the United States to Afghanistan in 2015. I spent time with Momena Billah, the daughter of the current *pir* of the Faizani community, in her apartment in Kabul's Karte Se neighborhood adjacent to Darul Aman. Home to the palace that was built by Afghanistan's modernizer Amanullah Khan in the 1920s, Darul Aman was a prestigious, comparatively quiet area of town. It was bombed to rubble during the successive periods of war.⁶⁷ Post-2001, the area, as well as adjacent neighborhoods, had gradually transformed again from ruins in which refugee returnees squatted to lively upper-middle-class neighborhoods with restaurants, cafés, cultural associations and a few high-rises. Several of the Faizani community, who were situated within the Afghan urban, educated middle class, lived in adjacent neighborhoods. Most members had at least a high school degree, a large portion of whom also went on to study at university and some of whom even became lecturers at universities. While the older women in the *zikr* circles showed an avid interest in education, they had fewer opportunities than their daughters for education, but they eagerly supported their daughters' educational goals.

After graduation from college, Momena Billah traveled the world. She was in Turkey when she talked to her sister, Manija (b. 1992), who had taken a job teaching at a private university in Kabul and persuaded Momena to join her in Afghanistan, where she could explore what the country was like post-2001. Three years after that decision, Momena was looking after her six-month-old son as we chatted until her husband, another Faizani Sufi devotee whom she had met in Kabul, came home and started cooking while they took turns looking after the baby. We talked first about her own winding path into Sufism. Her father was the *pir*, but she was initially not involved in the community, finding it difficult to position herself in the United States as a Muslim post-9/11:

> Personally, when I got into Sufism and God, that happened in college. I was trying to get away from all of this because of all the things that happened after 9/11. Islam was painted as so bad, and when you're an adolescent, you want to fit in. . . . But when I got to college, I had spiritual experiences myself; I had [*pauses*] certain experiences that sort of awakened me. I am not a holy person; I am a normal girl, maybe not normal, but I'm trying to get a college education, get a job [*laughs*]. I was not expecting this, and I think when that happened, I got into Rumi; that's when I fell in love with him. I have been reading him every night. I was looking into an explanation of what was happening. Of course, I will not say what these experiences were, because I believe they were really personal. So, I started reading, started looking for answers.⁶⁸

Evident in Momena's telling is that, despite growing up within a Sufi community and being exposed to *irfan* through her father, a spiritual path was not a foregone conclusion. Belonging to the family of the *pir* privileges access to information about the order, knowledge of the tradition and familiarity with ritual aspects; however, a position within the order itself as a knowledgeable teacher is not guaranteed through merely occupying a place in the genealogical line.[69] This is akin to processes that Shahla Haeri described historically for female leadership. The father-daughter relationship has been crucial in succession throughout Islamic history. However, as Haeri also aptly points out, these women not only inherited the position but also used their own acumen and charisma to get and remain in that position.[70] This was also the case for Momena when she became a teacher and leader within the community. It was her own interest, study and research of Sufi knowledge that led her to reengage with the Sufi community that her grandfather had established.

After returning to a country she had known primarily through the stories her parents told, Momena reconnected with her wider family and relatives and decided to become active within the Faizani Sufi community. She explained to me that the women in the Kabul chapter of the order had first been taught by one of the male *ustads* in their community, but that she saw it as their duty to educate a new generation of female Sufis who could take over the teaching of other women in the future.

Momena and Manija were not the only daughters within a family of religious scholars who became teachers within the Faizani community. Ustad Shukria, who led the Faizani *halqa-e zikr* (*zikr* circle) for women in Herat at the time of my research, had also been taught by her father, who was a follower of Allama Faizani. Shukria's father first instructed his daughter and son himself before hiring another *alim* (religious scholar) to teach them. After he met a similar fate to that of Allama Faizani—imprisonment during the Communist time—Shukria was left to her own devices and returned to reading Allama Faizani's books to continue her spiritual education.[71] She told me that the family had always practiced *zikr* privately but that, in 2005, she decided to open their *zikr* practice to other women outside her family. When asked about the decision to include nonfamily members in the practice, she recounted discussions within her family: "We always did *zikr* in our family. It was actually my brother who encouraged me to open up the *zikr* circle to other women as well. If you have that knowledge, and you are not sharing it, God will ask you later, 'I have given you this knowledge, you knew, but you didn't tell others. Why?'"[72]

The support that Ustad Shukria describes from her brother, who was affiliated with the men's *zikr* circle of the Faizani community and who leads the Faizani office in Herat, was mirrored in discussions I had with other nonkin male Sufi *murids*. As Line Nyhagen has pointed out, male allies are an important conduit for women to access gendered institutional spaces.[73] Ustad Shukria's daughters, who were college educated and had studied law and sociology (except the youngest, who was still in twelfth grade at the time of research), supported their mother in the *zikr* practice by serving the women who attended and vocally leading *zikr* recitations themselves. I asked Ustad Shukria whether they had experienced any negative reactions from men or other families after establishing a *halqa-e zikr* for women. Participants' male family members had voiced concerns, but it seemed that for every social critique that the group had faced, there was a remedy embedded within the spiritual exercise itself. Ustad Shukria told me that participants' male family members had been opposed to women participating based on erroneous accusations of impropriety and fears of leaders' financially profiting from followers. However, upon encountering "the good effects that the *zikr* had on them and their families, they changed and supported it." In Ustad Shukria's view, exposure to *zikr* ultimately benefited the community, which included the men who had been initially hostile to it.

When asked about whether they had experienced any criticism of the active engagement of women in *zikr*, Ustad Manija said that one imam in a nearby mosque had complained about hearing women's voices engaged in *zikr*. Among more conservative Muslims, a woman's voice is considered part of her *awrah* (lit., "nakedness"), "that which should be concealed (in public)."[74] In response to questions of security but also citing budget restraints, the community shifted locations to a backyard in the city center where the sounds of *zikr* might be drowned out by the city's general noise, sidestepping criticism that could have otherwise shut it down or could have brought out tensions.[75] These decisions were practical adaptations, a dexterity in navigating expectations and restrictions concerning women joining and leading Islamic practice.

The main female teachers discussed so far originated from within the family of *pir* Allama Faizani or his inner circle of followers. However, the community actively worked on expanding its base and training young women to lead *zikr* circles and teach Sufi insights. The women who initially joined the teaching circles were the wives and daughters of men who were already active in the community, but soon the circles widened and other women started to join who had no historical or kinship affiliation with the family of Allama Faizani. Some of them had heard of the *zikr* and Sufi teaching from other women at wedding receptions or at social gatherings; others were already searching for spiritual development and were referred to the gatherings through word of mouth. While the women in the Herat circle were predominantly of an older generation, often already mothers and grandmothers who brought their daughters along, the women in the Kabul circle were drawn from a younger group who still went to high school or attended university. Many Friday mornings I found them studying for course exams before joining the classes of the *tariqa*.

Teaching Authority: Leading Remembrance

Building up leadership skills and religious authority in a Sufi order is rooted in the ability to manage and direct the process of inner learning and experience for members of the group. Status and authority are not just assumed through titles and certificates but relationally produced and repeatedly demonstrated in the ability to teach and lead. One of the prime loci for this training is the leadership of *zikr* circles, which extends from the general development of awareness of how the self is connected to and reflective of the Divine to the actual instruction of *zikr* recitations. The practice of *zikr* is a meditative technique in which verses from the Qur'an, the names of God or the *shahada* are recited or chanted repeatedly, either in solitude or company, aloud or silently (loud *zikr* is called *zikr jahr* or *jahri zikr*, whereas silent *zikr* is called *khufya*).[76] All Sufi groups have *zikr*; however, not all of them practice it as a chant—for some it is "merely cadent speech," while others practice it with music.[77] The Faizani community follows the general Qadiriyyah tradition of vocal *zikr jahr* without any musical accompaniment.

While the weekly lessons among the Faizanis were partitioned into remembrance and thought (*zikr va fikr*), incorporating both topical talks and practical lessons, the example of how to teach the experiential side of holding a *zikr* circle enables us to see how leadership of *zikr* was used as a training ground for nurturing the leadership of female religious authority. Attaining authority over the leadership of a *zikr* circle within the Faizani community involved more than the command of written knowledge, even though the group organized exams in which the younger girls needed to show their level of learning, memorization of *zikr* formulas, as well as the Qur'anic references that are the basis for the *zikr* chants. The participants were trained to lead the group under supervision of the teachers and were given individual prayers and chants that they had to perform on their own. These *awrad* (singular, *wird*) are additional individual learning units, staggered along an incremental progression of required knowledge and command of inner states. Ustad Momena explained:

> It's a system that we follow, which is based on our school and on what my grandfather wrote. They're silent prayers that we do daily. Me and Manija, we still do it every day, on our own. That's our own individual prayer time, our connection with God. . . . Everyone has a different spiritual growth. Based on that, we see some of the girls who are in the first lesson for whom it might be more difficult to lead and take on this responsibility. But then another girl might be in the tenth or eleventh lesson. The eleventh lesson is where you finish off stage one. And then you go on to stage two, three, and it progresses from there. You go on to the names of Allah, chanting the names of God. It's all for spiritual purposes. That's one of the criteria you look for.

Teachers described this work on the inner self as an aspect of the inner abilities and experiences that are also necessary for the interpersonal leadership of a group to guide them through the spiritual states accessed through the practices. In the analysis of medieval Sufi manuals, Shahzad Bashir points out that "knowledge of the interior is predicated on the ability to understand and interpret the exterior correctly," which leads to a connected view of exterior action as reflective of interior developments.[78] Directing a *zikr* circle is therefore more than the outward orchestration of communal action; it is

Figure 4.3. Female *murid* speaking at Faizani conference, Kabul, 2019.

a cultivated ability to tend to and fine-tune adepts' internal development through external regulation.

The women in the Faizani community participate in their Sufi community and in the exploration of inner states to build the capacity to lead others on this path and to manage these states within a group setting. The person who leads the *zikr* circle needs to maintain control over the framework of the *zikr*, moving it from one level of rhythm and intensity to the next, because the framework "cannot be sustained liturgically in a limitless manner, and the speed and movement of the *dhikr* require careful evaluation in order to 'ride the waves' of the emotional and spiritual mood to *hal* (state of mystical experience)."[79]

"If it is one person leading [the *zikr*], they really need to be spiritually capable to manage that," Ustad Manija explained when I inquired about the choice of *murids* for leading a *zikr* session. Adepts needed to display several abilities, including knowledge in counting and meter, having a "good" (meaning clear and loud) voice that could help others in keeping the rhythm and remembering the phrasing and their meaning. All of the phrases used during a *halqa-e zikr* were of Qur'anic origin and were therefore recited in Arabic—remembering them and properly pronouncing them being no small feat for nonnative Arabic speakers. However, participants were doing more than just repeating them in rote memorization. Qur'anic phrases and idioms serve in *zikr* "as conduits for spiritual energy to the devotees' inner beings."[80] The collective, repeated enunciation of the *zikr* formulas did not only result in individual changes of emotions and personal dispositions but also created a particular group dynamic that the leaders of the *zikr* need to manage. Ustad Momena described the responsibility of "holding the space" of the *zikr* circle in one of our discussions:

> When you lead *zikr*, actually, there is a spiritual pressure that the person who leads the *zikr* feels. Sometimes that pressure is unbearable because there are a lot of souls sitting in a certain *zikr* circle, and there's sometimes darkness that comes in from the outside, from your regular day-to-day life. Contrarily, there is also a release of pressure as the *zikr* progresses, resulting in an opening of the heart when you feel elated.

Responding to the demands of the practice led Ustad Momena and Ustad Manija to decide to train a group of women to lead the *zikr* circle in rotation. The group of young women who were regularly leading the *zikr* practices and were tasked to give talks about specific dates of the religious calendar year, such as Ramadan, Muharram or the birthday of the Prophet, were also the young leaders involved in public-speaking engagements, for example, at the yearly public Faizani conferences as well as outreach of the Sufi community for new members.

The legitimacy the female teachers developed by leading their gender-segregated weekly meetings translated into an overall position of respect within the wider Faizani community and in their cultural organization. The example of the worldview and training program that the Faizani female Sufi leaders and teachers undergo to establish themselves as leaders illustrates that religious authority is linked to the mastery of certain techniques that direct the internal activation and development of the nongendered psychophysiological body. The next generation of female Sufi leaders were not established through a kinship connection to the *pir* but were required to demonstrate the ability to teach and lead as adepts themselves.

The case of the female teachers within the Qadiriyyah Faizani Sufi order shows how women as religious actors and leaders insert themselves and are active in institutional Islamic settings. Their own discourse of gender equality, indeed, of the transcendence of gender as a category in the spiritual realm, justifies not only women participating in but also leading *zikr*, Qur'an recitation and Islamic learning. While this discourse manifests itself in a strong ethos of male allyship and support from fellow male community members, it has to be said that the community adhered outwardly to the gendered expectations through setting up gender-segregated meetings and classes and retaining women as the main teachers for women in Afghanistan while holding gender-mixed meetings in the diaspora communities. These practical adaptations enabled women to participate in Sufi practice and to navigate expectations from Afghan society writ large. In comparison to other institutionally male-dominated settings, the Faizanis discursively legitimized women's participation and leadership through recourse to the spiritual/psychophysiological organs of the heart, soul and mind—the body, so often used to differentiate, is here rendered insignificant for the necessities of spiritual development and reduced to its nongendered parts, which overrides the gender difference.

Contrary to other examples in which women inhabit marginal spaces in their reinterpretation of Islam or become saintly after their death, the example of the Faizanis showed how women become a part of contemporary religious leadership within a community through their teaching. While this reinvigoration of the participation of women within the order is a post-2001 phenomenon, it has its origin in the inclusive vision and practices of the founder of the order in the 1970s.

The overall leadership within the community was set within the family of the *pir*; however, enlarging the group of teachers and leaders was seen as an active and ongoing task. Doing so necessitated navigating restrictive gendered notions of authority and passing on the ability to manage experiential aspects of learning within a group of students. While the Faizani community managed to navigate the killing of their leadership, migration and return in conjunction with a generational leadership change, not all Sufi communities manage this process so seamlessly. In some cases, as we see in the next chapter, leadership could be suspended altogether as the community and other Sufi groups negotiate a future for the order.

FIVE

Navigating the Divine through Dreams

"No one has taken over after our *pir*'s death. We currently don't have a leader." The words of the middle-aged medical doctor, who was a follower of a Sufi order in Herat and a teacher of Sufi poetry in his free time, stunned me. Their *pir* had died just a couple of years earlier, and no new leader had been appointed. The son of the *pir* was still present during my first year of research, and I, just like other outsiders to the group, initially mistook him to be the leader of the community. However, other *murids* corrected me. According to them, the community respected the son of the late *pir* because he was his offspring, but he was not seen as the leader of the order. Dr. Forough elaborated on this point: "This *tariqa* is not working through inheritance. The one who knows best and who completes this way can be the leader/*pir*. It's not that the one who is the son will be the leader. It's about their knowledge and capability."

"But how should it be decided?" I inquired, while sitting in Dr. Forough's examination room of the hospital and drinking tea with him after official consultation hours were over. "Has your late *pir* appointed a highest deputy [*khalifa*] who will take over?" I asked, toying with the different models of leadership succession that I had encountered.

He leaned on his desk, looking at me with the compassionate gaze of a man who often had to explain the obvious to patients who did not understand the medical procedures they were about to undergo: "No, he did not appoint anyone. There is one sign in this Salwatiyyah *tariqa*, that the Prophet Muhammad [PBUH; peace be upon him] will come to the dream of one of us, and when he sees the Prophet in his dreams, he will be selected as the *pir*.

"So, you say that you select your leader by a dream?"

"Yes. The one who reaches the top level [*shakhse ke muqam bala merasad*] will see the Prophet at night in a dream. Then he becomes selected as a leader."

This chapter delves into this extended moment of suspension, in which a leaderless Sufi order waits for a dream yet to come. Dreams open up a space of interaction, both within their ontological status as well as in the communal negotiation about who can have a dream and what the dream comes to mean in this social configuration. This space of interaction was twofold: On the one hand, the dreams themselves offered the meeting ground in which personages such as the Prophet Muhammad or luminaries otherwise considered long dead interacted with the dreamers. On the other hand, members of the group also engaged with each other about the interpretation, verification and discussion of guidance through dreams in worldly affairs.

The Sufi order's *khanaqah* was not the only place where the group's leaderless present and their questioned future were discussed. In an otherwise nondescript office, the members of Herat's Sufi Council discussed the Salwatiyyah order's predicament through assessing the community's self-portrayal in the history book that members of the order had published. The Shura-e Tasawwuf, to which I refer here as the Sufi Council, was established in 2004 with the goal to counter a discursive environment that was experienced by members as increasingly dismissive and potentially violent toward Sufi interpretations of Islam. The Sufi Council could be compared to a union or a professional board of Sufi teachers to both accredit practice and discuss challenges Sufi affiliates faced. The council published books on practices that have been divisive within Muslim communities and that were of specific interest concerning the legitimization of Sufism and boundary making of Islam. The books that the Sufi Council authored were distributed in bookstores in Herat, in mosques and to other religious authorities such as the Shura-e Ulama. But the council also worked as a reviewer of new books before or shortly after their publication. Authors within the Sufi community in Herat saw the Sufi Council as an organization convened for the approval of their publications.

Following the contestation of leadership in the Salwatiyyah Sufi order offers a glimpse into the wider Sufi sociosphere and how these contests in the religious public sphere were fought out. These intragroup dynamics shed light on the ways in which the discourses that we have seen develop and emanate within the regional history ricochet among Sufis and their discussions for rightful conduct, navigated through dreams. Dreams and visions have been an important sociocultural touchstone in Afghanistan and the broader region. In navigation of authority, dreams offer a potential potent claim to leadership. Their strength resides in their ontological status combined with their cultural and religious significance. Recourse to dreams offers a claim of authority in which orality trumps the written word, as "visionary interviews" with different past and long-gone luminaries can play important roles in community decision-making.[1] Insights gleaned from communication with the dead and knowledge of the past could have an impact on the present and give insights about the future. They thereby work with a not exclusive linear temporality: the dreamer has an exceptional access both to past and future, as the visions come from another time or outside time.[2]

The chapter builds on recent work by anthropologists on dreams within Muslim communities through interrogating how these dream practices interface with the navigation of authority.[3] In her work on an Egyptian Sufi community, Amira Mittermaier posits an anthropology of the imaginal, with a strong focus on what she calls a "*barzakhian* perceptive" that focuses on the extended community of the living and the dead, that can be experienced in the isthmus in which dreams and visions are accessed.[4] As Mittermaier has argued, "This interlinking of different temporalities, which is closely related to a different sense of what is real, imbues the dream vision with an exceptional epistemological value,"[5] something that Nile Green aptly summarized as "bringing the dead into speaking presence of the living."[6] Someone claiming a power like this would justifiably pose a threat to established orders, which makes dreams a medium affecting the navigation of succession and the legitimation of authority.

While the contestation over the authoritative use of dreams has a long history, the discomfort with revelatory dreams has become increasingly pronounced in the age of Muslim reformers. Mittermaier argues that reformers' insistence that dreams are intimately linked to the dreamer, with the goal of clearly distinguishing their experience from that of the Prophet Muhammad's Prophetic revelations, is also a response to the Orientalist contestation about the status and veracity of prophecy writ large.[7] Scholars opined that the Prophet Muhammad might have sincerely believed that he was the recipient of divine messages; however, they argue that the so-called revelation had actually come from his unconscious, making Muhammad a man with strong imagination instead of a Prophet.[8] Reformers' discomfort with contemporary divinatory insight through dreams might be a response to these refutations of the Prophet's overall revelation. No matter the actual reason for Muslim reformers' discomfort with divine dream insights, these controversies show that while dreams have immense social and religiously sanctioned power to inspire change, they are also not uncontested in their visionary and political potential.

Building on the insights of anthropologists who attended to the workings of dreams and the imaginal, the account of the Sufi order in Herat also differs from their work in crucial ways. Most of these works still view dreams akin to individual events, bounded in time and happening to an individual. However, I argue that an ethnographic approach that takes into account the various practices of dream invitation through *istikhara* and the Sufi epistemologies connected to purifying the heart to become receptive of dreams opens up a vista onto dreams as a field of vision whereby a whole community is engaged in dream practices that define their very constitution. The practices in which the Sufi group was involved are embedded in a worldview in which decisions were collectively negotiated through dreams. It also shows a social environment in which dreams can be suspended, awaited, delayed or expected and in which they can be a crucial part of navigating authority as well as deciding and legitimizing a potential future leader within a Sufi community.

Dream History: Perceiving Signs of the Divine

The dream that should mark out the future leader of the Sufi order had not yet come when I commenced my research and did not arrive over the ensuing months as I repeatedly visited the community. Mittermaier observes that a cosmological understanding of "true" (veridical) dreams as coming *from* God engenders a particular conception of agency. The prospective dreamers can invite true/divine dreams through preparatory actions, but they are not in control of whether the dream actually manifests. Therefore, "dream-visions can be invited, but they can never be demanded,"[9] as the dream is granted by God. But to whom is it granted?

Dreams have been recorded in Arabic and Persian chronicles; royal dreams have been immortalized in prose such as Ferdowsi's (d. AD 1020) *Shahnahmeh*; and dream manuals offer evidence of the practices that ensued from dreams.[10] Given the broader salience of dreams it seems hardly surprising that dreams turn up in the political history of a country such as Afghanistan that sits at the crossroads of these traditions.[11] While it seems self-evident that Sufi writers such as Herat's patron saint Khwaja Abdullah Ansari would write prolifically about dreams, not only saints and Sufi mystics ascribe divine provenance and significance to dreams.[12] Using dreams to justify leadership has precursors in Afghanistan's political history: Mughal ruler Babur (1483–1530), who founded a dynasty in Kabul in 1526 that would span three centuries, saw his successful takeover of Samarkand in a dream.[13] And Amir Abdur Rahman (1840/1844–1901), the so-called Iron Amir who united Afghanistan as a nation-state through the brutal elimination of internal dissent and persecution of minorities, used the narration of dreams prolifically in his writing to legitimize his own claims to rule.[14] He claimed to have seen the Prophet Muhammad in a dream, showing "an expression of consent" to appoint himself king. Several sources reference Mullah Omar as being inspired through a dream to rally the Taliban together at their very inception.[15] However, these examples, taken mainly from diaries and autobiographies of rulers, were a kind of "right to rule through oneiric verification of God's intentions";[16] they functioned as after-the-fact justifications and legitimizations. In the end, they already were rulers, no matter whether they gave themselves the air of divine acquiescence.

The case seemed to be different for the Salwatiyyah. The dream was not just an event of the past that was called on to justify leadership, as in the case of Afghanistan's rulers, but the Salwatiyyah shared a common field of perception in which dreams could be channels to reach the Divine, access long-dead luminaries or receive inspiration (*ilham*). From the Salwatiyyah's daily work as artists, doctors and students to the fundamental structures of their community and leadership, dreams offered a tool to interface with the Divine; they were part of a process and part of the navigation of authority in which the group was involved.

Months before the Salwatiyyah community published their community history that would introduce strife into the Sufi sociosphere about their leaderless existence, I learned how dreams were part of a repertoire in daily interactions as well as extraordinary occurrences for individual members of the order. A conversation with two *murids*, the calligrapher Bismillah and the miniaturist Habibi, who were at the time writing their community's history, pointed me to these instances in which signs of the Divine became perceptible. We had met in their workplace, an atelier located on a side wing of the imposing Qala Ikhtiaruddin, Herat's citadel founded by Alexander the Great in 330 BC and rebuilt by the Agha Khan Foundation into a nearly too-cleaned-up version of itself.[17] While most visitors stroll into the citadel, or Arg, as Heratis call it, through the imposing front gate and into the lower reaches where soldiers used to camp before ascending into the upper queen's and king's quarters, there was a side path that led along the outer wall to a shaded arcade with individual rooms housing a glassblower, a sesame mill driven by a camel and a few atelier rooms that doubled as workspace and teaching venues for the calligrapher and the miniaturist.[18]

Abdul Ghaffar Habibi had worked as a lecturer of fine arts at the university for the past eight years, and his friend Bismillah (Faramarz) Saruri had received a bachelor of arts in fine arts and was now teaching at the Behzad Institute.[19] In conversations in the downtown office I rented for interviews, they told me about their way into Sufism and art. While I had initially wanted to interview them individually, they came together and I quickly learned that they were inseparable, seeing their friendship as a twin-like life experience, or as Faramarz put it: "We have always been together since childhood, in the madrasa, in the class, at university and with our *murshid*.

We were neighbors and went to the mosque together. We have always been together, and now we are working on art together, too." Trying to gauge their trajectory better, I asked: "So, what was first, the *murshid* or the calligraphy and miniature painting?" Both smiled, answering in near unison: "First was the *murshid*, then the art." As I would later learn, choosing an occupation was a part of the Sufi way for these devoted followers. The occupation of their *pir* Osman (a shoemaker) had been chosen by his *pir* (Saudaii), and Pir Osman was in turn the one to discuss their profession with them so that they would choose a respectable line of work befitting to serving society.[20] Service for society was seen as a part of an upright spiritual path.[21] As much as everyday work was seen as part of one's service to God, divine guidance revealed itself in finding the right teacher and path as well.

When I asked how they had first met their *murshid* and become interested in Sufism, Bismillah, who was usually the one of the two who spoke when we met, explained:

> There are incidents that happen in your life, which later on form the cornerstones of your decisions. When I was twelve years old and I was living in poverty, I was praying and going to shrines [*ziyarats*]. I was praying to God that we will find a *murshid* to guide us. That was during the Taliban time. There is a poem by Mawlana that says, "If there is a painful heart, the doctor will follow / come to it." I saw a stranger in the street, and at the first look, I knew that he was a friend of God [*dost-e khuda*]. He asked me for the time. I told him that it was ten-fifteen. He asked me whether I studied. I said yes. He looked at me, and he hunted my heart with his look. We parted ways after that. After that I saw him again when I went to the mosque. There was a place empty next to him. I went and stood next to him [during *namaz*], and my heart got filled. I kept going to this mosque. At the time, no one was teaching Ibn Arabi's book *Futuhat al-Makkiyya* in Afghanistan, but he was teaching it.... He advised me to come and told me to call my friends if I had someone who was interested as well to join. He told me he would give me some *zikrs* so I could learn quicker. I told this to Agha Habibi. At the time there were three days a week to teaching of Ibn Arabi; on Fridays there was teaching of Mawlana and Maktubat-e Imam Rabbani and Mujaddidi's work at the *khanaqah*.[22]

Bismillah not only assigned finding his teacher in the form of his *murshid* Osman to divine guidance, seeing it as the outcome of a serious search through prayer, but also to his artistic work. Standing in the midday summer heat in his atelier at the Qala Ikhtiaruddin, a room dominated by a large table in the middle at which Abdul Ghaffar Habibi sat with a student explaining the structural design and composition of an image, Bismillah walked me from one calligraphic piece hanging on the wall to another.

"This is *Siyah Mashq* [Black Practice], which is my favorite calligraphic style." He pointed at a drawing that exuded a seductive darkness through brushstrokes filling the paper that retained their expressive movement even in their dried final form. *Siyah Mashq* was originally a warmup for calligraphers to refine their brushstrokes through repetition. When the adepts realized how stunning some of the pages filled with the progression of words and letters looked, they turned it into a style of its own. But not all scripts had their origin in the trial and error of calligraphic practice itself, as Ustad Bismillah told me: "This is a font I recently invented. I call it Niayesh [worship] style." Individual letters in the violet-blue calligraphic script seemed like arms outstretched, reaching beyond the confines of the otherwise meticulously kept line work. "The script is drawn with the pen inverted. The letters of the words and shapes visually express a message of humble supplication." While beholding the curvature of the letters that implicitly kept and occasionally expressively broke the lines that they visually created, he contemplated how the answer to the process of inventing a style was less rooted in the practice of aesthetic expression than in the apprehension of divine directives.

"When you walk on this path of Sufism, you receive direct indications, extra powers in what you are doing, and you receive *ilham* [inspiration]," Bismillah explained, referencing a sort of divinely inspired knowledge granted to friends of God (*awliya'allah*), the saints and holy personages of Islam. His answer indicated that inventing the script had been divinely inspired, describing a process of spiritual progression in which the daily life is suffused with signs of God and in which the conscious search for closeness to the Divine sets in motion interactions with it. Bismillah would later describe the writing of the community's history in a similar vein, when describing that the process of writing had been a process of divine inspiration.

He posited that while there were parts that were meticulously researched and pieced together through interviews within the Sufi community, he had also spent time at the grave of his late teacher. There, he had felt that his hand, like the calligrapher tracing out a new, divinely inspired style, had been moved by an invisible force.

While the book was the object that would later ignite the discussions between different Sufi groups, the calligrapher's experiences were by no means only individual outliers. Bismillah's claims and the Sufi community's perception of dreams and divine insights were rooted in Ibn Arabi's philosophy of the "oneness/unity of existence" (*wahdat al-wujud*), which was taught in weekly seminary-style lessons. In Ibn Arabi's view, the true, ultimate essence of God (*dhat*) cannot be known, only divine manifestations in the varying degrees in which they possess divine light.[23] He viewed imaginative impulses as an essential aspect of God's self-manifestation (*tajalli*).[24] The theophany, or *tajalli*, means that the Divine becomes perceptible to humans.[25] As Wendy Shaw eloquently summarizes an Ibn Arabi–inspired worldview (albeit with focus on Islamic art), "For somebody attuned to a reality beyond that of physicality, the so-called mystical is always immanent within the mundane; a practice of reception."[26] The perception of this divine manifestation, however, is linked to the different degrees of consciousness, which means that the same reality is perceived differently depending on the cultivated abilities of the receiver.

Dreams were thereby one way to perceive the Divine. In the Sufi community of the Salwatiyyah, dreams were often treated as a guiding principle for the order. When I first came to *zikr* meetings to interview members of the community, one of the teachers, Dr. Forough, asked whether I had had dreams that led me to do the research. He described that one of the ways to be led toward the path of Sufism was to have guiding dreams. Other members of the community described their own experiences of transforming from nonreligious lifestyles to devout Muslims because of dreams. For example, when I met Ustad Khoroq, he was a respectable teacher with his own library, but he harbored an unsavory past. He told me that he had been in the army and did not consider his lifestyle at that time as befitting a devout Muslim: "I was a soldier in Mazar-e Sharif; I was a misled person. I was not praying; I was not good. Then, in the night, I saw the Prophet Muhammad in a dream. I didn't see his face; I saw him from the chest down. He shook my hands. In the morning when I woke up, I changed one hundred eighty degrees and I became a good person. I started praying after that." It still took him a few years until he would join the Sufi order in Herat, but his own path had changed through this encounter. The dream had been a catalyst for his own path of becoming closer to and orienting his own life toward an alignment with God.

Seeing the Prophet Muhammad in dreams is a special occurrence, one that has even inspired its own genre of writing, dealing with the question of what it means to *see* and identify the Prophet in the absence of any rendering of his face.[27] Dreams of the Prophet Muhammad are regarded as the epitome of true dreams (*al-ru'ya al-sadiqa*), differentiated from common dreams (that are similar to psychologically interpreted everyday dreams) or dreams induced by Satan connected to the lower self, the *nafs*. One Hadith affirms: "Whoever sees me [the Prophet] in dreams will see me in wakefulness [the Hereafter] for Satan cannot take my shape."[28] This belief, that neither Satan nor a jinn can take on the shape of the Prophet Muhammad, directly marks out dreams in which the Prophet appears as undoubtedly true.[29] As in the case of Ustad Khoroq, dreams of the Prophet are seen as having the ability to usher in change in someone's life. In this instance, a dream had entered Ustad Khoroq's sleep and had changed the course of his life. However, not all dreams just appear by themselves. Some are invited into people's lives.

Istikhara: Conversations with the Divine

One way to invite guiding dreams is through *istikhara*, a widespread practice common in Afghanistan and in many Muslim communities worldwide.[30] *Istikhara* (lit., "the search for the good") has developed into a quasi-official form of futurological research in Muslim communities.[31] When believers are unsure about the correct course of action for their lives, they can ask God to send them a sign.[32] The practice differs from one region to another, but in Afghanistan the prospective dreamers perform a ritual ablution, pray two *rak'as* (cycles), followed by a prayer, and then meditate on the life choices in question.[33] The content of dreams that follow are then interpreted to answer the question to which the seekers set their mind while praying and falling asleep. While *istikhara* can be used for worldly decisions such as marriage choices and business deals, Sufis also use it to guide them toward their prospective teachers.[34]

Many instances of *istikhara* and dreams that impacted the Sufi order's development have been recorded in the community history (*Tarikh-e Alieh Salwatiyyah*; History of the perfected Salwatiyyah), which was written and published by the two *murids* Ustad Bismillah and Ustad Habibi in 2018 after the death of their *pir*. Pivotal moments in the history of the community connected to founding the order as well as its changes over time were recorded in the book, and indeed, the process of discovering the man who would become the future leader of the order had itself been precipitated through the search for a teacher via *istikhara*/dream induction.

According to the book, Hazrat Osman Mawdudi was born into a Sufi family of the Chishtiyyah line as well as into a family of Sadats in 1277 AH/1898 CE in the Pashtun Zargun area of Herat Province. He moved to the provincial capital to study Islamic jurisprudence at the madrasa Jameh Sharif, the Great Mosque of Herat. At that time, he made up his mind to meet "friends of God" (*awliya'allah*) and decided to find them through the practice of *istikhara*. The Salwatiyyah history describes how Hazrat Osman Mawdudi found his *pir* in this way, quoting him directly:

> In one night in which I did *istikhara*, a great and luminous person with a good appearance [*shamael-neko*] who had several *tasbeh* [prayer beads] in his hand and who was walking in the market came, and I asked a person close to me for his blessed name. This person said, "His name is Akhundzada Abdul Samad, known as Saudaii." The next night I asked my classmates whether they knew this person by the name of Akhundzada Abdul Samad Saudaii? They said, "Yes and his house is at the gate of Firozabad." I told them that I want to become a *murid* who is close to him. They answered, "Be careful and do not talk to him, as his talk is harmful for you." This advice from them created doubt in my heart.[35]

Heeding their warning, he decided to do *istikhara* for forty nights every Saturday at the shrine of Abdul Rahman Jami, a fifteenth-century poet, scholar and mystic, to decide whether he should abstain from seeking out Saudaii as a teacher. While *istikhara* is often done at home, the custom of sleeping next to tombs or in mosques to summon dreams is a practice common to Sufis and non-Sufi pilgrims.[36] Despite the warnings of his peers, his connection to the teacher, who visited him every night in dreams, only grew deeper, until at last he rejected the advice of his classmates and decided to become the teacher's *murid*.

Underlying the practice of *istikhara* is a cosmology that imbues dreams with having a future-oriented and creative potential. One of the most crucial indications of this potential is a Hadith according to which the Prophet Muhammad announced shortly before his death that once he was gone, no prophecy would remain except for righteous dream visions (*al-ru'ya al-saliha*) in which God would continuously reveal himself to the Muslim community.[37] John Lamoreaux shows that most Hadiths agree on the meaning and implications of the Qur'anic phrase "glad tidings" (Sura 10:64) as referring to true dreams ("those who believe and fear [God] . . . they will have glad tidings [*al-bushra*] in the life of this world and in the next"),[38] giving authority to dream interpretation as a form of understanding divine insight in Islam. The practice can also offer guidance about understanding the past. As Ismail Alatas shows in his work on *istikhara* in Indonesia, finding insight can be used to ascertain historical facts, such as the case of the *pir* who identified unmarked graves of saints through dream induction.[39] However, in the cases that I encountered, *istikhara* was not used to identify aspects of the past but to speak to situations in the present and to possible pathways in the future.

The communicative potential of dreams is anchored in the imagery of an in-between space in which dreams form the connective tissue between the everyday and the Divine. Several Qur'anic verses and Hadiths intertwine and were elaborated on by medieval Muslim thinkers to become the framework for understanding this in-between realm. The Qur'an itself connects dream experiences with a closeness to God (Sura 39:42, 6:60) when it tells believers that the souls of sleepers are taken into the presence of God and released upon waking.[40] Early Sufis spoke of visions as breaching "the world of the unseen" (*alam al-ghayb*), but later writers developed and codified a more comprehensive system of the dream and vision world.[41] Medieval Muslim scholars referred to this in-between or intermediary level as *alam*

Figure 5.1. Praying and dreaming at Khwaja Abdullah Ansari Shrine in Herat.

al-mithal (world of images or imaginal world) or as *alam al-barzakh* (world of isthmus).[42] The physician and philosopher Avicenna (Ibn Sina) used this concept "to explain the source of the foreknowledge of the Prophet,"[43] but Shihab al-din Suhrawardi (d. AD 1191) embedded dreams and visions in "a special sphere of existence of their own."[44] Nile Green, elaborating on Suhrawardi's systematization, concludes that this cosmic sphere was seen as an interface "between God's nondelimited knowledge and our own fragmentary understanding of the universe," a space where visionary meetings between the living and the dead could take place.[45]

Receiving Guidance and Ordaining Leaders

The vision of the Prophet Muhammad in a dream also figures prominently in other instances recounted in the Salwatiyyah *tariqa* history, connected to the establishment of authority of the *pir* as leader of the newly formed Sufi order. On one occasion, the Prophet Muhammad is said to have appeared to the late *pir* Osman Mawdudi in a dream vision while performing hajj (pilgrimage to Mecca). The intersection of the Prophet's dream visitation during the sacred act of pilgrimage demonstrated to Osman Mawdudi's followers that he had "reached the highest level of the blessed *tariqat* Salwatiyyah . . . gaining an openness of heart [*sharh-e sadr* (Arabic)] and becoming the leader/ruler/wali [*maqam-e walayat* (Arabic)]) while he was looking at the Kaaba Sharif."[46]

Seeing the Prophet Muhammad in a dream was a form of blessing (*baraka*) that marked out the teacher as a future leader: not only did he see the Prophet, but he also conversed with him, receiving guidance and blessings. *Baraka* is often defined as a "holy power inherent in a saintly figure that sets him/her apart from everyone else."[47] Muhammad Knight has made the shrewd observation of the Prophet Muhammad's body as a source of *baraka* that can materialize and dispense blessings, observing that "baraka is what the Prophetic body does."[48]

Unlike the experience of Ustad Khoroq, the soldier-turned-teacher whose encounter with the Prophet Muhammad in a dream had a life-transforming effect, the encounter between the Prophet and the future leader of the order, Pir Osman, was not as straightforward. Here, the *pir* recounts his experience of the dream vision:

> After circumambulating the Kaaba, we became very tired. I came with my friend, and we sat down across blessed Kaaba, and we were looking at the house when I saw between dream and revelation, excitement and rumble arising, and someone made a loud sound that the Prophet Muhammad—PBUH—and his companions (*moqeb*) arrived. I saw the best of the world [*behtarin-e allam*, meaning the Prophet Muhammad]—PBUH—with a group of companions who came close to me. I went and took the hand of the best of the world [hereafter, Prophet Muhammad], and kissed it and said to myself that maybe he is Hazrat Khizr—all health to him. I took his thumb to get to know whether he has any bone.[49]

Pir Osman doubted that the Prophet had actually appeared to him, expecting instead the distinguished figure of Hazrat Khizr, the guide among Sufi saints and the purported master of Ibn Arabi.[50] Some Muslims believe that Khizr lacked a bone in his thumb and could be identified this way. However, the Prophet Muhammad corrected Pir Osman: "In the middle of this, the Prophet Muhammad—PBUH—said: I am Muhammad—PBUH. Now I was shocked and threw myself to his feet and kissed him lovingly."

The encounter, however, did not end with this revelation but evolved into a discussion between the Prophet and the teacher Osman about rightful conduct within Islam:

> The Prophet Muhammad—PBUH—said: "What you did is forbidden in shariʿa."[51] I said to him: "Oh messenger of God—PBUH—it has been years that I do shariʿa; today I practice [lit., "act based on"] the fatwa of love." The Prophet—PBUH—was silent. After a long time of separation and waiting that this opportunity was given to me, I kissed the beautiful foot of Muhammad—PBUH—a lot, which was perfume producing [sweet smelling]. The Prophet—PBUH—said: "Rise. What kind of a request do you have, and what question you have?" I told the blessed: "My *pir janab* Hazrat Akhundzada Sahib said that whenever you reached the last part of cleaning/purifying your soul, Muhammad—PBUH—will be shown to you, and he will teach you the name of your specific *tariqa* [lit. says here: "beginning"]. Now I want you to show me that name." The blessed accepted, and he taught the beginning of my specification.[52]

The issue at play, often criticized by reformers as un-Islamic, was kissing the hand of an authority figure, in this instance, the Prophet himself, as a sign of respect and allegiance. The brief dream debate, as relayed by Pir Osman and written down in the community's history, shows the varying stances toward contested behavior. However, in the encounter, Pir Osman persuades the Prophet Muhammad of the rightfulness of this behavior. Furthermore, Pir Osman received communication and instructions directly through a dream-vision meeting with the Prophet Muhammad. The Prophet approves of Pir Osman's request and teaches him his name from his beginning (*mabda' ta'ayyun*).[53]

The meeting with the Prophet singled out Osman Mawdudi as the rightful leader of the Sufi order, his encounter promoting his status among other students.[54] The history of the Salwatiyyah describes the connection to the Prophet as a direct outcome of choosing the Salwatiyyah way, stating: "This meeting with the beloved of God [the Prophet] was the result of the way of *tariqat* of Salwatiyyah; he was honored with this position."

An aspect that is crucial for our understanding of the interlacing of dreamscape and immanent plane is the implicit understanding of why the *pir* was able to receive the dream of the Prophet Muhammad in the first place. As described by Mawdudi's teacher, "Whenever you reach the last part of cleaning/purifying your soul, Muhammad—PBUH—will be shown to you." Not just anybody can have veridical dreams that ordain a student as teacher and leader: the process of becoming is intimately tied to the individual adept's mastery of the self, purification and self-awareness reflective of a deep understanding of the Divine. The appearance of the Prophet Muhammad singled out the leader, marking this elevated spiritual state. But what happens when the dream is expected but remains unfulfilled?

A New Old Order

The community history of the Salwatiyyah shows several instances of visions and meetings with the Prophet Muhammad and other luminary figures who offered insights and instructed aspects of the *tariqa*, including its meditative practices. Pir Osman is described as being taught about the theory of *lata'if* in dreams as well. The theory of *lata'if*, a term that could be translated as "subtle spiritual centers,"[55] was developed in the Naqshbandi Sufi tradition and found a detailed explanation in Shah Wali Allah's writing.[56] While "some of the *lata'if* have names corresponding to body parts or faculties or are sometimes described as being located in specific areas of the body (liver, heart, or mind), they are not to be understood as identical with the organs located there."[57] They are instead "local manifestations of identically named parts of a higher realm of the cosmological structure."[58] These centers and their activation correspond to the psychological and spiritual progress of a follower of the Sufi path. The Salwatiyyah history recounts Pir Osman's spiritual quest to understand the concept and applications of the subtle spiritual centers:

> The sequence of the seven *lata'if* were not clear to him. Therefore, he went to other contemporary shaykhs, but they also did not know the answer, until one night in a dream Imam Ghazzali came to him and he asked him. He told him that this is the duty of Hazrat Khizr to solve this problem. So, in one of the nights in his house, Hazrat Khizr comes to him and Khizr

tells him, you don't need to seek. Whenever one *latifa* is completed, I come to you personally and teach you the next one. After that sometimes the shaykh would tell us that he had met Hazrat-e Khizr and had learned about another *latifa*.

However, while Pir Osman learned about these different practices through dream guidance and was immersed in the ways of multiple Sufi orders, he started to synthesize what he had learned from these different orders into a new path. The Salwatiyyah followers described this change as a process of simplification that would lead to quicker results in a spiritual aspirant's progress. Pir Osman shed the practice of *lata'if* and replaced earlier practices by focusing instead on sending prayers and good wishes to the Prophet Mohammad (*durud*). When discussing these changes with one of the *murids*, Bismillah, he pointed to Qur'anic references in which God instructs Muslims to send blessings (*salawat*) on the Prophet Muhammad: "Indeed, Allah confers blessing upon the Prophet, and His angels [ask Him to do so]. O you who have believed, ask [Allah to confer] blessing upon him and ask [Allah to grant him] peace."[59] The practice, anchored in Qur'anic example, was portrayed by *murids* as more effective and a faster way to work on the self than ascending through previous arduous processes.

This shift in focus is not only exemplified through changed practices but also signified by the Sufi order's name, Salwatiyyah. The order was previously known as the Chishtiyyah, which originated about AD 930 in Afghanistan's west, close to Herat in Chisht-e Sharif, from where it spread into India. The order is especially known for its use of music with commemorative *zikr*. Pir Osman was born into the Chishtiyyah way through membership in his family and was later initiated into the Qadiriyyah order.[60] He is said to have synthesized his knowledge together with the dream insights into the new Salwatiyyah *tariqa*. This strong focus on the Prophet Muhammad was also coupled with a change in *zikr* rituals. *Zikr* used to be communally practiced and oriented on the Chishtiyyah practice of *zikr*, often with musical accompaniment (one that was still practiced until the death of the son of the *pir*, as the Salwatiyyah affiliates told me, out of respect to the son of the late *pir* and his family). The whole system of practice changed to individualized *zikr* that everyone could practice on their own time in a place

Figure 5.2. Salwatiyyah *murids* drinking tea at Pir Osman's shrine, Herat.

of their convenience. This meant that the affiliates would no longer have to come into the *khanaqah* but could practice their *zikr* alone at home or in any place they found suitable. This system of *zikr* and prayer practice was described by Salwatiyyah affiliates as easier and "more suitable for the modern human beings." The individualization of practice was described as a part of becoming modern or modernization shifts from a communal practice in a public space to an individualized practice in a private setting.[61]

As becomes clear in this overview, many changes in the practice of the *tariqa*, including the new name and general self-definition of the order, were connected to insights gained through dreams that the order's late *pir* or his *pir* had experienced. The authors of the community's history, Bismillah and Habibi, did not claim to have had these dreams themselves but were the chroniclers of the dreams of their leaders who had instructed them on this new path. The instructions were one more level removed from their *pirs*, as they had gleaned them in dreams and were therefore only the receivers of the insight, not their creators.⁶² This description did not only date back to the establishment of the order but also anchored it in a claim that was difficult to dispute: the late *pir* was quoted, but only his experience of dreams as experienced and recorded in the history written down by the two *murids* who authored the book. He had not left any of these descriptions in writing himself.

Some Sufi students that I spoke to, however, were concerned about how their *tariqa* would be judged by outsiders, especially in view of the miracles and special abilities that the book ascribed to their late *pir*. The book mentioned special abilities of Pir Osman, such as the capability to discuss questions with long-dead saintly figures and authors such as Ibn Arabi and to therefore come to truthful insights about Ibn Arabi's writing because Pir Osman would have direct contact with him personally in his dreams. He was also described as having achieved special inner states that gave him specific powers to interpret dreams and make his dream interpretations come true. Some Sufi *murids* suggested that these were matters better left undiscussed in public.

Navigating the Sufi Sociosphere

It is understandable that some Sufi affiliates were especially worried about the publication of the book and the way the order would appear to the public: attributing such miraculous abilities is exactly what Salafi-inspired critics would see as the blasphemous usurpation of spiritual powers and divine abilities that aimed at deceiving people and creating a *pir* who is an intermediary between believers and God. And indeed, when I talked with Bismillah, one of the authors of the community history book, he conceded that he had received criticism and even threats since publishing and distributing the book. The criticism had been voiced online in posts on social media platforms. He was evasive in talking about the threats and said that "some people online" did not like what he had written but that they would not really understand.

But the online sphere was not the only place where the writing and establishment of the Salwatiyyah were seen critically. Shortly after the publication of the book I met with a member of the Sufi Council. To appreciate the tensions between the Salwatiyyah order and the Shura-e Tasawwuf, a short look into the rationale for the establishment of the council and its working is illuminating as it positions the council within the broader Sufi sociosphere of *tariqas* and *halqas*. The head of the Sufi Shura, Mawlawi Abdul Haleem Hosseini Wais, told me about the establishment:

> We had a big gathering in the blue mosque in Herat, which was in the time of Ismael Khan [2001–2004] where we decided to start a council, because there were some groups who were against Sufism and who started around that period in Herat.[63] So we decided to gather a *shura* of all three *tariqas* and stand against those who are against Sufism.... These groups still exist in Herat, and they are mostly Salafi, Wahhabi and Panjpiri. They say that mysticism [*irfan*] and Sufism [*tasawwuf*] are part of Hinduism and Buddhism. So we decided that it is important for somebody to stand against them and say that this is real Sufism and it is part of Islam. It has been in the past, and it is now, and there should be no action against it.... We discussed with them, saying, we are Sufi; we are not Salafi. There were arguments and even physical attacks. During the night, they even wrote leaflets and spread them around. I'm sure, if they were given the possibility to grow, there would be attacks every day.[64]

Since its establishment, the council had taken residence in a meeting house in Herat that was chosen when Wali Shah Bahrah was director of the Department of Information and Culture. The Sufi Council's house consisted of a few modest rooms, sparsely furnished with a few seating *toshaks* and a couple of bookshelves. One of the rooms was used as a library and storeroom for the council's publications. The Sufi Council's meetinghouse was the place that offered opportunities for discussions among Sufis about their own practices and beliefs as well as the possibility of bringing up incidents of hate speech and attacks that Sufi affiliates experienced. The Sufi Shura's goal was not only to monitor those instances but also to communally find ways to respond to them. The secretary of the Sufi Council, Ustad Irfani, a sinewy older imam with his own mosque and madrasa, described their position as a discussion board in comparison to the function of *khanaqahs* in the life of Sufi affiliates:

We gather together, and we discuss how to advise, but the practice [of Sufism itself such as *zikr* and instruction in Sufi learning] happens in the *khanaqahs*. In the *shura* it is all about theory, but when the people go back to the *khanaqah*, they practice. You can compare this, for example, to doctors. Doctors practice their medicine with patients, but when there is a special case, then they come together, and they discuss with each other how to go about it.

The Sufi Shura can be compared to a union or a professional board of Sufi teachers to both accredit their practice and discuss challenges that they faced. The members of this council were drawn from the main *tariqas* that were active in Herat, the Chishtiyya, Naqshbandiyyah and Qadiriyyah. While all members seemed to have one or more *tariqa* affiliations, some of the council members also preached at local mosques as the main imam. As many Sufi Council members were also part of the general ulama, as Ustad Irfani was himself, they could have theoretically also been represented by Afghanistan's Ulama Council. As formally a religious council, it was akin to other religious authorities, such as the semigovernmental Jamiyat al-Ulama (Society of Religious Scholars), also called the Ulama Council or Shura-e Ulama, which was established as a national council in 1931.[65] The Sufi Council was, however, not state connected as the traditional consultative councils were, which also set it apart from other examples regionally. Most other Sufi councils, such as in Pakistan or Egypt, show a divergent genesis and rationale because all of them were set up by the state itself or in close cooperation with the state, functioning more or less as a mouthpiece for certain groups in concert with the state.[66] In contrast, the Sufi Council in Herat was not a state initiative or directly connected to the Afghan government at that time. It was a grassroots organization arising out of a need that a community itself felt rather than a state-mandated organizing body. The Sufi Council members argued that there was a need for a separate Sufi Council as a platform for exchange: "Any social class or group needs discussion and exchange of ideas. That is the same with Sufis. Every Islamic society needs a Sufi Council. But because Herat is the earth of the saints [*khak awliyah*], that's why the Sufi Shura was created here for discussion."[67]

The Sufi Council's position was indeed unique in that it incorporated aspects of other organizational forms and combined them in a distinct manner. The council called itself by a traditional name of communal deliberation (*shura*);[68] however, it had taken on the form of a state-recognized organization, showing a response to the post-2001 environment in Afghanistan saturated by NGOs and international organizations. The council had designated a head, deputy and scribe for its weekly meetings, but it did not bring out reports as international NGOs did but instead published books like those of a traditional publishing house.

A survey of the content of the Sufi Council's books reveals the attempt to link its own view of Sufism to regional authority (principally the school of Deoband), historic and traditional precedent and legitimation of Sufi practices through reference to both the Qur'an and Sunna. The titles of the books ranged from *Some Selection of the Beliefs of Deoband Scholars*, *The Necessity of Following the Four Schools of Jurisprudence* [*mazhab*] / *Taqlid* [*following/imitation*], *Hanafi Opinions with Clear/Transparent Reasons*, to *The Place of Sufism in Islam*.[69] Some texts dealt in more detail with issues for which Sufis have often been criticized, such as *Judgment on Loud* Zikr, Tawasul/*Intermediaries*, *How to Celebrate the Prophet Muhammad's Birthday* and, of course, the thorny question of *Innovation*. These different texts had been published in an edited volume; however, they were also printed in individual books. These individual volumes were shorter, pocket-sized versions, which could be handed out to Sufis seeking arguments that would support the Sufi approach to one of these topics. For example, the third booklet, *Hanafi Opinions with Clear/Transparent Reasons*, locates practices and aspects of Sufism that might be viewed critically, such as visitation of graveyards, forecasting the future, proof of *karamat*, workings of amulets (*taweez*), respect for relics (*azsar*) and receiving cures from them (*shafa*) within largely unproblematic aspects of Islamic conduct such as practical matters of folding hands while at prayer, how far feet should be apart during prayer, special prayers during Ramadan, the advantage of the turban in Islam and the proper length for an Islamic beard. The focus on outward minutiae of practices and conduct surrounding controversial Sufi practices seems to parallel the Salafi strong focus on these aspects, which reflects the council's attempt to speak to a public that has been influenced by Salafi thought and practice.

The Sufi Shura was also concerned with delineating the line between allowable change and continuity within Islam. Which practices and ideas could be considered part of the religious tradition, and which should be considered innovations? One of the main books published by the Sufi Council is called *The Place of Sufism in Islam*.⁷⁰ It is a collection of scholarly opinions on Sufism, moving from a general description of Sufism to an analysis of the derivation and etymology of Sufism, a discussion of the roots of Sufism and its importance in Islam. Of specific interest concerning legitimization and boundary making is the section that deals with innovation, a crucial question generally within Islamic thought and in delineating what is correct tradition and what is forbidden. This section of the book starts with an appraisal of innovation from the point of view of the conservative early theologian Ibn Taymiyya, then proceeds to the understanding of innovation from the perspective of Islamic scholars of the University of al Azhar in Egypt, as well as from the point of view of other scholars focused on delineating what actual innovations might be and what things are not to be called innovation despite their novelty.⁷¹

The question of innovation was also at stake in the case of the changes within the Salwatiyyah, who had given their book to the Ulama Council and the Sufi Council, among other individual Sufi affiliates and scholars in Herat. The council was seen as a critical accreditation board for new publications. Ustad Karimi was one of the scholars on the Sufi Council who had read the book. He introduced himself as a practicing Sufi who devoutly followed his *pir* and had sought purification and insight through forty-day *chilla* retreats. He had written and published individually on the history of Sufism and had traveled regionally to research his writing. An accountant by day, he was a regular member of the Sufi Council and went to nightly *zikr* circles in the city. Talking with him about the establishment of the Salwatiyyah *tariqa*, however, upset him. He first remembered his own connection with the late *pir*:

> Karimi: I knew Sayed Osman myself for more than thirty years. Even at the time of the Taliban, he taught the book of Ibn Arabi, *Futuhat-e makiyah*, which is a difficult work. He also taught [Mawlana's] *Masnawi manawi*. I was a student of his for several years. His son was sitting in his

stead after Sayed Osman passed. He was Chishtiyyah, not Salwatiyyah. Sayed Osman was a good man when it comes to Sufis [ahl-e irfan]. But this business with the Salwatiyyah is new; this didn't exist in the original four *tariqas*. Naqshbandiyya, Qadiriyyah, Chishtiyyah, Suhrawardiyyah, . . . there is no Salwatiyyah. We didn't have this in the original. From the viewpoint of law this is not right.

Author: What do you mean by that?

Karimi: The case of the Salwatiyyah is new. The problem is that there is no *ussul* [knowledge of evidence of shari'a rulings/legal theory; e.g., this is not legally sound in Islam]. The Salwatiyyah is not related to any origin. There are some groups like Malamatya, Qalandariyah, Kubrawiyah—they have some kind of relation with the main four *tariqas*, but the Salwatiyyah doesn't. Everything has its own rules. For example, if you want to get a bachelor's degree, you need to study four years before you graduate. If someone would like to become a driver, he needs to learn and follow some rules. Same for the Salwatiyyah: there should have been some *ussul*, some rules, some origins or some laws that could be related to the other four *tariqas*. But unfortunately, it doesn't exist; they don't have those.

Author: So, on the one hand, we have the Chishtiyyah family with Sayed Osman and his son. But then as well, Sayed Osman and Ustad Saudai, who was the *pir* before him, they started this other *tariqa*. What do you think is happening there?

Karimi: Well, sometimes they said, "We belong to Chishtiyyah"; sometimes they said, "We belong to Salwatiyyah." All the other *tariqas* have lineages in how they connect to the Prophet and how the tradition was transmitted, but the Salwatiyyah does not have this; it is a new thing. Akhundzada was a *pir* who was in the Naqshbandiyyah. In the Naqshbandiyyah everything is done in silence [*sukkut*], the *zikr*, the sitting, everything in silence. Qadiriyyah has the *zikr jahr* [loud zikr], but Naqshbandiyyah doesn't have that. . . . When I went to Sayed Osman Agha's place twenty-five years ago to learn the *futuhat-e makkiyah*, nobody said then that they are the Salwatiyyah. They said that they are the Chishtiyyah *tariqat*.[72]

The change of the Sufi order, both in terms of their practices as well as their name and anchoring within Sufi history, seemed to unsettle the scholar. But there also seemed to be more than just the mere change that the history book proclaimed had already happened decades earlier when the late *pir* synthesized the various insights into a new path.

> Author: But why do you think they are saying now that they are the Salwatiyyah?

> Karimi: Now they say this because they want to change things themselves. They want more followers, more *murids*. They want an easy way, because the Salwatiyyah way is very easy. They are only reading and saying supplications to the Prophet. They say, send *durud* [blessings] to the Prophet Muhammad, but they don't have law and tradition [*shari'at wa sunnat*]. Sufism has laws. Other *tariqas* have rules and regulations for everything. But the Salwatiyyah are not like that. Why didn't they publish the book two years ago when Sayed Osman was still alive? He went to Iran; then he came here. Why didn't he write that book then about the Salwatiyyah? Why did they say that they are the Chishtiyyah?

The general change, however, was not the only aspect that the Sufi Council member criticized. I asked him what he thought about the selection of a new leader through a dream of the Prophet Muhammad. Ustad Karimi was not fazed by the method of dream divination of a future leader; however, he was appalled that the community was currently leaderless.

> Karimi: If you say that this Salwatiyyah is in the way of Sufism, Sayed Osman should have appointed a new leader after him. But he didn't do that. Every *tariqa* should have an action plan to tell them what they should do when their leader is dead. What characteristics should the newly appointed leader have? But this group doesn't have any principles. The *shura mutassawwufin* has religious specialists; we are studying the newly invented groups and we are comparing their practices to *shari'a*; and we are giving them allowance or not if it's not compatible.

> Author: So, the *shura* knows about this. What is the position of the Sufi Shura toward it?

Karimi: They came one or two weeks ago and brought their book for us to read and give feedback on. Most of the leaders [of the Sufi Shura] are traveling in different countries at the moment, but we have copies. We will read it and then make a decision. The one who follows the Qur'an and Sunna is the righteous one. A *murid* who doesn't follow the Qur'an and Sunna is not a *murid*. This is a rule. I have joined many circles of Osman Agha, but he never claimed anything like this during his speeches and lectures. It is his students who are making this new way. The *shura* has two viewpoints. The things about Sayed Osman Agha, they shouldn't be published. They should be removed from the book. Furthermore, Salwatiyyah does not have any base in the other four *tariqas*. If it doesn't have any origin or relation, that means it has been newly invented in the *tariqa*. In shari'a, we have a principle: every *bid'a*, or every newly invented tradition, is a wrong path; it is a misguidance. And every misguidance leads you to the fire of hell.

In his unease about the Salwatiyyah order, he brought up an important point that Sufism is a tradition in the sense of having an established line of transmission that is sanctioned through being part of one of the established "paths" (*tariqas*) that are known to other Sufi affiliates and to non-Sufi Muslims alike. In stepping out of these established pathways, the Salwatiyyah were visibly "new" in the marketplace of Sufism. But while the authors of the community history argued for their *tariqa* as having historical weight through the establishment by their *pir(s)* as received in their dreams, Ustad Karimi challenged this account as inaccurate because he had never heard their late *pir* positioning himself publicly toward the establishment of a new *tariqa*. What made the *tariqa* furthermore assailable was its status as currently leaderless. Ustad Karimi equated this with *bid'a*, wrongful innovation.

But what was at stake with this harsh criticism from a Sufi Council affiliate toward these Salwatiyyah Sufis? Why did they apparently intend to shut down publication and discussion of the Salwatiyyah history, since they were a council supporting and defending Sufism? Defense in this instance meant the preservation of a certain established orthodoxy and ortho-practice. Ustad Karimi remained vague about whether and how the Sufi Council would take a public stance, and at the time of my research, the Sufi Council had not issued a public statement. But his opinion was a window into the negotiations taking place within an institutional set up to defend Sufism. Ustad Karimi did not want to elaborate on his reason for his critique; for him, the questionable base within Islamic history and reasoning for establishing a new *tariqa* were evidence enough for accusing the Salwatiyyah of the crime of innovation.

There were multiple possible reasons for this critical stance against the Salwatiyyah claims, which intersect to varying degrees. The Sufi Council set itself up not only as a defender of Sufism but also as its arbiter in terms of defining correct Sufi practice and legitimacy. The power to define what Sufism is supposed to be might be threatened or undermined by someone (or another group) claiming to define a new path, especially if this claim were backed through a religiously sanctioned but difficult-to-falsify claim such as dream insight (albeit from a *pir* who is already deceased).

Furthermore, as Ustad Karimi pointed out, claims like those of the Salwatiyyah could be easily charged by outsiders as wrongful innovation, especially if too many other aspects of the Sufi order's practice and claims were seen as out of line with conventional customs. This opened the Salwatiyyah followers to criticism and possibly assault but also might be seen by the Sufi Council as bringing Sufism generally in disrepute if the Sawatiyyah were seen not as a fringe group but as representing Sufism more broadly. Critiquing the Salwatiyyah followers by more traditional Sufis was therefore also a strategy to preempt critique of Sufism from outside the Sufi circles.

Interesting in the whole contestation is that dreams as a medium for spiritual knowledge were generally not criticized by the Sufi Council member in his account of the Salwatiyyah. Dreams have been an established religio-cultural medium for claims of divine insight and guidance, and they also offered a convincing form for the establishment of the new *tariqa*. While Ustad Karimi did not critique the usage of dreams directly, he was skeptical about the timing of publishing the book and the claim that a new *tariqa* had been established after the death of the *pir* who was said to have had the inspirational dream. Ustad Karimi did not doubt the method of dream divination itself, but he showed skepticism toward its application in this instance since it was a dream that had been reported by the *pir*'s followers, who now founded (or claimed the prior foundation) of a new Sufi associational branch. While dreams are an effective all-Islamic idiom of legitimization, they have also been grounds for doubt and deception and for worries concerning how Muslim communities will be viewed from the outside by other Muslims or non-Muslims.

Dream Disturbances

Historically, dreams have often posed a threat for religious hierarchies and orthodoxies. They are powerful devices and difficult to counter. David Shulman and Guy Stroumsa therefore assert that "dreams are often the direct path to heresy. Indeed, the hallmark of a heretic is often the revelatory dream."[73] Dreams can become an arena in the challenges for leadership, but they can also provide mechanisms to voice critical or marginal opinions, as the dream reporters can always distance themselves from the content of the dream while retaining its subversive message.[74] Dreams receive their power through a chain of interlinked characteristics: their personal/private nature makes them impossible to either prove or disprove; in principle the dreamer is merely a receiver and reporter rather than creator of content; their oral nature has a contrarian but powerful status compared to the written word of scripture; and their special access to long-dead luminaries or divine future insights marks them out as especially powerful. This context explains why religious authorities often shy away from or fiercely oppose dreams (if they do not use the dream narrative for legitimization themselves) in an attempt to contain their divinatory power.

The example of the Salwatiyyah's use of dreams shows how the religious-cultural trope of "true dreams" and the cultural practice of dream interpretation as a social mechanism are efficacious in personal mystical experiences and in social settings. As an established and revered Islamic medium of transmission dreams navigate the realm of continuity within tradition while introducing change that is described and experienced by its affiliates as continuity. The community's temporary but extended in-between status as a leaderless group and writing of its community history show that it needed defending from other Sufi affiliates' opinions as well as those of non-Sufi Muslims who might see the use of the dream legitimization for change in leadership, practice and overall organization as a stretch or even as wrongful and heretical innovation (*bid'a*). The characteristics of dreams as well as the general acceptance of dreams as a method of divine connection within Islam made them the ideal mechanism to communicate shifts in practice, community formation and leadership. After all, when the new practices of changing *zikr*, the name of the *tariqa* and the leadership structure emerged, it was not the medium through which they were said to be conveyed that was attacked. Dreams and their agency had an impact in endorsing the changes in the first place and in positioning them as continuity within the order's history, a continuity with long-dead luminaries, the Prophet Muhammad and, ultimately, the Divine. They were challenged only by their status as not having been voiced *earlier* by the previous *pir* in his writing. It is not the status of dreams per se that is doubted—at least not in the intra-Sufi social sphere—but what they might bring with them as challengeable directives. Dreams and their agency mattered for the history writing that was part of the Salwatiyyah's navigation of the liminal space of succession. However, it remained to be seen how much of their dreams would carry into waking reality. The death of the *pir* was only the beginning in the negotiation of the future path of the Sufi order.

Conclusion and Epilogue on Transitions

IF THE DEATHS OF these *pirs* has taught me anything, it is that there are no conclusions, only transitions. When I first started looking into Sufi communities in Afghanistan in 2016, my well-meaning Herati friend Farhad, who himself had grown up in a Sufi community, told me that he liked the research topic but that I was too late, because all the great *pirs* had already passed away or were about to die. Indeed, my longest research stay in Afghanistan had been bookended by the deaths of two of the most prominent political Sufi leaders: Pir Sayyid Ahmed Gailani (1932–2017) died at the beginning, while the head of the Mujaddidi family, Sibghatullah Mojaddedi (1925–2019), passed away at the end of the nearly two-year research stay. When I had spent only a few months in various communities, news reached me that Ustad Mahjor, whom I had interviewed only a couple of weeks earlier, had passed away from a pulmonary edema. I pondered whether Farhad was right: Was I witnessing a decline of learning and community, the end of the age of *pirs* and the networks of followers gathered around them? But as death commemorations unfolded, I realized that these were the celebrations that the community coalesced around. Students and followers came together not only to remember but also to chart new pathways for the wider community. The rituals reinvigorated and reconstituted a sense of belonging and new directions. These moments of transition were also opportunities to confront challenges within the hierarchical structures of authority and learning, as inheritance of titles and positions was not an unquestioned given. Focusing on these internal transitions helped me delve more deeply into how Sufi groups had reacted to specters of change, both internal and external to their communities.

This book has sought to offer a window into the dynamics and processes within Sufi communities in Afghanistan that are part of an agentive civil sphere. It argues that tracking moments of transition and succession as they unfold enables us to see Afghan Sufis as dynamically adaptive to their changing environments, whose communities evolve to meet the challenges of the moment, even if they are also changed in the very process. The communities' internal struggles often reflect wider societal shifts and ongoing conversations about the acceptability of certain practices and about the type of authority suitable to represent the community to the outside world as well as the legitimacy of accession mechanisms and processes.

The book attempts to serve as a corrective to the simplistic narratives that haunt descriptions of religious communities and their leadership in Afghanistan. First, identifying leaders by their titles or honorifics tells us little about how authority was established, projected, submitted to or challenged, nor does it assist us in understanding what changes might have occurred within religious communities in past decades. Treating authority as a relationally defined ability to exert influence enables a view that does not take a leader's position as self-evident but offers insights into the navigational strategies and dynamics a leader utilizes within contested spaces. Second, several of the navigational strategies I have outlined would be easy to overlook given that they are often connected to integral characteristics of the Sufi communities. This is also what makes them often so particularly effective. An example is the oscillation between various positions of authority that can sometimes be inhabited by one and the same person, as the example of imam and *pir* Haji Saiqal showed. In Afghanistan, Sufis have sometimes been mullahs, and mullahs have sometimes been Sufis. The strong historical connection and practical intertwining of the two categories, which are often thought of as separate, have enabled Sufi groups to utilize mullahs to shield Sufi communities and, in other places such as Herat, to develop a Sufi

Council to shield Sufi practitioners. In an environment that increasingly privileges prescriptive authority, persons who are viewed as embodying such authority based on titles acquired through formal training can shield a community that practices experiential rituals such as *zikr*.

Leadership within Sufi communities is situated at the intersection of prescriptive and explorative authority. The cases in this book, in different ways, emphasize how these two forms of authority meet and intertwine and how we need to account for their existence and contestation at any given moment during periods of transformation. The exploration and command of spiritual interiority are what fuel a potential leader's authority. However, writing, charismatically conveying and intelligibly expressing experiences, beliefs and insights (as with poetry), channeling them (as in *zikr*) or sharing them with the community (as with dreams) confers legitimacy and authority. *Zikr* is one of the most physically involved rituals in the exploration of truth and meaning. However, to teach *zikr* and to practice it correctly, a teacher and *sar-e halqa* need to understand both its embedding within the *lata'if* system and its Qur'anic base; otherwise, as Momena and Manija asserted, it is "only movement that feels good, but you don't know why, and it doesn't gain any further meaning." Similarly, Chapter 5 shows how the Salwatiyyah community emphasized that divinely sanctioned dreams were anchored in the prescriptive authority of the Qur'an and Hadith. Dreams became the medium for change of practice, organizational form and questions of succession. Despite their explorative dimension, dreams provided a fitting medium because of their strong anchoring in sources acknowledged by most Muslims. However, asserting such authority, especially through experiential means, can be fraught with difficulty in an environment where prescriptive authority reigns supreme. A strengthening and valuing of "prescriptive authority" rather than "exploratory authority" has eroded Sufis' legitimacy within Afghanistan's society writ large and made them vulnerable to attacks, felt acutely in an environment of impunity and governmental indifference or ineffectiveness.

Media circles and policy makers describe Sufis often as inherently under threat for their practices and beliefs. While Sufis have indeed been targeted, this is only half the story, based on a misunderstanding of the ways Islam was, and in many cases still is, lived in Afghanistan. Sufism has been a vital part of Afghanistan's past and present interpretations of Islam for most Afghans, a deeply embedded feature of national heritage, religious education, artistic flowering and the negotiations between the state and religious leaders. Sufis *can* navigate the perilous waters of ever-changing ideological struggles and political upheavals because they have a sociocultural and religious foundation to draw on, a common root network with other non-Sufi Afghans. This common base extends even to individual Taliban members and commanders. It is not a straightforward correlation, of course, and should not be overstated to equate rulers such as the Taliban with Sufis (as has sometimes been suggested, for example, in the case of Mullah Omar). Nonetheless, they draw on similar sociocultural and religious bases when negotiating the space for communities and their practices and beliefs. I hope that future research can investigate these overlaps and mutual influences with the nuance they deserve.

The book also points to other aspects that still remain largely unexplored within anthropological writing. Most ethnographic studies of Sufi groups focus on a particular Sufi community, its practices as well as its individual and communal history. This leaves us with a dearth of insight pertaining to intergroup dynamics between different Sufi communities.[1] As the example of the Salwatiyyah community in Herat shows, Sufi communities are engaged in critical exchanges with one another, particularly concerning issues of outside perception and relations to non-Sufi Muslims or potential threats. Studying what I would call the wider Sufi sociosphere can be beneficial, as it highlights the push and pull these communities experience and how they react to it. Examining the perspectives of Sufi groups as part of the wider religious civil sphere enables us to see them as actors who influence one another and who react to the changing environment of instability.

Understanding and perceiving Sufi leaders and the groups they lead as part of the wider civil society sphere sheds light on the relationships and dynamics with other religious and secular actors. Particularly in environments of insecurity and conflict, Sufi groups are often characterized as "embattled," which places them as passive recipients of threats and violence and their responses as merely reactive. In Afghanistan, that has often been accompanied by a discourse of decline and perception of a replacement of Sufi Islam with other schools of thought, particularly Salafi and Wahhabi.

As *Sufi Civilities* shows, Sufis remained an integral part of Afghan society during all the decades of turmoil and hardship. They might have swapped guises, turning up in different capacities and professions, but they were still active within Afghanistan's public sphere. While individuals and communities were targeted for their work and practice, or for their positioning as public intellectuals, educators or artists, they were also key to shaping the existing civil sphere. In some instances, they became highly visible and shaped public discourse, operating as esteemed and respected voices for society. In other cases, they worked in the background, disseminating knowledge, building networks of solidarity and learning or distilling insights into artistic expression. In any case, they interacted with a large cross section of society ranging from intellectuals, politicians and religious leaders to businessmen, traders, workers, students and teachers, thereby crafting and articulating alternative visions for society.

An analysis of these local discourses on civility and the practices of artistic, religious and cultural expressions reveals a contextually embedded understanding of civil society actors, highlighting the dexterity with which they dealt with turbulent security setups as well as with the changing parameters of what was seen as respectable, disreputable or subject to debate. These navigations show how local actors attempted to bring change or preserve continuity in socially acceptable ways. Their successes and failures exemplify the plurality of ways to navigate but also the multiple influences that these navigations have on conceptualization of authority, communities and belonging.

Some shared characteristics of these navigational dynamics are worth pointing out. One of the underlying aspects that acquires salience in its absence is ambiguity. For example, with the Salwatiyyah, ambiguity, when present, played the role of peacemaker but, when removed, led to the very real possibility of confrontation. During the liminal phase after the death of the *pir*, external ambiguity about who was really in charge gave room for Sufi students to mourn as well as to position themselves in regard to succession. When two contenders for leadership published their own community history books and thus established their interpretation of their community's past (as well as making claims about their late *pir* and his abilities to wield miracles), ambiguity was removed and open confrontation over claims of leadership (or lack thereof) became a possibility.

In the realm of poetry, ambiguity offered the choice of multiple identities that could be donned as the need arose. Sufi poetry operates in multiple registers simultaneously. Read one way, it can be at the very core of religious education; read another way, it is a benign pastime or constitutive of national identity. Ambiguity about which register was being foregrounded operated like an emergency off-ramp that allowed one to drive the spiritual path while keeping the option of exiting into cultural/national heritage when needed. Thus, depending on how poetry was positioned vis-à-vis religious authority, Sufi affiliates had some wiggle room to navigate the pitfalls of a society where the limits of religiosity were in constant flux.

The ambiguity of the poetry not only offered interpretational room to maneuver but also the opportunity for a female teacher to assert herself without having to claim outright that she was a religious leader. This question of women in positions of authority was addressed explicitly in two chapters. In both cases, the women who were the primary teachers and leaders, or were aspiring to become teachers, were the daughters of previous teachers (although one community was also working to extend its teaching circle). As Shahla Haeri has shown in documenting queens in Islamic history, the father-daughter relationship has been crucial in succession throughout Islamic history.[2] However, as Haeri also aptly points out, women did not merely inherit the position but used their own acumen and charisma to ensure they would succeed and remain in power. The women leaders highlighted in this book were no different: They benefited from the advantageous father-daughter relationship. However, to actually teach or acquire positions of leadership, they—consciously or unconsciously—paired this position with other schemas, such as references to discourses of Sufi learning being nongendered, knowledge sharing in homosocial spaces, the use of publishing as an act of spiritual service and use of the internet as an interface to teach men in a highly gender-segregated society. The social navigation of establishing authority is thereby gendered in particular ways. While female leaders were able to assert their authority, they had to navigate the double binds of retaining a particular level of seclusion for respectability while showing publicly their capabilities to the communities they taught and led. Both publishing and technologies such as online teaching were helpful tools to extend their reach.

Another aspect that surfaced in several of the cases I discussed is the development of organizations. Traditionally, Sufis met in Sufi lodges (*khanaqahs*) that were the seat of their orders (*tariqas*). During the time of international intervention/occupation (post-2001) in which a plethora of NGOs populated urban Afghanistan, it was not surprising that Afghans themselves would form NGOs and foundations, especially if they lived in urban environments such as Herat or Kabul, had experienced international assistance in refugee camps in Pakistan or had lived abroad, such as the Faizani community. However, while the organizations they formed were modeled on NGOs with features such as national registration and interfaces with some of the international forms of educational accreditation (for instance, preparatory classes for English-language tests at the Faizani foundation), they were not directly connected to the international scene of funding and international NGOs. Funding was usually drawn from followers, who paid monthly support fees, and sometimes through local political connections that covered the costs of meeting places. However, owning and running an officially accredited and recognized organization gave a form of legitimacy in an environment where imitating and adopting such internationally recognized institutional forms offered symbolic capital. For some, institutionalization developed after experiences in Peshawar, where the community had offered support programs for fellow Afghans in exile during the Soviet occupation of Afghanistan. For other communities, the organization was akin to a professional board of Sufi teachers to both accredit their practice and discuss challenges they faced. In the way both of these formal organizations were set up, they were more an institutional extension of preexisting social structures than a restructuring of the group as such.

Overall, these various adaptations point to the fact that Sufi communities have long been a vital part of life in Afghanistan. They have retained, renewed and re-created their place in its history through resourcefully navigating threats as well as opportunities. Drawing on both prescriptive and exploratory authority, their leaders have found creative means to enable new ways forward for their communities.

It seems almost impossible to write a conclusion for research that was conducted at a moment in time in Afghanistan that has since been so irrevocably changed as to periodize the ethnographic present I experienced as the past. The research was conducted in Afghanistan during the time of the US-backed administration of President Ashraf Ghani and the presence of the international community and NATO mission. Interviewees reflected on regime changes that they had witnessed in the past and how these large-scale political upheavals impacted their communities. They also wrestled with an intensely insecure present marred by suicide attacks, targeted killings and a near total absence of accountability by their own government. Since then, another momentous change has happened: the US and NATO troop withdrawal, the collapse of the government and the takeover of the country by the Taliban in August 2021, who changed the name "Islamic Republic" to "Islamic Emirate" once again. The broader impacts of this watershed moment are now public record: The fiasco of the military withdrawal of the international forces from Afghanistan and the subsequent takeover of power by the Taliban was accompanied by the temporary dissolution of the donor-driven public sector and the imposition of sanctions against the Taliban's de facto government by the international community.[3] This led, not surprisingly, to an economic and humanitarian crisis with mass hunger exacerbated by climate change in the country, widespread unemployment, high inflation, displacement, a health crisis and arbitrary as well as targeted arrests, the disappearance of adults and minors, incarceration and torture as well as widespread vendetta killings and denunciation practices.[4]

Absent from the public record is what this has meant for individuals and communities such as the Sufis portrayed in this book. As has become clear in the course of the explorations of these groups, there is not one overarching answer because Afghanistan's Sufis are not a consolidated unit. They exist on a contested spectrum, from poor to rich, practice oriented to erudite, quietist to oppositional or government aligned. And just as their societal standings vary, so do their experiences.[5] Much remains unknown at the time of writing about the newly established, and still unrecognized, Taliban government. The domestic political situation remains in flux, and predicting how Sufi groups will adapt in this volatile environment is a difficult exercise. Nonetheless, the ongoing reflections of Sufi leaders of their experiences over the first years after the Taliban takeover, as well as the encounters between Sufis and the various governments over the past decades, including their navigation of the Taliban regime in the 1990s, can offer insight into these complex negotiations.

Many Sufi poets within Afghanistan's intellectual sphere found it difficult to sustain their lives under the Taliban in the 1990s. Most chose to go into exile after being targeted and imprisoned for their writing or prevented from publishing freely. These past experiences, coupled with an intimate acquaintance with two decades of violent insurgency post-2001, prompted many intellectuals to leave when the Taliban took over the country again. Some have found refuge in neighboring countries or in the West. A Herati *alim* recounted the fates of several Sufi teachers he knew who had migrated: "The people who have been writing and giving education, who have been teaching on Sufism in the past twenty or thirty years in Afghanistan, they are now working as laborers in Iran."[6] Traditional musicians, who were often aligned with Sufi orders that practiced *zikr* with musical accompaniment, also fled. Since coming to power, the Taliban have again outlawed music. This not only severs the link between musicians and their practice but more fundamentally prevents musicians from making a living. Musicians who were connected to international institutes such as the National Institute of Music have left the country, while others were forced into another profession to make a living for themselves and their families. Initial reports indicate that the loss of livelihoods combined with the lack of work opportunities in other sectors due to a faltering economy left many in extreme states of poverty.[7]

Others who have stayed in the country have done so with a defiant stance, committed to take care of their communities and the heritage they were building. When I spoke to female teachers such as Manija and Momena on the eve of the Taliban takeover about the expectations of female teachers remaining in Afghanistan, they were critical yet open to the possibility of negotiating space with the new rulers. Ustad Manija specifically pointed out that if the Taliban were to understand the history and mandates of their own religion, they would know that knowledge acquisition was important for women as well as men and that women had a place in communal life, just as the Prophet Muhammad had acknowledged women in his life.

As time went by, however, the inclusion of women in education and other public-sector jobs became increasingly circumscribed, potentially testifying to rifts within the Taliban movement itself, trying to appease disparate members and their stances toward women. Other female Sufi students and teachers expressed worry about the limitations placed on the public sphere as well as on their participation in education more broadly.[8] They protested the restrictions, yet they were not sure how successful their defiance would be and how the future would look for them in a Taliban-ruled Afghanistan.

The situation of Sufis remaining in country varied depending on their previous socioeconomic standing as well as the visibility of their practices within the wider society. Commemorations, celebrations and weekly practices in the *khanaqahs* described in this book were still taking place during the first months following the regime change. When I visited Haji Tamim in August 2021, just weeks before the Taliban takeover, he was unfazed by increasing Taliban influence. He noted that they had weathered previous governments and so would deal with any potential new one. One remark in particular has stuck with me ever since: "When they come, we will talk with them." Indeed, in the months after the return of the Taliban I received WhatsApp messages from him with videos from the commemorative events in the *khanaqah* and at the grave of Pahlawan *sahib*, as the community came together for *zikr* and celebrations.

Many events at the *khanaqah* continued even months after the Taliban assumed power. Then one of the main *khanaqahs* in Kabul's Darul Aman area was attacked in April 2022, which marked a watershed moment in Taliban government relations with Sufi communities. The *khanaqah* Allauddin, also known as the mosque of Khalifa Sahib, was a historic Sufi lodge from which Haji Saiqal had received his *ijaza* (authorization for transmitting knowledge) to teach, which connected the two Sufi lodges of Allauddin and Pahlawan through a line of teaching and learning. An explosion ripped through the Sufi lodge as a gathering was under way, damaging the roof, which caved in on worshippers. Official numbers recorded ten attendants killed and fifteen injured. However, local hospitals recorded far-higher casualty numbers with dozens killed, and news reports estimated the number to be at least fifty.[9] "There were many more. I knew them personally. There were over a hundred injured and so many of my friends killed," Haji Tamim sighed with the pained expression of someone who had buried too many friends in his lifetime. The attack took place at a time of renewed targeting of various religious minorities, such as the Hazara Shi'a community, Afghanistan's Sikh community and other Sufi lodges around the country.[10] In response to the attack on the Sufi lodge, the Taliban government ordered the closure of all *khanaqahs* nationwide. Not only Sufi lodges were closed but also religious foundations in which Sufi scholars were teaching weekly *Masnawi* classes, as well as Sufi institutions such as the Shura-e Tasawwuf in Herat, which published books in defense of Sufi practice and thought. The official reason for the closure was the same in all instances, citing the danger of attacks (presumably by ISIS-K, although none of the attacks on Sufi places had been officially claimed by them) and that security could not be guaranteed.

One of the Sufi *alims* in Kabul opined that the Taliban had used the attack as a convenient excuse to close the lodges because they were in reality against Sufism, arguing that if the Taliban had been concerned for the well-being of Sufi affiliates, then they would have given the lodges additional security personnel rather than completely shutting them down. After all, why would they want to shut down a place that offered support, spiritual edification, a warm meal and tea, pretty much the manifestation of community self-help at a time when Afghanistan was hard hit by an economic depression and many families were sliding into poverty? A university professor and teacher of Mawlana's poetry in Herat agreed. For him, these closures signified a change in ideology:

> In my opinion the current Taliban are different from the Taliban of the past. The current Taliban are almost like Salafis. They are not Salafi themselves, but they are very close to a Salafi or Daesh mentality. Talking about the past, even during the Communist time, *zikr* never stopped in the *masjid jameh* of Herat. Even at that time, nobody confronted the ones who came for *zikr* sessions there. If you went there during a Thursday, there would be *zikr*. People read Mawlana. But the Taliban have a different mentality now; they are against Sufism.[11]

Readers might be confounded by the conflation of Taliban with Salafi groups. After all, the Taliban had been actively engaged in a fight with

Daesh/ISIS-K for years before their eventual takeover of the government.[12] After that, they became actively engaged in attempting to curb the influence of Salafi imams and their followers' influence, perceiving them as a potential recruitment ground for Salafi jihadi groups such as Daesh/ISIS-K.[13] Regionally, Sufi communities also fell victim to attacks by Daesh, and the Taliban actively distanced itself from those ideologically motivated attacks. In his assessment, however, the professor was attempting to capture a process of ideological convergence that transcended the political competition between the Taliban and ISIS-K. Ever since the latter had established a presence in Afghanistan in 2015, it had presented a challenge to the Taliban's ideological authority. The fighting between the two groups can thus be seen as a struggle over who would lead the faithful, even as the ideological gap between them narrowed.

In the 1990s, when the Taliban were first in power, Sufis had indeed enjoyed some degree of tolerance. *Khanaqahs* had been open and were hosting Sufi gatherings. Now, in the post-2021 Taliban-governed Afghanistan, they were closed, an action exemplifying that not all was the same even if other actions—from banning music to erasing women from public life—were in line with the Taliban's first time in power. While it is unclear whether and how long the ban on Sufi lodges will last, it was more than the mere ban on *zikr* meetings that Sufi communities were experiencing. In a process akin to changes in perception of authority that had already begun in the 1980s with the attempts to legitimize the war effort against the Soviets (what one interlocutor called a process of "social erosion"), the delegitimization of Sufi practices had become more mainstream. This means that even if the Taliban did not justify the closure of Sufi lodges with an ideological stance against Sufism, they also did not stand for Sufi communities' rights to hold their meetings and practices anymore.

Challenges for Sufi affiliates not only arose from Taliban policies but also from changes in a discursive environment in which the range of opinions that could be publicly expressed were increasingly policed by Taliban officials and their supporters among ordinary citizens. During one of his classes, the same professor recounted just how fraught the environment had become:

There is a lot of control on what we teach. But it is not only that. Let me share a bad experience with you. I talked about education and that it is obligatory for everyone—men, women, children, everyone. Knowledge is not segregated. Since I mentioned these groups and particularly women, it became a problem. Most of the students are now Talibs. One day, one of them stood up and said, this should be your last time saying these things against the Taliban. And I told him that it is not against the Taliban; it is a general statement about education, which is something that can lighten up the community in the world. Then he said, this should be the last time for me to say this. Then I asked, if I said it again, what would happen? Then he said, I'd take out my gun and I shoot you twice in the forehead.[14]

Various parts of this book describe how Sufi affiliates (whether teachers, students, *pirs* or their followers) have had to contend with an environment of insecurity and impunity for many years, which made threats like these particularly potent. Equality of access to knowledge and the public sphere, something most Sufi groups favored, had become politicized so that arguments for them could be construed as criticism of the Taliban. Women's participation in education had become a lightning rod for conflict between the Taliban government and the international community. The space for voicing divergent opinions and tolerating a plurality of perspectives in the public sphere had become further curtailed in an environment in which teachers feared confrontations not only with the school administration and government but also with students themselves.

When I asked the professor whether he believed things would improve, he smiled wanly, suggesting that "maybe things will get better, but we might not be alive to see it. The challenges have become part of our life, and we have learned to deal with them."

Dealing with challenges, becoming used to and navigating them can easily sound like the resilience discourse of a people doomed to endure hardships, a discourse whose very terms this book has attempted to dislodge with a different perspective of presence, creative engagement, multidirectional impact and change. Even in the case of the professor, his apparent apathy was undercut by the fact that he kept writing books and articles in the hope that one day they might be published and might change the perspectives of prospective readers, investing in academic writing as a legacy even though he might not see these changes himself. His efforts were emblematic of a core belief of many of the Sufis I encountered throughout my research: political change is inevitable, but the beliefs and practices that form the bedrock of Sufi communities will endure.

Haji Tamim displayed a similar attitude when remarking about the closures of Sufi lodges: "The *khanaqahs* have been here before I was born, and they will exist long after we are gone." In his view, governments came and went, and Sufi groups endured—sometimes by simply outliving them, sometimes through engagement and clever navigations.

This attitude was reminiscent of his late colleague and friend Haji Saiqal, who had always found ways to keep the *khanaqah* open and his community safe through dialogue. He might not have agreed with the Taliban's interpretation of Islam, but he saw them as part of the wider negotiations within the community of disagreement. These negotiations were among the navigations of authority in which *pirs* had to demonstrate proficiency to establish themselves and their community. A core aspect that comes out of the variety of ways leaders navigate the changing situation is their belief in a potential for an otherwise, for transformation and change. The present situation, however dark and difficult, is always just a transition to another state; it is never the end destination. This is not disconnected, bright-eyed optimism but a sort of grounded hope enacted through action that directs individuals and communities toward a potentiality. In a very different context, Mariame Kaba speaks about hope as a discipline,[15] conceptualizing it neither as an emotion nor as optimism or positive rhetoric but as a practical orientation toward life that involves risk and experimentation. It is a chosen attitude enacted through the ways in which leaders and communities deal with restrictions in the public sphere, difficult economic situations, the targeting of infrastructure, practice or members. Far from being a fetishization of resilience, it acknowledges the challenging circumstances as well as the capacity of the people who find themselves in these situations and their determination to go on. The lives and navigations of the people we have met in the pages of this book are ongoing, unfinished and incomplete. But they point to the ability to adapt and, with these adaptations, to manifest hope for alternative futures.

It is fitting then, I believe, to close out this book with the person who opened it. I met Asma once again during a visit to Afghanistan after the Taliban takeover. She was concerned about the economic prospects of her community and the hardships it faced acquiring the basic necessities of life but was unfazed by what the changes might mean for community practice. More than that, she had redoubled her efforts for reinvigorating Sufism as a socioreligious force in the civil sphere. She kept editing her father's oeuvre, organizing the annual celebration, albeit in a private venue, and continued to engage in the wider community through online teaching and infrastructure projects. But she also made steps toward a more public-facing Bedil community through buying land on which she planned to build a cultural community center for Bedil lovers. Her vision was to host international and national scholars there, hold talks and further the religio-cultural dialogue.

The decision to set down deeper roots at a time when many others chose to leave the country for better prospects abroad seemed remarkable. At the time when I visited Asma, in November 2022, Afghan women had just been banned by the Taliban government from spending time in parks. When I inquired how she felt about such decisions, she laughed off my question. "It is winter now," she said. "Who wants to go into parks?" "But it will be summer again," I remarked, a little incredulously. "Exactly," she smiled as if explaining the most obvious truth to a child. Asma was not disputing the difficulties that she faced as an aspiring leader or woman in Afghanistan, but she faced them with an attitude that reflected a Sufi ethos, an orientation toward the unchangeable in faith in the face of changing political fortunes: "Just like it is winter now and will be summer, nothing stays," she added wryly. "Things change."

GLOSSARY

adab	politeness, refinement, decency, morals as part of Islamic etiquette
alim	a learned man (especially with religious knowledge), Islamic legal scholar
amir	lit., "military commander"; the title of Afghan rulers until King Amanullah introduced the title of king (shah)
amir al-Mu'minin	commander of the faithful
aql	mind, reason
arif/aref	gnostic/mystic
ashar	collective voluntary community labor
awliya	sing., wali; lit., "friends of God"; those close to God, often translated as "saints"
baraka	pl., barakat; blessing, grace, "beneficent force" (of divine origin); sanctity associated with individuals, places or objects
barzakh	intermediary realm, isthmus
batin	inner, concealed, hidden, secret realities; opposite of zahir
bay'a	oath of allegiance by a disciple to a pir
bid'at/bid'a	(wrongful) innovation; a belief or practice for which there is no precedent in the time of the Prophet; considered Islamic heresy

chilla	period of ascetic retreat, usually forty days
chilla khana	cave, room or building in which retreats take place
Chishtiyyah	Sufi order mainly found in South Asia; founded in Chisht-e Sharif close to Herat
darwish/dervish	religious mendicant; someone living an ascetic life
dastarbandi	ceremony of "tying the turban"; dastar: the sash or fine cloth wrapped around the turban
dhawq	taste, direct taste (of the Divine)
du'a/durud	prayer
faqir	poor, destitute; designates being poor in relation to God and hence being dependent on him
fana	extinction of the self before attaining final union with God
ghayb	unseen, unknown, divine mystery
Hadith	lit., "speech"; the collective body of traditions relating to Muhammad and his companions
hafiz	someone who has learned the Qur'an by heart
haji	a person who has performed hajj
hajj	the pilgrimage to Mecca
halqa	lit., "circle"; gathering
Hanafi	one of the four Sunni schools of Islamic law; named after Abu Hanifa
haqiqa	stage of Truth
haram	forbidden by Islamic law or custom
Hazrat	honorific religious title, given in Afghanistan to the Mujaddidi family
ijaza	authorization, license, permission; certificate of qualification for teaching, for example, from a Sufi pir or alim to be added to the existing chain of knowledge transmission
ilham	divine inspiration
imam	prayer leader; leader of a mosque and its community
irfan	mysticism, gnostic mysticism, gnosticism
ishq	irresistible desire and extreme, selfless and burning love (lustless love) toward a lover or God
istikhara	lit., "search for the good"; prayer for requesting God's help; dream divination, dream incubation
jihad	a holy war waged on behalf of Islam as a religious duty; in Afghan context usually refers to period of conflict with Soviet Union and PDPA; a jihadi is a fighter in a jihad (greater jihad: struggle with the inner soul)

jinn	supernatural race of good and evil spirits that may help or harm humans
jirga	group of Afghan tribal leaders or members of the community who meet to resolve problems or make decisions
Kaaba	cube-shaped building in Mecca at the center of Islam's most important mosque and holiest site; Muslims turn in its direction when praying
kafir	infidel; non-Muslim
karamat	miracles, allegedly performed by Sufi saints
khairat	support for people in need, good work, charity
khalifa	caliph, representative, vice-regent; one who is a successor to the Prophet in rulership; used in Sufism for highest-ranking students, successor to a pir
Khalq	lit., "masses"; Communist faction in the PDPA, members were called khalqis
khanaqah	Sufi lodge
khatm-e Qur'an	a reading of the entire Qur'an
Khwaja	patrilineal descendant of Abu Bakr
lata'if	sing. latifa, meaning "gentle or subtle"; subtle spiritual center,; special organs of perception in Sufi spiritual psychology, subtle human capacities for experience and action
Loya Jirga	an Afghan national assembly of notables that convenes when necessary and changes over time
madrasa	institution where Islamic sciences are taught
mahfil	assembly of people, often at a celebration or party
maktab	lower-level religious school or ordinary public school
malang	wandering ascetic
masjid	mosque
Mawlana	lit., "our master/lord"; scholar of religious learning; in Afghanistan, Iran and Turkey usually refers to Rumi
mawlawi	scholar of religious learning
mawlid	commemoration of the birth or death of a saint; birthday of the Prophet Muhammad; sometimes also called milad
mazhab	school of law; religious sect
mihrab	a niche in the wall of a mosque indicating the qibla, the direction of the Kaaba in Mecca, toward which the congregation faces to pray

muhajir	migrant
Mujahidin	sing. Mujahid; fighters in a jihad; in Afghan context the anti-Soviet and Taliban fighters
mullah	religious leader, often akin to an imam
murid	disciple
murshid	spiritual adviser; a guide toward salvation
na'at kwani	singing and poetry recitations in praise of the Prophet Muhammad
nafs	the ego, self, lower or passionate soul
namaz	Islamic worship or prayer
parcham	lit., "banner"; Communist faction in the PDPA
pir	lit., "elder"; spiritual guide, adviser or Sufi saint; see murshid
Qadiriyyah	Sufi order prevalent throughout the Islamic world, founded by Abd all-Qadir al-Jilani (d. 1166)
qawwali	a form of Sufi devotional music
qibla	direction of the shrine in Mecca toward which all Muslims turn in ritual prayer
ruh	spirit, soul
ruya	truthful dream visions
Salafi	member of a reform movement demanding the restoration of Islamic doctrines to a purer form by strict adherence to the Qur'an and practices of the "righteous ancestors" (al-salaf al-salih)
sama or sema	a form of worship; meditative ceremony as part of zikr; often includes singing, playing instruments, recitation of poetry and prayers, dancing movements
sar-e halqa	lit., "head" of circle/meeting; zikr leader
shah	king
shari'a	system of thought concerning how Muslims should live; Islamic law
shaykh	Sufi master; title of respect for a learned scholar
shirk	idolatry, polytheism
shura	council
silsila	line of spiritual succession in Sufi tariqa
suluk	a journey to attain closeness to God
Sunna	a precedent; normative legal custom; a tradition of the Prophet
Sura	Qur'anic chapter
tafsir	religious exegesis
tajalli	manifestation, revelation, disclosure, epiphany, theophany

tanzim	lit., "organization"; refers to the Afghan political parties (Mujahidin factions) that fought the Soviet Union in the 1980s
tariqa/tariqat	road, way, path; can mean the whole system of spiritual training or a Sufi order
tasawwuf	Sufism
tasbeh	prayer beads
tawhid	the oneness of God
toshak	seating cushion
ulama	Muslim scholars who have specialist knowledge of Islamic shariʿa and theology
ummah	"community"; collective community of Muslims
umrah	Islamic pilgrimage to Mecca
urs	commemorative festival on the occasion of a saint's death
ustad	teacher
wali	a friend of God; a saint
waqf	religious or charitable endowment
watan	homeland
zahir	revealed, outer
zikr (dhikr)	remembrance, invocation of God, Sufi ritual, devotional reciting, praying or chanting of ritual formula in praise of God as a means of achieving inner purification, closeness to God and/or attaining ecstatic experience; can also be carried out in silence
ziyarat	visit or pilgrimage to a sacred place or tomb; in Afghanistan refers mostly to the place (shrine or tomb of a Muslim saint)

NOTES

Introduction

1. Namoraadi refers to a young person dying and being buried along with all the person's desires and wishes.

2. Mashhad refers to a place of martyrdom, such as the western city of Mashad in Iran, which is the spot where Imam Reza's grave is located.

1. The terms "Afghan" and "Afghanistan" are contested. Critics in some ethnic groups, particularly the Hazara and Uzbek, note the terms' historically Pashtun origins and argue that they are exclusive of other ethnic groups. Other terms, such as "Khorasani" and "Afghanistani," have been proposed though have not yet gained large-scale traction domestically or internationally (Mousavi 1998; Faridullah Bezhan 2008; Abbasi 2015: 275). Throughout this book, I have used the terms "Afghan" and "Afghanistan" for two reasons: they remain the internationally accepted terms for the country and the people who call it home; and my interviewees and interlocutors themselves used these terms to denote national identity, without ethnic connotations.

2. Individuals and communities who identify as Sufi have been targeted for their religious persuasions, but as I am analyzing Sufis as a civil society, Marika Theros has aptly pointed out that the conflicts since 1978 can be read as a "long war against civil society" (2019: 148) because of the deliberate targeting of the educated elite, prominent community figures such as religious and tribal elders, artists and poets and others in the civil sphere.

3. F. Ahmed 2017; Barfield 2010; Dorronsoro 2005; Nawid 1999; Olesen 1995; Roy 1984; Tarzi 2017; particularly on gender, see Ahsan-Tirmizi 2017, 2021; Baldauf 1989, 2017; Bergner 2011: 95–144; Billaud 2009; Brodsky 2011: 74–89; M. Mills 2011: 60–73; Sultanova 2008, 2011.

4. Bergen and Tiedemann 2012; Coll 2018; Giustozzi 2000, 2008, 2019; Griffin 2001; Johnson 2010; Maley 2001; P. Marsden 2002; Magnus and Naby 1998; Rashid 2008, 2010; Roy 1990. For a critical appraisal of the varying notions of jihad, see Olesen 1995.

5. The term "religion" has been amply critiqued and deconstructed in the past decades, particularly concerning its historic genealogies (Asad 1993) and the impact of its application to non-Christian faiths (S. Ahmed 2016: 176–201). For an overview of the various categories of definitions of religion, see C. Martin 2009. What "religion" and "religious" come to mean varies significantly, but I am generally using the terms in the way that my interlocutors and their communities referred to them.

6. See Adelkhah 2011; Aharon 2011; Arify 2021; Baiza 2014, 2015; Brauer 1942; Bonotto 2021; Canfield 1973; Edwards 1986b; Emadi 2014; Koplik 2003, 2015; Monsutti 2010; Mousavi 1998; Perennes 2014; Shinwari 2002. However, Nile Green (2017: 31) argues that a recent process of dediversification has led to Afghanistan becoming one of the least religiously diverse Muslim-majority countries worldwide.

7. Afghanistan lies within what Shahab Ahmed called the "Balkans-to-Bengal complex" (2016: 83), where Sufism was an integral part of the way Islam was lived historically. However, Sufi communities can be found all over the world. For various global explorations of Sufism, see Corbett 2017; Diouf 2013; Ernst and Lawrence 2002; Bazzano and Hermansen 2020; Ogunnaike 2020; Piraino and Sedgwick 2019; Raudvere 2002; Raudvere and Stenberg 2008; Rozehnal 2007; Sharify-Funk 2018; Strothmann 2016; Xavier 2018; Werbner 2003.

8. *Irfan* is sometimes translated as "mysticism," "gnostic mysticism" or "Gnosticism." These terms are often used interchangeably; however, the differentiation between them is often followed in Afghanistan by an implicit evaluation of one form as a noble, metaphysical, gnostic form of inquiry (*irfan*), whereas the notion of Sufism (*tasawwuf*) has come to be associated with popular forms of belief, superstition and sometimes even antisocial behavior. For analogy in Iranian history, see Knysh 2017: 36–38.

9. Can 2020; De Bruijn 1997; Ahsraf Ghani 1988; N. Green 2012, 2017, 2019; Edwards 1993, 1996, 2002; Haroon 2007; Lewisohn 1993, 2018; Nasr 1999; Ziad 2017b, 2019, 2021.

10. Most poignantly remarked in N. Green 2017: 26; also see Edwards 2017. However, in the case of Afghanistan, the absence is largely not due to the decline

hypothesis, as espoused in earlier accounts in which scholars attested to a decline of Sufi orders (Arberry 1942, 1968; Geertz 1971; Gellner 1981) but to a total lack of scholarly attention to these groups.

11. Notable exceptions for work in country in the 1990s are Baldauf 2017 and Monsutti 2005. For an overview of themes and structures of the field of anthropology pertaining to Afghanistan, see Monsutti 2013.

12. For local politics and center-periphery interactions, see Coburn 2011; Coburn and Larson 2013; Schetter 2013; Sharan 2011, 2013; Sharan and Heathershaw 2011; Sharifi 2019. For gender relations, see Ahsan-Tirmizi 2017, 2021; Billaud 2009, 2012, 2015; Chiovenda 2020; Wimpelmann 2017. For memory, trauma and ethnicity, see Kerr-Chiovenda 2014, 2015, 2018; Dossa 2014. For the reconstruction and development nexus, see L. Martin 2021; W. Osman 2020; Mojaddedi 2016, 2019. For international economic and labor networks, see Coburn 2016, 2018; Lin 2021; Monsutti 2021.

13. Anthropologists David Edwards and Omar Sharifi have paid sustained attention to religious texts, the oral history of charismatic Islamic leaders and religiously coded celebrations around Newroz. See Edwards 1986a, 1986b, 1993, 1996, 2002, 2017; Sharifi 2019. A recent foray has also been made by Ahsan-Tirmizi 2021. When anthropological research on Afghanistan blossomed during the 1960s and 1970s, researchers mostly focused on rural and tribal religiosity. See Baldauf 1989; Einzmann 1977; Canfield 1973; L. Dupree 1976; Frembgen 1994; Penkala-Gawecka 1992; Rzehak 2004, 2007; Wilber 1952.

14. N. Green 2017: 26; Monsutti 2013.

15. Edwards 1996; Lizzio 2014; Wieland-Karimi 1998.

16. Ridgeon 2015: 1.

17. Much recent anthropological scholarship on Muslim communities developed in reference to the generative work of Talal Asad (1986), who proposed to conceptualize Islam as a discursive tradition. Based on Alasdair MacIntyre's formulation of tradition and a Foucaultian concept of "discourse," Asad's approach has given rise to the rich theoretical exploration of the production and transmission of authoritative textual and oral Islamic discourses (MacIntyre 1988: 12). For an overview of discourse according to Foucault's understanding, see S. Mills 2003: 53–66; also see Foucault 1978, 1995. For explorations based on these approaches, see Bowen 1993; Messick 1993; Soares 2005.

18. S. Ahmed 2016: 147.

19. I limit my discussion of Sufism to the Islamic tradition. In recent years, Sufism has become a trend as well in the West, often coupled with New Age instructions, which do not see embedding into Islam as a mandatory precondition to becoming and being a Sufi. While this development has opened up new vistas for scholarship (Geaves 2014), I am focused on how my interlocutors in Afghanistan

understood Sufism as part and parcel of Islam and as intense devotion as a Muslim.

20. The term comes from Arabic *tariqa* and is used in the Arab-speaking world most often with the plural *turuq*. However, this pluralization is less common in Persian. Most of my interlocutors pluralized the term as *tariqas*.

21. Papas 2020.

22. Usually, an enumeration of Sufi orders in Afghanistan includes Suhrawardiyyah as well. However, historical sources already show that this strain was comparatively weak, and apart from a few scholars who maintained that they had read Suhrawardiyyah texts, their prevalence was relatively circumscribed. I did not conduct research in any community that defined themselves as Suhrawardiyyah Sufis in Afghanistan. For more on the Suhrawardiyyah in South Asia, see Huda 2005. For brotherhoods and their founders, see N. Green 2012: 84–91.

23. There are of course also Sufi mendicants, wanderers, who are often called *malang*. They often only loosely associate with a particular order, although they might visit *khanaqahs* and *ziyarats*. The term *malang* can overlap with other categories. Homayun Sidky points to the spectrum that the term *malang* can refer to "*madaree* (stage-magicians), *fakir* (either beggar or holy-men), *qalandar* (wandering Sufis), *jadoogar* (sorcerers who, in some instances, are indistinguishable from shamans), *charsi* (hashish addicts), *divana* (possessed madmen) and *palang dar libasi malang* (lit., tigers in *malang* clothing: impostors and charlatans)" (1990: 290).

24. Knysh 2017: 71–73.

25. Anṣārī al-Harawī 2011; Beaurecueil 1988; Dallh 2011, 2013, 2017.

26. Masud, Salvatore and Bruinessen 2009: 125.

27. S. Ahmed, 2016: 20–26. However, one of the most frequent sayings I heard among Sufi students was that *shari'at* and *tariqat* were two sides of the same coin, binding them together for a holistic understanding of Islam.

28. Elphinstone 1815: 215–216, 220, 272. See Chapter 2 for a more in-depth discussion of this split. While I single out these writings, there is of course also a history of writing in Sufi poetry such as Mawlana Rumi's, which makes fun of mullahs and jurists, using their positionality to outline the limits of knowledge acquisition through particular pathways.

29. Ingram 2018; Ziad 2021: 18–20.

30. Zaman 2002, 2012; Ahmad 2017.

31. Asad 1986.

32. N. Khan 2012.

33. While I am going to name and analyze a few of the positions critical of Sufism, the list is by no means exhaustive, as a full historical, ideological and geographical spread of criticism is outside the scope of this work. Criticism could also be analyzed from the Mu'tazila, the Almohad, Kadizadeli and others who con-

tested Sufi beliefs, rituals or organizations. The following overview represents broader trends and groups who have criticized Sufi ideas and practices. For further reading, see Sirriyeh 1999; Knysh 2017: 36, 176.

34. Dandekar and Tschacher 2016: 7.

35. The Arabic lexical translation for "innovation" is *bid'a*, which is theologically seen as "a belief or practice for which there is no precedent in the time of the Prophet." While the term *bid'a* itself is not mentioned in the Qur'an, variations of it are, and there are several Hadiths attributed to the Prophet Muhammad that speak to innovations as misguidance and error (Qur'an 2:111–117, 6:101, 57:16, 57:27). For more on *bid'a*, see Robson 2012.

36. For an overview of the term and its applications, see Ali and Leaman 2008: 55; Robson 2012: 1199; Rispler 1991: 321; Kamrava 2011.

37. Saba Mahmood (2011) and Charles Hirschkind (2006) explored the ethical subjectivity of pious Muslims in Cairo who attempted to craft virtuous selves through bodily practices, listening to cassette sermons and adhering to strict moral codes. The study of revivalist movements has antecedents in research on the intersection of Islamism, modernity and secularism (for example, Gellner 1992; Eickelman and Piscatori 1996; Kepel 2012).

38. S. Ahmed 2016. Recent works that grapple with these questions for Islam in general, Islamic authority and Islamic art are Alatas 2021; Burak-Adli 2020; Hill 2018; Mittermaier 2011; Shaw 2019; Taneja 2018.

39. For examples in media reports, see Pollock and Wehrey 2018; Specia 2017; Ayoob 2019; Risemberg 2019; Conesa 2018.

40. This list could be extended to other places and times, for example, by pointing to the Catholic liberation theology in Latin America (Büschges, Müller and Oehri 2021; Wilde 2016). Although it is not uncommon to perceive Muslim groups as antithetical to civil society, few might be so glaring as Ernest Gellner's (1994) claims of Islam as a "rival" to civil society.

41. Borchgrevink 2007: 13.

42. The civil society mapping by the United Nation's Assistance Mission in Afghanistan (UNAMA) revealed that while the main focus continued to be service delivery, especially in education (47 percent) and agriculture sectors (33 percent), there is a significant increase in the number of CSOs working on governance, rule of law, policy advocacy, transparency, accountability and human rights monitoring (24 percent)" (European Union 2015: 25).

43. Howell and Lind 2009; Orjuela 2008; Konings 2009. For a critique of this process, see Borchgrevink et al. 2005; Borchgrevink 2007; Nojumi 2004; Harpviken, Strand and Ask 2002, 2005.

44. Howell and Lind 2009: 718. This trend has also been called a "Civil Society Industry." See Theros 2019: 143.

45. For an overview of the idea of civil society, see Seligman 1992. Also see Arato and Cohen 1992; Hagemann, Michel and Budde 2008; Hall 1995; Keane 1988. The concepts inherit particular assumptions as well as historic connotations: Alexis de Tocqueville saw the proliferation of voluntary organizations as a core strength of American democracy, and Robert Putnam attributed the variable strength of democratic society in Italy to the social capital developed in horizontal ties of trust that could provide mutual assistance. In a later study, he lamented the erosion of American civil engagement, stating that Americans had abandoned bowling in teams to go "bowling alone" (Putnam 1994, 2000; also see Tocqueville 2003). However, Robert Hefner presciently remarked that "these Enlightenment experiments in democratic civility failed to extend rights of participation to whole categories of people, including, most famously, women, the propertyless, and racial and ethnic minorities" (1998: 26).

46. Volpi 2011. Indeed, John Keane points out that "civility was a privileged discourse of the privileged; it supposed and required the exclusion of whole categories of the world's population because of such 'inferior' characteristics as skin colour, gender, religion or lack of upbringing" (2003: 190). However, Keane also argues that the term has undergone a marked connotative change toward "peaceful plurality of morals" (190). Margrit Pernau (2016) remarks that the ashraf in India took up civility as a distinguishing feature of a progressive class.

47. Glasius 2010. For a view into ongoing discussions about the concept of civil society, particularly in South America, see Biekart and Fowler 2022.

48. For a questioning of the civil sphere and its normative preconceptions and modernity, see Deeb 2006. Recently the term "uncivil civil society" or "uncivil society" has been used for "manifestations of civil society that challenge liberal democratic values" (Glasius 2010).

49. Norton 1995; Hefner 2000; Sajoo 2002; Wolff and Poppe 2015.

50. Seligman 1992; Weller 1999.

51. Powell 2001.

52. US Senate, Committee on Foreign Relations 2011: 5.

53. Bizhan, Ibrahimi and Bose (2019) outline three Hazara-led movements, starting with the Tabassum Movement (Junbesh-e Tabasum, 2015), the Enlightenment Movement (Junbesh-e Roshnayi-e, 2016–2017) and the Uprising for Change (Junbesh-e Rashtakhiz-e Taghir, 2017). On the Enlightenment Movement, see also Kerr-Chiovenda 2018; Jawad 2020.

54. The founding members of the Afghanistan 1400 Movement were a group of well-educated individuals who also held positions in government, NGOs and private companies or were students and civil society activists. Ibrahimi 2017: 137; see also S. Kazemi 2012; Reid 2021.

55. B. Osman 2014, 2015a; Ibrahimi 2017.

56. Ibrahimi 2017: 12.

57. Afghanistan 1400 was not formally registered, but it gained a highly visible public profile due to the political affiliations of many of its members.

58. Nojumi 2004: 22. Theros refers to non-formalized groups as "value-based networks" (2019: 150). For local organization structures, see also Murtazashvili 2016.

59. Theros 2019; Volpi 2011.

60. Weller 1999: 16; Hann and Dunn 1996. On tracing the origins of the term, see Hefner 1998. The term has also been taken up to describe a virtue in political conduct (Peterson 2019).

61. For the genealogy in social thought on civility, see Elias 1998; Shils 1991. For an alternative construction of *adab* as civility and of Sufi communities as establishing an urban civility, see Kostadinova 2018.

62. Volpi 2011: 838.

63. Borchgrevink 2007: 37. Resource distribution used to be a more pronounced part of *khanaqahs*, in which large *langars*, or communal kitchens, fed travelers and *murids*.

64. Salvatore 2016: 74.

65. Salvatore 2016: 88.

66. Salvatore 2016: 83–89; Levtzion 2002: 110.

67. Interview, Kabul, November 2022.

68. Azoy 2012; Barfield 2010; Christia 2012; Malejacq 2017, 2020.

69. In his study on power relations in Afghanistan, G. Whitney Azoy, for example, argues that authority in Afghanistan manifested "in individual men who relate to each other in transient patterns of cooperation and competition" rather than in institutions or permanent corporations. While he generally acknowledges Islam as a strong unifying force in Afghanistan, he argues (in contradistinction to his general approach), that Islam's "capacity for providing a unity of norms is more than offset, however, by its failure to structure institutions through which authority can work" (2012: 25, 26–27). Noah Coburn, however, points to the influence of religious leaders relative to *maliks*, the local government and commanders in the competition for resources (2011: 116–123).

70. Edwards 1996: 140–141.

71. There are particular religious titles that are more strongly circumscribed. The title "Sayyid" is reserved for descendants of the Prophet Muhammad, and "Hazrat" is used for descendants of the second Islamic caliph Umar. However, other names and titles are less strongly predetermined. On the historical social and economic position of village imams in Afghanistan, see Edwards 1996: 134.

72. Arendt 1968: 93. Hussein Agrama (2010) has explored through the case of fatwas how authority has become seen as synonymous with coercion, particularly

as obedience is pitted against free will in the contemporary liberal notion that "the true self is the free self."

73. Krämer and Schmidtke 2006: 2.

74. Arendt 1968: 93; Raz 2009: 141. While Hannah Arendt sees it as a general feature of authority, Joseph Raz sees it as a key characteristic of legitimating authority, or what he calls "preemptive" authority.

75. Cited in Schimmel 1975: 103–104.

76. Zaman 2012: 30 (italics in original).

77. Zaman 2012; Hallaq 2001.

78. Zaman 2012: 33.

79. Ismail Alatas builds on the Arendtian differentiation between labor and work, in which work denotes economic production and labor is seen as "the ongoing and recurring life-reproducing activities characteristic of farm or household" (2021: 5).

80. Alatas 2021: 60–61.

81. Alatas 2021: 4–5. On charisma as an emotional bond, see Werbner and Basu 1998; Lindholm 1990, 2013.

82. Miller 2017.

83. Gennep 1960: 11.

84. *Baraka* is often translated as "blessing or grace." It is a sanctity associated with individuals, places or objects and can be transmitted through proximity. See Knight 2020; Safi 2000.

85. Sedgwick 2005: 3.

86. Sedgwick 2005: 225. While charisma is often described as an innate quality of a person, Charles Lindholm has argued that "unlike physical characteristics, charisma appears only in interaction with others." Therefore, charisma is a relationship between the one who possesses it and others who perceive it and are affected by it (1990: 7). Lindholm also remarked that charisma in religious groups can have inverse valences, either through disrupting institutional settings or solidifying the social structure (2013: 8). See Werbner and Basu 1998 on the embodiment of charisma in Sufi groups.

87. The German political sociologist Ralf Dahrendorf builds on the Weberian idea of "social options" that are open to an individual in the person's positioning within society. As Henrik Vigh explains the connection between Dahrendorf's approach and social navigation, "Life chances are, in Dahrendorf's perspective, constituted by social options and ties. . . . When these are combined in an analytical perspective, they grant us the possibility to investigate situated action" (2007: 14).

88. Pierre Bourdieu's "theory of practice" posits that people and groups act in different, overlapping and interpermeating "fields." He describes the concept of a field as a structured social sphere or space of action. See Bourdieu 1977: 41. For the Bourdieuian field, see Fuchs-Heinritz and Koenig 2005: 76.

89. Vigh 2009: 428–429. Vigh compares this to approaches (such as Tim Ingold's) that use navigation through transposing physical landscapes onto social terrains, which implicitly assume the navigation of social, cultural or ethnic landscapes with layered topographies.

90. Vigh 2007: 13.

91. Vigh 2009: 420.

92. Montgomery 2016: 156.

93. Barth 2002; Montgomery 2016.

94. Montgomery 2016: 107–120, 124, 125, 133, 157, 166–169.

95. O'Brien 2017a: 281. The concept of resilience has also been critiqued particularly in its emergence as a twin binary with trauma. See Moghnieh 2021a, 2021b.

96. Walker and Cooper 2011. For a particularly sharp critique of the usage of the term, with an incisive overview of its application with subaltern studies, see Bracke 2016, who reads the term against the grain in light of Gayatri Spivak's development of the term "new subaltern" (Spivak 2000: 324).

97. Barnett 2013.

98. Neocleous 2013, 2015.

99. For an overview of these discussions, see Fraile-Marcos 2020. For the argument of retaining an altered version of resilience through her conception of "broken resilience," see O'Brien 2017a.

100. This debate also draws on and is indebted to prescient insights from North American indigenous critiques such as Gerald Vizenor's argument on Survivance. See Vizenor 2009.

101. Shahrani 1991. Herat-born Sunni theologian and Sufi poet Jami famously called Mawlana Rumi's magnus opus, the *Masnawi*, "the Qur'an in Persian language," which elevates it to "Qur'anic exegesis by other means." See Schimmel 1993: 367, 369, quoted in S. Ahmed 2016: 307. Shahab Ahmed traces "around 4,500 direct citations of verses of the Qur'an (quite aside from allusions thereto) as well as more than 700 Hadiths" (2016: 307).

102. Amira Mittermaier's (2011) work in Egypt in particular opened the doors for more widespread anthropological explorations of dreams within the anthropology of Islam.

103. John Lamoreaux argues that the Qur'an contains dream narratives; however, "it nowhere enjoins Muslims to interpret their dreams, nowhere suggests that God regularly communicates with Muslims through dreams, nowhere makes the interpretation of dreams one of the duties of Muslims" (2002: 108). Nonetheless, Lamoreaux shows that Hadiths complemented the Qur'an as "proof text" (116). Dream interpretation was not a fringe part of Islam "but at the center of the concerns of the ulema" (133). All of the canonical Hadith collections devote whole chapters to dream interpretation: Bukhari's *Bab al-ta'bir* (Bukhari Sahih 9:37–58),

Muslim's *Kitab al-ru'ya* (Muslim Sahih 15:6–35), Ibn Majah's *Kitab fi ta'bir al-ru'ya* (Ibn Majah Sunan 2:1286–1294), Abu Daud's *Bab fi al-ruya* (And Dawud Sunan 4:304–306), Tirmidhi's *Kitab al-ru'ya* (Tirmidhi Jami 4:532–543) and Nasa'i's *Kitab al-ta'bir* (Nasa'i Sunan 4:382–392).

104. Dreams have been a powerful medium in Muslim communities, embraced by the full spectrum of the varying interpretations of Islam, from Sufis to jihadists. However, dreams have been confronted by a rationalist-leaning public that doubts their validity. See Edgar (2011: 65–78), who analyzed jihadist dream interpretation and dreams of Al-Qaeda members in online messaging boards.

105. The term "community" is complex and has been questioned concerning its usefulness for describing groups of people, particularly as their social affiliation, scalar and spatial patterns vary (Amit 2002). From Ferdinand Tönnies, Emile Durkheim and Max Weber, to Benedict Anderson, Akhil Gupta and James Ferguson, the term has been used by social analysts for analyzing processes of social cohesion and transformation. In this book the term is used for groups such as Sufi orders and poetry circles but also for the wider networks that follow the guidance of Sufi teachers.

106. For a detailed and comprehensive overview of Herat and its manifold connections to Sufis, see Noelle-Karimi 2014.

107. Contrary to many studies on Afghanistan that focus on ethnicity, I decided not to record data on ethnic belonging, and it did not surface as a salient category in my interviews and interactions. For studies that focus on religiosity among particular ethnicities, see A. Ahmed 1976; Canfield 1973; Caron 2016; Baldauf 1989, 2017; Kopecky 1982, 1986.

108. Class formation is a crucial and cross-cutting issue of social analysis, yet we know little about it in Afghanistan. Some literature addresses class implicitly through focusing on the urban poor in Internally Displaced People (IDP) camps or the excesses of the political elite, but it is devoid of theorizing. This might be due to its anchoring in neoliberal humanitarian work that is embedded within the drive to develop Afghanistan with a particularly uncritical approach to modernization. For accounts that directly address class as a category, see Marsden 2018; W. Osman 2020. For accounts that directly address class through critically viewing the place of landownership, see Murtazashvili 2021.

109. According to UNESCO figures, the overall literacy rate in Afghanistan for the adult population over fifteen years old is 43 percent. While this is an overall increase since 1979 from 18 percent, a closer look at the gender as well as rural/urban divide shows stark differences in who has received education in the past decades. Overall male literacy is 55 percent, with a male literacy rate of 68 percent in Kabul and 41 percent in Helmand in Afghanistan's south. The general female literacy rate is lower at 29.8 percent. The regional breakdown shows an even starker

difference, with a literacy rate for women in Kabul of 34.7 percent, but plummeting to 1.6 percent in Afghanistan's south. For numbers from 2018, see UNESCO 2023; Central Asia Institute 2018.

110. For a discussion of the sectarian divide and the question of nomenclature pertaining to Shiʻa Sufis in Iran, see Knysh 2017: 36–38. For new anthropological research on Shiʻa Sufi communities in neighboring Iran, see Golestaneh 2022, 2023.

111. For more on dialogic ethnographic approaches, its prospects and challenges, see Brear 2019; Caretta and Perez 2019. For an exploration of dialogic approaches as part of writing feminist ethnographies, see Sanger 2003.

112. Al-Dewachi 2017; Al-Mohammad 2015; Aretxaga 1997; Daughtry 2015; Daniel 1996; Dewachi 2015, 2019; L. Green 1999; Henig 2012, 2020; Kwon 2008; Lin 2022; Navaro 2012; Nordstrom 2004; Nordstrom and Robben 1995; Rubaii 2020; Scheper-Hughes 1992; Scheper-Hughes and Bourgois 2004; Uk 2016; Zani 2019.

113. Zani 2019: 8.

114. Zani 2019: 6. See also Henig 2012, 2020.

115. See, for example, Rubaii in Hannun, Lin and Schmeding 2022 for shared military technologies in Iraq, Palestine and Afghanistan.

116. Rasmussen 2015. This point was also not lost on the Taliban, when they hung four presumed kidnappers as one of their first acts of deterrence in Herat in September 2021. See Talmazan 2021.

117. Billaud 2015: 22, adapted from Marcus 1995.

118. A suspicion of spying probably led to the death of Italian Cambridge University graduate and PhD researcher Guilio Regeni in Egypt in 2016. See BBC 2019; Walsh 2017.

119. Anthropological knowledge developed in an environment of European colonial expansion; however, as Talal Asad points out, its role in imperial domination was relatively unimportant as it was often deemed "too esoteric for government use" (1991: 315). As regional comparisons show, the use of anthropology and ethnography in Colonial rule varied (Steinmetz 2003). See also Gupta and Stoolman 2022; Said 1989; Stocking 1991; Price 2016. For reflections on the impact of the wider environment of the War on Terror on knowledge production in the social sciences and humanities, see Hannun, Lin and Schmeding 2022.

120. For a more recent involvement of anthropologists with the military and intelligence gathering, see contestations around the Human Terrain System in Albro et al. 2012; Joseph 2016; McFate and Fondacaro 2011; Manchanda 2017: 183.

121. Bayoumi 2015.

122. On spatial exclusion and passport elites within Afghanistan, see Fluri 2009.

123. Other female researchers have expressed annoyance at the question of

whether their gender was a liability or restricted their research because men are rarely asked to account for the impact of their gender on their research (Jackson 2021: 19). I would argue the opposite though, hoping that the discussion of positionality, which both enables and restricts certain research avenues, would become a normalized feature of any social scientist's inquiry regardless of the gender of the researcher.

124. My group of research assistants had all worked in different capacities with international organizations and were fluent in English, some even in German. They were in their twenties and thirties and studying at universities (medicine, international relations) or working independently on projects (as filmmakers, consultants, research managers, journalists).

125. Pinto 2002: 4. Also see Pinto 2010. The question concerning the observer's position in the study of religion has also provoked vehement anthropological debates in the past. While the anthropology of Islam is focused, among other things, on the study of Muslim societies and cultures or Islamic traditions and practices, there have been calls for an "Islamic anthropology," premised on Islam as the base and paradigm for research, privileging Islamic history and theology as the frame for analysis. This approach, which was most vocally proposed by Akbar Ahmed, developed as a response to the experience of the intertwining of colonialism and anthropology, of Orientalist depictions of "the Other" and as a native way to speak back. These approaches have received ample criticism because they were perceived to be reducing the scope and methodology of a discipline to an ideology. See A. Ahmed 1984: 2, 1986: 210; Tapper 1995: 191; Marranci 2008: 48.

126. Haraway 1988.

127. James 1902: 488.

Chapter 1

1. Heck 2007: 2–3. For a selection of approaches and configurations of Sufi engagement with the state, see Corbett and Ewing 2020; Ansari 1992; DeWeese and Gross 2018; N. Green 2012; Haroon 2007; Krämer and Schmidtke 2006; Ziad 2021.

2. Both James Caron and Shah Mahmoud Hanifi have been critical about the ways that historians have engaged in history writing in Afghanistan and have offered productive avenues for approaching Afghanistan's historiography. See Caron 2007, 2009, 2011, 2013, 2016; Caron and Ahmad 2016; Hanifi 2011.

3. See Rubin 1995; Ghani 2008; Goodson 2001. For a critique of these approaches, see W. Osman 2020; Manchanda 2017, 2020.

4. For alternative approaches, see F. Ahmed 2017; Caron 2007, 2009, 2013; Coburn 2018; Crews 2015; Hanifi 2011; Hannun 2020, 2021; Monsutti 2005, 2021.

5. N. Green 2017: 2.

6. It is particularly salient to point out the excellent works that foreground Islam and religious actors in the history of Afghanistan. See Nawid 1999; Olesen 1995; Ziad 2021.

7. For a focus on these interregional connections between Afghanistan, the Middle East and Asia, see F. Ahmed 2017; Crews 2015; Hannun 2020, 2021a, 2021b.

8. See Dale and Payind 1999; N. Green 2012: 132–154; Karamustafa 2007; Shaw 2019: 22–23; Knysh 2000: 4.

9. See Algar 2013; Arbabzadah 2017; Barry 2003; Gross 2001; Nasr 1999; Okten 2007; Ozdalga 1999; Paul 2011, 2016; Potter 1994; Weismann 2007.

10. See Paul 2017: 71; McChesney 1991; McChesney 2018: 201–202.

11. The Hanbali school is one of four traditional Sunni schools of Islamic jurisprudence, which was named after the scholar Ahmad Ibn Hanbal. He studied philology under al-Tibrizi (d. 502/1109); Ḥanbalite law under Abu 'l-Wafaʾ b. al-ʿAkil, who had come over from the Muʿtazila to the Ḥanbalite mazhab (d. 513/1121), and under the kazi Abu Saʿd al-Mubarak al-Mukharrimi; and Hadith under Abu Muh. Djaʿfar al-Sarradj, author of the *Maṣariʿ al-ʿUshahaḵ* (d. 500/1106). Abu 'l-Khayr Ḥammad al-Dabbas (d. 523/1131) introduced him to Sufism. See Braune 2012.

12. Hagiographies describe Abd al-Qader in such an exaggerated manner that it caused dismay to later writers. See Trimingham 1998: 40–44. Nile Green points out that the Qadiriyyah order emerged and was spread by his disciples by "means of multi-generational collusion," arguing that was "imagined as much as it was real" (2012: 87). Gailani was initially buried in a shrine within his madrasa in Bab al-Sheikh, Rosafa, in Baghdad, present-day Iraq. The shrine, however, was destroyed during the reign of Safavid shah Ismail I. The Ottoman sultan Suliman the Magnificent had a dome built over the shrine in 1535, which exists to this day. See Braune 2012.

13. Trimingham 1998: 73.

14. Ludwig Adamec gives Sayyid Hasan Gailani's genealogy as descending from Sayyid Ali Gailani, the son of Sayyid Salman Gailani, descendant of al-Imam Hasan, son of Caliph Ali, son of Abu Taleb (1987: 126). Adamec reports further that the move was apparently initially motivated by a disagreement with his elder brother, Sayyid Abdul Rahman Gailani, who was the Naqib of Baghdad at the time and who disagreed with his brother's choice in marriage. Because Afghanistan was outside the Ottoman Empire, it was beyond his brother's sphere of influence, but it did have an existing following of Qadiriyyah Sufis who also made pilgrimages to the mausoleum of Sheikh Abdul Qadir. Naqib Sahib is the title given to the spiritual leader of the Qadiriyyah *tariqat* by the Ottoman rulers. See Olesen 1995: 46.

15. The Naqshbandiyya are often called in their earlier history the Khwajagan-Naqshbandiyya, the additional moniker meaning "the teachers," which references the spiritual descent to the founder Abd al-Khaliq al Ghijduwani (thirteenth

century, Bukhara), who "is said to have experienced a spiritual initiation through the mysterious, immortal, 'green' prophet, Khidr (Khezr)" while being a disciple of Khaja Abu Ya'qub Yusuf Hamadani (Utas 1994: 119). Jürgen Paul remarks that it was a term that the spiritual teachers used for themselves and that the name "Naqshbandiyya" came to be used only toward the end of the fifteenth century, beginning in Herat. The name was not adopted by Transoxianian groups of Khwajagan until the sixteenth century. See Paul 2010, 2017: 75. For the Naqshbandi genealogical overview, see Trimingham 1998: 93. Twentieth-century writers remarked that Islamic teachers who were interested in Sufism still went north to Central Asia for education. See Sirat 1969.

16. Ziad 2017a: 108.

17. Senzil Nawid relays the genealogical descent of the Naqshbandi-Mujaddidis through Mohammad Fazl-Allah's Omdat al-Moqamat as traced to "Shahab al-Din Farrokhshah, a descendant of 'Omar, the second caliph, who settled in Afghanistan in the time of the Ghaznavids and was buried in the valley of Farrokhshah in Panjshir, north of Kabul. Imam Rafi'al-Din, a lineal descendant of this man, went from Kabul to Sirhind. One of his offspring, Sheikh Ahmad Mojaddad Alf al-Sani (the son of Mawlana 'Abd al-Ahad) was born in Sirhind" (1999: 15).

18. Sirhindi was himself a disciple of a Kabuli Sufi, Khwaja Baqi Billah Berang (1563–1603), who was influential in spreading Naqshbandi teachings in Mughal India. His family had migrated several centuries earlier from the vicinity of Kabul (Ziad 2017a: 108–109). However, Asta Olesen records that Sirhindi practiced as many as four *tariqas* (Chishtiyyah, Qadiriyyah, Suhrawardiyya and Naqshbandiyya), "but with strongest emphasis on the latter with which he has become identified" (1995: 47). Also see Trimingham 1998: 94; Bazmee Ansari 2012.

19. Haroon 2007: 34; Ziad 2017a: 109.

20. This depiction of the development of Naqshbandi-Mujaddidi history follows Waleed Ziad's insightful overview. See Ziad 2017a: 105–126. Kenneth Lizzio also offers the spiritual genealogy of the Naqshbandi-Mujaddidi in Afghanistan and outlines how the Naqshbandiyya already had *khalifas* in Afghanistan in the sixteenth century, especially in Balkh, Kabul, Badakhshan, Kohistan, Laghman, Ghorband and Logar. See Lizzio 2014: 44–45.

21. According to Ziad, Fazl Ahmad Ma'sumi was a descendant of Shaykh Ahmad Sirhindi's older brother. The *khanaqahs* and madrasas that formed a network ranging from Balkh to Khoqand, Ghazni to Kashmir, were sustained by land grants and *waqf* endowments from Durrani rulers as well as other regional authorities. Ziad 2017a: 111.

22. Apart from settling in Kabul and Peshawar, Hazrats also settled in Herat as the Hazrats of Karrokh and in Jalalabad as the Hazrats of Charbagh. See Nawid 1999: 16.

23. Nawid 1999: 17.

24. Ziad 2017a: 112; 2021: 9–10.

25. Ziad 2021. Waleed Ziad argues in his study of the Naqshbandi-Mujaddidi that more than a mere alliance between rulers and Sufis, the transregional institutional networks of the order constituted a hidden caliphate, a sovereignty integrating a two-tiered paradigm of a hidden and a manifest caliphate.

26. N. Green 2012: 7; Ziad 2021: 13.

27. For a tracing of different policy moves of the Hazrats in the 1930s–1950s and the critique of the Awaken Youth Party (AYP) toward the Mujaddidi family, see Frud Bezhan 2016: 176–184.

28. The Mujaddidis first supported the pan-Islamism of King Amanullah but then opposed Amanullah's modernizing edicts. See Roy 1990: 43, 47; Nawid 1999: 115, 155.

29. See Roy 1990: 43.

30. Abdur Rahman had already curbed the financial autonomy of the ulama by putting them on the payroll of the state. The extension of integrating the great religious families into the state through marriage, posts and gifts of land was the positive side of the coin, whereas arrests of the Mujaddidi family as in the late 1950s is the other side, evidencing the attempt of the state to remain in control regarding the influential Sufi families. See Roy 1990: 46–47.

31. Asta Olesen argues that a similar trend of state integration can be found among other prominent religious families, mentioning that Fazl Ahmad replaced Fazl Omar as minister in 1932 and later became chairman of the Senate. Other senators included Abdul Baqi and Mahroon and Hashem Mujaddidi. For other non-Mujaddidi religious family representatives who became integrated into the ruling establishment at the time, see Olesen 1995: 185.

32. Roy mentions not only Sebghatullah Mujaddidi but also Harun Mujaddidi, who was later arrested by Nassir as a Muslim Brother (1990: 43, 70).

33. Ernst 1997: 5; Haroon 2007.

34. Sirriyeh 1999: 29. Elizabeth Sirriyeh judges the anxieties among colonialists as unfounded and exaggerated paranoia of organized Sufism "in a period of notable Muslim weakness, in which Sufis had very little real opportunity to constitute the supposed 'Islamic Peril,' although many might engage in vain attempts to defend the umma" (28).

35. Masud, Salvatore and Bruinessen 2009: 131; Evans-Pritchard 1949.

36. Ernst 1997: 5; Sirriyeh 1999: 29–30, 38–42; Haroon 2007: 48; Edwards 1996: 176–219. While taking up arms against colonial powers might be the most famous response to the colonial takeover, many examples also show a quietist response or even collaboration. See Sirriyeh 1999: 32, 43–45.

37. Mountstuart Elphinstone described the hearsay about the power of an

army of mullahs in his writing: "Stories are told of the walls of towns falling down at the shout of an army of Moollahs; and swords are blunted, and balls turned aside when aimed at the lives of these holy personages" (1815: 216).

38. Ernst 1997: 5–7.

39. For an analysis of the terms and discursive strains used by the British against these religious leaders, see Edwards 1989.

40. Ernst 1997: 3–4; Schimmel 1983: 137; Sirriyeh 1999: 55.

41. Edwards 2002: 228.

42. Edwards 2002: 228.

43. Olesen 1995: 230.

44. Kakar 1995: 335.

45. Edwards 2002: 326.

46. Edwards 2002: 228.

47. Allama Faizani spent two years in prison after being accused by local clerics of claiming extraordinary spiritual powers and a year and a half in prison after participating in the organization of the Pul-i Khishti demonstration in 1969. See Edwards 2002: 228; Adamec 1987: 49.

48. Although Faizani has also been accused of having plotted to overthrow the government. See Edwards 2002: 229–230.

49. See, for example, Chiabotti et al. 2016; Eaton 1974, 2000; Papas 2020; Wolper 1960.

50. It is unclear what forced the jurist and *alim* Baha al-Din Walad, Mawlana Rumi's father, to flee Balkh. Some say it was a quarrel with the theologian Fakhr-e Razi; others, that he anticipated the Mongol invasion. See Lewis 2014: 103.

51. Kakar 1995: 79.

52. For an in-depth portrayal of the various factions at the time, see Sands and Qazizai 2019; Barfield 2010: 213.

53. Hasan Kakar describes the intellectual horizon of Afghanistan's Left as being influenced by Communist literature; however, Afghan leftists took a different, less antistate route than other typical leftists, influenced by the literature of the Tudeh Party of Iran, the Communist Party of the Soviet Union and the Communist Party of China. See Kakar 1995: 80–81.

54. Mohammad Sharifi notes that the naming after a month (Saur is the second month of the year in the solar calendar) falls into the pattern established by the Russian "Great October Revolution" (2019: 1).

55. The Communists formed the PDPA in 1965 under the leadership of Nur Muhammad Taraki and Babrak Karmal. By 1967 it had split into two factions. The Khalq (Masses) was largely Pashtun, under the leadership of Taraki and Hafizullah Amin, recruited among the disaffected Ghilzai Pashtuns in the Soviet-trained military, in favor of uprising and no marriage ties to old elite. The Parcham

(Banner) was mainly Persian speaking, under leadership of Babrak Karmal, center of power in the bureaucracy and educational institutions, more willing to cooperate with existing elite, multiethnic, mostly Kabul born and many tied by clientage or marriage to the Musahiban elite. See Barfield 2010: 213; Centlivres-Demont 2015: 8.

56. Barfield 2010: 228.

57. See Kakar 1995: 92; Roy 1990: 96–97. Also see "Mapping Report Afghanistan 3," n.d.

58. Roy 1983: 69.

59. Haji Tamim, interview, Kabul, April 2018.

60. Clark 2013.

61. Roy 1990: 95–97.

62. Haji Tamim, interview, Kabul, April 2018.

63. Sinno 2008: 34.

64. Olesen 1995: 257–258.

65. The Jamiat ul-ulama was reactivated in 1980 by Karmal and replaced in 1982 by the Department for Islamic Affairs (Edare-ye Sho'un-e Islami). Traditionally, the Jamiat ul-ulama functioned under the Ministry of Justice. In 1985 the Department for Islamic Affairs became the Ministry for Islamic Affairs and Religious Interests. See Lobato 1985: 113.

66. Olesen 1995: 258–259.

67. Lobato 1985: 112.

68. Lobato 1985: 117; Olesen 1995: 273n5.

69. Lobato 1985: 116.

70. Lobato 1985: 114. Chantal Lobato gives an overview of the different religious figures who were chosen by Babrak Karmal, including their biographical backgrounds. She concludes that "the communists hope to show themselves to be conciliatory by choosing mullahs who are representative of the diverse regions in Afghanistan" (116). Lobato also muses about the different motives that mullahs would have to join the regime and summarizes: "Those who had been taken in, the *farib khorda* as the Afghans would say, who thought that the regime was not anti-Islam and believed that the government would not take an anti-religious political stance; and the ungodly, the *molhed*, who have been true partisans of the communist regime since the beginning, although it is unknown whether their convictions in support of the regime arose before the coup d'etat in 1978 or not. The first category is on the way to disappearing" (115–116).

71. Olesen 1995: 263. This number increased over time: Najibullah claimed in 1987 that sixteen thousand mullahs were on the government's payroll and a year later declaring the number to have risen to twenty thousand, according to Barnett Rubin, with Najibullah announcing a 250 percent increase of salary for Islamic of-

ficials. See Rubin 2002: 166.

72. Mohammed Fahim (1957–2014), former vice president (2002–2004, 2009–2014), was a Tajik military commander of the Northern Alliance. While Wujudi did not specify the time of these advances, he most likely refers to the time when Fahim was head of the Afghan intelligence service (Khadamat-e Aetla'at-e Dawlati, or KHAD) under Sibghatullah Mojaddedi and Burhanuddin Rabbani.

73. Interview, Kabul, February 2018.

74. Interview, Kabul, February 2018.

75. Olesen 1995: 270.

76. Rubin judges Karmal's "jargon-bespattered speeches" as sounding "as if they had been written by Soviet advisors, as indeed they may have been." He contrasts them with Najibullah's oratory style: "Najibullah was most effective not when he merely spoke respectfully of Islam but when he spoke Islamically of everything. His speeches to elders, tribesmen, and ulama, broadcast over Kabul Radio, did not just begin with Qur'anic invocations; they referred continually to Qur'an, hadith, the practice of the early caliphate, and the Afghan folk tradition" (2002: 165).

77. Olesen 1995: 271.

78. See Monsutti 2021 for a perspective on migration as a defining feature of life for people from Afghanistan, particularly in past decades.

79. See Z. Ahmed 2012; Colville 1997; Pstrusinska 1987.

80. Centlivres-Demont 2015: 1. See also "Costs of War" 2021.

81. Olesen 1995: 280.

82. Interview, Kabul, 2018.

83. See "About/Ustad Mazhabi," n.d.

84. For Soviet views of the war, see Alexievich 1992.

85. Barfield 2010; Fein 1993; Maley 2002.

86. See Rubin 1995; Kakar 1995; Roy 1990; Maley 1993; Dorn 1989.

87. Roy 1990: 115.

88. Rubin 1995: 44, 203. Rubin further states that NIFA resembled the Mujaddidi's National Liberation Front: "The core of leadership consisted of the leader's brothers and sons. . . . Nearly all the rest of the staff was Pashtun. . . . Significant numbers attended elite high schools or were educated in the West. The ANFL, however, did not attract as many former high military officials as did NIFA" (211). On the constitution of the different segments of the Gailani and Mujaddidi constituency, see Roy 1983: 70–73.

89. Rubin 1995: 210.

90. Rubin 1995: 211.

91. Roy reports that the Naqshbandi, Chishtiyyah and Qadiriyyah in Herat Province "do not acknowledge the leadership of the two great families, and the

majority have joined the *Jamiat-e Islami* (Islamic society), a fundamentalist party created under the old regime.... A minority have joined the *Harakat-e enqelab-e Islami* (Islamic Revolutionary Movement), a highly traditionalist party in spite of its name" (1983: 71).

92. Roy 1983: 69.

93. Roy also recounts several miraculous tales about the sheltering capacity of *ziyarats* that were circulating among the local population (1983: 70).

94. Roy names the examples of three areas: "the following committees are certainly directed by *murids* (usually Naqshbandi): Injil—commander Sufi Ghaffur (one of the strongest personalities in the urban resistance); Haouz-e Kerbaz—commander Abdullah Karruk Ghoryan; and Barnabad—commander Khwaje Zabiullah" (1983: 74).

95. Interview, Kabul, 2016; interview, Herat, 2017.

96. Roy 1983: 70.

97. Barfield 2010: 240. For a recounting of a Soviet perspective of the conflict, see Alexievich 1992.

98. *Ullah* means "of God." Before 1986, Najibullah was known as Dr. Najib. See Barfield 2010: 239.

99. Maley 2002: 204–205.

100. Interview, Herat, March 5, 2018.

101. Sinno observes: "The larger fighting forces ... fought fiercely over Kabul, causing much destruction and many casualties. The consequence of all this was to tarnish the reputation and Islamic credentials of most *mujahideen* leaders and parties" (2008: 36).

102. Fatimah Gailani, interview, Kabul, January 2018.

103. Christia 2012.

104. The labeling of the Mujahidin as *munafiq* (hypocritical) has a longer genealogy with the Communist regime labeling their opponents as such, which, Olesen argues, "underlined the religious character of the conflict, the *munafiqin* being those who at the time of the Prophet outwardly professed to believe in his mission, but secretly denied the faith—i.e. the most treacherous and dangerous of enemies" (1995: 262).

105. The *khanaqah* also houses a mosque on the first floor.

106. Interview, Kabul, April 2018.

107. Giustozzi and Ibrahimi 2012.

108. The Taliban attempted an attack on Mazar in northern Afghanistan in May 1997 but were driven out with huge losses. A year later they regrouped and took Mazar in August and Bamiyan in September 1998. For massacres and atrocities, especially on Hazaras, see Chiovenda and Chiovenda 2018; Ibrahimi 2016.

109. Barfield 2010: 256–257.

110. On the usage of violence as necropolitical power under the Taliban, see Edwards 2017.

111. See Matinuddin 1999; Nojumi 2002; Rashid 2010.

112. *Iqra* is the first word spoken by God in the Qur'an. It is variably translated as "Read" or "Recite."

113. Fatima Gailani, interview, Kabul, January 2018.

114. One of the few exceptions in looking at civilian negotiations with the state is Ashley Jackson's (2021) work on civilian bargaining with the Taliban. However, Jackson focuses her work mainly on the post-2001 period.

115. Fatima Gailani, interview, Kabul, January 2018.

116. Linschoten and Gopal 2017: 11.

117. On *hujras*, see also Dam 2021.

118. Linschoten and Gopal 2017: 13. For more on the history of the Deobandi school and movement, see discussion in Chapter 2.

119. Individual Taliban officials referenced dreams; however, certain individuals were officially recognized as skilled dream interpreters, such as Mullah Omar's adviser Mullah Deobandi, who had his own dial-up program on Radio Shariat, to which Afghans sent all kinds of questions that were sometimes also related to dreams. He used dream manuals such as Ibn Sirin's (d. 110/728) texts on dream interpretation, which have been translated into Persian and Pashto and were available from most book sellers in Afghanistan. See Dam 2019: 157–158.

120. The former Taliban deputy minister of the Department for the Promotion of Virtue and the Elimination of Vice (Amr-e Bil M'arouf wa Nahi Anil Munkar), Maulvi Qalamuddin, explained to me how he had used dream divination/incubation (*istikhara*) as a device to make professional decisions, claiming that he had canceled a meeting in Tajikistan because of a dream (interview, Kabul, August 2018). Mullah Abdul Salam Zaeef, the Afghan ambassador to Pakistan prior to 2001, reports a foreshadowing dream in his memoir, although he does not give any additional explanation about his beliefs concerning dreams (2010: 166–167). The former finance minister of the Taliban, Mutasim Agha Jan, verified in an interview that Mullah Omar not only had dreams that he felt were insightful or impactful but also that dream interpretation itself was a common, even daily ritual practiced among Mullah Omar and his closest circle (interview, Kabul, 2018). Thanks to the Dutch journalist and author Bette Dam for introductions, as well as many instructive discussions and exchanges on this topic.

121. Mutasim Agha Jan, born in 1968, was the chief administrator in charge of political affairs of the Afghan Taliban and member of the Quetta Shura. He was the finance minister during the Taliban rule in Afghanistan. He remained in the Taliban movement until his split in 2009. See "Afghan Biographies: Motasim Agha Jan" 2010.

122. Interview, Kabul, 2018.

123. See "Afghan Biographies: Rohani Mawlawi Pir Mohammed" 2012. Also see Times Higher Education 1997.

124. Interview, Kabul, August 31, 2018.

125. Interview with Rohani, Kabul, August 31, 2018: "Sufism is not a *mazhab* [school of jurisprudence]. There are *tariqats* that exist in any *mazhab*. Sufism is all about thinking, remembrance [*zikr*] of the creator and how we were created, who created this world.... Sufis are observing all the aspects of Islam. So everything they do is regularly like other Muslims, their religious rituals. Sufis are not harming other Muslims, and others are safe from their actions and words; Sufis are not backbiting. Sufis are not violating anyone's rights. Sufis are not killing anyone. They want all the time good for others. At the same time, they do *zikr*, in a way that is very deep, in a way that they feel that they see God. They are very deep in their *zikr*. So in both ways, outer and inner, physically and spiritually, they are thinking about God."

126. Linschoten and Gopal 2017.

127. See Dam 2014, 2021.

128. Mutasim Agha Jan recounted a number of shrines that he had visited with Mullah Omar, including those who had been martyred in the fight against the Russians.

129. Interview, Kabul, May 31, 2018.

130. A few biographical books have recently been published by Afghan Arabs themselves, usually cowritten with a journalist. See Anas 2019; Farrall and Hamid 2015.

131. The number of "Arab Afghans" engaged in the various stages of the wars is contested. The number ranges from rather conservative estimates of ten thousand (made by journalist Jamal Khashoggi) to twenty thousand, thirty thousand or even thirty-five thousand. David Commins estimates roughly twenty thousand foreign fighters, most of them from the Gulf States (2006: 174). Ahmed Rashid estimates that "35,000 Muslim fighters went to Afghanistan between 1982 and 1992" overall (2010: 129). Arab Afghan Abdullah Anas sees many of these numbers as inflated and believes that there were "about a hundred or so Arab fighters inside Afghanistan at any one time—I mean committed fighters—while the rest based themselves in Peshawar" (2019: 144).

132. Edwards 2017.

133. Anas 2019.

134. Afghanistan also has a non-Arabic-speaking ethnic group known as Arab Afghans. See Barfield 1981, 2010.

135. Many of the Arab Afghans who had fought and learned on the Afghan jihad returned to their home countries or joined other wars and conflicts (Li 2020). This

was not always a centrally organized effort, but it was an outcome of their experience in Afghanistan that had global repercussions. Ahmed Rashid points out that "Bin Laden knew many of the perpetrators of these violent acts across the Muslim world, because they had lived and fought together in Afghanistan. His organization, focused around supporting veterans of the Afghan war and their families, maintained contacts with them. He may well have funded some of their operations, but he was unlikely to know what they were all up to" (2010: 136).

136. Nojumi 2002: 226–227.

137. Interview, Kabul, 2017.

138. Farrall and Hamid 2015: 74.

139. Edwards 2017: 108. On the tension between Arab Afghans and Afghans overall, see Rashid 2010: 132–133.

140. The Taliban were not the first to forbid music. The Mujahidin outlawed it first in parts of Afghanistan. "Outside the capital, mujahedeen rule veered into the tyrannical. A commander in the northwestern province of Faryab decreed it permissible to rape any unmarried girl over the age of twelve. In the western city of Herat, authorities curtailed musical performances, outlawing love songs and 'dancing music.' It was the mujahedeen—not the Taliban, who did not yet exist as a formal group—who first brought these strictures into politics" (Gopal 2014: 60). Also see Baily 2009: 143–164, quoted in Gopal 2014: 270; Rahmany et al. 2012: 131.

141. Matinuddin 1999: 36; Rashid 2010: 2, 50. Michael Griffin reports an unusual circumstance in 1999 when the Taliban allowed a song on Radio Sharia that mocked America (2001: 239).

142. One interviewee remembered *zikr* with music in Kabul during the Taliban time, but only in a private place and not in the private-public space of the *khanaqahs*.

143. Interview, Kabul, 2017; interview, Kabul, 2018.

144. Interview, Kabul, May 31, 2018.

145. Interview, Kabul, August 2017.

146. See Billaud 2015; Coburn 2016; Dorronsoro 2005; Fluri 2009, 2011; Salvatore 2011; L. Martin 2021; Monsutti 2021.

147. Billaud 2015: 14.

148. Otto 2010. While the main basis of law is Hanafi jurisprudence, Omar Sadr describes how the issue of the Shia Personal Status Law became a public discussion that adjudicated questions of multiculturalism in Afghanistan. See Sadr 2020: 195–201.

149. Rüttig 2019.

150. Coll 2009.

151. "Interview with Fatima Gailani" 2011.

152. Sharifi 2019.

153. In his tenure as the director of the Department of Information and Culture in Herat, Wali Shah Barah offered additional rooms for Sufi-affiliated calligraphers, miniaturists and artists at Qala Ikhtiaruddin to teach and practice their art, which is steeped in Sufi allegories. Renovations of Sufi shrines, however, were usually in the hands of foundations such as the Agha Khan Foundation, as they were historic buildings that were renovated by international organizations.

154. Giustozzi 2019; Jackson 2021.

155. Sinno 2010: 25–44.

156. Reactive stances can be seen, for example, in the case of the killing of Farkhunda, the burning of Qur'ans by American troops or the regulation of religious education at madrasas. See Graham-Harrison 2012; Kargar 2015; B. Osman 2015b.

157. Jackson 2021: 61.

158. Mashal and Sukhanyar 2017.

159. Azami 2013.

160. See Reuters 2018.

161. In a rare but insightful report, Kaja Borchgrevink not only outlines religious actors as overlooked agents in Afghan civil society but also laments the lack of support and protection that "middle grounders" within the ulama receive (2007:10). See also Mashal 2013.

162. Mashal and Sukhanyar 2018.

163. The birth of the Prophet is called *Mawlid*, *Mawlid al-Nabi al-Sharif* or colloquially *mevlid*, *mulut* or *milad*. Muhammad's birthday was not celebrated by most Muslims until about the thirteenth century, and the celebration held in 1207 is regarded by many Sunni Muslims as the first *Mawlid* festival. See *Encyclopaedia Britannica* (2017), s.v. "mawlid," https://www.britannica.com/topic/mawlid.

164. Nordland and Mashal 2018; Kumar and Noori 2018.

165. The response at the governmental and local levels was suspiciously subdued considering it was an eighth-century shrine that had been rebuilt by the Agha Khan Foundation in the mid-2000s and would be regarded as a historical treasure that in any other circumstance would merit an outcry. The shrine (*ziyarat*) was primarily used as a place for quiet contemplation and prayer but on Thursdays doubled as a *khanaqah*, where Sufis gathered for *zikr* with music. See AKTC 2003; Aga Khan Historic Cities Programme, n.d.

166. There is a growing literature concerned with the question of why certain terror attacks are being claimed and others not. Min (2013) argues for example: "While a dominant strategy of intimidation keeps claim rates low, extremists are more likely to claim responsibility for attacks that involve high costs (suicide and casualties), institutionally constrained states (democracy), and competitive environments." For other arguments, see Hoffman 2010; Kearns, Conlon and Young

2014; Kearns 2021.

167. Private discussion with musician in Herat, 2018. *Chilla khanas* are places of retreat found in Herat, where Sufis go for forty days of meditation, reading and practicing *zikr* to gain closeness to God. Schimmel 1978: 105.

168. See O'Donnel 2015; Harooni and Mahr 2015.

169. Zaman and Mohammadi 2014; Ibrahimi 2017.

170. Concept Note on the Coordination Unit on Promotion of Moderation (De-radicalization), May 15, 2017.

171. Concept Note on the Coordination Unit on Promotion of Moderation (De-radicalization), May 15, 2017.

172. Adviser to the president, pers. comm., June 2021.

173. Philippon 2020: 145.

174. Barelwis are members of a Sunni movement named after the Islamic scholar Mawlana Ahmad Raza Khan Barelwi (1856–1921). They are often described as antithetical to Deobandis. However, newer scholarship emphasizes similarities and similar roots within the same Islamic tradition. See Sanyal 2020.

Chapter 2

1. The term *mulla/mullah* (learned man) was used for graduates of a local madrasa. Senzil Nawid reports that "until the beginning of the twentieth century, all religious scholars were called *mollas*, but the term was later restricted to mosque functionaries" (1999: 11). The term *Dahmolla* (a learned man who can lead ten mullahs) was used in northern Afghanistan for religious scholars who had received their training in Bukhara.

2. For an academic example of the comparison of illiterate village mullahs with Cairo-educated urban theologians, see Roy 1983: 49–50, cited in Shahrani 1991. For a discussion of this trope of both mullah and *maulvi* within neighboring Pakistan, see Ahmad 2017: 196–200.

3. The phrase "rule of the mullahs" is often used in discussions of Iran's religious establishment. See, for example, Huggler 2003. "Rohani" (spiritual), a coined term free of pejorative connotations, seems to have been promoted among Shi'a clerics as an alternative to "Mullah" and "Akhoond." See Momen 1985: 203.

4. Groenhaug 1978: 97–98.

5. Reza Aslan describes the beginning of Sufism as a "reactionary movement against both the Imperial Islam of the Muslim Dynasties and the rigid formalism of Islam's 'orthodox' learned class, the Ulama" (2011: 205). Other examples are Werbner 2012: 83–94.

6. This is perceptively also observed in both Waleed Ziad's study of Naqshbandi-Mujaddidi (Ziad 2017a: 107) and Ingram's study on Deoband scholars and the

overlap of the categories of mullahs and Sufis, which parallels the ridicule that both Sufis and mullahs experience (Ingram 2018: 16).

7. Phillipon 2020: 154.

8. The findings are in line with Bauer et al.'s argument that the exposure to war-related violence tends to increase people's cooperative and altruistic behavior, generally called "prosocial behavior" (2016: 250).

9. The community placed an article like an advertisement in the local newspaper: "Khanaqah ya shafakhana amrazi qalbi," *Etebar*, Chahar Shanbe, 27 Qaws, 1396 shamsi (December 18, 2017).

10. The *khanaqah* was built as an extension to the original lodge and was enlarged a hundred years ago with additional land that bordered the lodge, which was gifted to the *khanaqah*.

11. The inscription details that the founder of the *khanaqah*, Sufi Sheer Mohammad, gained this *khalifa* position from Ahmadullah Laghmani, who was educated in the way of Naqshbandiyyah.

12. Examples abound of hereditary Sufi lineages, such as the two most prominent political Sufi families in Afghanistan, the Mujaddidi and Gailani, and in local and regional contemporary and former *khanaqahs*.

13. Weismann 2007:13.

14. Ziad 2017a: 109.

15. Edwards 2002: 43.

16. On the prevalence of jewelry among Afghan and Pakistani men and its religious significance, see Lin 2021.

17. One of the posters read: "Oh Darwish! A derwish is to protect the hearts. If you don't have the courage to protect the heart and give solace to it, be aware! Do not harm/upset a heart, because in our tariqa there is no sin bigger than that."

18. Interview, Kabul, August 16, 2018.

19. In the same volume, Elizabeth Corbett traces the funding of Islamic studies departments in North America through the Rockefeller Foundation, their closeness to the CIA and the impact on the conceptualization of Islam and Sufism in academic writing from the Cold War to the present. See Corbett 2020: 27–40.

20. Alix Philippon presents the "Sufi Islam versus mullah Islam" narrative, which developed in Pakistan in the Musharraf era's financing of Sufism as a cultural national heritage. She analyzes it as a rendering of Mahmood Mamdani's analysis of "good" Muslim versus "bad" Muslim essentialist tropes. Reifying "Sufism" and "extremist" expressions of Islam is posited as "a solution to extremism in all its forms." Phillipon 2020: 154; see also Tareen 2020: 179.

21. On the compartmentalization that emphasizes this split, see also S. Ahmed 2016: 94, 124.

22. "Moollaahs" are for Elphinstone a group of religious scholars who preached

austerity, educated youth, mediated conflicts, practiced law and administered justice. Holy men were termed by Elphinstone "Derweshes/Dervises," "Fuheers" or "Kulunders/Calenders," whose domain included miracles, occult sciences, prophecy, astrology and geomancy. See Elphinstone 1815: 215–216, 220, 272.

23. Elphinstone 1815: 272.
24. V. Cornell 1999; Ernst 1997: 3–4; Schimmel 1983: 137; Sirriyeh 1999: 55.
25. Ewing 2020: 4.
26. Ewing 2020: 4
27. Sirriyeh 1999: 59.
28. Sayyid Ahmad Khan spent his early life in a major Naqshbandiyyah *khanaqah* in Delhi. See Weismann 2015: 23.
29. Sirriyeh describes Sayyid Ahmad Khan's naturism: "Consequently, a religion that is truly ordained by Him would not contradict these laws of nature.... In a famous statement, Sayyid Ahmad declared, 'Islam is nature and nature is Islam.'" All alleged miracles had to be interpreted rationally, even if they were mentioned in the Qur'an (Sirriyeh 1999: 63–64). Miracles mentioned in the Qur'an (*mu'jizat*) were explained as being actually dreams. See Weismann 2015: 15.
30. Sirriyeh 1999: 60–62. Sirriyeh also points to Sayyid Jamal al-din al-Afghani (1838–1897) as a Muslim modernizer. However, his stance toward Sufism was changing and complicated, and his critique was somewhat implied rather than directly stated at certain stages of his writing. For further reading, see Sirriyeh 1999: 65–74.
31. S. Ahmed 2016: 517–518 (italics in original).
32. Another intellectual who falls into this category is the father of modern Pakistan, Mohammad Iqbal. See Bashir and Crews 2012: 190; Corbett 2020: 32–35; Phillipon 2020: 146.
33. Faiz Ahmed shows the influence and exchange of both the Ottoman Empire and British India on Afghanistan's political and legal development. For India he argues that the geographic proximity, trade routes and linguistic and cultural familiarity between the two countries contributed to Indian Muslims having a large and influential presence in Kabul. F. Ahmed 2017: 96.
34. F. Ahmed 2017: 99–100, 103–105, 112–116.
35. Hannun 2021b. For discourses during the Habibullah government, also see Caron 2009. For the role of Indian Muslims in Afghanistan's Higher Education, see Khan and Noor 2015.
36. F. Ahmed 2017: 101.
37. While I refer to these linkages, which have come to the fore in more recent historic analyses, a comprehensive intellectual history of Afghanistan is still lacking. Christine Noelle-Karimi captured the essence of this problem in 1997, observing that "while the Indian historian constantly encounters the colonial

heritage in the form of a well-established discourse, the student of Afghan history is largely preoccupied with the elementary task of reconstructing the bare bones of the historical narrative on the basis of thin and often contradictory data" (1997: xv).

38. Charles Kurzman defines modernist reformers as a movement that self-consciously adopted modern values (rationality, science, constitutionalism) and were proponents of modernity but also wished to preserve and improve Islamic faith in the contemporary world (2002: 4).

39. Roy 1990: 45. Habibia was founded in 1903 by King Habibullah Khan, and it has educated many of the former and current Afghan elite, including Afghan presidents such as Ashraf Ghani and Hamid Karzai and the famous musician Ahmad Zahir. See Haider 2018.

40. In an accounting overview of the first one hundred years of the Dar ul-'Ulum, Barbara Metcalf shows that Afghan students made up by far the majority of foreign students at Deoband. There were 109 students; the next-highest number was 44, from China. Metcalf 1982: 111; see also Roy 1990: 58.

41. While the influence can be traced through individual scholars, it has also manifested in scholar-state relationships with, for instance, the national association of religious scholars, Jami-e Ulama-i Afghanistan, established under Nadir Shah, echoing an identically named association established by Deoband scholars in India. The association was mandated to manage the religious studies curriculum in Afghanistan. See Haroon 2012: 48, 52; F. Ahmed 2017: 248.

42. Roy 1990: 58; Metcalf 1982: 87. Sana Haroon terms the Deobandi approach an Islamic revivalism that is "anti-imperialist in its motivations" (2012: 45).

43. Sikand 2013: 130.

44. Ron Geaves points out that Deoband scholarship changed in Pakistan: "From the early 1980s until the early 2000s, the Deobandi movement in Pakistan was a major recipient of funding from Saudi Arabia until it ceased in favor of the rival Ahl-i Hadith movement, who are today far more likely and accurately to be associated with the Salafi movement" (2015: 193).

45. Mandaville 2014: 314.

46. Ingram 2018: 209–210.

47. About the establishment of a network of schools as a measure of success of the Deoband's goals, see Metcalf 1982: 125–129, 136. Estimates of Deobandi madrasas range widely. Peter Mandaville cites an estimate ranging from ten thousand to forty thousand in Pakistan alone with a concentration in the former NWFP/Khyber Pakhtunkhwa (2014: 243). Geaves points to the contentious opinions on how these schools are linked to Deoband and the confusion engendered in their connection to the original school in Indian Deoband (2015: 204, 193). Although there is a general decline in the number of formal Sufi institutions and practices

that used to run parallel to the *dar al-ulum* in India, he argues that Sufism is still a part of today's Deoband curriculum (204).

48. Sirriyeh 1999: 47; Metcalf 1982: 99, 157.

49. See Sikand 2013: 130–131; Sirriyeh 1999: 47. Metcalf traces this approach of complementary shariʿa and *tariqat* back to al-Ghazali (d. 1111) (1982: 139).

50. Deobandis in general are often contrasted with Barelwis in South Asia, marking the former as anti-Sufis and the latter as defenders of traditional Sufism (Sirriyeh 1999: 48). Dale Eickelman and James Piscatori describe them as "primary competitors" (1996: 154). Also see Geaves 2015: 204–209. Brannon Ingram posits that Deobandis and Barelwis are "for all intents and purposes, identical to one another: Sunni Muslims, Hanafi in law, Ashʿari or Maturidi in theology, adhering to multiple Sufi orders, and sustained institutionally through madrasa networks." However, they differ in their divergent views on theological concepts on "the possibility of God creating another Prophet, or many prophets, on par with Prophet Muhammad . . . ; the possibility of God telling a lie . . . ; and the question of whether the Prophet has superhuman knowledge" (2018: 7).

51. Olivier Roy argues that "the historical influence of Deoband has certainly been crucial to the development of Islam in Afghanistan; the only opposition to this tradition has been provided by the secular parties and by the Islamists and the Wahhabites, who, in their turn, set about establishing *madrasa* in the north-west province from the fifties onwards" (1990: 58).

52. The discussion here is focused on the main Islamist parties who exerted the most influence. Other parties led by well-known clerics and the two parties led by the hereditary Sufi leaders drew on their existing authoritative positions established through their Sufi lineages and clerical learning. However, both in the jihad against the Soviets and the discourse on the jihad they remained a rather marginal force.

53. Edwards 2017: 62–68.

54. Farrall and Hamid 2015; Anas 2019.

55. Interview with male interviewee, Kabul, 2018.

56. Chiovenda 2020: 94.

57. Malejacq 2020: 59, 133.

58. See Olesen 1995: 249–250.

59. On the Soviet-built neighborhood of Microrayon and its development, see Beyer 2012.

60. "MOHRA reported approximately 5,000 of the estimated 160,000 mosques in the country were registered, including the registration of an additional 700 mosques during the year. According to MOHRA, the ministry lacked the financial resources to create a comprehensive registry of mullahs and mosques in the country." See US Department of State 2017.

61. Posocco 2014: 104, 106. Silvia Posocco follows Strathern's approach when describing scale switching and establishment of partial socialities (109).

62. Mutasim Agha Jan called these "bad types of *zikr*" that were forbidden (*haram*). In his perspective, the right kind of *zikr* was silent and performed only "in the heart, secretly." Interview, Kabul, May 2018.

63. In this section I am drawing on Michael Taussig's (1999) notion of the public secret, as in a shared secret, an essential aspect of life that is important to know but cannot be articulated, a feature of society in which persons know what not to know. However, while Taussig maintains that behind elaborate practices of secrecy, there is no actual secret, in this case, the actual hidden and shared secrets mattered, and keeping them secret kept a community from punitive response.

64. While this might be true in this particular Sufi community, other communities experienced arrests. See Chapter 1.

65. Short for al-Amr bi al-Ma'ruf wa al-Nahi 'an al-Munkir, in English known as the Ministry for the Promotion of Virtue and the Prevention of Vice.

66. Interview, Kabul, August 2021.

67. Jackson 2021: 20. Ashley Jackson's work looks at civilian-Taliban interactions post-2001 when the Taliban had become an insurgency. Power dynamics are therefore somewhat different at that time than when the Taliban were a government in the 1990s. The case of Haji Saiqal, however, points to the fact that Afghan civilians were always negotiating and bargaining with the Taliban, not only when they had become an insurgency but also when they were in power in the 1990s.

68. Interview, Kabul, August 2021.

69. Phone conversation, March 14, 2022.

70. Notably, the Alauddin *khanaqah* was led by a mullah as well. It was attacked in April 2022, a watershed moment for Sufi-Taliban relations, as I explore in the Conclusion of this book.

71. Interview, Kabul, August 2021.

72. Interview, Kabul, August 2021.

Chapter 3

1. The discussion took place in April 2018. Qalle Fatullah is a residential area close to the city center of Shahr-e naw, where many foreigners and middle-class Afghans lived. A significant number of NGO offices were located in this area, which used to be lower profile in terms of security than Wazir Akbar Khan but became a target zone for kidnapping due to its economic profile. See Foschini 2019.

2. Abenante 2017: 129–148; Yazid and Demiri 2018: 304–307.

3. The experience of teachers as individual remainders from a great era who were seen as repositories of knowledge resembles Andrew Shryock's description of

oral history telling in Jordan. In Shryock's depiction, men claimed that there were "no more shaykhs" because the age of shaykhs had ended. However, his interlocutors established their preeminence through linking themselves to the glorious past. Lineages of learning function in a similar way in Afghanistan, where teachers point to past influential teachers to establish their own position through belonging as a link to the chain of transmission (*silsila*). Shryock 1997: 14.

4. Discussion in Kabul, September 2017.
5. Lindholm 2013.
6. Ahmed categorizes Sufi poetry as a prime locus for the exploration of the Divine, arguing that exploratory authority resided in the historical freedom of Muslims to explore meaning, value and truth through a multiplicity of ways, such as philosophy, Sufism or artistic expressions steeped in Islam, which informed such explorations. S. Ahmed 2016: 282–283.
7. See N. Haeri 2021; Marsden 2005; Mittermaier 2007; Shryock 1997; Olszewska 2007, 2015.
8. Koepke 2001.
9. Smith, Wetherell and Campbell 2018.
10. Breed and Iğmen 2020.
11. Dubuisson 2020: 89, 90.
12. Smith 2006.
13. See Wieland-Karimi 1998: 154; Loewen and McMichael 2010: 79.
14. Full poem in Persian quoted from the Diwan of Haidari Wujudi: دیشب کتاب طاقت من پاره پاره بود / دل درمیان سینه ی من بی اداره بود / در آرزوی دیدنت ای کعبه ی مراد / ورد و وظیفه دل من استخاره بود / از داغ های هجر تو ای مهر و ماه من/ دامان آسمان دلم پر ستاره بود/ می ریخت اشک حسرت من تا سپیده دم/ جانا، دو چشم من به مثال فواره بود/ دل آب گشته بود، سر و سینه ام کباب/ از بسکه آتش غم تو پرشراره بود/ دل نام، طفلکی که پدرخوانده ام بود/ از سینه ام برآمده و بی گاهواره بود/ نی شایق جمال و نه آقای عشقری/ نی عارف و امین و نه یک ماه پاره بود / نی نغمه ی مجید و نه آوای دلکشش/ جز آدمی که هیچ ندانم چه کاره بود/ نی از دیار لوگرو نی خاک پنجشیر/ نی کس انیس صحبت من از هزاره بود/ بردوش حیدری که ز یادم نمیرود/ القصه روز شد غم عالم اجاره بود

15. The general importance of poetry as a national cultural heritage is also described in N. Dupree 2002.
16. N. Haeri 2021: 45.
17. N. Haeri 2021: 30.
18. Lawrence 2006: 124.
19. Arjana 2020.
20. Moaveni 2017.
21. Lawrence 2006: 119.
22. Transliteration of Persian original: "Masnawi Mawlawi Manawi, ast qur'an dar lasaan pahlawi; Man che guyem vasif-e an ali-janab, nist peghumbar vali darad kitab."

23. Ali 2017.

24. Barks seems to work either from scholarly translations such as the ones of Nicholson and Arberry (who go uncredited) or transcriptions supplied by John Abel Moyne (born Java Moin), a professor emeritus of linguistics at City University of New York. Franklin Lewis comments sharply: "It is difficult to estimate the accuracy of the cribs Moyne supplied to Barks.... Barks holds some terminological misconceptions ... [and] often seems at times to have imprecisely or even incorrectly apprehended the meaning of the original. At other times he fudges culturally or religiously specific details." See Lewis 2014: 1, 127.

25. Ali 2017.

26. Schimmel 1983: 130; Nwyia 1970, 1972: 46.

27. Omid Safi, quoted in Ali 2017.

28. While examples of educational history are still patchy for some eras, Marya Hannun details the teaching of Amina al-Rasul (b. 1873), daughter of Mir Ghulam Faruq, who was an administrator/overseer of mosques in Kabul. She taught religious studies (*diniyat*) in the first school for girls in Afghanistan in the 1920s, including Mawlana Rumi's *Masnawi*, which "according to one of her students, imparting to hundreds of girls a consciousness of God and love of religion and the secrets of Sufism and guidance of mysticism." Hannun 2021b: 253. Hannun references here a quote from an oral history conducted by May Schinasi with students and teachers from the first school for girls in Kabul in the 1920s.

29. Shahrani 1991: 168.

30. About the varying conceptions and different institutional setups of madrasas in Afghanistan during the past century, see Karlsson and Mansonry 2007a, 2018.

31. Changes in education over the next decades are uneven. While the Communist government "introduced a modern education almost free from Islam (but with plenty of Communist propaganda)," it "wisely left the traditional madrasas to the local communities." The Civil War years show a highly uneven access to education, while the Taliban, as students of Islam, focused on their own particular reading of Islam. Karlsson and Mansory 2007b: 20.

32. See Shahrani 1991: 167–168. Indeed, Richard Tapper and Nancy Lindisfarne-Tapper (2020) report on the widespread use of the Chahar Kitab as well among Pashtun communities in the north before the war.

33. Peter Avery remarked that "the Persian language has changed less since the death of the poet Rūdakī in 940–1 AD than has English since that of Chaucer in 1400; Chaucer, of course, was Hāfiz's contemporary" (Avery 2010: xiii).

34. L. Dupree 1980: 75.

35. Wujudi's son Ghulam Naqshband pointed out a poem in his Diwan, which he saw as guiding Haidari's own approach to teaching and leadership: "You are my

beloved and I am yours / You will be my helper and I will be yours / You'll hold my hand, I'll hold yours / You are my leader and I am yours." Persian original: تو دلبر من باشی و من دلبر تو// تو یاور من باشی و من یاور تو// تو دست مرا بگیر// من دست ترا // تو رهبر من باشی و من رهبر تو

36. Conversation, Kabul, April 9, 2018.

37. Knysh 2017: 71–73. For *hal*, see also Gardet 2012. Adapted from the technical vocabulary of early Muslim scholars, al-Muhasibi (d. 857) of Basra is thought to be the first to have employed the term in relation to mystical experience. Contrary to a spiritual station (*maqam*), *hal* cannot be attained through efforts but is a grace bestowed by God.

38. Shahab Ahmed argues that the notion of specialized knowledge that sets particular groups apart was not exclusive to Sufis and philosophers but could also be found among "*kalam*-theologians" who cautioned against exposing commoners to knotty theological questions. Furthermore, the *amm/khass* divide has been used in Shi'ism to refer to Shi'ites themselves as *khassa*/elect and to Sunnis as *amman* commoners. See S. Ahmed 2016: 372–373.

39. From Haidari Wujudi's Diwan: تو چه دانی که در آتشکده عشق و هنر/ چقدر سوخته ام تا سخنی ساخته ام

40. From Haidari Wujudi's Diwan: به یاد آن مه گم گشته اندر عالم رویا/ که دارد آرزوی آسمان گردی که من دارم

41. Barfield 2005: 213.

42. Barfield 2005: 237.

43. Interview, twenty-five-year old Afghan female interviewee, New York, March 2016. Interviewee reconstructed that the memory might be from 1999.

44. Interview, male interviewee, Kabul, August 2016.

45. Pia Karlsson and Amir Mansory (2007b), for example, mention the differential time allotments for religious education between government-run, NGO-supported and former Taliban schools and give a general overview of subjects that are usually taught. However, they do not offer a comprehensive review of curricula or of actually taught subjects nationwide. While a full assessment of the changing position of Sufi poetry within the Afghan education system lies outside the purview of this chapter, the concern about its (partial) erasure or marginalization was voiced throughout my research in a variety of interviews.

46. "Radicalization" is an elusive term that people seem quick to use when referring to violent fundamentalism, or antecedents of jihadism, though it often remains ill defined. The discussion of indoctrination was often also connected to the funding of madrasas and the question of influence on perspectives that were taught. For example, Carlotta Gall (2016) emphasized: "Saudi Arabia is offering the Afghan government substantial defense and development agreements, while Afghans say sheikhs from Saudi Arabia and other Arab Persian Gulf states are qui-

etly funneling billions in private money to Sunni organizations, madrasas and universities to shape the next generation of Afghans."

47. See Quraishi and Doran 2014.
48. See "Open Letter," n.d.
49. Zaman and Mohammadi 2014.
50. Interview with Abdul Hafiz Mansoor, Kabul, June 2017.
51. In comparison, Sufi poetry used to be part of the Taliban's first generation's educational background in the 1990s, and poetry evenings were still held across the country at that time. See Dam 2021: 69–70, 156; Linschoten and Gopal 2017.
52. Alarabiya News 2022; Arif 2022.
53. Schimmel 1975: 2.
54. TOLO News Afghanistan 2016.
55. Change.org, n.d.
56. Frud Bezhan 2016.
57. For an insightful exploration of the struggle between a shared but contested language and literary heritage between Afghan migrants and Iranian crafting of national heritage, see Olszewska 2015: 12.
58. Smith 2006: 5; Kuutma 2013: 2.
59. Smith 2006: 3. Laurajane Smith has argued in the same book against the differentiation of material/tangible and intangible heritage, because all heritage would be intangible due to the value ascribed to it. She sees the differentiation into these two categories as an institutional and political application of the terms.
60. Bedil's full name is Mawlana Abul-Ma'ani Mirza Abdul-Qadir Bedil, but he is also known as Bidel Dehlavi. Both ways of writing the name as either Bedil or Bidel can be found in the reference literature. Some sources state that Bedil got his name in reference to Qadiriyyah Pir Shaikh Abdul Qadir Jilani, because Bedil's father (Mirza Abdul Khaliq) was a follower of the Qadiriyyah Sufi order. See Abdul Ghani 1960: 4.
61. Wieland-Karimi 1998: 154.
62. Interview, Kabul, June 9, 2017.
63. His year of birth is quoted as either 1642 or 1644: Sidiqqi 1989.
64. See Sidiqqi 1989. Abdul Ghani discusses the various Tazkirahs (biographical sources) and comes to the same conclusion. Ghani 1960: 1–3.
65. See Allworth 1990: 74: "His family in Putna (Azimabad) was descended from Uzbeks who had evidently migrated to Hindustan much earlier." See also *Encyclopedia Britannica* (2022), s.v. "South Asian arts," http://www.britannica.com/EB-checked/topic/556016/South-Asian-arts/65196/Persian?anchor=ref532393.
66. See Sidiqqi 1989.
67. Rypka and Jahn 1968: 519.
68. See Sidiqqi 1989.

69. Persian original: نهفت معنی مکشوف بیتاملیام/ نبستن مژه آفاق را معما کرد.

70. For a recent development in interest in Bedil in Iran, see reports on international seminars on Bedil, for example, SCRIBD, n.d.; and on its political ripple effects, see Agha 2016.

71. See Rypka and Jahn 1968: 517; also see the opinion piece in M. Kazemi 2015.

72. See Rypka and Jahn 1968: 517; "Mirza Abdul-Qader Bedil" 2011.

73. Almut Wieland-Karimi mentions a circle focused on Khushhal Khan Khattak in Peshawar, which was highly frequented after 1978 by Afghan literati and intellectuals (1998: 155). For Ghazni as an important center in the past, see Hosain and Massé 2012.

74. Interviews, Kabul, 2017.

75. The arguments about Persian as a language and whether Dari and Farsi are two different variants or their own individual languages have been fought publicly and been politically ideologically charged in recent years. Nile Green's historical overview refers to the political decision to rename Farsi/Persian as Dari as a nationalistic decision. Even though there are differences between Afghan and Iranian Persian, he argues that differences were "exacerbated by distinct literary trajectories pursued by Iranian and Afghan writers in the twentieth century" (2017: 13).

76. Green and Arbabzadah 2013: 13–16.

77. Green and Arbabzadah 2013: 10.

78. Green and Arbabzadah 2013: 13.

79. See "Mahmud Tarzi: His Life" 2004.

80. See Ashraf Ghani 1988: 432–433.

81. See Ashraf Ghani 1988: 432–433.

82. A sketch of Efendi's life can be found in Hosseini 2017.

83. He later moved to Jad-e Maiwand.

84. Khalilullah Khalili (1907–1987) was an "Afghan 'poet laureate' whose collected works (*diwan*) were published in three parts in 1960, 1975, and 1984. . . . He held various offices under the Tajik king [Habibullah Kalakani], but then lived as a refugee in Tashkent and later with his uncle" in Herat. He "became lecturer at Kabul University (1948) and secretary of the Shah Mahmud cabinet (1949). In 1951 he became minister of press and information and chief advisor for press and information to King Zahir (1953). In 1965 he was elected a member of Parliament . . . and founded the centrist Wahdat-i-milli (National unity) party. He was appointed Afghan ambassador to Saudi Arabia and Iraq from 1969–1978" (Adamec 2006: 217–218).

85. Sufi Abdul Bitab (1892–1958, though Ghani [1988: 444] quotes 1888–1971) was a "poet laureate (*Malik al-Shu'ara*) of Afghanistan who attained the status of master (*khalifa*) of the Naqshbandi Sufi fraternity. . . . He was awarded the title of

poet laureate in 1951 but was also respected as a commentator of hadith and author of numerous publications in a variety of fields" (Adamec 2006: 63).

86. Mawlawi Khal Muhammad Khasta (1902–1973) was a calligrapher, poet, writer, author of *Mo'asserin-e Sokhanwar* (Contemporary poets) and publisher as well as editor of Wahdat. See Adamec 2006: 220.

87. Interview with granddaughter of Efendi, Nilab Mubarez, Kabul, 2018. For coverage of the *urs* of Bedil, which mentions the beginning through Efendi, see Musharraf 2013.

88. These Afghan scholars are also mentioned in the Indian scholar Abdul Ghani's account on Bedil, who traveled to Kabul and met Sardar Faiz, Muhammad Khan Zakariya, Khalilullah Khan Khalili, Hashim Shaiq Efendi (though written Afandi in his account) and Dr. Ans. See Ghani 1960: ix.

89. Qandi Agha came originally from Badakhshan, but his life centered around Kabul. For political reasons he had to leave Kabul and lived for a while in Kandahar. He was a student at Armani High School and was fluent in German and Arabic. See Wieland-Karimi 1998: 154.

90. Sakata 1985: 138. For more on the musicality of Sarahang, see Sarmast 2009. Ustad Sarahang (2000) also authored a book on music titled *Qanun-i tarab* (Law of music).

91. Interview, Kabul, August 2016.

92. Loewen and McMichael 2010: 259. Ustad Sarahang was not the only one to use poetry in the early days of Afghan radio. Poetry recitation as an art form was celebrated in programs such as *Az Har Chaman Samaney* in the 1960s and 1970s and hosted by personalities such as Anisa Durrani (pers. comm., Mejgan Massoumi, Department of History, Stanford University; also see Massoumi 2021, 2022). Almut Wieland-Karimi reports about one such radio program titled *Zamzameh-e Shab-hangam* (Hummed melodies of the evening) in which a speaker recited verses of Mawlana Rumi and Hafiz while someone played calming music in the background. Wieland-Karimi 1998: 156.

93. The radio transmitter was first introduced during the reign of Amanullah Khan (1919–1929). In 1941 a government radio station, Radio Kabul, was established, known since 1964 as Radio Afghanistan. See Sakata 2002: xv.

94. The literature on Sufism and music is vast. More classic anthropological and ethnomusicological literature deals with communities surrounding musical performance and experience (see, for example, Abbas and Fernea 2002; Burney Abbas 2007; Pannke 2014; Jankowsky 2017; Manuel 2008; Ogunnaike 2018; Qureshi 2006; Senay 2014; Waugh 2005). Clinical studies have also been conducted on the impact of Sufi music on mental health (for example, Gurbuz-Dogan et al. 2021).

95. Ernst 2011; Ernst and Lawrence 2002; Rozehnal 2007.

96. See Sakata 2002: 190.

97. Ernst 2011: 228.

98. John Baily (2010) makes a similar argument but concerning why Afghans and foreign music connoisseurs tend to prioritize different products in the music market.

99. Baily 2010: 74; 2015: 29, 186.

100. See "Mohammed Hussain Sarahang" 2003.

101. Loewen and McMichael 2010: 259.

102. Kuutma 2013: 3.

103. For an overview of contested heritage studies, see Silverman 2010.

104. Sharifi 2018: 68–69.

105. Baily 2015: 49.

106. For an exploration of the environment that enabled some artists to flourish but suppressed others, see Baily 2016. For an exploration of the resulting exile for some, and the ways that music has incorporated these experiences as themes, see Jafari and Schuster 2019; Karimi 2017.

107. For Farhad Darya's recollection of Gorohe Bayan, see "Farhad Darya," n.d.

108. Online interview, April 2022.

109. The song that the interviewee referenced is "Baz amadam," which is based on a poem by Mawlana and available on YouTube at https://www.youtube.com/watch?v=xbPehzvYzao.

110. See Naderi 2022.

111. See Sharifi 2018: 69–70. For poetry collections from the refugee camps, particularly in the Pashto Landay format, see Majrouh 2003.

112. Sewing was one of the few allowed activities for women in the 1990s under the Taliban. An underground network of writers and poets met in hidden literary associations. See Lamb 2003.

113. Partaw Naderi (2000) mentions specifically the burning of fifty-five thousand Persian manuscripts in the Pul-e Khomri Library.

114. Sharifi 2018: 71. For more on the poetry of the Taliban, see Rahmany et al. 2012; Weinreich and Pelevin 2012.

115. Kabul, August 24, 2017.

116. Lindholm 2002: 185.

117. Kabul, July 19, 2018.

118. Ahmad (2011) presents a beautiful illustration on the usage of arguing through stories in the setting of a *jirga/shura* in the Afghan-Pakistani borderland.

119. Mallya 2014.

120. S. Haeri 2020: 25.

Chapter 4

1. See, for instance, N. Dupree 1992; Moghadam 1992; Ahmed-Ghosh 2003.
2. Billaud 2015: 5.
3. This development has been analyzed and critiqued by many feminist scholars, for example, Abu-Lughod 2002, 2013; Amin and Alizada 2020; Arat-Koc 2002; Lindisfarne 2002; Kandiyoti 2005, 2007; Stabile and Kumar 2005; Daulatzai 2008; Heath and Zahedi 2011; Fluri 2011, 2014; Fluri et al. 2017; Wimpelmann 2017.
4. On this point, also see Manchanda 2020: 143–179.
5. D. Holland, Lucile Martin and Saeed Parto (2016) describe the realization among international development actors that a human-rights-based discourse drawing on international standards had little resonance among the general public. This led to an increased concern about the "cultural appropriateness" of program design, leading to a repackaging of issues surrounding human rights and women's rights as "rights from an Islamic perspective." This approach often translated into the selection of elements of language from the Qur'an and/or the Hadith to legitimize the content of interventions by stating that "human rights are in the Qur'an."
6. My argument contributes to an ongoing debate on women as actors with agency. See Deeb 2006; Göle 2013; Mahmood 2011; Salime 2011.
7. This notion builds on what the novelist Chimamanda Ngozi Adichie (2009) called the danger of a "single story."
8. While I am providing specific examples, it needs emphasizing that individual journalists are not pushing this narrative, but it is a discursive field in which a particular trope has gained salience. See, for example, Faizi and Nordland 2019; Rajagopalan 2019; Breuer 2019; Glinski 2019; Luxner 2019; Brain 2013.
9. Carolyn G. Heilbrun sharply observes that "exceptional women are the chief imprisoners of non-exceptional women, simultaneously proving that any woman could do [remarkable things] and assuring, in their uniqueness among men, that no other woman will." Reality might not be so bleak, and success stories can bring the representation that motivates change, but they should also not blind us to the structural impediments to women's participation or leadership. Heilbrun 1988 quoted in R. Cornell 2005: 18.
10. Sherry Ortner critiqued structure/agency debates for seeing agency as a heroic quality set against a Borg-like determining suprastructure. I am building here on her approach of a more complex rendering of agency as enmeshed and determined in conjunction with the multiple social relations in which a person is implicated. See Ortner 2006: 129–139.
11. For a succinct overview, see Sehlikoglu 2017.
12. Deeb 2006: 29; also see Abu-Lughod 1998; L. Ahmed 1993; Spivak 1988; Puar 2008.

13. Mahmood 2011: 15.

14. Mahmood 2011: 29.

15. Mahmood's approach has been critiqued for being too specific to be used as a model for all Muslim gendered agency, for the reach of her ethnographic analysis and for the problematic narrowing of the field due to the *piety turn* associated with Mahmood's seminal work. See Bangstad 2011; Bautista 2008; Deeb 2015; Fadil and Fernando 2015; Schielke 2009a, 2009b, 2010; Schielke and Debevec 2012.

16. Serta Sehlikoglu (2017) sees this as a fourth wave of research on agency that develops away from too strong a focus on piety.

17. See, for example, Heath and Zahedi 2011, 60; Nordberg 2014. For a study on the shifts and pressure on masculinity, see Chiovenda 2020. Sonia Ahsan-Tirmizi directly builds on Mahmood's work (2021: 36).

18. See, for example, Bergner 2011: 95–144; Brodsky 2011: 74–89. The same volume also offers some rare writing on women's complex (and religious) agency in a patriarchal society. As Margaret Mills points out, women's controlled and disempowered status mainly enables them to assume the role of the subversive trickster in social settings, as evidenced in oral traditions (2011: 60–73).

19. The narrowing of Islam as prescriptive authority akin to orthodoxy is described by Shahab Ahmed in his critique of Asad's rendering of Islam as a discursive tradition. Ahmed argues that Asad's focus on text-based authority "effectively collapses the categories of 'Islam' and 'orthodoxy,'" which fails to capture the multiplicity of trajectories in Muslims' lives (2016: 290, 281).

20. Jinns are a supernatural species of good and evil creatures that may help or harm humans. For more on jinns, see El-Zein 2009; Beattie 1983; Einzmann 1977.

21. Baldauf 1989; Centlivres, Centlivres and Slobin 1971.

22. Sultanova's main research focus is Uzbekistan; however, she refers to female musical ceremonies in Afghan Uzbek communities in Afghanistan's north in the mid-2000s. While both celebrations are accompanied by collective music, women in Uzbekistan combine "pre-Islamic mythological beliefs of a Zoroastrian, Manichean, or Shamanic nature," while Afghan Uzbek female communities performed "predominantly Islamic rituals with Quranic reading as the main functional element in those gatherings" (2011: 194; also see Sultanova 2008).

23. Centlivres, Centlivres and Slobin 1971: 172.

24. A rare exception to this are the observations of Afghan businesswomen's discursive positioning within Islamic precepts. See Rahman 2018: 60–70. Robert Crews has offered an insightful media analysis of rhetorical strategies of Sunni (Jamiat-i Islah) and Shi'a (Tebyan) organizations to legitimize female religious authority through recourse to the family of the Prophet and reference to Iranian and Egyptian models (2021: 360–376).

25. Baldauf 2017: 210.

26. Ahsan-Tirmizi 2017: 225–241; 2021.

27. For a historic overview of women in mosque spaces, see Katz 2014. For an insight into the changing patterns concerning women and religious leadership, see Badran and Moghadam 2012; Bano and Kalmbach 2012; Gabbay 2020.

28. See R. Cornell 2005, 2019; Helminski 2003; Nurbakhsh 2004.

29. Frembgen 2008: 54–56.

30. Sedgwick 2005: 143.

31. Pemberton 2006: 74.

32. Some rare contemporary examples showcase appointed female *pirs* and *sheikhas* in Turkey and Senegal. See Burak-Adli 2020; Hill 2018.

33. Wieland-Karimi 1998.

34. The only other Sufi community I am aware of with this level of women's involvement includes the followers of Akhtar Mohammad Jan, also known as Baba Jan, a *pir* who died in 2009 in Kabul. The Baba Janis, as they are often called, have separate *zikr* and teaching circles for women. While I was able to interview a follower from one of the Baba Jani families, the wider community is more secretive and was not open to research about their community at this time. A combination of their secrecy and the active involvement of women might also have contributed to strongly critical views about their community by others, who viewed the participation of women as questionable, even alleging that *pir* Baba Jan had been involved in abuse of power toward women through forced marriages between male and female followers. Interview with Baba Jan follower, Kabul, 2016; interview with Mujaddidi family member, Kabul, 2016.

35. For more on the politics of the Communist regime toward religious orders, see Kakar 1995: 92; Roy 1983: 69; 1990: 96; Schmeding 2020: 109–115. For Faizani dates, see Edwards 2002: 228. However, his biography on the website of the organization lists his birth date as April 17, 1923. See "About Mawlana Faizani" 2015. Allama Faizani was imprisoned many times during his life. In an interview that David Edwards conducted with a Faizani *murid* in the 1980s in Peshawar, Pakistan, and that he kindly shared with me, the *murid* recounted that during the time of imprisonment, "*murids* and devotees helped his [Allama Faizani's] family. Everyone helped according to his own capacity." To make ends meet, "the members of the family taught the smaller ones how to make carpets. As they knotted the carpets, they simultaneously did *zikr*."

36. Olesen 1995: 230.

37. Edwards 2002: 228. While Faizani had a large following among military and government officials, he also had notable enmities, such as with PDPA-founding member Sulaiman Layeq (1930–2020), whose father was a well-known religious scholar and follower of the Naqshbandiyyah Abdul Ghani (d. 1979). Adamec 1987;

Rüttig 2020; interviews conducted by David Edwards in Peshawar in the 1980s (transcripts shared with me).

38. For a portrayal of this time in the Faizani community, see Cochran 2015: 63. Even more recent work on Faizani's writing and the community surrounding him both historically and currently found scarce documentary evidence of any female followers of Faizani, even though these followers do exist. The errors in these accounts, I believe, result because none of the authors interviewed the women of the Faizani community or focused specifically on the gender dimension within the Sufi sphere. Their accounts were based mainly on conjectural knowledge of his general political affiliations or on literary and digital analysis of the community's publishing (75).

39. Momena Billah, interview, Kabul, June 4, 2018.

40. Interviews conducted by David Edwards in Peshawar in the 1980s (transcripts shared with me).

41. Internal document of Faizani's community history written by Hasibullah Mowahed and shared with me, p. 7; Ustad Mazhabi, interview, Kabul, December 2019.

42. Ustad Mazhabi, interview, Kabul, December 2019.

43. Mann 2006: 8–10; see also Gopal 2014: 60, 270.

44. Burak-Adli 2020: 64–73, 179–197.

45. Laidlaw 2014: 87.

46. Kakar 1995: 79.

47. Barfield 2010: 213; Kakar 1995: 80–81.

48. Rachel Cochran argues that most writing on Faizani does not consider how Faizani evaluates science. She asserts that he often used it "as a literary tool to juxtapose the scientific expertise with the spiritual incompetence of man, particularly in those activities which have traditionally been within the purview of Sufi thought" (2015: 123). This approach "gained him considerable influence among the young educated who, when exposed to the results of the scientific revolution, were losing faith in the dogmatism of the traditionalists" (Olesen 1995: 230).

49. Interview, Kabul, July 2018.

50. R. Cornell 2007: 257–280.

51. Hill 2018: 144.

52. Shahzad 2007: 512–514.

53. Informal online conversation with Momenah and Manija Billah, July 30, 2020.

54. Ernst 1997: 106–111; Vicini 2017: 123.

55. Bashir 2011: 44–45.

56. Kugle 2003: 222–226.

57. Al-Ghazali 1993: 22.

58. Bashir 2011: 29.
59. Kamrava 2011: 126.
60. Kugle 2003: 48.
61. For an exploration of the heart in Sufi cosmology, see Kugle 2003.
62. Frembgen 2000: 14; Schimmel 1978: 17.
63. The Faizani approach is an adaptation of a much older tradition that can be found in classic Sufi writing such as Attar's introduction to Rabi'a or Sulami's biography of Sufi women, in which women's religious authority is legitimized within the nongender specificity of the Sufi path. See R. Cornell 2019: 254, 277.
64. Interview, Kabul, 2018.
65. Ustad Mazhabi entered the presidential race in 2009. See "Mazhabi, Motasim Billah" 2012.
66. The combination of Sufism and religion within neoliberal economic contexts has been analyzed elsewhere as expressions of individual empowerment and self-transformation. However, the Faizani interface with the capitalist and developmentalist milieu seems comparatively more utilitarian by using it as a recruitment ground for joining the community than a complete recasting of religion as individualized therapy and self-improvement. On these contrasting trends, see Altglas 2014; McCloud 2007.
67. For a historic overview of the area, see Schinasi 2017.
68. Momena Billah, informal interview discussion in English, Kabul, 2018.
69. Pemberton 2006: 68.
70. S. Haeri 2020: 25.
71. His death was never confirmed, similarly to Allama Faizani's death after vanishing at Pul-e Charkhi prison.
72. Ustad Shukria, interview, Herat, July 2018.
73. Nyhagen 2019: 321.
74. Hoel 2013: 32.
75. Ustad Manija, interview, 2018, and informal discussion, 2019.
76. Ernst 1997: 92; Utas 1999: 122.
77. Waugh 2005: 22.
78. Bashir 2011: 28.
79. Waugh 2005: 24–25.
80. Waugh 2005: 25. On the power of orality of the Qur'an, see Lawrence 2006: 7.

Chapter 5

1. N. Green 2003: 298.
2. Mittermaier 2011: 237.

3. Hill 2018; Mittermaier 2007, 2011, 2015; see also Ewing 1990, 1994, 1997.
4. Mittermaier 2007, 2011, 2015.
5. Mittermaier 2011: 239.
6. N. Green 2003: 298.
7. Mittermaier 2011: 243.
8. Rodinson 1980: 77; Watt 1974: 17. While Maxime Rodinson and Montgomery Watt might have conceded this point in contrast to earlier suggestions that the Prophet Muhammad might have been crazy, epileptic or schizophrenic, they nonetheless did not grant him the status of Prophethood.
9. Mittermaier 2011: 110.
10. Dream manuals constitute a particular subgenre of divinatory literature in Islam that can be traced to the influence of the translation of the Greek manuals of Artemidorus. See Bulkeley 2001.
11. Elphinstone records the belief in the efficacy of dreams in Afghanistan: "They believe in dreams, in which a sufficient latitude of interpretation is allowed, to admit of their easy application to any event. A man of some consequence told me, that at one time while he was flying from the persecution of Waffadar Khan (then Grand Vizier), he dreamed that he saw the Vizier dressed entirely in black, with a melancholy countenance, and with his hands shriveled, and so weak that he attempted in vain to untie his own girdle. Soon after the dream awoke, a man broke in on a private interview between him and another great man, with intelligence that the Vizier was deposed and taken prisoner" (1815: 223).
12. Khwajah Abd Allah Ansari 1983: 196–197, quoted in Islam 2002: 27–28.
13. Thackston 2002: 98–99.
14. A. Khan 1900.
15. Iain Edgar writes about Mullah Omar being inspired through a dream to rally the Taliban as a force, citing as a source Mariam Abou Zahab, a French political scientist who had studied in Pakistan (2011: 79). Thomas Johnson references dream insights of Mullah Omar for the inception of the Taliban, for taking the cloak of the Prophet to wear it in a public rally and for destroying the Bamiyan Buddhas; however, he does not cite any sources for the connection to dreams (2017: 282). Only Bette Dam gives a direct source for this foundation myth, referencing an audio recording of the inauguration speech of Omar as the amir in April 1996: "As the tape played, I heard Omar fall silent after describing the angels in his dream. A moment later, I heard him fighting back his tears. My Pashto teacher confirmed that he had seen Mullah Omar become emotional as he talked about his dream. The room was deathly quiet. But Omar regained control of himself and continued, 'Then I said the angels should touch me.' At these words, the audience jumped up and cheered as if he had told them that these angels were a sign Allah himself had chosen him. The audience started to chant rallying cries such as 'Allah

is great' and 'long live Islam.' Mullah Omar called on them to be silent and concluded his talk: 'So that was the start of the movement, and everything got going within twenty-four hours. That's what happened" (2021: 115).

16. Shaw 2019: 192.

17. Qala Ikhtiaruddin is located at the center of Herat city. The foundations date back to 330 BC when Alexander the Great and his troops arrived in Herat after the Battle of Gaugamela. The fort was destroyed and rebuilt many times over the centuries and saved from demolition in the 1950s. It was restored by UNESCO between 1976 and 1979. Between 2006 and 2011 it was completely renovated again with funds from Agha Khan Trust for Culture and the US and German governments. At the time of research it housed the Herat National Museum, and the Ministry of Information and Culture was the caretaker.

18. *Arg* means "citadel." Arg also referred to the presidential palace in Kabul. However, as the citadel in Herat was a former main royal palace, it also retained this name. The rooms in which the ateliers were located were added to the Arg during the time when Wali Shah Bahrah was director of the Department of Information and Culture. At the time, several Sufi-affiliated projects and arts found support.

19. Both affiliates added the name of their *tariqa* to their name: Bismillah (Faramarz) Salwati Saruri and Abdul Ghaffar Salwati Habibi. Bismillah/Faramarz told me that his legal name/birth name was Faramarz but that his *murshid* changed his name to Bismillah. I use the two names interchangeably but give preference to his chosen name.

20. There were distinct overlaps between occupation lines that used to function in a guild system in Afghanistan and Sufi affiliations. Micheline Centlivres-Demont (1997) has pointed out that each guild used to have a patron saint, whose name was inscribed in the *risala* that each guild affiliate would carry. Mohammad Sharifi has described in his study on the Newroz celebration in Mazar-e Sharif that the guilds were part of organizing Qur'an and Sufi poetry recitation as well as other rituals that accompany the festivities (2019: 21, 81, 157, 168).

21. These attitudes of understanding work as service to society and part of the spiritual path were also expressed in the *Tarikh-e Ali Salwatiyyah* as lawful and honest (*halal*) work being the basis of the *tariqa*: "Hazrat Akhundzada Sahib told me that the base of the *tariqat* is lawful honest/*halal* work and you need to work and earn your food. According to his will, I went and started some work that I liked, but I didn't continue any of it. I left that work and it was boring to me. I went to him and asked which profession I should take? Mubarak said, 'In the past time many sheikhs were shoemakers; you will also learn this profession.' I accepted. Then I went to an experienced shoemaker and became his student and learned his profession." Salwati Saruri and Salwati Habibi 2018: 122.

22. Interview, Herat, August 1, 2017.

23. Ibn Arabi 1980: 211.

24. Toshihiko Izutsu summarizes: "Self-manifestation' (*tajalli*) . . . is the very basis of his world view. . . . His entire philosophy is, in short, a theory of *tajalli*" (1983: 152). See also S. Ahmed 2016: 27, 30–31. Also on Ibn Arabi and his views on imagination, see Sviri 1999: 257–261; Chittick 1994; Corbin 1969: 184–190. On the imagination in Arabic philosophical tradition, see Meisami 1998: 393–394; N. Green 2003: 296.

25. Barry 2003: 14.

26. Shaw 2019: 19.

27. Knight 2016: 146–147.

28. *Sahih al-Bukhari*, vol. 9, book 87, no. 125. Leah Kinberg asserts that each of the canonical Hadith collections cites this hadith in support of the reliability of dreams (2008: 27).

29. Michael Knight discusses the implications of "seeing" and the ability to recognize and correctly identify Muhammad without having a visual record of him (2016: 146–47).

30. *Istikhara* is a widely known practice in Pakistan and Afghanistan, as well as in other locations such as Morocco, where it is called *stikhara*; in northeastern Sierra Leone, where it is referred to as *an-listikhaar*; and in Senegal, as *listikhaar*. See Crapanzano 1975: 148–149; Dilley 1999: 74–75.

31. Schimmel 1998: 16.

32. Schimmel 1998: 41; Hermansen 2001: 75.

33. Fahd 2012.

34. Edgar 2011.

35. See Salwati Saruri and Salwati Habibi 2018. Translations from Persian my own.

36. N. Green 2003: 308; Schimmel 1998: 41.

37. "The Prophet, now quite ill, is carried into the mosque on the shoulders of two companions. He tries to lead the prayer, but is too weak. He delegates his duties to Abu Bakr and as he leaves, proclaims: '[When I am gone] there shall remain naught of the glad tidings of prophecy, except for true dreams. These the Muslim will see or they will be seen for him'" (Lamoreaux 2002: 84).

38. Lamoreaux 2002: 110–113. For more on the connection of "glad tidings" and dreams as well as linguistic etymologies, see Kinberg 2008: 27n8.

39. Alatas 2020.

40. Schimmel 1998: 28.

41. N. Green 2003: 294.

42. See Bashier 2004; Hermansen 2001: 81; Lange 2011.

43. Hermansen 2001: 81.

44. N. Green 2003: 295.

45. N. Green 2003: 295. On the connection of the Barzakh with communication with the dead, see Marlow 2008: 5; Mittermaier 2007: 235; Lange 2011.
46. Salwati Saruri and Salwati Habibi 2018. Translations from Persian my own.
47. Karamustafa 2007: 130.
48. Knight 2020: 7.
49. Salwati Saruri and Salwati Habibi 2018. Translations from Persian my own.
50. Corbin 1969.
51. This part is written in Arabic.
52. Salwati Saruri and Salwati Habibi 2018. Translations from Persian my own.
53. The issue of Origin (*mabda*) has been of intense interest in Sufi thought. The technical term *ta'ayyun* (edification) plays an important role in discussions of Ibn Arabi's thought: "The word is derived from *'ayn*, entity, and it means to become an entity. Given that an entity is a thing, one might translate it as 'reification', not in the sense of a human cognitive process, however, but as a designation for the manner in which Nondelimited Being becomes determined, limited, defined, and 'thingish' in the process of disclosing itself as everything other than God" (Chittick 2020). *Ta'ayyun* is a key term in Ibn Arabi's ontology connected to the determination of Being and the process by which the Absolute is manifesting itself (*tajalli*) into concrete forms (Izutsu 1983: 152).
54. Sirriyeh 1999: 140.
55. I am following here Annemarie Schimmel's translation. See Schimmel 1985: 248. Marcia Hermansen traces the term *latifa* (plural, *lata'if*) to the Arabic word *latif*, meaning "gentle or subtle." While not Qur'anic in origin, the concept of the subtle body (*jism latif*) seems to have arisen in the third Islamic century. Other translations for *latifa* have been "subtlety," "tenuous body," "subtle point" or "subtle essence." Hermansen 1988: 1–2.
56. See Wali Allah al-Dihlawi 1982.
57. Hermansen 1988: 2.
58. Fusfels 1981, cited in Hermansen 1988: 2.
59. Qur'an Sura 33, 56.
60. Salwatiyyah history details: "He also did *suluk* in the Chishtiyyah and Qadiriyyah way. He learned about Chishtiyyah from his father, and his father had learned from his own predecessors. And after years of learning about Salwatiyyah, he got to know the Qadiriyyah way from Janab Hazrat Haji Mawlawi Sahib Abdalhalim Ghurani."
61. The line of argument that the practice was more "modern" due to its individualized character deserves fuller attention than this chapter can afford. Changes within religious practices and how they are anchored within perceptions of the urban and modern character of followers or, alternatively, parallel security concerns, is a promising avenue for future research.

62. On the question of authorship in dreams, see Hill 2018: 36; Mittermaier 2007: 235.

63. Mohammad Ismail Khan was a Mujahidin leader who served as a governor of Herat Province post-2001 until he was removed from his post in 2004. The time frame that Hosseini Wais refers to is the governorship until his removal. Ismail Khan then served as a minister of water and energy in Karzai's government from 2005 to 2013.

64. Malawi Abdul Haleem Hosseini Wais, head of Sufi Shura, Herat, interview, August 2016.

65. The Ulama Council has progenitors in the advisory board of ulama (Mizan al-Tahqiqat) that existed under Amir Habibullah (1827–1919) and King Amanullah (1892–1960), but it was a more comprehensive, national organization that has been described as a "pressure group for religious interests within the state" (Olesen 1995: 184). Post-2001 the Ulama Council was a semigovernmental body that was not mandated in the constitution but registered with the Ministry of Justice as a social and cultural organization. See also Dorronsoro 2005; Borchgrevink 2007: 27–28.

66. See Drage 2015; Ladjal and Bensaid 2015; Philippon 2014; Stjernholm 2010.

67. Interview, Herat, August 21, 2017.

68. For a view on the tradition of *shuras* and how the concept has been revitalized and used in the concept of development projects, particularly the NSP, see Noelle-Karimi 2013: 39–58.

69. The books were self-published by the council and then distributed to booksellers as well as institutions in the religious public sphere and religious personnel in mosques and *khanaqahs*.

70. The book mainly summarizes scholarly opinions, justifying the place of Sufism within Islamic history and Islamic religious practice and belief overall. The books of the Sufi Shura rely mainly either on established scholarly opinions or attempts to legitimize Sufi practices directly through reference to the Qur'an, Hadith and opinion of jurists, such as in the chapter on loud *zikr*, which legitimizes the practice mainly through reference to the Qur'an, Hadith and Islamic jurisprudence.

71. Imam Sabaki, Zahib Fatawil Faqahiattul Kubra.

72. Interview, Herat, 18.September 2018.

73. Shulman and Stroumsa 1999: 5.

74. Marlow 2008: 6.

Conclusion

1. For an exception to this, see Pinto 2002, 2010.
2. S. Haeri 2020.
3. Since the military withdrawal of NATO, international organizations and NGOs have begun to transport humanitarian aid again to Afghanistan. See, for example, UN News 2021a, 2021b; UNHCR 2021; Abdulkerimov 2021; Menon 2022. However, humanitarian aid has also become subject to negotiation, as witnessed in the suspension of aid activities when Afghan women were barred from working in NGOs. See UN 2022; Wintour 2023.
4. See in particular Aich et al. 2017; CBS 2022; International Federation of Journalists 2022; Qutbudin et al. 2019; Human Rights Watch 2021, 2022a.
5. The change of government in 2021 brought up challenging discussions among researchers pertaining to the ethics of research in de facto Taliban-governed Afghanistan. Control and surveillance of researchers have increased, as well as the pressure on communities and research assistants, facing potential endangerment through association with foreign researchers. I remained in contact with leaders and Sufi affiliates and visited most communities in Kabul and Herat in late 2022. Any meetings that I conducted in this setting were accompanied by careful back-and-forth between me, my research assistants and the communities we interfaced with, in which we assessed collectively what they considered acceptable or too risky. Previous long-standing relationships of trust were crucial in navigating the changing environment, in which I listened and followed their advice.
6. Conversation, Herat, November 2022.
7. Armangue 2021; Azim 2022; Synovitz 2021.
8. Bollag 1997.
9. Siddique 2022; UN News 2022.
10. On the attack on Sikh Gudwara, see Kumar 2022. On the attack on the mosque frequented by Sufis in Kunduz in April 2022, see Al Jazeera 2022; Goldbaum and Rahim 2022; Human Rights Watch 2022b.
11. Interview, Herat, November 2022.
12. Sands and Qazizai 2022.
13. Siddique 2021; Sirur 2021.
14. Interview, Herat, November 2022.
15. Kaba 2021.

REFERENCES

Abbas, Shemeem Burney, and Elizabeth Warnock Fernea. 2002. *The Female Voice in Sufi Ritual: Devotional Practices of Pakistan and India*. Austin: University of Texas Press.

Abbasi, Khadija. 2015. "Young Afghanistani Refugees in Iran: Professional Training, Work and Perspectives." In *Afghanistan / Identity, Society and Politics since 1980*, edited by Micheline Centlivres-Demont, 275–278. London: I. B. Tauris.

Abdulkerimov, Bakhtiyar. 2021. "UN Sends 100 Tons of Aid to Afghanistan via Uzbekistan." Anadolu Agency, October 18. https://www.aa.com.tr/en/asia-pacific/un-sends-100-tons-of-aid-to-afghanistan-via-uzbekistan/2395696.

Abenante, Paola. 2017. "Tasting Islam: Religious Aesthetics and Modernity in a Contemporary Egyptian Sufi Brotherhood." *Culture and Religion* 18 (2): 129–148.

"About: Mawlana Faizani." 2015. *Mawlana Faizani*. http://www.faizani.com/about/mawlana_faizani.html.

"About: Ustad Mazhabi." n.d. *Mawlana Faizani*. Accessed November 30, 2019. http://www.faizani.com/about/ustad_mazhabi.html.

Abu-Lughod, Lila. 1998. *Remaking Women: Feminism and Modernity in the Middle East*. Princeton, NJ: Princeton University Press.

———. 2002. "Do Muslim Women Really Need Saving? Anthropological Reflections on Cultural Relativism and Its Others." *American Anthropologist* 104 (3): 783–790.

———. 2013. *Do Muslim Women Need Saving?* Cambridge, MA: Harvard University Press.

Adamec, Ludwig W. 1987. *Biographical Dictionary of Contemporary Afghanistan.* Graz, Austria: Akademische Druck- u. Verlagsanstalt.

———. 2006. *Historical Dictionary of Afghanistan.* 3rd ed. New Delhi: Manas Publications.

Adelkhah, Fariba. 2011. "Religious Dependency in Afghanistan: Shia Madrasas as a Religious Mode of Social Assertion?" In *The Moral Economy of the Madrasa: Islam and Education Today*, edited by Keiko Sakurai and Fariba Adelkhah, 115–141. London: Routledge.

Adichie, Chimamanda Ngozi. 2009. "The Danger of a Single Story." TEDGlobal.

"Afghan Biographies: Motasim Agha Jan." 2010. March.

"Afghan Biographies: Rohani Mawlawi Pir Mohammed." 2012. December 5.

Aga Khan Historic Cities Programme. n.d. "Asheqan and Arefan Shrine Restoration." ArchNet. Accessed March 8, 2023. https://archnet.org/sites/5594.

Agha, Eram. 2016. "ICCR's International Seminar on Sufi Poet to Keep Pakistan Out." News18, November 6. https://www.news18.com/news/india/iccrs-international-seminar-on-sufi-poet-to-keep-pakistan-out-1308501.html.

Agrama, Hussein Ali. 2010. "Ethics, Tradition, Authority: Toward an Anthropology of the Fatwa." *American Ethnologist* 37 (1): 2–18.

Aharon, Sara Y. 2011. *From Kabul to Queens: The Jews of Afghanistan and Their Move to the United States.* Mount Vernon, NY: Decalogue Books.

Ahmad, Irfan. 2017. *Religion as Critique: Islamic Critical Thinking from Mecca to the Marketplace.* Chapel Hill: University of North Carolina Press.

Ahmadi, Arif. 2022. "MoHE to Implement New Curriculum in Accordance with Islamic Law." Khaama Press, August 12. https://www.khaama.com/mohe-to-implement-new-curriculum-in-accordance-with-islamic-law/.

Ahmadi, Belquis, and Sadaf Lakhani. 2016. *Afghan Women and Violent Extremism: Colluding, Perpetrating, or Preventing?* United States Institute of Peace Special Report, November 30. https://www.usip.org/publications/2016/11/afghan-women-and-violent-extremism.

Ahmed, Akbar. 1976. *Millennium and Charisma among the Pathans: A Critical Essay in Social Anthropology.* London: Routledge and Kegan Paul.

———. 1984. "Defining Islamic Anthropology." *RAIN* 65:1–4.

———. 1986. "Toward Islamic Anthropology." *American Journal of Islamic Social Sciences* 3 (2): 181–230.

Ahmed, Faiz. 2017. *Afghanistan Rising: Islamic Law and Statecraft between the Ottoman and British Empires.* Cambridge, MA: Harvard University Press.

Ahmed, Leila. 1993. *Women and Gender in Islam: Historical Roots of a Modern Debate.* Reissue ed. New Haven, CT: Yale University Press.

Ahmed, Shahab. 2016. *What Is Islam? The Importance of Being Islamic*. Princeton, NJ: Princeton University Press.

Ahmed, Zahid Shahab. 2012. "The Future of Afghan Refugees in Pakistan." Open Democracy, October 23. https://www.opendemocracy.net/en/opensecurity/future-of-afghan-refugees-in-pakistan/.

Ahmed-Ghosh, Huma. 2003. "A History of Women in Afghanistan: Lessons Learnt for the Future or Yesterdays and Tomorrow: Women in Afghanistan." *Journal of International Women's Studies* 4 (3): 1–14.

Ahsan-Tirmizi, Sonia. 2017. "When Muslims Become Feminists: Khana-Yi Aman, Islam and Pashtunwali." In *Afghanistan's Islam: From Conversion to the Taliban*, edited by Nile Green, 225–241. Oakland: University of California Press.

———. 2021. *Pious Peripheries: Runaway Women in Post-Taliban Afghanistan*. Stanford, CA: Stanford University Press.

Aich, Valentin, Noor Ahmad Akhunzadah, Alec Knuerr, Ahmad Jamshed Khoshbeen, Fred Hattermann, Heiko Paeth, Andrew Scanlon and Eva Nora Paton. 2017. "Climate Change in Afghanistan Deduced from Reanalysis and Coordinated Regional Climate Downscaling Experiment (CORDEX)—South Asia Simulations." *Climate* 5 (2): 1–25.

Akbar, Shaharzad. 2018. "Afghan Youth and 'Soft Radicalisation': Emerging Social Forces." In *Afghanistan—Challenges and Prospects*, edited by Srinjoy Bose, Nishank Motwani and William Maley, 143–156. London: Routledge.

AKTC (Aga Khan Trust for Culture), Historic Cities Support Programme. 2003. "*Asheqan Wa Arefan* Rehabilitation Programme, Kabul." Paper presented at the UNESCO International Coordination Committee for the Safeguarding of Afghanistan's Cultural Heritage Plenary Session, Paris, June 16–18. http://afghandata.org:8080/xmlui/bitstream/handle/azu/4309/azu_acku_pamphlet_na1492_a84_2002_w.pdf?sequence=1&isAllowed=y.

Al Jazeera. 2022. "Explosion at Afghan Mosque Kills Dozens of People." April 22. https://www.aljazeera.com/news/2022/4/22/explosion-at-afghan-mosque-kills-or-wounds-dozens.

Alarabiya News. 2022. "Taliban Adds More Compulsory Religion Classes to Universities in Afghanistan." August 16. https://english.alarabiya.net/News/world/2022/08/16/Taliban-adds-more-compulsory-religion-classes-to-universities-in-Afghanistan-.

Alatas, Ismail Fajrie. 2020. "Dreaming Saints: Exploratory Authority and Islamic Praxes of History in Central Java." *Journal of the Royal Anthropological Institute* 26 (1): 67–85.

———. 2021. *What Is Religious Authority? Cultivating Islamic Community in Indonesia*. Princeton, NJ: Princeton University Press.

Albro, Robert, George Marcus, Laura A. McNamara and Monica Schoch-Spana, eds. 2012. *Anthropologists in the Securityscape: Ethics, Practice, and Professional Identity*. Walnut Creek, CA: Left Coast Press.

Al-Dewachi, Omar. 2017. *Ungovernable Life: Mandatory Medicine and Statecraft in Iraq*. Stanford, CA: Stanford University Press.

Alexievich, Svetlana. 1992. *Zinky Boys: Soviet Voices from the Afghanistan War*. 1st American ed. New York: W. W. Norton.

Algar, Hamid. 2013. *Jami*. New Delhi: Oxford University Press.

Al-Ghazali, Abu-Hamid Muhammad. 1993. *The Alchemy of Happiness*. Translated by Claude Field and Elton L. Daniel. Armonk, NY: M. E. Sharp.

Ali, Kecia, and Oliver Leaman. 2008. *Islam: The Key Concepts*. New York: Routledge.

Ali, Rozina. 2017. "The Erasure of Islam from the Poetry of Rumi." *New York Times*, May 1. http://www.newyorker.com/books/page-turner/the-erasure-of-islam-from-the-poetry-of-rumi.

Allworth, Edward. 1990. *The Modern Uzbeks from the Fourteenth Century to the Present: A Cultural History*. Stanford, CA: Hoover Institution Press.

Al-Mohammad, Hayder. 2015. "Poverty beyond Disaster in Postinvasion Iraq: Ethics and the Rough Ground of the Everyday." *Current Anthropology* 56 (S11): S108–115.

Altglas, Veronique. 2014. *From Yoga to Kabbalah: Religious Exoticism and the Logics of Bricolage*. New York: Oxford University Press.

Amin, Sara N., and Nazifa Alizada. 2020. "Alternative Forms of Resistance: Afghan Women Negotiating for Change." *Journal of International Women's Studies* 21 (6): 358–375.

Amit, Vered, and European Association of Social Anthropologists. 2002. *Realizing Community: Concepts, Social Relationships and Sentiments*. London: Routledge.

Anas, Abdullah. 2019. *To the Mountains: My Life in Jihad from Algeria to Afghanistan*. Edited by Tam Hussein. London: Hurst.

Anṣārī al-Harawī, 'Abd Allāh ibn Muḥammad. 2011. *Stations of the Wayfarers / Manāzil al-Sā'irīn*. Paris: Albouraq.

Ansari, Sarah. 1992. *Sufi Saints and State Power*. Cambridge: Cambridge University Press.

Arat-Koc, Sedef. 2002. "Imperial Wars or Benevolent Interventions? Reflections on 'Global Feminism' post September 11th." *Atlantis* (Wolfville, Nova Scotia) 26 (2): 53–65.

Arato, Andrew, and Jean L. Cohen. 1992. *Civil Society and Political Theory*. Cambridge, MA: MIT Press.

Arbabzadah, Nushin. 2017. "Women and Religious Patronage in the Timurid Empire." In *Afghanistan's Islam: From Conversion to the Taliban*, edited by Nile Green, 56–70. Oakland: University of California Press.

Arberry, A. J. 1942. *An Introduction to the History of Sufism*. London: Longmans, Green.

———. 1968. *Sufism: An Account of the Mystics of Islam*. London: Allen and Unwin.

Arendt, Hannah. 1968. *Between Past and Future: Eight Exercises in Political Thought*. New York: Penguin Books.

Aretxaga, Begona. 1997. *Shattering Silence: Women, Nationalism, and Political Subjectivity in Northern Ireland*. Princeton, NJ: Princeton University Press.

Arify, Mujtaba. 2021. "Cultural and Ethnic Characteristics of Sikhs in Afghanistan." *Advances in Anthropology* 11 (1): 25–35.

Arjana, Sophia Rose. 2020. *Buying Buddha, Selling Rumi: Orientalism and the Mystical Marketplace*. New York: Oneworld Publications.

Armangue, Bernat. 2021. "Under Taliban, Thriving Afghan Music Scene Heads to Silence." *The Diplomat*, September 23. https://thediplomat.com/2021/09/under-taliban-thriving-afghan-music-scene-heads-to-silence/.

Asad, Talal. 1986. *The Idea of an Anthropology of Islam*. Washington, DC: Georgetown University Center for Contemporary Arab Studies.

———. 1991. "Afterword: From the History of Colonial Anthropology to the Anthropology of Western Hegemony." In *Colonial Situations: Essays on the Contextualization of Ethnographic Knowledge*, edited by George W. Stocking, 314–324. Madison: University of Wisconsin Press.

———. 1993. *Genealogies of Religion: Discipline and Reasons of Power in Christianity and Islam*. Baltimore: Johns Hopkins University Press.

Aslan, Reza. 2011. *No God but God: The Origins, Evolution, and Future of Islam*. Updated ed. New York: Random House Trade Paperbacks.

Avery, Peter. 2010. "Foreword: Hafiz of Shiraz." In *Hafiz and the Religion of Love in Classical Persian Poetry*, edited by Leonard Lewisohn. London: I. B. Tauris.

Ayoob, Mohammed. 2019. "Caught between Two Extremisms." *The Hindu*, February 11. https://www.thehindu.com/opinion/lead/caught-between-two-extremisms/article26231338.ece.

Azami, Dawood. 2013. "The 'Dissenting' Clerics Killed in Afghanistan." *BBC World*, November 19. https://www.bbc.com/news/world-asia-22885170.

Azim, Abdul Karim. 2022. "The Lives Impacted by Taliban Takeover." *Alive-in*, April 6. https://www.alive-in.org/the-lives-impacted-by-taliban-takeover/.

Azoy, G. Whitney. 2012. *Buzkashi: Game and Power in Afghanistan*. 3rd ed. Long Grove, IL: Waveland Press.

Badran, Margot, and Valentine Moghadam. 2012. *Women, Leadership, and Mosques: Changes in Contemporary Islamic Authority*. Leiden, Netherlands: Brill.

Baily, John. 2009. "Music and Censorship in Afghanistan, 1973–2003." In *Music and the Play of Power in the Middle East, North Africa and Central Asia*, edited by Laudan Nooshin, 143–164. Farnham, Surry, UK: Ashgate.

———. 2010. "Two Different Worlds: Afghan Music for Afghanistanis and Kharejis." *Ethnomusicology Forum* 19 (1): 69–88.

———. 2015. *War, Exile and the Music of Afghanistan*. SOAS Musicology Series. Surrey, UK: Ashgate Publishing.

———. 2016. "The Religious Persecution of Musicians in Afghanistan (1978–2014)." *Redefining Community in Intercultural Context* 5 (1): 17–22.

Baiza, Yahia. 2014. "The Hazaras of Afghanistan and Their Shi'a Orientation: An Analytical Historical Survey." *Journal of Shi'a Islamic Studies* 7 (2): 151–171.

———. 2015. "The Shi'a Isma'ili *Da'wat* in Khurasan: From Its Early Beginning to the Ghaznawid Era." *Journal of Shi'a Islamic Studies* 8 (1): 37–60. https://doi.org/10.1353/isl.2015.0013.

Baldauf, Ingeborg. 1989. "Zur Religiosen Paxis Ozbekischer Frauen in Nordafghanistan." In *Religious and Lay Symbolism in the Altaic World and Other Papers: Proceedings of the 27th Meeting of the Permanent International Altaistic Conference*. Wiesbaden: Otto Harrassowitz.

———. 2017. "Female Sainthood between Politics and Legend: The Emergence of Bibi Nushin of Shiberghan." In *Afghanistan's Islam: From Conversion to the Taliban*, edited by Nile Green, 207–224. Oakland: University of California Press.

Bangstad, Sindre. 2011. "Saba Mahmood and Anthropological Feminism after Virtue." *Theory, Culture & Society* 28 (3): 28–54.

Bano, Masooda, and Hilary Kalmbach. 2012. *Women, Leadership and Mosques: Changes in Contemporary Islamic Authority*. Leiden, Netherlands: Brill.

Barfield, Thomas J. 1981. *The Central Asian Arabs of Afghanistan: Pastoral Nomadism in Transition*. Austin: University of Texas Press.

———. 1993. *The Nomadic Alternative*. Englewood Cliffs, NJ: Prentice Hall.

———. 2005. "An Islamic State Is a State Run by Good Muslims: Religion as a Way of Life and Not as an Ideology in Afghanistan." In *Remaking Muslim Politics: Pluralism, Contestation, Democratization*, edited by Robert Hefner, 213–239. Princeton, NJ: Princeton University Press.

———. 2010. *Afghanistan: A Cultural and Political History*. Princeton, NJ: Princeton University Press.

Barnett, Michael N. 2013. "Humanitarian Governance." *Annual Review of Political Science* 16 (1): 379–398.
Barry, Michael A. 2003. *Figurative Art in Medieval Islam and the Riddle of Bihzad of Herat (1465–1535)*. English language ed. Paris: Flammarion.
Barth, Fredrik. 2002. "An Anthropology of Knowledge." *Current Anthropology* 43 (1): 1–18.
Bashier, Salman H. 2004. *Ibn Al-'Arabi's Barzakh: The Concept of the Limit and the Relationship between God and the World*. Albany: State University of New York Press.
Bashir, Shahzad. 2011. *Sufi Bodies: Religion and Society in Medieval Islam*. New York: Columbia University Press.
Bashir, Shahzad, and Robert D. Crews, eds. 2012. *Under the Drones: Modern Lives in the Afghanistan-Pakistan Borderlands*. Cambridge, MA: Harvard University Press.
Bauer, Michal, Christopher Blattman, Julie Chytilov, Joseph Henrich, Edward Miguel, and Tamar Mitts. 2016. "Can War Foster Cooperation?" *Journal of Economic Perspectives* 30 (3): 249–274.
Bautista, Julius. 2008. "The Meta-theory of Piety: Reflections on the Work of Saba Mahmood." *Contemporary Islam* 2 (1): 75–83.
Bayoumi, Moustafa. 2015. *This Muslim American Life: Dispatches from the War on Terror*. New York: NYU Press.
Bazmee Ansari, A. S. 2012. "Kh̲wādj̲a Bāḳī Bi'llāh." In *Encyclopaedia of Islam*, 2nd ed., edited by P. Bearman, Th. Bianquis, C. E. Bosworth, E. van Donzel and W. P. Heinrichs. Leiden: Brill.
Bazzano, Elliott, and Marcia K. Hermansen. 2020. *Varieties of American Sufism: Islam, Sufi Orders, and Authority in a Time of Transition*. Albany: State University of New York Press.
BBC. 2019. "Giulio Regeni: Egypt Tried to Cover up Student Murder, Italy Says." BBC, December 18. https://www.bbc.com/news/world-europe-50835174.
Beattie, Hugh. 1983. *Tombs and Footprints: Islamic Shrines and Pilgrimages in Modern Iran and Afghanistan*. London: University of London, School of Oriental and African Studies.
Beaurecueil, Serge de. 1988. "Abdullah Ansari de Herat (1006–1089)." In *Herat: Une ville d'art et d'histoire, victime du conflit: Recueil des communications faites au colloque organise par Afrane et Ceredaf*, edited by Afrane and Ceredaf, 44–45. Paris: Amitié Franco-Afghane.
Bergen, Peter, and Katherine Tiedemann. 2012. *Talibanistan: Negotiating the Borders between Terror, Politics, and Religion*. Oxford: Oxford University Press.
Bergner, Gwen. 2011. "Veiled Motives: Women's Liberation and the War in Afghanistan." In *Globalizing Afghanistan: Terrorism, War, and the Rhetoric of*

Nation Building, edited by Zubeda Jalalzai and David Jefferess, 95–116. Durham, NC: Duke University Press.

Beyer, Elke. 2012. "Competitive Coexistence: Soviet Town Planning and Housing Projects in Kabul in the 1960s." *Journal of Architecture* (London) 17 (3): 309–332.

Bezhan, Faridullah. 2008. "Obedient and Resistant: Afghanistani Women in Maryam Mahboob's Short Stories." *Women's Studies International Forum* 31 (5): 373–382.

———. 2017. "Nationalism, Not Islam: The 'Awaken Youth' Party and Pashtun Nationalism." In *Afghanistan's Islam: From Conversion to the Taliban*, edited by Nile Green, 163–186. Oakland: University of California Press.

Bezhan, Frud. 2016. "Cultural Tug-of-War Erupts over Persian Poet Rumi." Radio Free Europe/Radio Liberty, June 10. https://www.rferl.org/a/afghanistan-rumi-poet-turkey-iran-unesco/27791137.html.

Biekart, Kees, and Alan Fowler. 2022. *A Research Agenda for Civil Society*. Cheltenham, UK: Edward Elgar Publishing.

Billaud, Julie. 2009. "Visible under the Veil: Dissimulation, Performance and Agency in an Islamic Public Space." *International Journal of Women's Studies* 11 (2): 120–135.

———. 2012. "Suicidal Performances: Voicing Discontent in a Girls' Dormitory in Kabul." *Culture, Medicine, and Psychiatry* 36 (April): 264–285.

———. 2015. *Kabul Carnival: Gender Politics in Postwar Afghanistan*. Philadelphia: University of Pennsylvania Press.

Bizhan, Nematullah, Niamatullah Ibrahimi and Srinjoy Bose. 2019. *Youth Protest Movements in Afghanistan : Seeking Voice and Agency*. Washington, DC: United States Institute of Peace.

Bollag, Burton. 1997. "Afghanistan's Universities to Reopen, but for Men Only." *Chronicle of Higher Education*, February 21. https://www.chronicle.com/article/afghanistans-universities-to-reopen-but-for-men-only.

Bonotto, Riccardo. 2021. "The History and Current Position of the Afghanistan's Sikh Community." *Iran and the Caucasus* 25 (2): 154–167.

Borchgrevink, Kaja. 2007. *Religious Actors and Civil Society in Post-2001 Afghanistan*. Oslo: International Peace Research Institute (PRIO).

Borchgrevink, Kaja, Kristian Berg Harpviken, M. Nawabi and Arne Strand. 2005. *Disconnected and Discounted? Religious Actors and Civil Society in Post-2001 Afghanistan*. Oslo: Peace Research Institute.

Bourdieu, Pierre. 1977. *Outline of a Theory of Practice*. Cambridge: Cambridge University Press.

Bowen, John. 1993. *Muslims through Discourse: Religion and Ritual in Gayo Society*. Princeton, NJ: Princeton University Press.

Bracke, Sarah. 2016. "Is the Subaltern Resilient? Notes on Agency and Neoliberal Subjects." *Cultural Studies* (London) 30 (5): 839–855.

Brain, Jon. 2013. "Afghanistan's First Female Aeroplane Pilot." BBC, August 2. https://www.bbc.com/news/av/world-middle-east-23556958/afghanistan-s-first-female-aeroplane-pilot.

Brauer, Erich. 1942. "The Jews of Afghanistan: An Anthropological Report." *Jewish Social Studies* 4:121–138.

Braune, W. 2012. "Abd Al-Ḳādir al-Dj īlānī." In *Encyclopaedia of Islam*, 2nd ed., edited by P. Bearman, Th. Bianquis, C. E. Bosworth, E. van Donzel and W. P. Heinrichs. Leiden, Netherlands: Brill.

Brear, Michelle. 2019. "Process and Outcomes of a Recursive, Dialogic Member Checking Approach: A Project Ethnography." *Qualitative Health Research* 29 (7): 944–957. https://doi.org/10.1177/1049732318812448.

Breed, Ananda, and Ali Iğmen. 2020. "Introduction: Making Culture in (Post) Socialist Kazakhstan, Kyrgyzstan, and Xinjiang." In *Creating Culture in (Post) Socialist Central Asia*, edited by Ananda Breed, Eva-Marie Dubuisson and Ali Iğmen, 1–12. Cham, Switzerland: Springer International.

Breuer, Theresa. 2019. "Inside the First Afghan Women's Ascent of Mount Noshaq." *Outside Journal*, April 8. https://www.outsideonline.com/2393332/noshaq-afghanistan-first-women-ascent.

Brodsky, Anne E. 2011. "Centuries of Threat, Centuries of Resistance: The Lessons of Afghan Women's Resilience." In *Land of the Unconquerable: The Lives of Contemporary Afghan Women*, edited by Jennifer Heath and Ashraf Zahedi, 74–89. Berkeley: University of California Press.

Bulkeley, Kelly. 2001. *Dreams: A Reader on Religious, Cultural, and Psychological Dimensions of Dreaming*. New York: Palgrave.

Burak-Adli, Feyza. 2020. *Trajectories of Modern Sufism: An Ethnohistorical Study of the Rifai Order and Social Change in Turkey*. Boston: Boston University.

Burney Abbas, Shemeem. 2007. "Risky Knowledge in Risky Times: Political Discourses of Qawwali and Sufiana-Kalam in Pakistan-Indian Sufism." *Muslim World* 97 (4): 626–639.

Büschges, Christian, Andrea Müller and Noah Oehri. 2021. *Liberation Theology and the Others: Contextualizing Catholic Activism in 20th Century Latin America*. Lanham, MD: Lexington Books.

Can, Lale. 2020. *Spiritual Subjects: Central Asian Pilgrims and the Ottoman Hajj at the End of Empire*. Stanford, CA: Stanford University Press.

Canfield, Robert L. 1973. *Faction and Conversion in a Plural Society: Religious Alignments in the Hindu Kush*. Anthropological Papers (University of Michigan, Museum of Anthropology), No. 50. Ann Arbor: University of Michigan.

Caretta, Martina Angela, and Maria Alejandra Perez. 2019. "When Participants

Do Not Agree: Member Checking and Challenges to Epistemic Authority in Participatory Research." *Field Methods* 31 (4): 359–374.

Caron, James. 2007. "Afghanistan Historiography and Pashtun Islam: Modernization Theory's Afterimage." *History Compass* 5 (2): 314–329.

———. 2009. "Cultural Histories of Pashtun Nationalism, Public Participation, and Social Inequality in Monarchic Afghanistan, 1905–1960." PhD diss., University of Pennsylvania.

———. 2011. "Reading the Power of Printed Orality in Afghanistan: Popular Pashto Literature as Historical Evidence and Public Intervention." *Journal of Social History* 45 (1): 172–194.

———. 2013. "Elite Pasts and Subaltern Potentialities." *International Journal of Middle East Studies* 45 (1): 138–141.

———. 2016. "Sufism and Liberation across the Indo-Afghan Border, 1880–1928." *South Asian History and Culture* 7 (2): 135–154.

Caron, James, and Mahvish Ahmad. 2016. "Activism, Knowledge and Publishing: Some Views from Pakistan and Afghanistan." *South Asian History and Culture* 7 (1): 30–36.

CBS. 2022. "Afghanistan Women's Rights Activist Says Taliban Tortured Her in Prison, but She 'Had to Speak Out.'" CBS News, August 16. https://www.cbsnews.com/news/afghanistan-womens-rights-activist-alleges-taliban-torture/.

Centlivres-Demont, Micheline. 1997. "Un corpus de Risala du Turkestan Afghan." In *Madrasa: La transmission du savoir dans le monde musulman*, edited by Nicole Grandin and Marc Gaborieau, 84–91. Paris: Éditions arguments.

———. 2015. *Afghanistan: Identity, Society and Politics since 1980*. London: I. B. Tauris.

Centlivres, Micheline, Pierre Centlivres and Mark Slobin. 1971. "A Muslim Shaman of Afghan Turkestan." *Ethnology* 10 (2): 160–173.

Central Asia Institute. 2018. "Gender Equality in Afghan Education: Building a New Start for a Nation in Turmoil." December 20. https://centralasiainstitute.org/gender-equality-in-afghan-education-building-a-new-start-for-a-nation-in-turmoil/.

Change.org. n.d. "Petition: Dear UNESCO, Rumi's Masnavi Belongs to Afghanistan's Heritage." Accessed February 16, 2021. https://www.change.org/p/dear-unesco-rumi-belongs-to-afghanistan.

Chiabotti, Francesco, Eve Feuillebois-Pierunek, Catherine Mayeur-Jaouen and Luca Patrizi. 2016. *Ethics and Spirituality in Islam: Sufi Adab*. Vol. 1. Leiden, Netherlands: Brill.

Chiovenda, Andrea. 2020. *Crafting Masculine Selves: Culture, War, and Psychodynamics in Afghanistan*. New York: Oxford University Press.
Chiovenda, Andrea, and Melissa Chiovenda. 2018. "The Specter of the 'Arrivant': Hauntology of an Interethnic Conflict in Afghanistan." *Asian Anthropology* 17 (3): 165–184.
Chittick, William C. 1994. *Imaginal Worlds: Ibn al-Arabi and the Problem of Religious Diversity*. Albany: State University of New York Press.
———. 2020. "Ibn 'Arabî." In *Stanford Encyclopedia of Philosophy*, Spring ed., edited by Edward N. Zalta. https://plato.stanford.edu/archives/spr2020/entries/ibn-arabi/.
Christia, Fotini. 2012. *Alliance Formation in Civil Wars*. Cambridge: Cambridge University Press.
Clark, Kate. 2013. "Death List Published: Families of Disappeared End a 30 Year Wait for News." Afghanistan Analysts Network, September 26. https://www.afghanistan-analysts.org/death-list-published-families-of-disappeared-end-a-30-year-wait-for-news.
———. 2020. *The Cost of Support to Afghanistan: Considering Inequality, Poverty and Lack of Democracy through the "Rentier State" Lens*. Afghanistan Analysts Network, May. https://www.afghanistan-analysts.org/en/wp-content/uploads/sites/2/2020/05/20200528-Rentier-2.pdf.
Clifford, James, and George E. Marcus. 1986. *Writing Culture: The Poetics and Politics of Ethnography*. Berkeley: University of California Press.
Coburn, Noah. 2011. *Bazaar Politics Power and Pottery in an Afghan Market Town*. Stanford Studies in Middle Eastern and Islamic Societies and Cultures. Stanford, CA: Stanford University Press.
———. 2016. *Losing Afghanistan: An Obituary for the Intervention*. Stanford, CA: Stanford University Press.
———. 2018. *Under Contract: The Invisible Workers of America's Global War*. Stanford, CA: Stanford University Press.
Coburn, Noah, and Anna Larson. 2013. *Derailing Democracy in Afghanistan: Elections in an Unstable Political Landscape*. New York: Columbia University Press.
Cochran, Rachel Alexandra. 2015. "Batin, Activism, and the Maktab-e Tawhid: Uncovering Persianate Sufi Thought in the Constitutional Decade of Afghanistan (1963–1973)." Dissertation Order No. 10305876, American University of Paris (France).
Coll, Steve. 2009. "Talking Afghan Politics." *New Yorker*, January 11. https://www.newyorker.com/news/steve-coll/talking-afghan-politics.
———. 2018. *Directorate S: The C.I.A. and America's Secret Wars in Afghanistan and Pakistan*. New York: Penguin Press.

Colville, Rupert. 1997. "The Biggest Caseload in the World." *Refugees* Magazine 108 (Afghanistan: The Unending Crisis), June 1. http://www.unhcr.org/3b-680fbfc.html.

Commins, David Dean. 2006. *The Wahhabi Mission and Saudi Arabia*. London: I. B. Tauris.

Conesa, Pierre. 2018. "Inside the Saudi Terror Machine: Understanding Wahhabism and Salafism." *Salon*, September 13. https://www.salon.com/2018/09/13/inside-the-saudi-terror-machine-understanding-wahhabism-and-salafism/.

Corbett, Rosemary R. 2017. *Making Moderate Islam: Sufism, Service, and the "Ground Zero Mosque" Controversy*. Stanford, CA: Stanford University Press.

———. 2020. "Anti-Colonial Militants or Liberal Peace Activists? The Role of Private Foundations in Producing Pacifist Sufis during the Cold War." In *Modern Sufis and the State: The Politics of Islam in South Asia and Beyond*, edited by Katherine Pratt Ewing and Rosemary R. Corbett, 27–39. New York: Columbia University Press.

Corbett, Rosemary R., and Katherine Pratt Ewing. 2020. *Modern Sufis and the State: The Politics of Islam in South Asia and Beyond*. New York: Columbia University Press.

Corbin, Henry. 1969. *Creative Imagination of the Sufism of Ibn Arabi*. Bollingen Series XCI. Princeton, NJ: Princeton University Press.

Cornell, Rkia Elaroui. 2005. *Early Sufi Women: Dhikr an-Niswa al-Muta 'abbidat as-Sufiyyat*. Lahore, Pakistan: Suhail Academy.

———. 2007. "'Soul of a Woman Was Created Below': Woman as the Lower Soul (Nafs) in Islam." In *Probing the Depths of Evil and Good: Multireligious Views and Case Studies*, edited by Jerald Gort, Henry Jansen and Hendrik M. Vroom, 33:257–280. Amsterdam: Rodopi.

———. 2019. *Rabi'a: From Narrative to Myth*. London: Oneworld Academic.

Cornell, Vincent J. 1999. "Faqīh versus Faqīr in Marinid Morocco: Epistemological Dimensions of a Polemic." In *Islamic Mysticism: Thirteen Centuries of Controversies and Polemics*, edited by Ferdinand de Jong and Bernd Radtke, 207–224. Leiden, Netherlands: Brill.

"Costs of War." 2021. Watson Institute, Brown University, August. https://watson.brown.edu/costsofwar/costs/human/refugees/afghan.

Crapanzano, Vincent. 1975. "Saints, Jnun, and Dreams: An Essay in Moroccan Ethnopsychology." *Psychiatry* (Washington, DC) 38 (2): 145–159.

Crews, Robert D. 2015. *Afghan Modern: The History of a Global Nation*. Cambridge, MA: Belknap Press.

———. 2021. "Gender, Religious Authority, and Media in Afghanistan." In *The Written and the Spoken in Central Asia / Mündlichkeit Und Schriftlichkeit in*

Zentralasien-Festschrift for Ingeborg Baldauf, edited by Redkollegiia, 360–376. Potsdam: edition tethys.

Dale, Stephen F., and Alam Payind. 1999. "The Ahrari Waqf in Kabul in the Year 1546 and the Mughul Naqshbandiyyah." *Journal of the American Oriental Society* 119 (2): 218–233.

Dallh, Minlib. 2011. "A Mystical Encounter of a Dominican Friar, Serge de Beaurecueil (d. 2005), and a Hanbalī Sūfī, 'abdullāh Ansārī of Herāt (d. 1089)." PhD diss., University of Exeter.

———. 2013. "Path to the Divine: Ansārī's Sad Maydān and Manāzil al-Sā'irīn." *Muslim World* (Hartford, CT) 103 (4): 464–478.

———. 2017. *The Sufi and the Friar: A Mystical Encounter of Two Men of God in the Abode of Islam.* Albany: State University of New York Press.

Dam, Bette. 2014. "Death of a Sahebzada: A Story of Different Strands of Thought in the Taleban Movement." Afghanistan Analysts Network, May 25. https://www.afghanistan-analysts.org/en/reports/context-culture/death-of-a-sahebzada-a-story-of-different-strands-of-thought-in-the-taleban-movement/.

———. 2019. *Op Zoek Naar de Vijand: Het Verhaal van Een Terrorist Die Een Vriend Wilde Zijn.* Amsterdam: Bezige Bij.

———. 2021. *Looking for the Enemy.* Noida, Uttar Pradesh: HarperCollins India.

Dandekar, Deepra, and Torsten Tschacher. 2016. *Islam, Sufism and Everyday Politics of Belonging in South Asia.* New York: Routledge.

Daniel, E. Valentine. 1996. *Charred Lullabies: Chapters in an Anthropography of Violence.* Princeton, NJ: Princeton University Press.

Daughtry, J. Martin. 2015. *Listening to War: Sound, Music, Trauma and Survival in Wartime Iraq.* New York: Oxford University Press.

Daulatzai, Anila. 2008. "The Discursive Occupation of Afghanistan." *British Journal of Middle Eastern Studies* 35 (3): 419–435.

De Bruijn, Johannes Thomas Pieter. 1997. *Persian Sufi Poetry: An Introduction to the Mystical Use of Classical Poems.* Richmond, Surrey, UK: Curzon.

Deeb, Lara. 2006. *An Enchanted Modern: Gender and Public Piety in Shi'i Lebanon.* Princeton, NJ: Princeton University Press.

———. 2015. "Thinking Piety and the Everyday Together: A Response to Fadil and Fernando." *HAU: Journal of Ethnographic Theory* 5 (2): 93–96.

Dewachi, Omar. 2015. "When Wounds Travel." *Medicine Anthropology Theory* 2 (3): 61–82.

———. 2019. "Iraqibacter and the Pathologies of Intervention." *Middle East Report* 49 (290): 8–12.

DeWeese, Devin A., and Jo-Ann Gross. 2018. *Sufism in Central Asia: New Perspectives on Sufi Traditions, 15th–21st Centuries.* Leiden, Netherlands: Brill.

Dilley, Roy. 1999. "Ways of Knowing, Forms of Power." *Cultural Dynamics* 11 (1): 33–55.

Diouf, Mamadou. 2013. *Tolerance, Democracy, and Sufis in Senegal*. New York: Columbia University Press.

Dorn, Allen E. 1989. *Countering the Revolution: The Mujahideen Counterrevolution*. New York: Afghanistan Forum.

Dorronsoro, Gilles. 2005. *Revolution Unending: Afghanistan, 1979 to the Present*. New York: Columbia University Press in association with the Centre d'Etudes et de Recherches Internationales, Paris.

Dossa, Parin. 2014. *Afghanistan Remembers: Gendered Narrations of Violence and Culinary Practices*. Toronto: University of Toronto Press, Scholarly Publishing Division.

Drage, Theresa Ann. 2015. "The National Sufi Council: Redefining the Islamic Republic of Pakistan through a Discourse on Sufism after 9/11." PhD diss., Religion and Society Research Centre, University of Western Sydney.

Dubuisson, Eva-Marie. 2020. "Poets of the People: Learning to Make Culture in Kazakhstan." In *Creating Culture in (Post) Socialist Central Asia*, edited by Ananda Breed, Eva-Marie Dubuisson and Ali Iğmen, 87–113. Cham, Switzerland: Springer International.

Dupree, Louis. 1976. *Saint Cults in Afghanistan*. Hanover, NH: American Universities Field Staff.

———. 1980. *Afghanistan, 1980 Edition*. New Delhi: RAMA Publishers.

Dupree, Nancy Hatch. 1992. "Afghanistan: Women, Society and Development." *Journal of Developing Societies* 8 (1): 30–42.

———. 2002. "Cultural Heritage and National Identity in Afghanistan." *Third World Quarterly* 23 (5): 977–989.

Eaton, Richard M. 1974. "Sufi Folk Literature and the Expansion of Indian Islam." *History of Religions* 14 (2): 117–127.

———. 2000. *Essays on Islam and Indian History*. New Delhi: Oxford University Press.

Edgar, Iain R. 2011. *The Dream in Islam: From Qur'anic Tradition to Jihadist Inspiration*. Oxford: Berghahn Books.

Edwards, David B. 1986a. "Charismatic Leadership and Political Process in Afghanistan." *Central Asian Survey* 5 (3–4): 273–299.

———. 1986b. "The Evolution of Shi'i Political Dissent in Afghanistan." In *Shi'ism and Social Protest*, edited by Juan Ricardo Cole, Nikki R. Keddie, 201–229. New Haven, CT: Yale University Press.

———. 1989. "Mad Mullahs and Englishmen: Discourse in the Colonial Encounter." *Comparative Studies in Society and History* 31 (4): 649–670.

———. 1993. "The Political Lives of Afghan Saints: The Case of the Kabul

Hazrats." In *Manifestations of Sainthood in Islam*, edited by Grace Martin Smith and Carl W. Ernst, 171–192. Istanbul: Isis Press.

———. 1996. *Heroes of the Age: Moral Fault Lines on the Afghan Frontier*. Berkeley: University of California Press.

———. 2002. *Before Taliban Genealogies of the Afghan Jihad*. Berkeley: University of California Press.

———. 2017. *Caravan of Martyrs/Sacrifice and Suicide Bombing in Afghanistan*. Oakland: University of California Press.

Eickelman, Dale F., and James Piscatori. 1996. *Muslim Politics*. Princeton Studies in Muslim Politics. Princeton, NJ: Princeton University Press.

Einzmann, Harald. 1977. *Religioses Volksbrauchtum in Afghanistan: Islamische Heiligenverehrung Und Wallfahrtswesen Im Raum Kabul*. Wiesbaden: Franz Steiner.

Elias, Norbert. 1978. *The Civilizing Process*. 1st American ed. New York: Urizen Books.

Elphinstone, Mountstuart. 1815. *Account of the Kingdom of Caubul, and Its Dependencies in Persia, Tartary, and India: Comprising a View of the Afghaun Nation, and a History of the Dooraunee Monarchy*. Cambridge: Cambridge University Press.

El-Zein, Amira. 2009. *Islam, Arabs, and the Intelligent World of the Jinn*. Syracuse, NY: Syracuse University Press.

Emadi, Hafizullah. 2014. "Minorities and Marginality: Pertinacity of Hindus and Sikhs in a Repressive Environment in Afghanistan." *Nationalities Papers* 42 (2): 307–320.

Ernst, Carl W. 1997. *The Shambhala Guide to Sufism*. Boston: Shambhala.

———. 2011. *Sufism: An Introduction to the Mystical Tradition of Islam*. Reprint ed. Boston: Shambhala.

Ernst, Carl W., and Bruce Lawrence. 2002. *Sufi Martyrs of Love: The Chishti Order in South Asia and Beyond*. New York: Palgrave Macmillan.

European Union. 2015. *Afghanistan: EU Country Roadmap for Engagement with Civil Society, 2015–2017*. https://www.acbar.org/upload/1471260026304.pdf.

Evans-Pritchard, E. E. 1949. *The Sanusi of Cyrenaica*. Oxford: Oxford University Press.

Ewing, Katherine P. 1990. "The Dream of Spiritual Initiation and the Organization of Self Representations among Pakistani Sufis." *American Ethnologist* 17 (1): 56–74.

———. 1994. "Dreams from a Saint: Anthropological Atheism and the Temptation to Believe." *American Anthropologist* 96 (3): 571–583.

———. 1997. *Arguing Sainthood: Modernity, Psychoanalysis, and Islam*. 2nd ed. Durham, NC: Duke University Press.

———. 2020. "Introduction. Sufis and the State: The Politics of Islam in South Asia and Beyond." In *Sufis and the State: The Politics of Islam in South Asia and Beyond*, edited by Katherine Pratt Ewing and Rosemary R. Corbett, 1–24. New York: Columbia University Press.

Fadil, Nadia, and Mayanthi Fernando. 2015. "Rediscovering the 'Everyday' Muslim: Notes on an Anthropological Divide." *HAU: Journal of Ethnographic Theory* 5 (2): 59–88.

Fahd, T. 2012. "Istikhara." In *Encyclopaedia of Islam*, 2nd ed., edited by P. Bearman, Th. Bianquis, C. E. Bosworth, E. van Donzel and W. P. Heinrichs. Leiden, Netherlands: Brill.

Faizi, Fatima, and Rod Nordland. 2019. "Afghan Town's First Female Mayor Awaits Her Assassination." *New York Times*, October. https://www.nytimes.com/2019/10/04/world/asia/zarifa-ghafari-afghanistan-maidan-shar.html.

"Farhad Darya." n.d. Accessed April 29, 2022. https://m.facebook.com/FarhadDaryaOfficialPage/photos/قصه-های-که-زگره-به-کس-نی-گفته-ما-2-طلوع-و-غروب-گرگ-باراںrise-fall-of-baranسول-د/10152820934490176/.

Farrall, Leah, and Mustafa Hamid. 2015. *The Arabs at War in Afghanistan*. London: C. Hurst.

Fein, Helen. 1993. "Discriminating Genocide from War Crimes: Vietnam and Afghanistan Reexamined." *Denver Journal of International Law and Policy* 22 (1): 29–62.

Fluri, Jennifer. 2009. "'Foreign Passports Only': Geographies of (Post)Conflict Work in Kabul, Afghanistan." *Annals of the Association of American Geographers* 99 (5): 986–994.

———. 2011. "Armored Peacocks and Proxy Bodies: Gender Geopolitics in Aid/Development Spaces of Afghanistan." *Gender, Place and Culture* 18 (4): 519–536.

———. 2014. "States of (In)Security: Corporeal Geographies and the Elsewhere War." *Environment and Planning D, Society & Space* 32 (5): 795–814.

Fluri, Jennifer L., Rachel Lehr, Mathew Coleman, Sapana Doshi and Nik Heynen. 2017. *The Carpetbaggers of Kabul and Other American-Afghan Entanglements: Intimate Development, Geopolitics, and the Currency of Gender and Grief*. Athens: University of Georgia Press.

Foschini, Fabrizio. 2019. "Kabul Unpacked: A Geographical Guide to a Metropolis in the Making." Afghanistan Analysts Network, March 2. https://www.afghanistan-analysts.org/en/special-reports/kabul-unpacked-a-geographical-guide-to-a-metropolis-in-the-making/.

Foucault, Michel. 1978. *The History of Sexuality*. 1st American ed. New York: Pantheon Books.

———. 1995. *Discipline and Punish: The Birth of the Prison.* 2nd Vintage Books ed. New York: Vintage Books.
Fraile-Marcos, Ana María, ed. 2020. *Glocal Narratives of Resilience.* New York: Routledge.
Frembgen, Jürgen Wasim. 1994. "Nachbildungen von Bettelschalen: Ihre Bedeutung Im Islamischen Volksglauben Afghanistans Und Pakistans." *Munchener Beitrage Zur Volkerkunde* 4:49–55.
———. 2000. *Reise zu Gott: Sufis und Derwische im Islam.* Munich: C. H. Beck.
———. 2008. *Journey to God: Sufis and Dervishes in Islam.* Oxford: Oxford University Press.
Fuchs-Heinritz, Werner, and Alexandra Koenig. 2005. *Pierre Bourdieu/Eine Einführung.* Konstanz, Germany: UVK/UTB.
Gabbay, Alyssa. 2020. *Gender and Succession in Medieval and Early Modern Islam: Bilateral Descent and the Legacy of Fatima.* London: I. B. Tauris.
Gall, Carlotta. 2016. "Saudis Bankroll Taliban, Even as King Officially Supports Afghan Government." *New York Times*, June 12. https://www.nytimes.com/2016/12/06/world/asia/saudi-arabia-afghanistan.html.
Gardet, L. 2012. "Ḥāl." In *Encyclopaedia of Islam*, 2nd ed., edited by P. Bearman, Th. Bianquis, C. E. Bosworth, E. van Donzel and W. P. Heinrichs. Leiden, Netherlands, Brill.
Geaves, Ron. 2014. *Sufism in the West.* Cambridge: Cambridge University Press.
———. 2015. "The Contested Milieu of Deoband: 'Salafis' or 'Sufis.'" In *Sufis and Salafis in the Contemporary Age*, edited by Lloyd Ridgeon, 191–216. London: Bloomsbury Academic.
Geertz, Clifford. 1971. *Islam Observed: Religious Development in Morocco and Indonesia.* Phoenix ed. Terry Lectures. Chicago: University of Chicago Press.
Gellner, Ernest. 1981. *Muslim Society.* Cambridge Studies in Social Anthropology No. 32. Cambridge: Cambridge University Press.
———. 1992. *Postmodernism, Reason and Religion.* London: Routledge.
———. 1994. *Conditions of Liberty: Civil Society and Its Rivals.* 1st American ed. New York: Allen Lane/Penguin Press.
Gennep, Arnold van. 1960. *The Rites of Passage.* Chicago: University of Chicago Press.
Ghani, Abdul. 1960. *Life and Works of Abdul Qadir Bedil.* Lahore: Publishers United.
Ghani, Ashraf. 1988. "The Persian Literature of Afghanistan, 1911–78, in the Context of Its Political and Intellectual History." In *Persian Literature*, edited by Ehsan Yarshater, 428–543. Albany: Persian Heritage Foundation/SUNY Press.

———. 2008. *Fixing Failed States: A Framework for Rebuilding a Fractured World.* Oxford: Oxford University Press.
Giustozzi, Antonio. 2000. *War, Politics and Society in Afghanistan, 1978–1992.* Washington, DC: Georgetown University Press.
———. 2008. *Koran, Kalashnikov, and Laptop: The Neo-Taliban Insurgency in Afghanistan.* New York: Columbia University Press.
———. 2019. *The Taliban at War: 2001–2018.* London: C. Hurst.
Giustozzi, Antonio, and Niamatullah Ibrahimi. 2012. *Thirty Years of Conflict: Drivers of Anti-government Mobilisation in Afghanistan, 1978–2011.* Kabul: Afghanistan Research and Evaluation Unit.
Glasius, Marlies. 2010. "Uncivil Society." In *International Encyclopedia of Civil Society,* edited by Helmut K. Anheier and Stefan Toepler, 1583–1588. New York: Springer.
Glinski, Stefani. 2019. "Afghanistan Woman Breaks Ground with Kabul Recycling Plant." *Los Angeles Times,* November 25. https://www.latimes.com/world-nation/story/2019-11-25/afghanistan-woman-breaks-ground-with-kabul-recycling-plant.
Goldbaum, Christina, and Najim Rahim. 2022. "Mosque Explosion Kills 33 as Deadly Week in Afghanistan Continues." *New York Times,* April 22. https://www.nytimes.com/2022/04/22/world/asia/afghanistan-mosque-attack.html.
Göle, Nilüfer. 2013. *The Forbidden Modern: Civilization and Veiling.* Ann Arbor: University of Michigan Press.
Golestaneh, Seema. 2022. "And the Master Answered? Deferrals of Authority in Contemporary Sufism in Iran." *Iranian Studies* 56 (2): 1–22.
———. 2023. *Unknowing and the Everyday: Sufism and Knowledge in Iran.* Durham, NC: Duke University Press.
Goodson, Larry P. 2001. *Afghanistan's Endless War: State Failure, Regional Politics, and the Rise of the Taliban.* Seattle: University of Washington Press.
Gopal, Anand. 2014. *No Good Men among the Living: America, the Taliban, and the War through Afghan Eyes.* New York: Metropolitan Books/Henry Holt.
Graham-Harrison, Emma. 2012. "Qur'an Burning Protests: Two US Soldiers Shot Dead by Afghan Colleague." *The Guardian,* February 23. https://www.theguardian.com/world/2012/feb/23/quran-burning-afghanistan-us-soldiers-dead.
Green, Linda. 1999. *Fear as a Way of Life: Mayan Widows in Rural Guatemala.* New York: Columbia University Press.
Green, Nile. 2003. "The Religious and Cultural Roles of Dreams and Visions in Islam." *Royal Asiatic Society/JRAS* 13 (3): 287–313.
———. 2012. *Sufism: A Global History.* Chichester, West Sussex, UK: Wiley-Blackwell.

———, ed. 2017. *Afghanistan's Islam: From Conversion to the Taliban*. Oakland: University of California Press.

———. 2019. *The Persianate World: The Frontiers of a Eurasian Lingua Franca*. Berkeley: University of California Press.

Green, Nile, and Nushin Arbabzadah. 2013. *Afghanistan in Ink : Literature between Diaspora and Nation*. New York: Columbia University Press.

Griffin, Michael. 2001. *Reaping the Whirlwind: The Taliban Movement in Afghanistan*. London: Pluto Press.

Groenhaug, Reidar. 1978. "Scale as a Variable in Analysis: Fields in Social Organization in Herat." In *Scale and Social Organization*, edited by Fredrik Barth, 78–121. Bergen: Universitetsforlaget.

Gross, Jo-Ann. 2001. "Naqshbandi Appeals to the Herat Court: A Preliminary Study of Trade and Property Issues." In *Studies on Central Asian History in Honor of Yuri Bregel*, edited by Devin DeWeese, 113–128. Bloomington: Indiana University Research Institute for Inner Asia Studies.

Gupta, Akhil, and Jessie Stoolman. 2022. "Decolonizing US Anthropology." *American Anthropologist* 124 (4): 778–799.

Gurbuz-Dogan, R. N., A. Ali, B. Candy and M. King. 2021. "The Effectiveness of Sufi Music for Mental Health Outcomes: A Systematic Review and Meta-analysis of 21 Randomised Trials." *Complementary Therapies in Medicine* 57:1–16.

Haeri, Niloofar. 2021. *Say What Your Longing Heart Desires: Women, Prayer, and Poetry in Iran*. Stanford, CA: Stanford University Press.

Haeri, Shahla. 2020. *The Unforgettable Queens of Islam*. Cambridge, MA: Cambridge University Press.

Hagemann, Karen, Sonya Michel and Gunilla-Friederike Budde. 2008. *Civil Society and Gender Justice: Historical and Comparative Perspectives*. New York: Berghahn Books.

Haider, Arwa. 2018. "Ahmad Zahir: The Enduring Appeal of the Afghan Elvis." BBC World News, December 6. https://www.bbc.com/culture/article/20181206-ahmad-zahir-the-enduring-appeal-of-the-afghan-elvis.

Hall, John A. 1995. *Civil Society: Theory, History, Comparison*. Cambridge, UK: Polity Press.

Hallaq, Wael B. 2001. *Authority, Continuity and Change in Islamic Law*. Cambridge: Cambridge University Press.

Hanifi, Shah Mahmoud. 2011. *Connecting Histories in Afghanistan: Market Relations and State Formation on a Colonial Frontier*. Stanford, CA: Stanford University Press.

Hann, C. M., and Elizabeth C. Dunn. 1996. *Civil Society: Challenging Western Models*. London: Routledge.

Hannun, Marya. 2020. "From Kabul to Cairo and Back Again: The Afghan

Women's Movement and Early 20th Century Transregional Transformations." *Genre & Histoire* 25. https://journals.openedition.org/genrehistoire/5017?/lang=en.

———. 2021a. "From Afghan Pan-Islamism to Turkish Feminism." *Journal of Middle East Women's Studies* 17 (3): 466–472.

———. 2021b. "States of Change: Women, Islamic Reform, and Transregional Mobility in the Making of Modern Afghanistan." PhD diss., Georgetown University.

Hannun, Marya, Ping-Hsiu Alice Lin and Annika Schmeding. 2022. "Disentangling the 'War on Terror': Pushing Boundaries of Inquiry." *International Journal of Middle East Studies* 54 (2): 338–339.

Haraway, Donna. 1988. "Situated Knowledges: The Science Question in Feminism and the Privilege of Partial Perspective." *Feminist Studies* 14 (3): 575–599.

Haroon, Sana. 2007. *Frontier of Faith: Islam in the Indo-Afghan Borderland*. New York: Columbia University Press.

———. 2012. "Religious Revivalism across the Durand Line." In *Under the Drones: Modern Lives in the Afghanistan-Pakistan Borderlands*, edited by Shahzad Bashir and Robert D. Crews, 45–59. Cambridge, MA: Harvard University Press.

Harooni, Mirwais, and Krista Mahr. 2015. "Six Killed in Gunmen Attack on Sufi Place for Worship in Kabul." Reuters, March 7. https://www.reuters.com/article/us-afghanistan-attack/six-killed-in-gunmen-attack-on-sufi-place-of-worship-in-kabul-idUSKBN-0M30PO20150307.

Harpviken, Kristian Berg, Arne Strand and Karin Ask. 2002. *Afghanistan and Civil Society*. Bergen: Chr. Michelsen Institute. https://www.cmi.no/publications/1765-afghanistan-and-civil-society.

Heath, Jennifer, and Ashraf Zahedi, eds. 2011. *Land of the Unconquerable: The Lives of Contemporary Afghan Women*. Berkeley: University of California Press.

Heck, Paul L. 2007. *Sufism and Politics: The Power of Spirituality*. Princeton, NJ: Markus Wiener Publishers.

Hefner, Robert W. 1998. *Democratic Civility: The History and Cross-cultural Possibility of a Modern Political Ideal*. New Brunswick, NJ: Transaction Publishers.

———. 2000. *Civil Islam: Muslims and Democratization in Indonesia*. Princeton, NJ: Princeton University Press.

Heilbrun, Carolyn G. 1988. *Writing a Woman's Life*. New York: Ballantine.

Helminski, Camille Adams. 2003. *Women of Sufism: A Hidden Treasure: Writings and Stories of Mystic Poets, Scholars & Saints*. Boston: Shambhala Publications.

Henig, David. 2012. "'Knocking on My Neighbour's Door': On Metamorphoses of Sociality in Rural Bosnia." *Critique of Anthropology* 32 (1): 3–19.

———. 2020. *Remaking Muslim Lives: Everyday Islam in Postwar Bosnia and Herzegovina*. Urbana: University of Illinois Press.

Hermansen, Marcia K. 1988. "Shāh Walī Allāh's Theory of the Subtle Spiritual Centers (Laṭā'if): A Sufi Model of Personhood and Self-Transformation." *Journal of Near Eastern Studies* 47 (1): 1–25.

———. 2001. "Dreams and Dreaming in Islam." In *Dreams: A Reader on Religious, Cultural, and Psychological Dimensions of Dreaming*, edited by Kelly Bulkeley, 73–91. New York: Palgrave Macmillan.

Hill, Joseph. 2018. *Wrapping Authority: Women Islamic Leaders in a Sufi Movement in Dakar, Senegal*. Toronto: University of Toronto Press.

Hirschkind, Charles. 2006. *The Ethical Soundscape: Cassette Sermons and Islamic Counterpublics*. New York: Columbia University Press.

Hoel, Nina. 2013. "Sexualising the Sacred, Sacralising Sexuality: An Analysis of Public Responses to Muslim Women's Religious Leadership in the Context of a Cape Town Mosque." *Journal for the Study of Religion* 26 (2): 25–42.

Hoexter, Miriam, S. N. Eisenstadt and Nehemia Levtzion. 2002. *The Public Sphere in Muslim Societies*. Albany: State University of New York Press.

Hoffman, Aaron M. 2010. "Voice and Silence: Why Groups Take Credit for Acts of Terror." *Journal of Peace Research* 47 (5): 615–626.

Holland, D., Lucile Martin and Saeed Parto. 2016. *Rights in Afghanistan: "Human" or "Fundamental"?* Kabul: Afghanistan Public Policy Research Organization (APPRO).

Hosain, Hidayet, and H. Massé. 2012. "Hud̲j̲wīrī." In *Encyclopaedia of Islam*, 2nd ed., edited by P. Bearman, Th. Bianquis, C. E. Bosworth, E. van Donzel and W. P. Heinrichs. Leiden, Netherlands: Brill.

Hosseini, Nemat. 2017. "Sheikh Mohammad Hashem Efendi." Aryana Database, December 26. http://database-aryana-encyclopaedia.blogspot.com/2009/01/blog-post_15.html.

Howell, Jude, and Jeremy Lind. 2009. "Manufacturing Civil Society and the Limits of Legitimacy: Aid, Security and Civil Society after 9/11 in Afghanistan." *European Journal of Development Research* 21 (5): 718–736.

Huda, Qamar-Ul. 2005. *Striving for Divine Union: Spiritual Exercises for Suhraward Sufis*. London, Routledge.

Huggler, Justin. 2003. "Iranian Students Openly Defy Rule of the Mullahs." *The Independent*, June 14. https://www.independent.co.uk/news/world/middle-east/iranian-students-openly-defy-rule-of-the-mullahs-108799.html.

Human Rights Watch. 2021. "'No Forgiveness for People like You:' Executions and Enforced Disappearances in Afghanistan under the Taliban." November 30. https://www.hrw.org/report/2021/11/30/no-forgiveness-people-you/executions-and-enforced-disappearances-afghanistan.

———. 2022a. "Afghanistan: Herat Women's Prison Head Missing 6 Months." April 20. https://www.hrw.org/news/2022/04/20/afghanistan-herat-womens-prison-head-missing-6-months#.

———. 2022b. "Afghanistan: ISIS Group Targets Religious Minorities." September 6. https://www.hrw.org/news/2022/09/06/afghanistan-isis-group-targets-religious-minorities.

Ibn Arabi. 1980. *The Bezels of Wisdom*. Translated by R. W. J. Austin. New York: Paulist Press.

Ibrahimi, Niamatullah. 2016. "Framing Ethnicity under Conditions of Uncertainty: The Case of Hazaras during Afghanistan's 2014 Presidential Elections." *Conflict, Security & Development* 16 (6): 635–652.

———. 2017. "Dynamics of Contentious Politics in Afghanistan, 2001–2016." PhD diss., Australian National University. https://openresearch-repository.anu.edu.au/bitstream/1885/141336/1/N%20Ibrahimi%20PhD%20Thesis%202017.pdf.

Ingram, Brannon D. 2018. *Revival from Below: The Deoband Movement and Global Islam*. Oakland: University of California Press.

International Federation of Journalists (IFJ). 2022. "Afghanistan: Journalist Sentenced to Prison for Criticism of Taliban Regime." May 12. https://www.ifj.org/media-centre/news/detail/category/press-releases/article/afghanistan-journalist-sentenced-to-prison-for-criticism-of-taliban-regime.html.

"Interview with Fatima Gailani." 2011. *International Review of the Red Cross* 93 (881). https://international-review.icrc.org/sites/default/files/irrc-881-interview.pdf.

Islam, Riazul. 2002. *Sufism in South Asia: Impact on Fourteenth-Century Muslim Society*. Karachi: Oxford University Press.

Izutsu, Toshihiko. 1983. *Sufism and Taoism*. Berkeley: University of California Press.

Jackson, Ashley. 2021. *Negotiating Survival: Civilian-Insurgent Relations in Afghanistan*. New York: Oxford University Press.

Jafari, Belgheis Alavi, and Liza Schuster. 2019. "Representations of Exile in Afghan Oral Poetry and Songs." *Crossings* (Bristol) 10 (2): 183–203.

Jalalzai, Zubeda, and David Jefferess. 2011. *Globalizing Afghanistan: Terrorism, War, and the Rhetoric of Nation Building*. Durham, NC: Duke University Press.

James, William. 1902. *The Varieties of Religious Experience: A Study in Human Nature*. Auckland: Floating Press.

Jankowsky, Richard C. 2017. "Absence and Presence: El-Hadhra and the Cultural

Politics of Staging Sufi Music in Tunisia." *Journal of North African Studies* 22 (5): 860–887.
Jawad, Ali Aqa Mohammad. 2020. "Dynamics of Protest Mobilization and Rapid Demobilization in Post-2001 Afghanistan: Facing Enlightening Movement." *International Journal of Humanities and Social Sciences* 14 (8): 564–577.
Jawad, Nassim. 1992. *Afghanistan: A Nation of Minorities*. Vol. 209. London: Minority Rights Group.
Johnson, Thomas H. 2010. "Religious Figures, Insurgency, and Jihad in Southern Afghanistan." In *Who Speaks for Islam? Muslim Grassroots Leaders and Popular Preachers in South Asia*, edited by Mumtaz Ahmad, Dietrich Reetz and Thomas H. Johnson, 41–65. Seattle: National Bureau of Asian Research.
———. 2017. *Taliban Narratives: The Use and Power of Stories in the Afghanistan Conflict*. New York: Oxford University Press.
Joseph, Paul. 2016. "'Soft Power' Does Not Always Mean 'Smart Power': An Investigation of Human Terrain Teams in Iraq and Afghanistan." *Palgrave Communications* 2 (1): 1–9.
Kaba, Mariame. 2021. *We Do This 'til We Free Us: Abolitionist Organizing and Transforming Justice*. Chicago: Haymarket Books.
Kakar, Hasan Kawun. 1995. *Afghanistan: The Soviet Invasion and the Afghan Response, 1979–1982*. Berkeley: University of California Press.
Kamrava, Mehran. 2011. *Innovation in Islam: Traditions and Contributions*. Berkeley: University of California Press.
Kandiyoti, Deniz. 2005. "The Politics of Gender and Reconstruction in Afghanistan." Occasional Papers (4). Geneva: United Nations Research Institute for Social Development (UNRISD).
———. 2007. "Old Dilemmas or New Challenges? The Politics of Gender and Reconstruction in Afghanistan." *Development and Change* 38 (2): 169–199.
Karamustafa, Ahmet T. 2007. *Sufism: The Formative Period*. Edinburgh: Edinburgh University Press.
Kargar, Zarghuna. 2015. "Farkhunda: The Making of a Martyr." BBC World News, August 11. http://www.bbc.com/news/magazine-33810338.
Karimi, Ali. 2017. "Medium of the Oppressed: Folk Music, Forced Migration, and Tactical Media." *Communication, Culture & Critique* 10 (4): 729–745.
Karlsson, Pia, and Amir Mansory. 2007a. *An Afghan Dilemma: Education, Gender and Globalisation in an Islamic Context*. Stockholm: Institute of International Education, Department of Education, Stockholm University.
———. 2007b. *Islamic and Modern Education in Afghanistan—Conflictual or Complementary?* Stockholm: Institute of International Education, Stockholm University.
———. 2018. "Islamic Education in Afghanistan." In *Handbook of Islamic*

Education, edited by Holger Daun and Reza Arjmand, 7:685–697. Cham, Switzerland: Springer.

Katz, Marion Holmes. 2014. *Women in the Mosque: A History of Legal Thought and Social Practice*. New York: Columbia University Press.

Katz, Steven T. 1983. *Mysticism and Religious Traditions*. New York: Oxford University Press.

Kazemi, Mohammad Kazemi. 2015. "دلایل گمنامي 'بیدل' در ایران [The Reason behind the Anonymity of 'Bedil' in Iran]." Mehr News Agency, July 20. https://www.mehrnews.com/news/351274/دلایل-گمنامي-بیدل-در-ایران.

Kazemi, S. Reza. 2012. "The 'Afghanistan 1400' Movement: Changing Youth Politics in Afghanistan?" Afghanistan Analysts Network, December 30. https://www.afghanistan-analysts.org/en/reports/political-landscape/the-afghanistan-1400-movement-changing-youth-politics-in-afghanistan/.

Keane, John. 1988. *Civil Society and the State: New European Perspectives*. London: Verso.

———. 2003. *Global Civil Society?* Cambridge: Cambridge University Press.

Kearns, Erin M. 2021. "When to Take Credit for Terrorism? A Cross-national Examination of Claims and Attributions." *Terrorism and Political Violence* 33 (1): 164–193.

Kearns, Erin M., Brendan Conlon and Joseph K. Young. 2014. "Lying about Terrorism." *Studies in Conflict & Terrorism* 37 (5): 422–439.

Kepel, Gilles. 2012. *Le prophète et le pharaon: Les mouvements islamistes dans l'Egypte contemporaine*. Paris: Folio Histoire.

Kerr-Chiovenda, Melissa. 2014. "The Illumination of Marginality: How Ethnic Hazaras in Bamyan, Afghanistan Perceive the Lack of Electricity as Discrimination." *Central Asian Survey* 33 (4): 449–462.

———. 2015. "Memory, History, and Landscape: Ethnic Hazaras' Understanding of Marginality in Bamyan, Afghanistan." In *State, Society, and Minorities in South and Southeast Asia*, edited by Sunil Kukreja, 1–12. Lanham, MD: Lexington Books.

———. 2018. "Hazara Civil Society Activists and Local, National, and International Political Institutions." In *Modern Afghanistan: Forty Years of War and Rebellion*, edited by M. Nazif Shahrani, 251–270. Bloomington: Indiana University Press.

Khan, Abd al-Rahman Khan. 1900. *The Life of Abdur Rahman, Amir of Afghanistan*. London: John Murray.

Khan, Naveeda. 2012. *Muslim Becoming: Aspiration and Skepticism in Pakistan*. Durham, NC: Duke University Press.

Khan, Sarfraz, and Noor Ul Amin. 2015. "Prelude to Higher Education in Afghanistan: The Role of Indian Muslims (1901–33)." *Central Asia* 77 (2): 1–28.

Khorasan zameen. 2015. http://www.khorasanzameen.net/php/read. php?id=1274.

Kinberg, Leah. 2008. "Qur'an and Hadith: A Struggle for Supremacy as Reflected in Dream Narratives." In *Dreaming across Boundaries: The Interpretation of Dreams in Islamic Lands*. Boston: Ilex Foundation, Harvard University Press.

Knight, Michael Muhammad. 2016. *Magic in Islam*. New York: Tarcher Perigee.

———. 2020. *Muhammad's Body: Baraka Networks and the Prophetic Assemblage*. Chapel Hill: University of North Carolina Press.

Knysh, Alexander. 2000. *Islamic Mysticism: A Short History*. Leiden, Netherlands: Brill.

———. 2017. *Sufism: A New History of Islamic Mysticism*. Princeton, NJ: Princeton University Press.

Koepke, Bruce. 2001. "Intangible Cultural Heritage in Afghanistan." *Historic Environment* 15 (3): 56–66.

Konings, Piet. 2009. *Neoliberal Bandwagonism: Civil Society and the Politics of Belonging in Anglophone Cameroon*. Leiden, Netherlands: African Studies Centre.

Kopecky, Lucas-Michael. 1982. "The Imami Sayyed of the Hazarajat: The Maintenance of Their Elite Position." *Folk* 24:89–110.

———. 1986. "Die Saiyid und die Imamitischen Hazara Afghanistans: Religiose Vergemeinschaftung und Ethnogenese." In *Die Ethnischen Gruppen Afghanistans: Fallstudien zu Gruppenidentität und Intergruppenbeziehungen*. Wiesbaden: Dr. Ludwig Reichert Verlag.

Koplik, Sara. 2003. "The Demise of Afghanistan's Jewish Community and the Soviet Refugee Crisis (1932–1936)." *Iranian Studies* 36 (3): 353–379.

———. 2015. *A Political and Economic History of the Jews of Afghanistan*. Leiden, Netherlands: Brill.

Kostadinova, Zora. 2018. "'And When the Heart Is Sick, the Whole Body Is Sick': Repairing the Person and the Urban Fabric through Everyday Sufi Ethics in Postwar Sarajevo." *Comparative Southeast European Studies* 66 (1): 69–93.

Krämer, Gudrun, and Sabine Schmidtke, eds. 2006. *Speaking for Islam: Religious Authorities in Muslim Societies*. Leiden, Netherlands: Brill.

Kugle, Scott. 2003. "The Heart of Ritual Is the Body: Anatomy of an Islamic Devotional Manual of the Nineteenth Century." *Journal of Ritual Studies* 17 (1): 42–60.

———. 2011. *Sufis and Saints' Bodies: Mysticism, Corporeality, and Sacred Power in Islam*. Chapel Hill: University of North Carolina Press.

Kumar, Ruchi, and Hikmat Noori. 2018. "Kabul Reels in Grief after Wedding Hall Attack." *The National*, November 21. https://www.thenational.ae/world/asia/kabul-reels-in-grief-after-wedding-hall-attack-1.794365.

———. 2022. "Deadly Attack on Sikh Temple in Kabul Leaves Community in Fear." Al Jazeera, June 18. https://www.aljazeera.com/news/2022/6/18/deadly-attack-on-sikh-temple-in-kabul-leaves-community-in-fear.

Kurzman, Charles. 2002. *Modernist Islam, 1840–1940: A Sourcebook*. Oxford: Oxford University Press.

Kuutma, Kristin. 2013. "Concepts and Contingencies in Heritage Politics." In *Anthropological Perspectives on Intangible Cultural Heritage*, edited by Lourdes Arizpe and Cristina Amescua, 1–15. Cham: Springer International Publishing.

Kwon, Heonik. 2008. *Ghosts of War in Vietnam: Heonik Kwon*. Cambridge: Cambridge University Press.

Ladjal, Tarek, and Benaouda Bensaid. 2015. "Sufism and Politics in Contemporary Egypt: A Study of Sufi Political Engagement in the Pre and Post-revolutionary Reality of January 2011." *Journal of Asian and African Studies* 50 (4): 468–485.

Laidlaw, James. 2014. *The Subject of Virtue: An Anthropology of Ethics and Freedom*. Cambridge: Cambridge University Press.

Lamb, Christina. 2003. *The Sewing Circles of Herat: My Afghan Years*. London: HarperCollins.

Lamoreaux, John C. 2002. *The Early Muslim Tradition of Dream Interpretation*. New York: State University of New York Press.

Lange, Christian. 2011. "Barzakh." In *Encyclopaedia of Islam*, 3rd ed., edited by Kate Fleet, Gudrun Krämer, Denis Matringe, John Nawas and Devin J. Stewart. Leiden, Netherlands: Brill.

Lawrence, Bruce. 2006. *The Qur'an: A Biography*. New York: Atlantic Monthly Press.

Lewis, Franklin D. 2014. *Rumi—Past and Present, East and West: The Life, Teachings, and Poetry of Jalal Al-Din Rumi*. London: Oneworld Publications.

Lewisohn, Leonard. 1993. *Classical Persian Sufism: From Its Origins to Rumi*. 1st British ed. London: Khaniqahi Nimatullahi Publications.

———. 2018. *The Heritage of Sufism: Classical Persian Sufism from Its Origins to Rumi (700–1300)*. Vol. 1. New York: Oneworld Publications.

Li, Darryl. 2020. *The Universal Enemy: Jihad, Empire, and the Challenge of Solidarity*. Stanford, CA: Stanford University Press.

Lin, Ping-hsiu Alice. 2021. "Precious Economies: Gems and Value Making in and from the Pakistan-Afghanistan Borderlands." PhD diss., Chinese University of Hong Kong.

———. 2022. "Between a Rock and a Hard Place: Ethics of Fieldwork in Northwest Pakistan." *International Quarterly for Asian Studies* 53 (4): 587–612.

Lindholm, Charles. 1990. *Charisma*. Oxford, UK: Basil Blackwell.

———. 2002. *The Islamic Middle East: Tradition and Change*. Malden, MA: Blackwell Publishers.

———. 2013. *The Anthropology of Religious Charisma: Ecstasies and Institutions.* New York: Palgrave Macmillan.
Lindisfarne, Nancy. 2002. "Gendering the Afghan War." *Eclipse: The Anti-war Review* 4:2–3.
Linschoten, Alex Strick van, and Anand Gopal. 2017. "Ideology in the Afghan Taliban." Afghanistan Analysts Network. https://www.afghanistan-analysts.org/wp-content/uploads/2017/06/201705-AGopal-ASvLinschoten-TB-Ideology.pdf.
Lizzio, Kenneth P. 2014. *Embattled Saints: My Year with the Sufis of Afghanistan.* Wheaton, IL: Quest Books.
Lobato, Chantal. 1985. "Islam in Kabul: The Religious Politics of Babrak Karmal." *Central Asian Survey* 4 (4): 111–120.
Loewen, Arley, and Josette McMichael. 2010. *Images of Afghanistan: Exploring Afghan Culture through Art and Literature.* Karachi: Oxford University Press.
Luxner, Larry. 2019. "Afghanistan's First Female Ambassador to U.S. Insists Peace Is Still Possible." *Washington Diplomat*, December 3. https://washdiplomat.com/afghanistans-first-female-ambassador-to-us-insists-peace-is-still-possible/.
MacIntyre, Alasdair C. 1988. *Whose Justice? Which Rationality?* Notre Dame, IN: University of Notre Dame Press.
Magnus, Ralph H., and Eden Naby. 1998. *Afghanistan: Mullah, Marx, and Mujahid.* Boulder, CO: Westview Press.
Mahmood, Saba. 2011. *Politics of Piety: The Islamic Revival and the Feminist Subject.* Princeton, NJ: Princeton University Press.
"Mahmud Tarzi: His Life." 2004. http://www.mahmudtarzi.com/type1.php?menu_id=17.
Majrouh, Sayd Bahodine. 2003. *Songs of Love and War: Afghan Women's Poetry.* New York: Other Press.
Malejacq, Romain. 2017. "From Rebel to Quasi-state: Governance, Diplomacy and Legitimacy in the Midst of Afghanistan's Wars (1979–2001)." *Small Wars & Insurgencies* 28 (4–5): 867–886.
———. 2020. *Warlord Survival: The Delusion of State Building in Afghanistan.* Ithaca, NY: Cornell University Press.
Maley, William. 1993. "The Future of Islamic Afghanistan." *Security Dialogue* 24 (4): 383–396.
———, ed. 2001. *Fundamentalism Reborn? Afghanistan and the Taliban.* New York: New York University Press.
———. 2002. *The Afghanistan Wars.* London: Macmillan Education UK.
Mallya, Vinutha. 2014. "In Afghanistan, Fledgling Publishing Industry Takes

First Step." *Growth Markets*, October 14. https://publishingperspectives.com/2014/10/in-afghanistan-fledgling-publishing-industry-takes-first-steps/.

Manchanda, Nivi. 2017. "Rendering Afghanistan Legible: Borders, Frontiers and the State of Afghanistan." *Politics* (Manchester, UK) 37 (4): 386–401.

———. 2020. *Imagining Afghanistan: The History and Politics of Imperial Knowledge*. Cambridge: Cambridge University Press.

Mandaville, Peter. 2014. *Islam and Politics*. 2nd ed. New York: Routledge.

Mann, Carol. 2006. "Models and Realities of Afghan Womanhood: A Retrospective and Prospects." Paper for the Gender Equality and Development Section, Social and Human Sciences Sector, UNESCO. https://www.academia.edu/6324163/Models_and_Realities_of_Afghan_Womanhood_A_Retrospective_and_Prospects.

Manuel, Peter. 2008. "North Indian Sufi Music in the Age of Hindu and Muslim Fundamentalism." *Ethnomusicology* 52 (3): 378–400.

"Mapping Report Afghanistan 3." n.d. Internet Archive. Accessed February 22, 2019. https://archive.org/stream/MappingReportAfghanistan3/Mapping%20Report%20Afghanistan-3_djvu.txt.

Marcus, George E. 1995. "Ethnography in/of the World System: The Emergence of Multi-sited Ethnography." *Annual Review of Anthropology* 24 (1): 95–117.

Marlow, Louise, ed. 2008. *Dreaming across Boundaries: The Interpretation of Dreams in Islamic Lands*. Boston: Ilex Foundation, Harvard University Press.

Marranci, Gabriele. 2008. *The Anthropology of Islam*. Oxford, UK: Berg.

Marsden, Magnus. 2005. *Living Islam: Muslim Religious Experience in Pakistan's North-West Frontier*. Cambridge: Cambridge University Press.

———. 2018. "Civility and Diplomacy: Trust and Dissimulation in Transnational Afghan Trading Networks." *Anthropological Theory* 18 (2–3): 175–197.

Marsden, Peter. 2002. *The Taliban: War and Religion in Afghanistan*. Cape Town: Spearhead.

Martin, Craig. 2009. "Delimiting Religion." *Method & Theory in the Study of Religion* 21 (2): 157–176.

Martin, Lucile. 2021. *Iran as Model and Countermodel: Migration, (Re)Definition of Identity and Transfer of Social Norms in Urban Afghanistan*. Ghent, Belgium: University of Ghent, Faculty of Political and Social Sciences.

Mashal, Mujib. 2013. "Missed Opportunity in Afghanistan: We Forgot to Pay the Preachers." *Time*, February 27. https://world.time.com/2013/02/27/missed-opportunity-in-afghanistan-we-forgot-to-pay-the-preachers/.

Mashal, Mujib, and Jawad Sukhanyar. 2017. "Taliban Target: Scholars of Islam." *New York Times*, May 28. https://www.nytimes.com/2017/05/28/world/asia/

uptick-in-killing-of-religious-scholars-as-taliban-look-to-curtail-their-influ-ence.html?_r=0.
———. 2018. "Bomber Attacks Afghan Scholars Gathered to Denounce Violence." *New York Times*, June 4. https://www.nytimes.com/2018/06/04/world/asia/afghanistan-bombing-clerics.html.
Massoumi, Mejgan. 2021. "The Sounds of Kabul: Radio and the Politics of Popular Culture in Afghanistan, 1969–79." PhD diss., Stanford University.
———. 2022. "Soundwaves of Dissent: Resistance through Persianate Cultural Production in Afghanistan." *Iranian Studies* 55 (3): 697–718.
Masud, Muhammad Khalid, Armando Salvatore and Martin van Bruinessen. 2009. *Islam and Modernity: Key Issues and Debates*. Edinburgh: Edinburgh University Press.
Matinuddin, Kamal. 1999. *The Taliban Phenomenon: Afghanistan 1994–1997*. Karachi: Oxford University Press.
"Mazhabi, Motasim Billah." 2012. Our Campaigns, October 16. https://www.ourcampaigns.com/CandidateDetail.html?CandidateID=322759.
McChesney, Robert D. 1991. *Waqf in Central Asia: Four Hundred Years in the History of a Shrine*. Princeton, NJ: Princeton University Press.
———. 2018. "Reliquary Sufism: Sacred Fiber in Afghanistan." In *Sufism in Central Asia: New Perspectives on Sufi Traditions, 15th–21st Centuries*, edited by Devin DeWeese and Jo-Ann Gross, 191–237. Leiden, Netherlands: Brill.
McCloud, Sean. 2007. *Divine Hierarchies: Class in American Religion and Religious Studies*. Chapel Hill: University of North Carolina Press.
McFate, Montgomery, and Steve Fondacaro. 2011. "Reflections on the Human Terrain System during the First 4 Years." *Prism* (Washington, DC) 2 (4): 63–82.
Meisami, Julie Scott. 1998. "Imagination." In *Encyclopedia of Arabic Literature*, edited by Julie Scott Meisami and Paul Starkey, 393–394. London: Routledge.
Menon, Shruti. 2022. "Afghanistan: What Humanitarian Aid Is Getting In?" BBC, July 8. https://www.bbc.com/news/world-asia-59518628.
Mervin, Sabrina, and Institut français du Proche-Orient. 2010. *Shia Worlds and Iran*. London: Saqi, in association with Institut français du Proche-Orient.
Messick, Brinkley. 1993. *The Calligraphic State: Textual Domination and History in a Muslim Society*. Berkeley: University of California Press.
Metcalf, Barbara Daly. 1982. *Islamic Revival in British India: Deoband, 1860–1900*. Princeton, NJ: Princeton University Press.
Miller, Simone Rosa. 2017. "Autorität Heute–Mit Arendt Über Sie Hinaus." *Deutsche Zeitschrift für Philosophie* 65 (3): 490–503.
Mills, Margaret A. 2011. "Between Covered and Covert: Traditions, Stereotypes, and Afghan Women's Agency." In *Land of the Unconquerable: The Lives of*

Contemporary Afghan Women, edited by Jennifer Heath and Ashraf Zahedi, 60–73. Berkeley: University of California Press.

Mills, Sara. 2003. *Michel Foucault*. London: Routledge.

Min, Eric. 2013. "Taking Responsibility: When and Why Terrorists Claim Attacks." Paper prepared for the 2013 annual meeting of the American Political Science Association, Chicago, August.

Mittermaier, Amira. 2007. "The Book of Visions: Dreams, Poetry and Prophecy in Contemporary Egypt." *International Journal of Middle East Studies* 39:229–247.

———. 2011. *Dreams That Matter: Egyptian Landscapes of Imagination*. Berkeley: University of California Press.

———. 2015. "How to Do Things with Examples: Sufis, Dreams, and Anthropology." *Journal of the Royal Anthropological Institute* 21 (S1): 129–143.

Moaveni, Azadeh. 2017. "How Did Rumi Become One of Our Best-Selling Poets?" *New York Times*, January 20. https://www.nytimes.com/2017/01/20/books/review/rumi-brad-gooch.html.

Moghadam, Valentine M. 1992. "Patriarchy and the Politics of Gender in Modernising Societies: Iran, Pakistan and Afghanistan." *International Sociology* 7 (1): 35–53.

Moghnieh, Lamia. 2021a. "Infrastructures of Suffering: Trauma, Sumud and the Politics of Violence and Aid in Lebanon." *Medicine Anthropology Theory* 8 (1): 1–26.

———. 2021b. "(Interrupted) Writing in Apocalyptic Times: Suffering, Survival, and Rebuilding." *Perpetual Postponement*, December 20. https://perpetual-postponement.org/interrupted-writing-in-apocalyptic-times-suffering-survival-and-rebuilding/.

"Mohammed Hussain Sarahang." 2003. Wikipedia. https://en-academic.com/dic.nsf/enwiki/2894245.

Mojaddedi, Fatima. 2016. "Terrestrial Things: War, Language and Value in Afghanistan." PhD diss., Columbia University.

———. 2019. "The Closing: Heart, Mouth, Word." *Public Culture* 31 (3): 497–520.

Momen, Moojan. 1985. *An Introduction to Shiʻi Islam*. New Haven, CT: Yale University Press.

Monsutti, Alessandro. 2005. *War and Migration: Social Networks and Economic Strategies of the Hazaras of Afghanistan*. New York: Routledge.

———. 2010. "Islamism among the Shiʻa of Afghanistan: From Social Revolution to Identity-Building." In *The Shiʻa Worlds and Iran*, edited by Sabrina Mervin, 45–62. London: Saqi Books.

———. 2013. "Anthropologizing Afghanistan: Colonial and Postcolonial Encounters." *Annual Review of Anthropology* 42 (June): 269–285.

———. 2021. *Homo Itinerans: Towards a Global Ethnography of Afghanistan*. New York: Berghahn Books.
Montgomery, David W. 2016. *Practicing Islam: Knowledge, Experience, and Social Navigation in Kyrgyzstan*. Pittsburgh: University of Pittsburgh Press.
Mousavi, Sayed Askar. 1998. *The Hazaras of Afghanistan: An Historical, Cultural, Economic and Political Study*. Richmond, Surrey, UK: Curzon.
Murtazashvili, Jennifer Brick. 2016. *Informal Order and the State in Afghanistan*. New York: Cambridge University Press.
———. 2021. *Land, the State, and War: Property Institutions and Political Order in Afghanistan*. Cambridge: Cambridge University Press.
Musharraf, Ghadeer. 2013. "Qadamat Urs Bedil Dar Afghanistan Wa Mantaqah" [Bedil tradition of urs in Afghanistan and the region]. *Dari VOA*, December 6. https://www.darivoa.com/a/urse-bedil-in-kabul-and-region/2535962.html.
Naderi, Partaw. 2000. "Kitab Suzaan Deegar" [Another book burning]. Khorasan Zameen, http://www.khorasanzameen.net/php/read.php?id=1274.
———. 2022. *Poetry and Politics*. https://iwp.uiowa.edu/sites/iwp/files/naderi.draftfinal.whereiwrite.fortheweb.pdf.
Nasimi, M. Najim. 2020. "Climate and Water Resources Variation in Afghanistan and the Need for Urgent Adaptation Measures." *International Journal of Food Science and Agriculture* 4 (1): 49–64.
Nasr, Seyyed Hossein. 1999. "Persian Sufi Literature: Its Spiritual and Cultural Significance." In *The Heritage of Sufism*, edited by David Morgan and Leonard Lewisohn, vol. 2, *The Legacy of Medieval Persian Sufism (1150–1500)*, 1–10. Oxford, UK: Oneworld.
Navaro, Yael. 2012. *The Make-Believe Space: Affective Geography in a Postwar Polity*. Durham, NC: Duke University Press.
Nawid, Senzil K. 1999. *Religious Response to Social Change in Afghanistan, 1919–1929: King Aman-Allah and the Afghan Ulama*. Costa Mesa, CA: Mazda Publishers.
Neocleous, Mark. 2012. "'Don't Be Scared, Be Prepared': Trauma-Anxiety-Resilience." *Alternatives: Global, Local, Political* 37 (3): 188–198.
———. 2015. "Resisting Resilience: Against the Colonization of Political Imagination." Der Resilienzdiskurs in der Politik und in der Hilfe. 10jähriges Jubiläum Der Stiftung Medico International Und Symposium, June 5–6. https://www.medico.de/fileadmin/user_upload/media/Neocleous_Resisting_Resilience.pdf.
Noelle-Karimi, Christine. 1997. *State and Tribe in Nineteenth-Century Afghanistan: The Reign of Amir Dost Muhammad Khan (1826–1863)*. London: Routledge.
———. 2013. "Jirga, Shura and Community Development Councils: Village

Institutions and State Interference." In *Local Politics in Afghanistan: A Century of Intervention in the Social Order*, edited by Conrad J. Schetter, 39–58. London: Hurst.

———. 2014. *The Pearl in Its Midst: Herat and the Mapping of Khurasan (15th–19th Centuries)*. Veröffentlichungen Zur Iranistik 74. Vienna: Verlag der Österreichischen Akademie der Wissenschaften.

Nojumi, Neamatollah. 2002. *The Rise of the Taliban in Afghanistan: Mass Mobilization, Civil War, and the Future of the Region*. New York: Palgrave.

———. 2004. *The Prospect of Justice and the Political Transition of Civil Society: The Recovery Process of Afghanistan*. Washington, DC: Asia Program Special Report, Asia and Middle East Program at the Woodrow Wilson Center.

Nooshin, Laudan, ed. 2009. *Music and the Play of Power in the Middle East, North Africa and Central Asia*. Farnham, Surrey, UK: Ashgate.

Nordberg, Jenny. 2014. *The Underground Girls of Kabul: In Search of a Hidden Resistance in Afghanistan*. New York: Crown Publishing.

Nordland, Rod, and Mujib Mashal. 2018. "At Least 55 Killed in Bombing of Afghan Religious Gathering." *New York Times*, November 20. https://www.nytimes.com/2018/11/20/world/asia/afghanistan-wedding-hall-bombing.html.

Nordstrom, Carolyn. 2004. *Shadows of War: Violence, Power, and International Profiteering in the Twenty-First Century*. California Series in Public Anthropology 10. Berkeley: University of California Press.

Nordstrom, Carolyn, and Antonius C. G. M. Robben. 1995. *Fieldwork under Fire: Contemporary Studies of Violence and Survival*. Berkeley: University of California Press.

Norton, Augustus Richard, ed. 1995. *Civil Society in the Middle East*. Leiden, Netherlands : Brill.

Nurbakhsh, Javad. 2004. *Sufi Women*. London: Khaniqahi Nimatullahi Publications.

Nwyia, Paul. 1970. *Exegese coranique et langage mystique*. Beirut: Université Saint-Joseph.

———. 1972. *Ibn "Ata" Allah (m. 709/1309) et la naissance de la confrerie Shadilite*. Beirut: Dar el-Machreq.

Nyhagen, Line. 2019. "Mosques as Gendered Spaces: The Complexity of Women's Compliance with, and Resistance to, Dominant Gender Norms, and the Importance of Male Allies." *Religions* (Basel, Switzerland) 10 (5): 1–15.

O'Brien, Susie. 2017a. "Resilience." In *Fueling Culture: 101 Words for Energy and Environment*, edited by Jennifer Wenzel and Patricia Yaeger, 281–284. New York: Fordham University Press.

———. 2017b. "Resilience Stories: Narratives of Adaptation, Refusal, and Compromise." *Resilience* (Lincoln, NE) 4 (2–3): 43–65.

O'Donnel, Lynne. 2015. "Killing of 11 Sufis at Afghan Mosque Mystifies Authorities." Associated Press, December 3. https://apnews.com/article/228c701e1cc743d7bdd1db8441395ce2.

Ogunnaike, Oludamini. 2018. "Performing Realization: The Sufi Music Videos of the Taalibe Baye of Dakar." *African Arts* 51 (3): 26–39.

———. 2020. *Deep Knowledge: Ways of Knowing in Sufism and Ifa, Two West African Intellectual Traditions*. University Park: Pennsylvania State University Press.

Okten, Ertugrul. 2007. *Jami (817–898/1414–1492): His Biography and Intellectual Influence in Herat*. Chicago: University of Chicago Press.

Olesen, Asta. 1995. *Islam & Politics in Afghanistan*. London: Routledge.

Olszewska, Zuzanna. 2007. "'A Desolate Voice': Poetry and Identity among Young Afghan Refugees in Iran." *Iranian Studies* 40 (2): 203–224.

———. 2015. *The Pearl of Dari: Poetry and Personhood among Young Afghans in Iran*. Bloomington: Indiana University Press.

"Open Letter: 'نامه سرگشاده به رییس جمهور و وزیر معارف'." n.d. http://8am.af/1392/12/18/letter-to-president-and-ministry-introduction/ [site discontinued].

Orjuela, Camilla. 2008. *The Identity Politics of Peacebuilding: Civil Society in War-Torn Sri Lanka*. New Delhi: SAGE Publications.

Ortner, Sherry B. 2006. *Anthropology and Social Theory: Culture, Power and the Acting Subject*. Durham, NC: Duke University Press.

Osman, Borhan. 2014. "Afghan Youth for Democracy? Not All of Them." Afghanistan Analysts Network, April 2. https://www.afghanistan-analysts.org/en/reports/political-landscape/afghan-youth-for-democracy-not-all-of-them/.

———. 2015a. "Beyond Jihad and Traditionalism: Afghanistan's New Generation of Islamic Activists." Afghanistan Analysts Network. https://www.afghanistan-analysts.org/wp-content/uploads/2015/06/AAN-Paper-012015-Borhan-Osman-.pdf.

———. 2015b. "The Killing of Farkhunda (2); Mullahs, Feminists and a Gap in the Debate." Afghanistan Analysts Network, April 29. https://www.afghanistan-analysts.org/the-killing-of-farkhunda-2-mullahs-feminists-and-a-gap-in-the-debate/.

Osman, Wazhmah. 2020. *Television and the Afghan Culture Wars: Brought to You by Foreigners, Warlords, and Activists*. Urbana: University of Illinois Press.

Otto, Jan Michiel. 2010. *Sharia Incorporated: A Comparative Overview of the Legal Systems of Twelve Muslim Countries in Past and Present*. Leiden, Netherlands: Leiden University Press.

Ozdalga, Elisabeth, ed. 1999. *The Naqshbandis in Western and Central Asia: Change and Continuity.* Istanbul: Swedish Research Institute in Istanbul.

Pannke, Peter. 2014. *Saints and Singers: Sufi Music in the Indus Valley.* Karachi: Oxford University Press.

Papas, Alexandre. 2020. *Sufi Institutions.* Boston: Brill.

Paul, Juergen. 2010. "Abd Al-Khāliq al-Ghijduwānī." In *Encyclopaedia of Islam*, 3rd ed., edited by Kate Fleet, Gudrun Krämer, Denis Matringe, John Nawas and Devin J. Stewart. Leiden, Netherlands: Brill.

———. 2011. "The Khwajagan in Herat during Shahrukh's Reign." In *Horizons of the World: Festschrift for Isenbike Togan*, edited by İlker Evrim Binbaş and Nurten Kılıç-Schubel, 217–250. Istanbul: İthaki Yayınları.

———. 2017. "The Rise of the Khwajagan-Naqshbandiyya Sufi Order in Timurid Herat." In *Afghanistan's Islam: From Conversion to the Taliban*, edited by Nile Green, 71–86. Oakland: University of California Press.

Pemberton, Kelly. 2006. "Women Pirs, Saintly Succession, and Spiritual Guidance in South Asian Sufism." *Muslim World* 96 (1): 61–87.

Penkala-Gawecka, Danuta. 1992. "Pilgrimage as Cure: Shrines in Afghanistan." *Etnografia Polska* 17:35–45.

Perennes, Jean-Jacques. 2014. *Passion Kaboul: Le père Serge de Beaurecueil.* Paris: Cerf.

Pernau, Margrit. 2016. "Provincializing Concepts: The Language of Transnational History." *Comparative Studies of South Asia, Africa, and the Middle East* 36 (3): 483–499.

Peterson, Andrew. 2019. *Civility and Democratic Education.* Birmingham, UK: Springer.

Philippon, Alix. 2014. "A Sublime, yet Disputed, Object of Political Ideology? Sufism in Pakistan at the Crossroads." *Commonwealth & Comparative Politics* 52 (2): 271–292.

———. 2020. "Sufi Politics and the War on Terror in Pakistan: Looking for an Alternative to Radical Islamism?" In *Modern Sufis and the State: The Politics of Islam in South Asia and Beyond*, edited by Katherine Pratt Ewing and Rosemary R. Corbett, 140–160. New York: Columbia University Press.

Pinto, Paulo. 2002. "Mystical Bodies: Ritual, Experience and the Embodiment of Sufism in Syria." ProQuest Dissertations Publishing. http://search.proquest.com/docview/304802272/.

———. 2010. "The Anthropologist and the Initiated: Reflections on the Ethnography of Mystical Experience among the Sufis of Aleppo, Syria." *Social Compass* 57 (4): 464–478.

Piraino, Francesco, and Mark J. Sedgwick. 2019. *Global Sufism: Boundaries, Structures and Politics.* London: Hurst.

Pollock, Katherine, and Frederic Wehrey. 2018. "The Sufi-Salafi Rift." Carnegie Middle East Center, January 23. https://carnegie-mec.org/diwan/75310.
Posocco, Silvia. 2014. *Secrecy and Insurgency: Socialities and Knowledge Practices in Guatemala*. Tuscaloosa: University of Alabama Press.
Potter, Lawrence G. 1994. "Sufis and Sultans in Post-Mongol Iran." *Iranian Studies* 27 (4): 77–102.
Powell, Colin L. 2001. "Remarks to the National Foreign Policy Conference for Leaders of Nongovernmental Organizations." U.S. Department of State Archive, October 26. https://2001-2009.state.gov/secretary/former/powell/remarks/2001/5762.htm.
Price, David H. 2016. *Cold War Anthropology: The CIA, the Pentagon, and the Growth of Dual Use Anthropology*. Durham, NC: Duke University Press.
Pstrusinska, Jadwiga. 1987. "Movements of Population in Afghanistan since 1978." Paper presented at Second European Seminar on Central Asian Studies, London, April 7–10.
Puar, Jasbir. 2008. "Feminists and Queers in the Service of Empire." In *Feminism and War: Confronting US Imperialism*, edited by Chandra Talpade Mohanty, Robin L. Riley and Minnie Bruce Pratt, 103–116. London: Zed Books.
Putnam, Robert. 1994. *Making Democracy Work: Civic Traditions in Modern Italy*. Princeton, NJ: Princeton University Press.
———. 2000. *Bowling Alone: The Collapse and Revival of American Community*. New York: Simon and Schuster.
Quraishi, Najibullah, and Jamie Doran. 2014. "The Girls of the Taliban." Al Jazeera English, December 24. http://www.aljazeera.com/programmes/specialseries/2014/12/girls-taliban-2014121716718177928.html.
Qureshi, Regula. 2006. *Sufi Music of India and Pakistan: Sound, Context and Meaning in Qawwali*. Karachi: Oxford University Press.
Qutbudin, Ishanch, Mohammed Sanusi Shiru, Ahmad Sharafati, Kamal Ahmed, Nadhir Al-Ansari, Zaher Mundher Yaseen, Shamsuddin Shahid and Xiaojun Wang. 2019. "Seasonal Drought Pattern Changes due to Climate Variability: Case Study in Afghanistan." *Water* 11 (5): 1–20.
Rahman, Farhana. 2018. "Narratives of Agency: Women, Islam, and the Politics of Economic Participation in Afghanistan." *Journal of International Women's Studies* 19 (3): 60–70.
Rahmany, Mirwais, Hamid Stanikzai, Alex Strick van Linschoten and Felix Kuehn, eds. 2012. *Poetry of the Taliban*. London: Hurst.
Rajagopalan, Megha. 2019. "Grounded." *BuzzFeed*, December 14. https://www.buzzfeednews.com/article/megharа/the-badass-afghan-pilot-who-went-massively-viral-is-now.

Rashid, Ahmed. 2008. *Descent into Chaos: The United States and the Failure of Nation Building in Pakistan, Afghanistan, and Central Asia*. New York: Viking.

———. 2010. *Taliban: Militant Islam, Oil, and Fundamentalism in Central Asia*. New Haven, CT: Yale Nota Bene.

Rasmussen, Sune Engel. 2015. "Afghanistan's Model City Is Also Its Kidnapping Capital." *Global Post*, July 27. https://theworld.org/stories/2015-07-27/afghanistans-model-city-also-its-kidnapping-capital.

Raudvere, Catharina. 2002. *The Book and the Roses: Sufi Women, Visibility, and Zikir in Contemporary Istanbul*. Istanbul: Swedish Research Institute.

Raudvere, Catharina, and Leif Stenberg. 2008. *Sufism Today: Heritage and Tradition in the Global Community*. London: I. B. Tauris.

Raz, Joseph. 2009. *Between Authority and Interpretation: On the Theory of Law and Practical Reason*. Oxford: Oxford University Press.

Redkollegiia, ed. 2021. *The Written and the Spoken in Central Asia / Mündlichkeit Und Schriftlichkeit in Zentralasien–Festschrift for Ingeborg Baldauf*. Vol. 4. Potsdam: edition tethys.

Reid, Rachel. 2021. "Afghanistan 1400: The Dawn and Decline of a Political Movement." Afghanistan Analysts Network, March 24. https://www.afghanistan-analysts.org/en/reports/rights-freedom/afghanistan-1400-the-dawn-and-decline-of-a-political-movement/.

Reuters. 2018. "Senior Cleric in Afghanistan's Top Religious Body Killed." Reuters, November 24. https://www.reuters.com/article/us-afghanistan-attack-religion/senior-cleric-in-afghanistans-top-religious-body-killed-idUSKCN1NT0IH.

Ridgeon, Lloyd, ed. 2015. *Sufis and Salafis in the Contemporary Age*. London: Bloomsbury Academic.

Risemberg, Annie. 2019. "In Mali, Tolerant Islam Runs Deeper than Jihadism." *Bright Magazine*, February 19. https://brightthemag.com/in-mali-tolerant-islam-runs-deeper-than-jihadism-extremism-religion-west-africa-c939427060c2.

Rispler, Vardit. 1991. "Toward a New Understanding of the Term Bid'a." *Der Islam* 68 (2): 320–328.

Robson, J. 2012. "Bid'a." In *Encyclopaedia of Islam*, 2nd ed., edited by P. Bearman, Th. Bianquis, C. E. Bosworth, E. van Donzel and W. P. Heinrichs. Leiden, Netherlands: Brill.

Rodinson, Maxime. 1980. *Muhammad*. New York: Pantheon Books.

Roy, Olivier. 1983. "Sufism in the Afghan Resistance." *Central Asian Survey* 2 (4): 61–79. http://dx.doi.org/10.1080/02634938308400447.

———. 1984. "Islam in the Afghan Resistance." *Religion in Communist Lands* 12 (1): 55–68. DOI: 10.1080/09637498408431111.

———. 1990. *Islam and Resistance in Afghanistan*. 2nd ed. Cambridge: Cambridge University Press.
Rozehnal, Robert Thomas. 2007. *Islamic Sufism Unbound: Politics and Piety in Twenty-First Century Pakistan*. New York: Palgrave Macmillan.
Rubaii, Kali. 2020. "Trust without Confidence: Moving Medicine with Dirty Hands." *Cultural Anthropology* 35 (2): 211–217.
———. 2022. "'Concrete Soldiers': T-Walls and Coercive Landscaping in Iraq." *International Journal of Middle East Studies* 54 (2): 357–362.
Rubin, Barnett R. 1995. *The Fragmentation of Afghanistan: State Formation and Collapse in the International System*. New Haven, CT: Yale University Press.
———. 2002. *The Fragmentation of Afghanistan: State Formation and Collapse in the International System*. 2nd ed. New Haven, CT: Yale University Press.
Rüttig, Thomas. 2019. "From Sufi Sheikh to President: Historic Mujahedin Leader Mujaddedi Passes Away." Afghanistan Analysts Network, February 13. https://www.afghanistan-analysts.org/en/reports/political-landscape/from-sufi-sheikh-to-interim-president-historic-mujahedin-leader-mujaddedi-passes-away/.
———. 2020. "AAN Obituary: PDPA Leader and Poet Sulaiman Layeq (1930–2020)." Afghanistan Analysts Network, August 19. https://www.afghanistan-analysts.org/en/reports/context-culture/aan-obituary-pdpa-leader-and-poet-sulaiman-layeq-1930-2020/.
Rypka, Jan, and Karl Jahn. 1968. *History of Iranian Literature*. Dordrecht: Springer Netherlands.
Rzehak, Lutz. 2004. "Narrative Strukturen des Erzählers über Heilige und ihre Gräber in Afghanistan." *Asiatische Studien: Zeitschrift der Schweizerischen Asiengesellschaft Etudes Asiatiques: Revue de la Societe Suisse—Asie* 58 (1): 195–229.
———. 2007. "Verheiratet mit Dschinns: Formen Der Volksfrommigkeit in Afghanistan." *Sudasien* 2:74–77.
Sadr, Omar. 2020. *Negotiating Cultural Diversity in Afghanistan*. Oxford, UK: Routledge.
Safi, Omid. 2000. "Bargaining with Baraka: Persian Ṣūfism, 'Mysticism,' and Pre-modern Politics." *Muslim World* 90 (3–4): 259–287.
Sahih al-Bukhari. n.d. Vol. 9, book 87, no. 125. Accessed May 4, 2023. https://www.sahih-bukhari.com/Pages/Bukhari_9_87.php.
Said, Edward W. 1989. "Representing the Colonized: Anthropology's Interlocutors." *Critical Inquiry* 15 (2): 205–225.
Sajoo, Amyn B. 2002. *Civil Society in the Muslim World: Contemporary Perspectives*. London: I. B. Tauris.

Sakata, Hiromi Lorraine. 1985. "Musicians Who Do Not Perform." *Asian Music* 17 (1): 132–142.

———. 2002. *Music in the Mind: The Concepts of Music and Musician in Afghanistan*. Washington, DC: Smithsonian Institution Press.

Salime, Zakia. 2011. *Between Feminism and Islam: Human Rights and Sharia Law in Morocco*. Minneapolis: University of Minnesota Press.

Salvatore, Armando. 2016. *The Sociology of Islam: Knowledge, Power and Civility*. Chichester, West Sussex, UK: Wiley Blackwell.

Salwati Sarwari, Bismillah Faramarz and Abdul Ghaffar Salwati Habibi. 2018. *Tarikh-e Alieh Salwatiyyah* [History of the perfected Salwatiyyah]. Herat: Ahrari Publishing.

Sands, Chris, and Fazelminallah Qazizai. 2019. *Night Letters: Gulbuddin Hekmatyar and the Afghan Islamists Who Changed the World*. Oxford, UK: C. Hurst.

———. 2022. "Faith and Vengeance: The Islamic State's War in Afghanistan." *New Lines Magazine*, August 1. https://newlinesmag.com/reportage/faith-and-vengeance-the-islamic-states-war-in-afghanistan/.

Sanger, Pamela Chapman. 2003. "Living and Writing Feminist Ethnography: Threads in a Quilt Stitched from the Heart." In *Expressions of Ethnography: Novel Approaches to Qualitative Methods*, edited by Robin Patric Clair, 29–44. Albany: State University of New York Press.

Sanyal, Usha. 2020. "Sufism through the Prism of Sharia: A Reformist Barelwi Girls' Madrasa in Uttar Pradesh, India." In *Modern Sufis and the State: The Politics of Islam in South Asia and Beyond*, edited by Katherine Pratt Ewing and Rosemary R. Corbett, 92–105. New York: Columbia University Press.

Sarahang, Muhammad Husayn. 2000. *Qanun-i Tarab*. Stockholm: Shura-yi Farhangi-i Afghanistan.

Sarmast, Ahmad. 2009. *A Survey of the History of Music in Afghanistan: Special Reference to Art Music from c. 1000 A.D.* Saarbrücken, Germany: VDM Verlag.

Scheper-Hughes, Nancy. 1992. *Death without Weeping: The Violence of Everyday Life in Brazil*. Berkeley: University of California Press.

Scheper-Hughes, Nancy, and Philippe I. Bourgois. 2004. *Violence in War and Peace*. Malden, MA: Blackwell.

Schetter, Conrad, ed. 2013. *Local Politics in Afghanistan: A Century of Intervention in the Social Order*. London: C. Hurst.

Schielke, Samuli. 2009a. "Ambivalent Commitments: Troubles of Morality, Religiosity and Aspiration among Young Egyptians." *Journal of Religion in Africa* 39 (2): 158–185.

———. 2009b. "Being Good in Ramadan: Ambivalence, Fragmentation, and the Moral Self in the Lives of Young Egyptians." *Journal of the Royal Anthropological Institute* 15:S24–40.

---. 2010. "Second Thoughts about the Anthropology of Islam, or How to Make Sense of Grand Schemes in Everyday Life." Zentrum Moderner Orient Working Papers (no. 2), 1–16. https://d-nb.info/1019243724/34.
Schielke, Samuli, and Liza Debevec. 2012. *Ordinary Lives and Grand Schemes: An Anthropology of Everyday Religion*. New York: Berghahn Books.
Schimmel, Annemarie. 1975. "Sufi Literature." The Afghanistan Council of the Asia Society Occasional Paper/Special Paper Based on Lecture, New York City, April 28.
---. 1978. *Mystical Dimensions of Islam*. Chapel Hill: University of North Carolina Press.
---. 1983. "Sufism and the Islamic Tradition." In *Mysticism and Religious Traditions*, edited by Steven T. Katz, 131–147. Oxford: Oxford University Press.
---. 1985. *Mystische Dimensionen Des Islam: Die Geschichte Des Sufismus*. Cologne: Eugen Diederichs Verlag.
---. 1993. *A Triumphant Sun: A Study of the Works of Jalaloddin Rumi*. Albany: State University of New York Press.
---. 1998. *Die Träume Des Kalifen: Träume Und Ihre Deutung in Der Islamischen Kultur*. Munich: C. H. Beck.
Schinasi, May. 2017. *Kabul: A History 1773–1948*. Leiden, Netherlands: Brill.
Schmeding, Annika. 2020. "Sufis in Afghanistan: Religious Authority and Succession in an Insecure Age." PhD diss., Boston University.
SCRIBD. n.d. "Seminar Abdul Qadir Bedil." Accessed June 20, 2020. https://www.scribd.com/doc/138682884/Seminar-Abdul-Qadir-Bedil.
Sedgwick, Mark. 2005. *Saints and Sons: The Making and Remaking of the Rashidi Ahmadi Sufi Order, 1799–2000*. Leiden, Netherlands: Brill.
Sehlikoglu, Serta. 2017. "Revisited: Muslim Women's Agency and Feminist Anthropology of the Middle East." *Contemporary Islam* 12 (1): 73–92.
Seligman, Adam B. 1992. *The Idea of Civil Society*. New York: Free Press.
Senay, Banu. 2014. "The Fall and Rise of the Ney: From the Sufi Lodge to the World Stage." *Ethnomusicology Forum* 23 (3): 405–424.
Shahzad, Qaiser. 2007. "Ibn 'Arabi's Metaphysics of the Human Body." *Islamic Studies* 46 (4): 499–525.
Sharan, Timor. 2011. "The Dynamics of Elite Networks and Patron-Client Relations in Afghanistan." *Europe-Asia Studies* 63 (6): 1109–1127.
---. 2013. "The Network Politics of International Statebuilding: Intervention and Statehood in Post-2001 Afghanistan." Open Research Exeter, March. https://ore.exeter.ac.uk/repository/handle/10871/14542.
Sharan, Timor, and John Heathershaw. 2011. "Identity Politics and Statebuilding in Post-Bonn Afghanistan: The 2009 Presidential Election." *Ethnopolitics* 10 (3–4): 297–319.

Shahrani, Nazif. 1991. "Local Knowledge of Islam and Social Discourse in Afghanistan and Turkistan in the Modern Period." In *Turko-Persia in Historical Perspective*, edited by Robert Canfield, 161–188. New York: Cambridge University Press.

Sharifi, Mohammad Omar. 2018. "Language, Poetry, and Identity in Afghanistan: Poetic Texts, Changing Contexts." In *Modern Afghanistan: The Impact of 40 Years of War*, edited by M. Nazif Shahrani, 56–76. Bloomington: Indiana University Press.

———. 2019. "The Nauroz Festival as a Social Site: Understanding Faith, Ethnicity and Nation-ness in Afghanistan." PhD diss., Boston University.

Sharify-Funk, Meena. 2018. *Contemporary Sufism: Piety, Politics, and Popular Culture*. Abingdon, UK: Routledge.

Shaw, Wendy M. K. 2019. *What Is "Islamic" Art? Between Religion and Perception*. Cambridge: Cambridge University Press.

Shils, Edward. 1991. "The Virtue of Civil Society." *Government and Opposition* 26 (1): 3–20.

Shinwari, Jakar. 2002. *Afghani Hinduwan Aw Sikhan*. Amrika: Pushto Yun.

Shryock, Andrew. 1997. *Nationalism and the Genealogical Imagination: Oral History and Textual Authority in Tribal Jordan*. Comparative Studies on Muslim Societies 23. Berkeley: University of California Press.

Shulman, David, and Guy G. Stroumsa, eds. 1999. *Dream Cultures: Explorations in the Comparative History of Dreaming*. New York: Oxford University Press.

Siddiqi, Moazzam. 1989. "Bīdel, ʿAbd-al-Qāder." In *Encyclopædia Iranica*, online ed. http://www.iranicaonline.org/articles/bidel-bedil-mirza-abd-al-qader-b. Available in print: vol. IV, fasc. 3, 244–246.

Siddique, Abubakar Ayadi. 2021. "Taliban Wages Deadly Crackdown on Afghan Salafists as War with IS-K Intensifies." Radio Free Europe/Radio Liberty, October 22. https://www.rferl.org/a/taliban-crackdown-salafis-islamic-state-khorasan/31524687.html.

———. 2022. "Fear Grips Afghanistan's Sufi Community Following Deadly Attacks." Radio Free Europe/Radio Liberty, May 16.https://www.rferl.org/a/afghanistan-sufis-attacks-is-k/31853526.html https://www.rferl.org/a/afghanistan-sufis-attacks-is-k/31853526.html.

Sidky, M. Homayun. 1990. "Malang, Sufis, and Mystics: An Ethnographic and Historical Study of Shamanism in Afghanistan." *Asian Folklore Studies* 49 (2): 275–301.

Sikand, Yoginder. 2013. "The Reformist Sufism of the Tablighi Jama'at: The Case of the Meos of Mewat, India." In *Sufism and the "Modern" in Islam*, edited by Martin van Bruinessen and Julia Day Howell, 129–149. London: I. B. Tauris.

Silverman, Helaine. 2010. *Contested Cultural Heritage: Religion, Nationalism, Erasure, and Exclusion in a Global World.* New York: Springer New York.
Sinno, Abdulkader H. 2008. *Organizations at War in Afghanistan and Beyond.* Ithaca, NY: Cornell University Press.
———. 2010. "The Strategic Use of Islam in Afghan Politics." In *Religion and Politics in South Asia*, edited by Ali Riaz, 53–75. New York: Routledge.
Sirat, Abdul Satar. 1969. "Sharia and Islamic Education in Modern Afghanistan." *Middle East Journal* 23 (2): 217–219.
Sirriyeh, Elizabeth. 1999. *Sufis and Anti-Sufis: The Defence, Rethinking and Rejection of Sufism in the Modern World.* London: Routledge.
Sirur, Simrin. 2021. "Pakistani Salafi Clerics Are Upset with Taliban after Imam Killing and Mosque-Closing Spree." *The Print*, September 15. https://theprint.in/go-to-pakistan/pakistani-salafi-clerics-upset-with-taliban-after-imam-killing/733935/.
Smith, Laurajane. 2006. *Uses of Heritage.* London: Routledge.
Smith, Laurajane, and Natsuko Akagawa. 2009. *Intangible Heritage.* London: Routledge.
———. 2018. *Safeguarding Intangible Heritage: Practices and Politics.* Oxford, UK: Routledge.
Smith, Laurajane, Margaret Wetherell and Gary Campbell. 2018. *Emotion, Affective Practices, and the Past in the Present.* Oxford, UK: Routledge.
Soares, Benjamin. 2005. *Islam and the Prayer Economy: History and Authority in a Malian Town.* Ann Arbor: University of Michigan Press.
Specia, Megan. 2017. "Who Are Sufi Muslims and Why Do Some Extremists Hate Them?" *New York Times*, November 24. https://www.nytimes.com/2017/11/24/world/middleeast/sufi-muslim-explainer.html.
Spivak, Gayatri C. 1988. "Can the Subaltern Speak?" In *Marxism and the Interpretation of Culture*, edited by Cary Nelson and Lawrence Grossberg, 271–313. Urbana: University of Illinois Press.
———. 2000. "The New Subaltern: A Silent Interview." In *Mapping Subaltern Studies and the Postcolonial*, edited by Vinayak Chaturvedi, 324–340. London: Verso.
Stabile, Carol A., and Deepa Kumar. 2005. "Unveiling Imperialism: Media, Gender and the War on Afghanistan." *Media, Culture & Society* 27 (5): 765–782.
Steinmetz, George. 2003. "'The Devil's Handwriting': Precolonial Discourse, Ethnographic Acuity, and Cross-identification in German Colonialism." *Comparative Studies in Society and History* 45 (1): 41–95.
Stjernholm, Simon. 2010. "Sufi Politics in Britain: The Sufi Muslim Council and

the 'Silent Majority' of Muslims." *Journal of Islamic Law and Culture* 12 (3): 215–226.
Stocking, George W. 1991. *Colonial Situations: Essays on the Contextualization of Ethnographic Knowledge*. Madison: University of Wisconsin Press.
Strothmann, Linus. 2016. *Managing Piety: The Shrine of Data Ganj Bakhsh*. Karachi: Oxford University Press.
Sultanova, Razia. 2008. "Female Celebrations in Uzbekistan and Afghanistan: The Power of Cosmology in Musical Rites." *Yearbook for Traditional Music* 40:8–20.
———. 2011. *From Shamanism to Sufism: Women, Islam and Culture in Central Asia*. London: I. B. Tauris.
Sviri, Sara. 1999. "Dreaming Analyzed and Recorded: Dreams in the World of Medieval Islam." In *Dream Cultures / Explorations in the Comparative History of Dreaming*, edited by David Shulman and Guy G Stroumsa, 235–251. New York: Oxford University Press.
Synovitz, Ron. 2021. "'I Feel like a Dead Fish': Silenced by the Taliban, Afghanistan's Musicians Despair." Radio Free Europe/Radio Liberty, October 13. https://www.rferl.org/a/musicians-silenced-taliban/31507522.html.
Talmazan, Yuliya. 2021. "Taliban Hang Bodies of Alleged Kidnappers in Afghan City of Herat." NBC News, September 26. https://www.nbcnews.com/news/world/taliban-hang-bodies-alleged-kidnappers-afghan-city-herat-n1280106.
Taneja, Anand Vivek. 2018. *Jinnealogy: Time, Islam, and Ecological Thought in the Medieval Ruins of Delhi*. Stanford, CA: Stanford University Press.
Tapper, Richard. 1995. "'Islamic Anthropology' and the 'Anthropology of Islam.'" *Anthropological Quarterly* 68 (3): 185–193.
Tapper, Richard, and Nancy Lindisfarne-Tapper. 2020. *Afghan Village Voices: Stories from a Tribal Community*. London: I. B. Tauris.
Tarzi, Amin. 2017. "Islam, Shari'a, and State Building under 'Abd al-Rahman Khan." In *Afghanistan's Islam*, edited by Nile Green, 129–144. Oakland: University of California Press.
Taussig, Michael T. 1999. *Defacement: Public Secrecy and the Labor of the Negative*. Stanford, CA: Stanford University Press.
Thackston, Wheeler M. 2002. *The Baburnama: Memoirs of Babur, Prince and Emperor*. New York: Modern Library Paperback Edition.
Theros, Marika. 2019. "Reimagining Civil Society in Conflict: Findings from Post-2001 Afghanistan." *Journal of Civil Society* 15 (2): 143–161.
Tocqueville, Alexis de. 2003. *Democracy in America*. London: Penguin Classics.
TOLO News Afghanistan. 2016. "Afghanistan to Turkey, Iran: Rumi Is Afghanistan's Heritage." TOLO News, June 8. https://tolonews.com/afghanistan/afghanistan-turkey-iran-rumi-afghanistans-heritage.

Trimingham, J. Spencer. 1998. *The Sufi Orders in Islam*. New York: Oxford University Press.

Uk, Krisna. 2016. *Salvage: Cultural Resilience among the Jorai of Northeast Cambodia*. Ithaca, NY: Cornell University Press.

UN. 2022. "Afghanistan: Taliban's Targeting of Women and NGOs Preventing Delivery of Life-Saving Assistance Is Deplorable, Say UN Experts." United Nations, December 30. https://www.ohchr.org/en/statements/2022/12/afghanistan-talibans-targeting-women-and-ngos-preventing-delivery-life-saving.

UN News. 2021a. "First Humanitarian Flight to Kabul Marks 'Turning Point' in Crisis: WFP." UN News, September 14. https://news.un.org/en/story/2021/09/1099862.

———. 2021b. "Security Council Paves Way for Aid to Reach Desperate Afghans." UN News, December 22. https://news.un.org/en/story/2021/12/1108642.

———. 2022. "Deadly Mosque Explosion: 'Another Painful Blow to the People of Afghanistan.'" UN News, April 29. https://news.un.org/en/story/2022/04/1117322.

UNESCO. 2023. "Afghanistan: Education and Literacy." UNESCO Institute for Statistics. http://uis.unesco.org/country/AF.

UNHCR. 2021. "UNHCR Begins Airlifting Aid to Kabul." UNHCR, November 2. https://www.unhcr.org/news/briefing/2021/11/618101074/unhcr-begins-airlifting-aid-to-kabul.html.

US Department of State. 2017. "2017 Report on International Religious Freedom: Afghanistan." https://www.state.gov/reports/2017-report-on-international-religious-freedom/afghanistan/.

US Senate, Committee on Foreign Relations. 2011. *Evaluating US Foreign Assistance to Afghanistan: A Majority Staff Report Prepared for the Use of the Committee on Foreign Relations United States Senate*. https://www.govinfo.gov/content/pkg/CPRT-112SPRT66591/pdf/CPRT-112SPRT66591.pdf.

Utas, Bo. 1999. "The Naqshbandiyya of Afghanistan on the Eve of the 1978 Coup d'Etat." In *Naqshbandis in Western and Central Asia: Change and Continuity*, edited by Elizabeth Özdalga, vol. 9, *Transactions of the Swedish Research Institute in Istanbul*, 117–127. Richmond, Surrey, UK: Curzon.

Vicini, Fabio. 2017. "Thinking through the Heart: Islam, Reflection and the Search for Transcendence." *Culture and Religion* 18 (2): 110–128.

Vigh, Henrik. 2007. *Navigating Terrains of War: Youth and Soldiering in Guinea-Bissau*. New York: Berghahn Books.

———. 2009. "Motion Squared: A Second Look at the Concept of Social Navigation." *Anthropological Theory* 9 (4), 419–438.

———. 2011. "Vigilance: On Conflict, Social Invisibility, and Negative Potentiality." *Social Analysis: The International Journal of Social and Cultural Practice* 55 (3): 93–114.
Vizenor, Gerald. 2009. *Native Liberty: Natural Reason and Cultural Survivance*. Lincoln: University of Nebraska Press.
Volpi, Frederic. 2011. "Framing Civility in the Middle East: Alternative Perspectives on the State and Civil Society." *Third World Quarterly* 32 (5): 827–843.
Wali Allah al-Dihlawi. 1982. *The Sacred Knowledge of the Higher Functions of the Mind: Altaf al-Quds*. London: Octagon Press.
Walker, Jeremy, and Melinda Cooper. 2011. "Genealogies of Resilience: From Systems Ecology to the Political Economy of Crisis Adaptation." *Security Dialogue* 42 (2): 143–160.
Walsh, Declan. 2017. "Why Was an Italian Graduate Student Tortured and Murdered in Egypt?" *New York Times Magazine*, August 15. https://www.nytimes.com/2017/08/15/magazine/giulio-regeni-italian-graduate-student-tortured-murdered-egypt.html.
Watt, W. Montgomery. 1974. *Muhammad: Prophet and Statesman*. London: Oxford University Press.
Waugh, Earle H. 2005. *Memory, Music, and Religion: Morocco's Mystical Chanters*. Columbia: University of South Carolina Press.
Weinreich, Matthias, and Mikhail Pelevin. 2012. "The Songs of the Taliban: Continuity of Form and Thought in an Ever-Changing Environment." *Iran & the Caucasus* 16 (1): 45–70.
Weismann, Itzchak. 2007. *The Naqshbandiyya: Orthodoxy and Activism in a Worldwide Sufi Tradition*. London: Routledge.
———. 2015. "Modernity from Within: Islamic Fundamentalism and Sufism." In *Sufis and Salafis in the Contemporary Age*, edited by Lloyd Ridgeon, 9–31. London: Bloomsbury Academic.
Weller, Robert P. 1999. *Alternate Civilities: Democracy and Culture in China and Taiwan*. Boulder, CO: Westview Press.
Werbner, Pnina. 2003. *Pilgrims of Love: The Anthropology of a Global Sufi Cult*. Bloomington: Indiana University Press.
———. 2012. "Du'a: Popular Culture and Powerful Blessings at the 'Urs.'" In *South Asian Sufis*, edited by Clinton Bennett and Charles M. Ramsey, 83–93. London: Continuum.
Werbner, Pnina, and Helene Basu, eds. 1998. *Embodying Charisma: Modernity, Locality and the Performance of Emotion in Sufi Cults*. London: Routledge.
Wieland-Karimi, Almut. 1998. *Islamische Mystik in Afghanistan: Die Strukturelle Einbindung Der Sufik in Die Gesellschaft*. Berlin: Humboldt University.

Wilber, Donald. 1952. "The Structure and Position of Islam in Afghanistan." *Middle East Journal* 6:41–48.

Wilde, Alexander. 2016. *Religious Responses to Violence: Human Rights in Latin America Past and Present.* Notre Dame, IN: University of Notre Dame Press.

Wimpelmann, Torunn. 2017. *The Pitfalls of Protection: Gender, Violence and Power in Afghanistan.* Oakland: University of California Press.

Wintour, Patrick. 2023. "Afghan Aid at Risk from Taliban Ban on Women, Warns United Nations." *The Guardian*, January 6. https://www.theguardian.com/world/2023/jan/06/afghan-aid-at-risk-from-taliban-ban-on-women-warns-united-nations.

Wolff, Jonas, and Annika E. Poppe. 2015. *From Closing Space to Contested Spaces: Re-assessing Current Conflicts over International Civil Society Support.* Vol. 137. Frankfurt am Main: Hessische Stiftung Friedens- und Konfliktforschung.

Wolper, Ethel Sara. 1960. *Cities and Saints: Sufism and the Transformation of Urban Space in Medieval Anatolia.* University Park: Pennsylvania State University Press.

Xavier, Merin Shobhana. 2018. *Sacred Spaces and Transnational Networks in American Sufism: Bawa Muhaiyaddeen and Contemporary Shrine Cultures.* London: Bloomsbury Academic.

Yazid, Said, and Lejla Demiri. 2018. *The Future of Interfaith Dialogue: Muslim-Christian Encounters through a Common Word.* Cambridge: Cambridge University Press.

Zaeef, Abdul Salam. 2010. *My Life with the Taliban.* New York: Columbia University Press.

Zaman, Muhammad Qasim. 2002. *The Ulama in Contemporary Islam: Custodians of Change.* Princeton, NJ: Princeton University Press.

———. 2012. *Modern Islamic Thought in a Radical Age: Religious Authority and Internal Criticism.* Cambridge: Cambridge University Press.

Zaman, Robert, and Abdul Ahad Mohammadi. 2014. *Trends in Student Radicalization across University Campuses in Afghanistan.* Kabul: Afghan Institute for Strategic Studies. https://kar.kent.ac.uk/47807/1/Trends%20in%20Student%20Radicalization%20across%20University%20Campuses%20in%20Afghanistan_Zaman.pdf.

Zani, Leah. 2019. *Bomb Children: Life in the Former Battlefields of Laos.* Durham, NC: Duke University Press.

Ziad, Waleed. 2017a. "Transporting Knowledge in the Durrani Empire: Two Manuals of Naqshbandi-Mujaddidi Sufi Practice." In *Afghanistan's Islam: From Conversion to the Taliban*, edited by Nile Green, 105–126. Berkeley: University of California Press.

———. 2017b. "Traversing the Indus and the Oxus: Trans-regional Islamic

Revival in the Age of Political Fragmentation and the 'Great Game' 1747–1880." PhD diss., Yale University.

———. 2019. "From Yarkand to Sindh via Kabul: The Rise of Naqshbandi-Mujaddidi Sufi Networks in the 18th–19th Century Durrani Empire." In *The Persianate World: Rethinking a Shared Sphere*, edited by Abbas Amanat and Assef Ashraf, 125–168. Leiden, Netherlands: Brill.

———. 2021. *Hidden Caliphate: Sufi Saints beyond the Oxus and Indus*. Cambridge, MA: Harvard University Press.

INDEX

Academy of Science, 129
adab, 14, 225n61
adaptation, 3–4, 10, 18, 20–1, 23, 28, 33–4, 37–9, 102, 128, 141, 154, 158, 162, 167, 198, 203–4, 210, 259n63; dexterity, 3, 16, 20–1, 33, 37–8, 201
Afghanistan
—Baghlan, 44, 151
—Balkh, 40, 46, 121, 232n20, 234n50. *See also* Mazar-e Sharif; Pul-i Khumri, 44, 151
—Charharbagh, 40
—Chisht-e Sharif, 184
—Dehsabz, 54
—Ghazni, 23, 125, 232n21
—Helmand, 228n109
—Herat, 10, 23, 26, 29–30, 35, 40, 43–4, 49, 54–6, 60, 64, 69–72, 125, 144–5, 150, 159, 161–3, 168–73, 177–8, 184, 187–90, 198, 200, 203, 207, 229n116, 232n22, 236–7n91, 240n140, 241n153, 242n167, 252n84, 261nn17–8, 264n63, 265n5; Gazargah, 40, 69
—Jalalabad, 40–1, 60, 145, 232n22
—Kabul, 1–2, 13, 23, 26, 33, 41–4, 48–51, 54–8, 60, 62–3, 67, 69–71, 74, 77, 87, 90, 99, 103–4, 106–7, 113, 116, 120, 123, 125–6, 129, 131, 149–51, 154, 158–61, 163, 165, 172, 203, 206–7, 228–9n109, 232nn17–22, 235n55, 236n76, 237n101, 240n142, 244n33, 257n34, 261n18; Asheqan-o-Arefan, 33, 77; Bagh-e Ali Mardan, 126; Bagh-e Babur, 123; Bagh-e Rais, 1–2, 123; Chilsetoon, 123; Darul Aman, 62, 159, 206; Karte Se, 159; Kharabat, 108, 129; Microrayon, 33, 74, 89, 92, 95, 97, 100, 246n59; Qala-e Fatullah, 103, 247n1; Shahr-e Naw, 129, 247n1; Shor Bazar, 42, 43, 49; Wazir Akbar Khan 247n1

—Kandahar, 23–4, 49, 51, 61, 63–5, 77, 150, 253n89
—Logar, 49, 232n20
—Mazar-e Sharif, 23, 40, 45, 69, 130, 145, 176–7, 237n108, 261n20. *See also* Balkh; Hazrat Ali mosque. *See* mosque
—Panjshir, 107, 109, 232n17
Agha Khan Foundation, 173, 241, 261n17
Ahmed, Shahab, 84, 105, 220n5, 227n101, 250n38, 256n19
Ahsan-Tirmizi, Sonia, 149, 221n13, 256n17
akhund, 17, 101
al-Afghani, Sayyid Jamal al-din, 244n30
Alatas, Ismail Fajrie, 18, 179, 226n79
Al-Azhar, 51
Al-Ghazali, 17, 156, 246n49
alim, 8, 101, 161, 205, 207, 234n50
Ansari, Khwaja Abdullah, 7, 40, 115, 172, 180
Arab Afghan, 65, 87, 239nn131–4, 239–40n135
Arendt, Hannah, 17, 226n74
arif, 104
Arg, 62, 173, 261n18
arrest, 49–50, 60, 79–80, 204, 233n30, 247n64
Asad, Talal, 221n17, 229n119
authority, 2–4, 7, 9–10, 16–23, 33–5, 38, 42, 45–6, 55, 73, 75–6, 84, 86–8, 98, 102, 104–6, 119, 121–2, 133–4, 137–8, 140–3, 145, 163–4, 166–7, 170–1, 173, 180, 189, 198–9, 201–3, 208, 210, 225n69, 225–6n2, 248n6, 256n19, 257n34; explorative, 9, 102, 105, 199; female 137–41, 143, 148–9, 202, 205, 259n63; prescriptive, 9, 102, 152, 199, 203, 256n19
Avicenna (Ibn Sina), 180
Awaken Youth Party, 233n27
awliya, 23, 175, 178, 188
awrad, 164
Azzam, Abdullah, 65

Babur, 172
Baily, John, 129–30, 254n98
Baldauf, Ingeborg, 148
batin. *See* religion
baraka. *See* blessing
Barelwis, 72, 242n174, 246n50
Barfield, Thomas J, 49
Barth, Fredrik, 20
Bashir, Shahzad, 164
bay'a. *See* Sufism
Bedil, Mawlana Abul-Ma'ani Mirza Abdul-Qadir (Bedil Dehlavi), 1–3, 15, 51, 53, 104, 115, 122–9, 133–4, 136–7, 140–3, 211, 251nn60–5, 252n70, 253n88
belonging, 14, 52, 81, 120–1, 124, 130, 161, 201, 228n107, 247–8n3
bid'a, 9, 193–4, 196, 223n35
Bilateral Security Agreement (BSA), 68
Billah, Momena, 27, 151, 156, 159–60, 164, 166
Billaud, Julie, 146
Bin Laden, Osama, 65, 239–40n135
blessing, 19, 42, 181, 184, 192, 226n84
body, 77, 109, 128, 145, 156–8, 166–7, 181, 183, 223n37, 263n55; embodying, 2, 82, 199; imaginal, 156; *nafs*, 155–6, 177; physical, 155–8; psychophysiological, 35, 145, 166–7; *qalb*, 118, 144, 155–6; *ruh*, 128, 155–6
bomb. *See* violence

Index

book, 2, 9, 15, 27, 97, 106–14, 124–5, 132, 134, 137–44, 158, 161, 169–70, 174–6, 178, 186–94, 201, 207, 209, 238n119, 239n130, 253n86, 264n69–70; Sufi manual, 158, 164
Bourdieu, Pierre, 19, 226n88

calligraphy, 90, 173–6, 241n153, 253n86; Siyah Mashq, 175; Niayesh, 175
capital, 2, 42, 138, 203, 224n45; cultural, 2, 138; financial, 2, 138; symbolic, 42, 203
celebration, 1–3, 7, 15, 26–7, 53, 70, 80–1, 86, 97–8, 126, 134, 137, 141–3, 197, 206, 211, 256n22, 261n20; *urs*, 1–3, 7, 10, 26, 53, 124, 126, 135, 137–8, 141–2, 253n87; *mahfil*, l 2, 128; *mawlid*, 7, 70, 97, 241n163
Central Asia, 5, 20, 33, 41, 90, 114, 124-125, 232n15
charisma, 18–9, 44, 105, 161, 199, 202; religious, 105, 221n13, 226n86
chilla khana, 70, 190, 242n167
civil society, 1–2, 6, 10–16, 30, 34, 47, 68, 120, 200–1, 219n2, 223n40, 223–4n44–48, 241n161; and neoliberal development/NGO-ization, 1–2, 11–4, 16; and counterinsurgency 12; disobedience, 13
class: elite, 12–3, 24, 29–30, 39, 43, 48, 51, 68, 126, 142, 147, 219n2, 228n108, 229n122, 234–5n55, 236n88, 245n39; middle, 24, 84, 123, 160, 247n1; socioeconomic, 5, 24, 37, 206; working, 24, 205
colonialism, 8, 12, 29, 34, 38, 43–5, 75, 82–6, 101, 106, 147, 229n119, 230n125, 233n34–36, 244–5n37; postcolonial, 8
communication, 14, 95, 116–7, 170, 182, 196, 227n103, 263n45

Communism, 26, 45, 48–9, 52–3, 56–7, 59, 80–1, 87, 130, 132, 150–1, 153, 161, 207, 234–5nn53–55, 235n70, 237n104, 249n31, 257n35
community: decision-making, 3, 22, 30, 35, 47, 69, 81, 97, 99, 100, 114, 153, 161-2, 170-1, 193;   discourse, 16, 142, 155, 166–7; dissent, 8, 45, 172; of disagreement, 6–10, 210; concealment, 92, 94
conflict, 3–4, 8, 10, 14, 28, 60, 64, 86, 96, 101, 133, 142, 152, 200, 209, 219n2, 237n101–8, 239n131; postconflict, 4, 28
contestation, 3–4, 6, 16, 20, 22–4, 33–4, 43, 48, 59, 118, 129, 132-3, 141–3, 149, 170–1, 182, 194, 198–9, 204, 229n120, 239n131, 251n57
cooperation, 22, 76, 101, 126, 188, 225n69, 235n55, 243n8
criticism, 8–10, 12, 21, 29, 43–5, 63, 75, 77, 84, 86–7, 98, 101, 125, 130, 135–6, 147, 151, 162, 182, 186, 189–95, 200, 205, 209, 222–3n33, 228n108, 230n5, 237n104, 257n34
curriculum. *See* education

Dahrendorf, Ralf, 19, 226n87
Darya, Farhad, 131
Dastarbandi, 42
Dastageer, Daud, 81, 90, 92–94
death, 1–3, 40, 49, 53, 65, 80, 98, 102, 110, 124, 129, 133–4, 137, 141, 143, 167–8, 178–9, 184, 194, 196–7, 201, 259n71
Dervish, 82, 214
desecularization, 52
development, 11–2; neoliberal, 11, 14, 228n108
diplomacy, 5, 11–2, 14, 16, 84, 86, 146, 154, 203

distribution, 14, 90, 137–8; resource, 14, 35, 72, 114, 225n63

dream, 20, 22–3, 33, 35, 61–2, 103, 117, 144, 168–96, 199, 227–8n103, 238nn119–20, 244n29, 260n11–15, 262n37; awaited, 23, 35, 169, 171, 183; *barzakh*, 170, 180; divination, 20, 33, 171, 192–5, 238n120, 260n11; dreamer, 169–72, 177, 195; *istikhara*, 22, 61, 171, 177–9, 238n120, 262n30; of the Prophet, 169, 171–2, 176–7, 179–83, 192, 196; personal, 184, 186, 195;   receiver, 176, 185, 195; reporter, 195; revelatory, 22, 171, 195; true, 172, 177, 179, 195, 262n37

Dupree, Louis, 49, 114

durud, 184, 192

economy, 21, 205

education. *See also* madrasa; Aligarh, 84–5; curriculum, 61, 71, 84, 119–20, 141, 245–6n47, 250n45; Dar al-ʿUlum Haqqaniyya, 85; Deobandi, 61, 83, 85–6, 88, 189, 238n118–9, 242n174, 242–3n6, 245–6nn41—7; educational background, 62, 83, 87, 251n51; Habibia College, 84, 245n39; high school, 25, 160, 163, 236n88, 253n89; *hujra*, 61, 63; Kabul University, 48, 62, 162, 252n84; literacy/illiteracy, 20, 25, 114, 151, 154, 228–9n109; memorization, 22, 34, 85, 114, 164, 166; primary, 25, 85, 151, 156, 202; religious, 16, 22, 33, 34, 75, 79, 101, 105, 111, 113–5, 118–20, 127, 129, 133, 142, 161, 202, 232nn17–8, 241n156, 249n28, 250n45; school, 58, 71, 87, 94, 209, 249n28, 250n45; university, 25, 48, 71–2, 86, 120, 153, 160, 163; vocational, 24, 53, 174

Edwards, David, 17, 65, 87, 221n13, 225n71, 257n35, 257–8n37

elite. *See* class

Elphinstone, 82, 222n28, 233–4n37, 243–4n22, 260n11

endorsement, 19, 104

Enlightenment, 12, 13, 224n53

epistemology, 7, 29, 75, 170–1

ethics, 87, 99, 105, 265n5; Islamic, 14, 30, 87, 105, 114, 118, 223

Ewing, Katherine, 82-3, 230n37

exclusion, 12, 23, 27, 35, 81, 121, 141, 224n46, 229n122

exile, 53–9, 66, 68, 81, 203, 205

expression: artistic, 5, 9–10, 23, 45, 59, 90, 105, 109, 111, 113–4, 120, 122, 124, 132, 175, 201, 248n6; open debate, 2, 135; restricting, 47, 67, 98, 132, 206; symbolic, 42, 157

Faizani: Allama Faizani, 44–5, 49, 142, 144, 150–9, 161, 163, 234nn47–8, 257n35, 259nn63–6;   Community, 24, 53, 144–5, 150–67; Hizb-e Tawheed, 151

fana, 7

Fatima Gailani. *See under* Gailani

Female: agency, 34–5, 144–67, 255–6nn5–18; authority, 137–41, 143, 148–9, 202, 205, 259n63;   *awrah*, 162; empowerment, 146, 259n66

Ferdowsi, 172

fighter, 5, 26, 54, 56–7, 64–5, 87, 92, 239–40nn131–5. *See also* conflict; war

fieldwork: dialogic, 27, 29; ethnography, 25–7; interviews, 24, 26–32, 39; research assistants, 24, 29, 31, 70, 92,

112, 129, 230n124, 265n5; security, 2–4, 28–30, 24n,1, 265n5

Gailani: Abd-al Qadir Gailani, 40, 231; family, 25, 39–42, 56–60, 68, 150, 231n12–4, 243n12; Fatima Gailani, 56, 59–60, 68; Sayyid Ahmad Gailani, 41, 54, 56, 66, 197; Sayyid Hasan Gailani, 40–1, 231
gender, 5, 23, 30–1 34–5, 59, 68, 142–55, 166–7, 202, 224n46, 228–9n109, 22–30n123, 256n15, 258n38; equality, 144–67; mixed, 145, 167; nongendered, 35, 142, 145, 155, 166–7, 202; relations, 5, 30–1, 34–5, 141–2, 144–67, 229–30n123, 256n15, 258n38; segregation, 30, 34, 145, 166–7, 202, 209
genealogy, 7, 14, 40, 61, 77–8, 122, 140, 146–7, 220n5, 231–2n14—15; lineage, 19, 41, 77–8, 86, 191, 243n12, 246n52, 248n3
Ghafari, Rahimi 142
Ghulam Nabi. *See* Sufi Ashqari
gnosticism, 5, 104, 220n8
Gopal, Anand, 61, 240n140
Government: Abdullah Abdullah, 71, 132; Afghan, 13, 25–6, 28–9, 40–5, 48–73, 86–100, 102, 112, 119–21, 129–32, 153, 188, 203–11, 234–8nn52–114, 240nn140–1, 243n20, 247n65, 249n31, 250n45, 252n84; Amrullah Saleh, 130, 132; Ashraf Ghani, 69, 71–2, 204, 245n39; Babrak Karmal, 50, 52, 234–5n55; constitution, 68, 126, 171, 236n88, 264n65; Hamid Karzai, 69, 97, 245n39, 264n63; Daoud Khan, 43, 48–9, 54, 78, 153; Democratic Republic, 37; Hafizullah Amin, 49, 50–1, 79, 234n55; Islamic Emirate, 26, 37, 204; Islamic Republic, 28, 37, 204; Ismael Khan, 187; Marshall Fahim, 51, 236n72; Mullah Omar, 61, 63–4, 67, 93, 96–7, 172, 200, 238n119–20, 239n128, 260–1n15. *See also* Taliban; Dr. Najibullah, 51-2, 55-6, 131, 235–6n71–6, 237n98; Republic, 28, 37, 204; Abdulrab Rasul Sayyaf, 66; Taliban, 4, 24, 26, 28, 35, 37, 58–69, 71–2, 85, 88–90, 93–8, 100, 102, 119–20, 132, 134, 137, 152, 158, 172, 174, 190, 200, 204–11, 229n116, 237n108, 238nn110–21, 240nn141–2, 247nn66–70, 249n31, 250n45, 251n51, 254n112–4, 260–1n15, 265n5; Secret service, 50, 54, 56, 131, 236n72; Taraki, 50, 234n55; Zahir Shah, 129, 252n84
Green, Nile, 38, 125, 170, 180, 220n10, 231n12, 252n75
grave, 7, 9, 15, 23, 27, 64–5, 77, 87, 176, 179, 189, 206, 219nn1–2. *See also* shrine
Gul Agha. *See* Mujaddidi

Habibi, Abdul Ghaffar, 173–5, 178, 185, 261n19
Hadith, 7, 22, 34, 67, 88, 113–4, 119, 126, 177, 179, 199, 223n34, 227n101, 231n11, 236n76, 252–3n85, 255n5, 262n28, 264n70
Haeri, Niloofar, 111
Haeri, Shahla, 161, 202
Hafiz, 22, 34, 114–5, 249n33, 253n92
Haji Ahmad Jan, 49, 79–80
Haji Baba, 63–4
Haji Saiqal, 8, 67, 73–9, 81, 88–102, 198, 206, 210, 247n67

Haji Tamim, 49, 57, 67, 78–80, 88–9, 94, 97–8, 100, 206, 210
hajj, 50–2, 71, 180. *See also* pilgrimage
hal, 115, 117, 165, 250n37
halqa, 2, 6, 26, 60, 94, 105, 117, 122, 124, 127–8, 134, 141–2, 144, 159, 161–2, 165, 187, 199; *sar-e halqa*, 144, 159, 199
Harakat-e Afghanistan 1400 (Afghanistan 1400 Movement), 13, 224n54
Hazara, 13, 49, 207, 219, 224n53, 237n108
Hazrat, 43, 49, 54, 61, 69, 178, 181–4, 225n71, 232n22, 233n27, 261n21, 263n60
Helmand Peace Convoy, 13
heresy, 9–10, 195. *See also bid'a*
heritage: cultural, 5, 22, 52, 105–6, 121–3, 127–9, 133, 141–2, 202, 243n20; intangible, 22, 34, 105–6, 121–7, 141–2, 251n59; *miras*, 124, 133; national, 5, 16, 22, 105, 111, 120–7, 132, 200, 202, 243n20, 248n15, 251n59; political, 52, 105–6, 121–2, 129–30, 243n20; regional, 121; religious, 52; tangible, 121, 251n59
Hill, Joseph, 155
Hinduism, 4, 187
Hirschkind, Charles, 223n37
historiography, 33, 37–9, 230n2

Ibn Arabi, 156, 174, 176, 181, 186, 190, 262n24, 263n53; *wahdat al-wujud*, 176; *tajalli*, 176, 262n2, 263n53
Ibn Taymiyya, 190
identity, 24, 69, 121, 132, 134, 202, 219; cultural, 21
ideology, 3-4, 13, 38, 44, 47–8, 50, 58–5, 61, 64–5, 69–71, 73, 76, 87, 101–2, 130, 132, 200

ilham, 173, 175; inspiration, 44, 83, 173, 175
imagination, 21, 171
imprison, 45, 66, 91, 158, 161, 205, 257n35. *See also* arrest; prison
India: Aligarh, 84–5; Azimabad, 124; British, 43, 44, 84–5, 102, 244n33; Mughal, 40–1, 124, 172, 232n18; Patna, 124; Sirhind, 78, 232nn17–8
Ingram, Brannon, 85, 242–3n6, 246n50
insecurity, 10, 33–4, 73–102, 200, 204, 209. *See also* conflict; war
Iran: Tehran, 121, 133
Iraq: Baghdad, 40-1, 149, 231n12
irfan, 5, 115, 133, 161, 187, 191, 220n8; mysticism, 5, 32, 101, 111, 115, 133, 187, 220n8, 249n28
Islam: boundary making, 6, 9–10, 147, 169, 190; disputation, textual, 2, 8, 84, 221n17; innovation, 9, 63, 154, 189–96, 223n35; Islamist, 5, 13, 38, 44, 48–9, 54–5, 65, 69, 83, 86, 89, 153, 233n28, 246n52; Ismaili, 4; Panjpiri, 187; Salafism, 9, 10, 64, 69, 86, 186–7, 189, 200, 207-8, 245n44; Shi'a, 4, 25, 154, 207, 229n110, 242n3, 256n24; Sufism. *See* Sufism; Sunni, 4, 10, 25, 40, 154, 227n101, 231n11, 241n163, 242n174, 246n50, 250n38, 250–1n46, 256n24; Wahhabi, 51, 64–6, 187, 200, 246n51

Jackson, Ashley, 69, 96, 229–30n123, 238n114, 247n67
Jamal, Shayiq, 109
James, William, 32
Jami, Abdur Rahman, 40
Jamiat-e Eslah, 13, 26, 256–7n24
Jan, Mutasim Agha, 63–4, 67, 93, 238,120–1, 247n62

Jews, 4
jinn, 148, 177, 256n20; possession, 148
jirga, 13, 51, 68, 100, 254. See also *shura*; *loya*, 68; *meshrano*, 68
Junbesh-e Roshnayi (Enlightenment Movement), 13, 224n53
jurisprudence, 63, 71, 85, 178, 189, 231n11, 239n125, 240n148, 264n70; Hanafi, 71, 189, 240n148, 246n50; Hanbali, 40, 231n11; Wahhabi, 71
jurist, 8, 17, 222n28, 234n50, 264n70

Kaba, Mariame, 210
KHAD, 50, 131, 236n72
Khalis, Maulvi, 65
khalifa, 41, 46, 78, 99, 168, 206, 232n20, 243n11, 252–3n85
Khan, Sayyid Ahmad, 83–5, 244n29
khanaqah, 7, 26–8, 41–2, 44, 49–50, 53, 56–8, 60, 63, 67, 70, 73–4, 76–83, 88–100, 102, 104, 149–51, 169, 174, 185, 187–8, 203, 206–8, 210, 222n23, 225n63, 232n21, 237n105, 240n142, 241n165, 243nn9-12, 244n28, 247n70, 264n69; Alauddin, 99, 206, 247n70; leaderless, 169, 173, 192–3, 195; Pahlawan, 49, 57, 73, 75–80, 83, 90, 92–3, 98–100, 102, 206
khudshenasi/khudashenasi, 158
Khattak, Khushhal Khan, 252n73
khutbah, 96–7; sermon, 45, 69, 96, 223n37
king, 41–3, 77, 126, 172–3, 252n84; Amanullah, 42, 159, 233n28, 253n93, 264n65; Amir Abdur Rahman, 172, 233; Amir Habibullah, 41, 126, 245n39, 264n65; Nadir Shah, 43, 245n41; Timur Shah, 42, 125; Zaman Shah, 42
Knight, Muhammad, 181, 262n29

Kugle, Scott, 156
Kuutma, Kristin, 129
Kyrgyzstan, 20

Laidlaw, James, 153
Lamoreaux, John, 179, 227–8n103, 262n37
Language: Arabic, 114, 165, 172, 181, 222n20, 223n35, 239n134, 253n89, 263n51; Dari/Farsi/Persian, 24, 81, 111–4, 122, 124–6, 132, 154, 172, 222n20, 227n101, 238n119, 248n14, 249n33, 252n75, 254n113; Pashto, 24, 31, 59, 114, 125, 132, 154, 238n119, 254n111
lata'if, 183–4, 199, 263n55
law, 58, 68, 223n42, 240n148. See also *shari'a*; national, 68
legitimacy, 10, 17, 19, 33, 40, 42, 44–5, 50, 72–3, 88–9, 91, 102, 132, 138, 145, 166, 170, 189, 194, 198–9, 203; delegitimization, 44, 59, 87, 89, 208
library, 26, 44, 47, 51, 53, 97, 102, 106–7, 109–11, 118, 123, 132, 151, 176, 187, 254n112
life: everyday, 20–2, 34, 83, 87, 119, 174, 179
Lindholm, Charles, 140, 226n86
literary device, 114, 124
Lobato, Chantal, 50, 235n70
love, 1, 15, 57, 102, 120, 134, 140, 157, 160, 182, 240n140, 249n28; beloved, 117, 120, 124, 182; lover, 77, 109, 112, 117, 122, 126, 211

madrasa, 5, 22, 34, 41, 44, 61, 71, 85, 114, 119, 141, 173, 178, 187, 231n12, 232n21, 241n156, 242n1, 245–6n47–51, 249nn30-1, 250–1n46; Dar ul-

'Ulum, 85; Jameh Sharif, 178; radical, 61, 71–2, 249–50n46
mahfil. See celebration
Mahjor: Abdul Qadir Arezo Mahjor, 127–9, 133–4, 136, 138; Asma Mahjor, 1–2, 4, 7, 15–6, 102, 127, 129, 133–43, 211; Ustad Majhor, 7, 26, 123–124, 127–129, 133–135, 138, 197
Mahmood, Saba, 147, 223n37, 256n15
male, 19, 31, 34, 77, 81, 134, 137, 140–2, 145, 148, 153–5, 158, 161–2, 167, 228–9n109, 257n34; allyship, 34, 145, 162, 167
malang, 222n23
Malejacq, Romain, 88
masjid. See mosque
mawlawi, 17, 101
media, 3, 10, 27, 30, 70, 72, 85, 103, 105, 120–1, 141, 146, 186, 199, 256n24; audiocassette, 66, 129, 223,37; CD, 94, 97; Facebook, 15–6, 111, 140; film/movie, 94, 119, 127; photograph, 27, 87, 134, 140—1; radio, 66, 121, 128–30, 236n76, 253nn9–3; Radio Afghanistan, 128, 253n93; Radio Kabul, 66, 129, 253n93; Radio Shariat, 66, 238n119, 240n141; Skype, 134, 140; social media, 3, 27, 70, 120–1, 141, 186; television, 71, 130, 134; Twitter, 121; video, 27, 66, 93, 97, 100, 206; website, 53, 257n35; WhatsApp, 206
mediation, 10, 13–4, 42; political, 12–3, 65
meditation, 66, 93, 128, 144, 163, 177, 183, 242n167
Mevlevi, 40
migration, 3, 25, 33, 47, 53, 76, 80, 101–2, 167, 205, 232n18, 236n78, 251n65
ministry, 13, 50, 71, 96–7, 121, 127, 130, 235n65, 246n60; Ministry of Culture, 127, 130, 261n17; Ministry of Foreign Affairs, 121; Ministry of Hajj and Religious Affairs, 71; Ministry of Justice, 13, 96–7, 235n65, 264n65; Ministry for the Promotion of Virtue and the Prevention of Vice, 58, 238n120, 247n65; Wizarat-e Shun-e Islami wa Auqaf, 50
Mir Mohammad (Pahlawan), 49, 57, 73, 75–80, 83, 90, 92–3, 98–100, 102, 206
miracle, 7, 44, 84, 186, 201, 237n93, 244n29
misdirect, 67, 92
Mittermaier, Amira, 170–2, 227n102
Montgomery, David W, 20
moral exemplar, 34, 152-3
mosque, 15, 41, 44, 46, 50, 57, 60, 65, 69–71, 74–5, 78–9, 81, 89–92, 95–7, 102, 119, 147–9, 151, 162, 169, 174, 178–9, 187–8, 206-7, 237n105, 242n1, 246n60, 249n28, 262n37, 264n69; Great Mosque of Herat, 178, 207; Hazrat Ali mosque, 69; *mihrab*, 90; Pul-I Khishti, 44, 151, 234n47; *qibla*, 90
Muhammad (Prophet), 5–7, 9, 70, 96–7, 169, 171–2, 176–7, 179–84, 189, 192, 196, 205, 223n35, 225n71, 241n163, 246n50, 260n8, 262n37
Muharram, 166
Mujaddidi: family, 25, 39–45, 49, 59, 68, 130, 150, 174, 197, 232n17–20, 233n25–32, 236n72, 242–3n6, 257n34; Fazl Ahmad Ma'sumi, 42; Fazl Omar Mujaddidi, 43; Gul Agha, 43, 57; Sibghatullah Mojaddedi, 54, 68, 197, 233n32, 236n72;

Khwaja Safiullah Mujaddidi, 42;
Muhammad Ibrahim Mujaddidi, 49
mujahidin, 26, 53, 55–8, 66, 79, 87–90,
  94, 102, 131–2, 152, 237n101–4,
  240n140, 264n63. *See also* resistance
mullah, 5, 33, 51, 61, 67, 74–8, 82, 88–9,
  96, 101–2, 198, 222n28, 235–6nn70–1,
  242–3nn1–6, 246n60, 247n70;
  Hadda, 43; Islam, 75, 243n20; mad,
  44, 101-2, 233–4n37; Nasruddin, 75
murid, 6–7, 14, 30–1, 49, 55, 63–4, 93–4,
  97–100, 116, 140, 150–1, 153–5, 162,
  165, 168, 173, 178–9, 184–6, 192–3,
  225n63, 237n94, 257n35
murshid, 6, 61, 140, 173–5, 261n19. See
  also *pir*; *ustad*
mystic. See *arif*

na'at, 97, 99–100
namaz, 114, 174. *See also* prayer
NATO, 11–2, 25, 28, 72, 204, 265n3. *See
  also* government
navigation, social, 19–20, 33–4, 105,
  140, 144–67, 170, 173, 196, 201–2,
  205, 210, 226n87, 227n89; restriction, 10, 20, 34, 47, 67, 145, 162–3,
  167, 206, 210
Nawa'i, Ali Shir ,40
Nawid, Senzil, 42, 232n17, 242n1
negotiation, 19, 22, 24, 35, 55, 59–60,
  66–8, 70, 96–7, 102, 106, 119, 167, 169,
  171, 194, 196, 200, 205, 210, 247n63,
  265n3; bargaining, 94, 238n114,
  247n67; communal, 164, 169, 187;
  peace, 1, 11, 13, 28, 55, 62, 68, 70, 72,
  109
network, 25, 41–2, 45, 78, 96, 197, 200–1,
  254n112; economic, 5, 221n12;
  horizontal, 14–6, 224n45; international, 5, 41, 232n21, 233n25,

245–6n47; social, 5, 14, 30, 96, 147;
  Sufi, 5, 14, 41–2, 45, 78, 197, 201,
  228n105, 233n25; translocal, 14
Nojumi, Neamatollah, 13
nongovernmental organization
  (NGO), 1–2, 7, 11–3, 15–6, 25, 74, 103,
  154, 159, 189, 203, 224n54, 247n1,
  250n45, 265n3
Nuristani, 49

Obama, Barack, 12
occupation, 37–8, 54, 203, 261n20
Olesen, Asta, 53, 150, 232n18, 233n31,
  237n104
opposition, 43–4, 49, 54, 59, 75, 132,
  149, 154, 195, 204, 246n51
orality, 20, 22, 27, 34, 37, 39, 57, 106, 119,
  147, 151, 170, 195, 256n18; oral history,
  37, 39, 57, 147, 151, 221n13, 247–8n3,
  249n28
order, Sufi. See *tariqa*
Orientalism, 8, 82-83, 101, 171, 230n125
orthodoxy, 8, 22, 34, 86, 101, 148, 193,
  195, 199, 242n5, 256n19
Ottoman Empire, 40, 231n12, 244n33

Pakistan, 6, 42, 53–4, 58, 61, 72, 81, 85,
  87, 91–2, 102, 119, 125, 128, 132, 134,
  137, 152, 188,
  203, 238n120, 242n2, 243n20, 244n32,
  245n44–7, 254n118, 257n35, 260n15,
  262n30; Lahore, 84, 114; Peshawar,
  42, 53–4, 86, 114, 125, 152, 158, 203,
  232n22, 239n131, 252n73, 257n35
Pashtun, 63, 178, 219n1, 234n55, 236n88,
  249n32
peace, 1, 11, 13, 28, 47, 53, 55, 62, 68, 70,
  72, 98, 109, 169, 184; peace-building,
  11; High Peace Council, 62, 68
pedagogy, 7, 120. *See also* education

People's Democratic Party of Afghanistan (PDPA), 26, 48–55, 58, 90, 130, 132, 151, 234–5n55, 257–8n37; Parcham, 48, 130, 234–5n55; Khalq, 48, 234–5n55
Pemberton, Kelly 149
Philippon, Alix, 72, 243n20
pilgrimage, 40, 50, 92, 148, 180–1, 231n14. See also *hajj*; *umrah*
pir, 2, 6–7, 9, 14, 17, 33–4, 40–4, 46, 55–6, 62–4, 66, 75, 77, 82, 90, 98–100, 102, 104, 145, 149–54, 156, 158–61, 166–9, 174, 178–81, 183–6, 190–4, 196–8, 201, 209–10, 257n34. See also *murshid*; Allama Faizani. See Faizani; Fazl Ahmad, 42–3, 98, 232n6; Osman Mawdudi, 174–5, 178, 180–6, 190–3; Sayyid Ahmad Gailani. See Gailani
pledge. See Sufism; *bay'a*
poetry, 1, 7, 20, 22–3, 26, 33–4, 40, 46–7, 51–3, 61, 82–3, 101–6, 109, 111–34, 140–2, 168, 199, 202, 207, 222n28, 228n105, 248n3, 249–50n35–45, 251n51, 253n92, 254n11–2, 261n20; *aitys*, 106; allegory, 1, 117; ambiguity, 124, 201–2; *ghazal*, 122, 128-9; intertextuality, 112; *landay*, 254n111; metaphor, 124, 154, 156; meter, 1, 165; mystical, 82–3, 108, 111; oral, 22, 46, 106; *Panj Ganj*, 113–4, 119; Persian and Qur'an, 7, 22, 34, 111–4, 119; propaganda, 47, 52, 132;   recitation, 20, 53, 93, 118, 126, 128, 134, 156, 162–3, 167, 253n92, 261n20; register, 140, 202;   sentence structure, 124; social commentary, 101, 104, 131, 140; wordplay, 124
politeness, 100, 136
politics, 5, 33, 37, 40, 45, 47, 49, 62, 68, 82–3, 85–6, 91, 129–31, 150, 240n140, 257n35; nonalignment, 46–7, 91; state alignment 33, 39-43, 49, 54, 59, 204
possession. See *jinn*
practice: calligraphic, 175; devotional, 7; dreams as, 62, 170–2, 179, 184; individualization of, 184–5; legitimation, 9, 19, 59, 64–6, 76–7, 93, 189–90, 192–4, 198; ritual, 2, 4, 14, 22, 34, 63, 81, 89, 144, 199, 238,120; theory of, 19, 226n88
prayer, 7, 60, 62, 65, 67, 74–5, 81, 88, 90, 92, 96, 99, 111, 113–4, 116, 130, 136, 152, 164, 174-8, 184–5, 189, 241n165, 262n37; as social critique, 136; at gravesites, 7, 64-5; *dua*, 115, 136, 175, 192
president, 43, 51, 68, 71–2, 119, 130, 132, 204, 245n39. See also government
prison, 45, 49, 79–80, 131, 150, 152–3, 234n47. See also imprison; Pul-e Charkhi, 49, 79, 150, 259n71
publication, 2, 16, 108, 125, 138, 170, 186–7, 190, 193, 252–3n85–6; patron, 40, 42, 138
pure, 108, 117, 138

qal, 115
qalandar, 82, 191, 222n22
Qandi Agha (Ustad Muhammad 'Abd al-Hamid "Asir"), 122–4, 126–8, 133–7, 253n89
Qur'an, 5, 7, 22, 34, 44–5, 67, 84–5, 88, 100, 111–4, 119, 134, 144–5, 163, 167, 179, 189, 193, 199, 223n35, 227n101, 236n76, 238n112, 241n156, 244n29, 255n5, 261n20, 263n55, 264n70; in Persian, 112

radical, 48, 54, 61, 132, 155; radicalization, 71–72, 119–120, 250–1n46; deradicalization, 71–72
Ramadan, 166, 189
reform, 11, 13, 45, 48, 71–2, 75, 84–6, 88, 120, 151, 153; reformer, 8–9, 13, 34, 83–8, 102, 171, 182, 245n38
refugee, 5, 39, 46, 53, 58, 61, 121, 132, 152, 160, 203, 252n84
relic, 79–80, 189
religion, 4, 8–9, 13, 31, 45, 68–9, 71, 101, 111, 113, 205, 220n5, 224n46, 230n125, 244n9, 249n28, 259n66; actor, 14, 20, 69, 145–9, 166, 200–1, 231n6, 241n161; *batin*, 156; martyr, 65, 87, 239n128; *zahir*, 63, 101, 156
repetition. *See* literary device
resilience, 20-1, 209-210, 227nn95–9
resistance, 2, 5, 33, 37, 39, 43–5, 51, 53–5, 73, 87, 101, 130–2, 147, 237n94. *See also* Mujahidin; fighter, 5, 54, 56–7, 64–5, 87, 92, 239n128; Hizb-e Islami, 54; Jamiat-e Islami, 54–56, 236–7n91; National Islamic Front, 54, 68; National Liberation Front, 54, 236n88
revelation, 22, 171, 174, 179, 181–2, 195; divine, 22
revolution, 37, 45, 48–9, 234n54, 237n91
ritual, 2, 6–7, 47, 52, 60, 66, 82–3, 89, 114, 136, 151, 161, 177, 184, 197, 199, 222–3n33, 238n120, 239n125, 256n22, 261nn20–1; cleansing, 114, 117, 144, 157–8, 182–3; rhythm, 66–7, 93, 165
Rocketi, Abdul Salam, 60
Rohani, Mawlawi Pir Mohammad, 62, 66, 239n125
Roy, Olivier, 49, 54, 246
Rumi, Jalal ad-din (Mawlana), 22, 34, 46, 51, 104, 109, 111–2, 114–5, 121–3, 125, 127, 131, 160, 174, 190, 207, 222n28, 227n101, 234n50, 249n28, 253n92; *Masnawi*, 51, 71, 111, 121, 151, 190, 207, 227n101, 249n28
ruya, 35, 117

Saadi, 22, 34, 114
Safavid dynasty, 40, 124, 231n12
Safi, Omid, 113
Sahib, 17, 42, 61, 64, 79, 98–9, 124, 151, 182, 206, 231n14, 261n21, 263n60
saint, 1, 7, 23, 40–1, 44, 72, 77, 86, 97, 124, 149, 172, 175, 179, 181, 186, 188, 261n20; *khak-e awliya*, 23, 188
Sakata, Lorraine, 128
Salvatore, Armando, 14
sama. *See* Sufism; music
Samadi, Husnia, 80–1
Sarahang, Mohammad Hussain, 127–8, 129, 253nn90–2
Saruri, Bismillah (Faramarz), 173–6, 178, 184–6, 261n19
Satan, 157, 177
Saudi Arabia: Mecca, 90, 92, 109, 149, 180
Saur Revolution, 48–9, 234n54
Sayyid, 40–1, 43, 54, 66, 82–5, 197, 225n71, 231n14, 244nn28–30
Schimmel, Annemarie, 112, 263n55
school. *See* education
secrecy, 26, 50, 54–5, 67, 90, 92–4, 103, 136, 148, 237n104, 247nn62–3, 249n28, 257n34
security, 10, 12, 14, 21, 23–4, 27–31, 33–4, 58, 68, 70, 73–102, 106, 162, 200–1, 204, 207, 209, 247n1, 263–4n61
Sedgwick, Mark, 19
Seljuqs, 40
service, 11–2, 15, 33, 53, 69, 78, 138, 140, 152, 174, 202, 261n21; act of, 138, 140,

202; delivery, 11, 15, 223n42; soup kitchen, 39, 41; spiritual, 33, 78, 140, 174, 202
shahada, 144, 163
shaman, 148, 222n23, 256n22; cure, 148, 189; divination, 148; exorcism, 148; obstetrics, 148
Shahnahmeh, 172
Shahrani, Nazif, 114
shari'a, 8, 41, 77, 86, 182, 191–3, 222n27, 246n49. See also law
shirk, 9, 65
shrine, 6, 9, 23, 33, 40–1, 46, 60, 63–5, 69–70, 85, 87, 148–50, 174, 178, 180, 185, 231n12, 239n128, 241n153. See also grave; *ziyarat*; Abdul Rahman Jami, 40, 178, 227n101; Bibi Nushin, 149; Chardah Massoum, 70; Gazargah, 40, 69; Sayyid Hasan Gailani, 40; Tamim Ansar, 150; visitation, 7, 9, 2, 65, 150, 189, 222n23
shura, 13, 20, 50–51, 70, 100, 169–70, 187–90, 192–3, 207, 254n118, 264nn68–70. See also *jirga*: Shura-e Tasawwuf, 169, 187–90, 192–5, 207; Shura-ye 'ali-ye 'ulama wa ruhaniyun, 50; Quetta Shura, 238n121
Sikhs, 4
Sinno, Abdulkader H, 69, 237n101
Sirriyeh, Elizabeth, 83, 233n34, 244n29
Smith, Laurajane, 106, 121, 251n59
sociosphere, 8, 35, 102, 145, 170, 173, 186, 187, 200
spirituality, 7–8, 14–5, 22, 28, 32, 33–5, 41–2, 44–5, 53, 64, 77–8, 85, 103–4, 112–3, 115–6, 126, 128, 134, 138, 140–5, 149, 153–67, 174, 183–4, 186, 194, 199, 202, 207, 231–2nn14–5, 234n47, 239n125, 242n3, 250n37, 258n48;

development, 8, 153, 156, 163–7; path of, 7, 103, 144, 161, 174, 261n21
state: altered, 128; building, 1, 4, 11, 12, 68, 125, 132, 159; failure, 38
status, 2, 21, 31, 39, 78, 89–90, 106, 146–7, 163, 169–71, 182, 193, 195–6, 240n148, 252–3n85, 256n18, 260n8; genealogical, 78, 89, 137, 140, 161; hereditary, 77–8, 81, 89, 137, 143, 243n12, 246n52
strategic distance, 33, 37, 39, 45–7, 53, 66–7, 73, 91, 130
Strick van Linschoten, Alex, 61
student. See *murid*
subaltern, 227n96
succession, 3, 18–9, 35, 77–8, 99, 137–8, 143, 161, 168, 170, 196, 198–9, 201–2
Sufism. See also Islam.
—*bay'a*, 6, 64, 151
—decline hypothesis, 5, 200
—diaspora, 6, 15, 27, 35, 60, 67, 129, 145, 150, 167
—hierarchy, 7, 14, 115–6, 134, 195; *amm*, 7, 116, 250n38; *khass*, 7, 116, 250n38; *khass al-khass*, 7
—music, 7, 66–7, 88, 93–4, 108, 127–9, 131, 152, 163, 184, 205, 208, 240nn140–1, 241n165, 253–4n90–106, 256n22; Qawwali, 128, 142; *sama*, 128; Ustad Sarahang, 127–128, 129, 253nn90–2
Sufi Council, 8, 10, 35, 169–70, 186–90, 192–4, 199
Sufi Ashqari (Ghulam Nabi), 97–8, 107–10, 122
Suhrawardi, Shihab al-din, 180
Sultanova, Razia, 148, 256n22
suluk, 7, 263n60
Sunna, 18, 189, 192–3
superstition, 9, 220n8

survivance, 227n100

tafsir, 151
Tajik, 70, 236n72, 252n84
tariqa, 2, 6–7, 9, 14, 19, 22, 25–6, 33–5, 39–43, 49–50, 55, 61–2, 67, 77–8, 85–6, 91, 128, 134, 143–5, 148–51, 154, 158, 161, 163, 166–9, 170–3, 176–8, 180–8, 190–4, 196, 203, 205, 222n20, 231n14, 232n18, 243n17, 261n19
—'Aisawa, 149
—Chishtiyyah, 7, 26, 31, 35, 49, 55, 66, 151, 178, 184, 191–2, 232n18, 236–7n91, 263n60
—Muhammadiyya, 43; Sayyid Ahmad Barelwi, 43
—Naqshbandiyyah, 7, 26, 40–3, 49, 55, 59, 61, 64, 77–8, 86, 122, 151, 183, 188, 191, 231– 3nn15–25, 236–7n91, 242–4n6, 252–3n85, 258n37; Fazl Ahmad Ma'sumi, 42, 232n21; Shaykh Ahmad Sirhindi, 41, 78, 232nn17–21; Qandi Agha. See Qandi Agha
—Qadiriyyah, 7, 26, 34, 40, 44, 57, 59–61, 63, 86, 148, 150–1, 163, 166, 184, 188, 191, 231nn12–4, 232n18, 236–7n91, 251n60, 263n60. See also Faizani; Naqib of Baghdad, 40, 231n14; Naqib of Charharbagh, 40, 151;
—Rahmaniyya, 149
—Rifai, 153
—Safaviyya, 40
—Salwatiyyah, 26, 35, 169–70, 173, 176, 178, 180–7, 190–6, 199–201, 261n19, 263n60; Akhundzada Abdul Samad Saudaii, 174, 178; Pir Osman Mawdudi, 174–175, 178, 180–186, 190–193; Suhrawardiyyah, 151, 191, 222n22

Tarzi, Mahmud, 126
tasawwuf. See *murshid*, Sufism
technology, 20, 86, 153–4, 202. See also media
temporality, 170
Timurid dynasty, 40,
theology, 75, 140, 223n35; Islamic, 75, 230n125, 246n50, 250n38
theory, 19, 22, 115, 183, 188, 191, 226n88, 262n24. See also practice; dream, 22, 183
transition, 3, 18–20, 33, 35, 37–8, 50, 57, 73, 76, 100, 142, 197–8, 210
trauma, 5, 227n95
Turkmen, 148

ulama, 8, 33, 49–51, 63, 69–71, 75, 83, 85, 88, 170, 188, 190, 233n30, 235n65, 236n76, 241n161, 242n5, 245n41; Ulama Council, 50, 69, 71, 188, 190, 264n65
ummah, 6, 18, 233n34
umrah, 92
UN, 25, 55, 69, 121, 223n42, 265n3; UNESCO, 121–2, 228–9n109, 261n17
United States, 11–2, 54, 72, 81, 98, 111, 137, 138, 145, 158-60
urs. See celebration,
Ustad, 7, 17, 26–7, 51, 72, 102, 104, 106–7, 113, 115–6, 118, 121–4, 126–30, 133–5, 138–9, 142, 144–5, 151–2, 158, 161–2, 164–6, 175–8, 181, 187–8, 190–4, 197, 205. See also *murshid*;   Ustad Rahim Bakhsh, 128; Ustad Bitab, 126; Ustad Hasham Sheiq Efendi, 126, 253n88; Ustad Haidari Wujudi, 26, 51–2, 97, 102, 104–5, 111, 113, 115,

118, 121–2, 129–32, 134–6, 142, 236n72, 249–50n35; Ustad Irfani, 187–8; Ustad Khalili, 126, 252n84; Ustad Khoroq, 176–7, 181; Ustad Mahjor. *See* Mahjor; Ustad Abdullah Mowafaq, 133, 134, 136–7, 140–3; Ustad Manija Billah, 27, 159, 160–2, 164–6, 199, 205; Ustad Mutasim Mazhabi Billah, 145, 151–2, 158; Ustad Muhammad 'Abd al-Hamid "Asir" (Qandi Aga). *See* Qandi Agha; Ustad Momena Billah, 27, 151, 156, 159–61, 164, 166, 199, 205; Ustad Shukria, 144–5, 161–2; Ustad Mawlawi Abdul Haleem Hosseini Wais, 187

Uzbekistan, 20, 41; Bukhara, 41, 114, 126, 231–2n15, 242n1; Samarkand, 172; Uzbeks, 124, 148, 219, 251n65, 256n22

Vigh, Henrik, 19–20, 226n87, 227n89
violence, 3, 10, 17, 21, 28–9, 46, 54, 76, 85, 88, 92, 101, 169, 200, 205, 239–40n135, 243n8, 250–1n46; attack, 3, 6, 9–10, 34, 37, 57, 64, 69–71, 85, 187, 199, 204, 206–8, 237n108, 241–2n166; bomb, 5, 28–9, 34, 38, 54–5, 61–2, 69–70, 76, 91, 101, 159; disappearance, 45, 49–50, 52, 54, 57, 80, 204; hate speech, 187; kidnapping 29, 94, 229n116, 247n1; killing, 28, 45, 49, 56, 69–71, 76, 101, 148, 150, 167, 204, 206, 239n125, 241n156; military waste, 28; suicide 5, 28, 38, 70; torture, 54, 91, 204

vision, 7–8, 18, 22, 105, 122, 138, 147, 152–3, 167, 170–172, 179–83, 201, 211; inspirational, 22, 194

waqf, 40, 50, 232n21
war: Civil War, 33, 37, 53, 56–9, 75, 88, 92, 110, 249n31; Cold War, 54, 82, 243n9; counterinsurgency, 12, 37; insurgency, 4, 68–9, 71–2, 94, 96, 205, 247; invasion, 33, 37, 48, 53, 55, 57, 113, 130, 146, 154, 158; jihad, 4, 43, 55–9, 64–5, 86–8, 102, 131, 208, 220n4, 228n104, 239–40n135, 246n52, 250–1n46; War on Terror, 29, 72, 82, 229n119

weapon, 54–5, 62, 87
Wieland-Karimi, Almut, 150, 252n73
zahir. *See* religion
Zaman, Muhammad Qasim, 17–8
Zani, Leah, 28
Zia ul-Haq, Muhammad 54
Ziad, Waleed, 42, 232nn20–1, 232n25, 242–3n6
zikr, 7, 22–4, 26–7, 31, 34, 44, 47, 53, 55, 60, 63, 66–7, 78–81, 86, 90, 93–4, 96–7, 99–100, 109, 144–5, 148, 150–2, 154, 156–67, 174, 176, 184–5, 188–91, 196, 199, 205–8, 239n125, 240n142, 241n165, 242n167, 257nn34–5; *zikr jahr*, 66–7, 86, 93–4, 96, 163, 189, 191, 264n70; *zikr khufya*, 86, 93, 163, 247n62
ziyarat, 7, 55, 86, 148, 150, 174, 222n23, 237n93, 241n165

The authorized representative in the EU for product safety and compliance is:
Mare Nostrum Group
B.V Doelen 72
4831 GR Breda
The Netherlands

www.ingramcontent.com/pod-product-compliance
Lightning Source LLC
Chambersburg PA
CBHW031755220426
43662CB00007B/408